2001

GERMAN AND ENGLISH IDIOMS

SECOND EDITION

2001 DEUTSCHE UND ENGLISCHE REDEWENDUNGEN

ZWEITE AUSGABE

D1320152

BARRON'S
FOREIGN LANGUAGE GUIDES

2001
GERMAN AND ENGLISH IDIOMS

SECOND EDITION

2001 DEUTSCHE UND ENGLISCHE REDEWENDUNGEN

ZWEITE AUSGABE

Henry Strutz

All inquiries should be addressed to:
Barron's Educational Series, Inc.
250 Wireless Boulevard
Hauppauge, New York 11788

ISBN-13: 978-0-7641-4224-6
ISBN-10: 0-7641-4224-0

Library of Congress Catalog Card Number 2009930986

PRINTED IN THE UNITED STATES OF AMERICA

9 8 7 6 5 4 3 2 1

INHALT

CONTENTS

TEIL I
DEUTSCH-ENGLISCH

PART I
GERMAN-ENGLISH

VORWORT

Idiom ist aus dem Griechischen "sich aneignen" abgeleitet. Um sich eine Sprache anzueignen, ist das Erlernen von Redewendungen, die das Eigenartige einer Sprache widerspiegeln, unumgänglich. Ohne solche Kenntnisse kann man keine Sprache eigentlich beherrschen, selbst wenn man mit deren Grundlagen schon vertraut ist. In der Urbedeutung hat *Idiom* auch mit "privat" zu tun. Wenn man der Idiomatik einer Sprache mächtig ist, besitzt man den Schlüssel zum Eintritt in Sprachbereiche, die sonst nur Muttersprachlern oder Eingeweihten vorbehalten sind. Wörterbücher der Idiomatik, wie die schon in anderen Sprachen von Barrons herausgegebenen, bieten Studenten, Reisenden und Geschäftspersonen Definitionen, die in Wörterbüchern im Taschenformat meist nicht enthalten sind, und die nur mit großer Mühe mehrbändigen Wörterbüchern abzugewinnen sind.

Dieses Buch, wie die anderen in der Serie, bietet eine bunte Mischung aus bildhaften Redensarten, die alle, einschließlich Muttersprachlern zur Idiomatic zählen würden, zusammen mit einfacheren Ausdrücken, die Sprachstudenten idiomatisch vorkommen, weil wörtliche Übersetzungen unmöglich sind. Daher wird man Einfaches wie *to be afraid/right* (Angst/recht haben) neben Phantasievollerem finden. Viele Sprüche und Redensarten, entstammen altem Sprachgut und können manchmal veraltet wirken. Daher wurde versucht, Redewendungen in einem zeitgenössischen Zusammenhang anzuwenden mit Rücksicht auf aktuelle Themen aus Gesellschaft, Politik, Finanz und Umwelt. Ob es sich um alte Sprüche, bildhafte Ausdrücke, oder grammatische Bildungen handelte, die dem Sprachstudenten sonderbar oder gar "idiotisch" scheinen könnten, war das Ausschlaggebende für deren Aufnahme die Eigenartigkeit, das Idiomatische an ihnen. Es liegt daher auf der Hand, dass Sätze wie: *He is here. We drink beer. The grass is green.* und dergleichen nicht aufgenommen wurden.

Wenn Redensarten anhand eines herkömmlichen Wörterbuches übersetzt werden, ist das Ergebnis oft völlig irreführend. Zum Beispiel, das deutsche "über den Berg" könnte leicht irrtümlicherweise als *over the hill* übersetzt werden. Eigentlich heißt es: *out of the woods.* Kleinere Wörterbücher bringen nur eine beschränkte Zahl an Redensarten und bei größeren Wörterbüchern müssen Benutzer oft durch Wortdickichte stolpern. Mit einem herkömmlichen Wörterbuch, könnte man leicht zu dem Schluss kommen, dass der Ausdruck "auf den Busch klopfen" mit *to beat about the bush* übersetzt werden sollte. In diesem Buch werden Sie schnell erfahren, dass es *to sound out* heißt. Auch wird man schnell feststellen können, dass: "um den heißen Brei herumreden," *to beat about the bush* heißt. Dieses Buch verschafft Ihnen leichten Zugang zu idiomatischen Ausdrücken und wird Ihnen helfen, Irrtümer zu vermeiden. Da der Gebrauch von Redewendungen oft von einem Zusammenhang abhängig ist, sind den mehr als 2500 hier aufgezeichneten Redewendungen Anwendungsbeispiele zugeordnet.

Im Englischen und vielleicht noch mehr im Deutschen, wird im heutigen Sprachgebrauch reichlich Gebrauch von Redewendungen, Sprichwörtern und bildhaften Ausdrücken gemacht. Sehr oft treten Redewendungen in Abwandlungen auf, d.h. in Umformungen, Anspielungen, Persiflagen, Wortspielen verschiedenster Art. Um das alles schätzen zu können, müssen Ihnen die idiomatischen Ausgangspuntkte vertraut sein.

Dieser Band enthält mehr als 2000 englische und deutsche Redewendungen. Die Redewendungen sind nach Stichwörtern alphabetisch geordnet. Jeder Eintrag besteht aus vier Teilen: eine Redewendung (in Fettdruck), ihre Bedeutung beziehungsweise Übersetzung in der anderen Sprache (kursiv), ein Anwendungsbeispiel, das den Gebrauch der Redewendung in einem Zusammenhang zeigt (in Antiqua), und eine Übersetzung des Satzes in die andere Sprache (kursiv). Obwohl die Stichwörter wörtlich übersetzt sind, wird es Ihnen vielleicht auffallen, dass ihre Bedeutungen sich erheblich ändern können, wenn sie in Redewendungen auftreten.

Die zur Vorbereitung dieses Buches meistbenutzten Nachschlagewerke waren: *Duden; Redewendungen und sprichwörtliche Redensarten; Wörterbuch der deutschen Idiomatik,* Band 11 des zwölfbändigen Duden Standardwerkes zur Deutschen Sprache, sowie die mehrbändigen Duden und Langenscheidt Deutsch-Englisch/Englisch-Deutsch Wörterbücher.

Das bloße Wort für Wort Übersetzen aus einer Sprache in eine andere hat es Komikern von Mark Twain bis Art Buchwald erlaubt, Lächerliches hervorzubringen. Um eine Sprache zu beherrschen, und um nicht ausgelacht zu werden, sind Kenntnisse von Redewendungen unerlässlich. Sie werden sich gut amüsieren, und auch richtiger als die Komiker vorgehen, wenn Sie die verschiedenen Berührungs- und Ausgangspunkte zwischen dem Deutschen und dem Englischen vergleichen und unterscheiden. Bei seltenen Gelegenheiten gleichen sich deutsche und englische Redewendungen in allen Punkten. Normalerweise, jedoch, begegnet man Variationen über ein Grundthema. Daher wird der "Elefant im Porzellanladen" zu einem *bull in a china shop.* Deutsche Säufer sehen "weiße Mäuse,'" statt *pink elephants.* Werden die Trunkenbolde zu Krawallmachern, holt sie dann die Polizei in der "Grünen Minna" ab, die auf englisch eine *Black Maria* ist. Das "goldene Eier" legende Federvieh ist ein deutsches Huhn, aber eine englische *goose.* Ob man den "Bock zum Gärtner" oder, wie im Englischen, "den Fuchs zum Vorgesetzten des Hühnerhauses" macht, ist die Grundidee bei den meisten Redewendungen oft dieselbe, obwohl Tiere, Farben, Namen, Bilder, Einzelheiten jeder Art, verschieden sind. Um Ihren sprachlichen Tierpark zu vergrößern, um das Farbspektrum der Sprachgalerie mit einer Vielfalt von bildhaften Ausdrücken zu erweitern, müssen Ihnen Redewendungen ein Begriff sein. Wenn sie Redensarten gut anbringen können, werden Sie Ihrem Sprechen Farbe verleihen. Das Studium von Redewendungen ist auch eine interessante, anschauliche Weise, die grundlegende menschliche Einheit wahrzunehmen, so wie sie in sprachlicher Mannigfaltigkeit offenbart wird.

DEUTSCHE REDEWENDUNGEN
(German Idioms)

A — *das A*

Wer A sagt, muss auch B sagen. *Once you've started something you've got to follow through.*

das A und O sein — *to be essential, indispensable.*

Beim Studium der vergleichenden Religionswissenschaft ist Toleranz das A und O. *Tolerance is indispensable when studying comparative religion.*

---

aasen — *to be wasteful*

mit dem Geld aasen — *to throw money around.*

Eine Zeitlang aaste er mit dem Geld jede Nacht in der Kneipe. *For a time he threw money around every night in the tavern.*

mit seiner Gesundheit aasen — *to burn the candle at both ends.*

Weil er an nichts außer sich glaubt, aast er mit seiner Gesundheit. *Because he believes in nothing outside himself, he burns the candle at both ends.*

---

die Abbitte — *pardon*

Abbitte leisten — *to ask for pardon; to make amends.*

Mit den Blumen wollte er ihr Abbitte leisten. *He wanted to make amends to her with the flowers.*

---

abbrechen — *to break off*

sich keinen abbrechen — *not to strain o. s.*

Er hat mir ein bisschen geholfen; aber dabei hat er sich keinen abgebrochen. *He helped me a little, but he didn't strain himself.*

---

der Abbruch — *demolition*
   Abbruch tun — *to do damage.*
   Durch ihre Schriften und Reden hat sie der Bewegung viel Abbruch getan.
   By her writings and speeches she's done much damage to the
   movement.

der Abend — *evening*
   Es ist noch nicht aller Tage Abend. — *Nothing is definite yet.*
   Sie haben keine Kinder, aber es ist noch nicht aller Tage Abend. *They*
   don't have children, but it's not over yet.

aber — *but; really*
   Die Chefin duldet kein Aber. *The boss won't put up with any objections.*
   Das war aber schön! *That was really nice!*

abermals — *once again; once more*
   Sieben Jahre waren abermals verstrichen, und der Holländer trat wieder
   ans Land. *Seven years had passed once more, and the Dutchman came*
   on shore again.

abessen — *to eat up; clear plates*
   abgegessen haben — *to have worn out one's welcome.*
   Dein Onkel hat bei uns abgegessen. *Your uncle has worn out his welcome*
   with us.

abfahren — *to depart*
   Der letzte Zug nach Marienbad ist abgefahren. *The last train for*
   Marienbad has left.
   Dein Freund bekommt den Posten nicht — für ihn ist dieser Zug
   abgefahren. *Your friend won't get the position — he's missed the boat.*

die Abfuhr — *removal; rebuff*
   sich eine Abfuhr holen — *to be rejected*
   Mit seinen Vorschlägen für die Giftmüllabfuhr holte er sich eine Abfuhr.
   His proposals for toxic waste removal were rejected.

der Abschluss — *conclusion*
einen Abschluss haben — *to graduate; have a degree.*
Er hat keinen Universitätsabschluss. *He has no university degree.*

zum Abschluss bringen — *to conclude.*
Wir hoffen, das Geschäft bald zum Abschluss zu bringen. *We hope to conclude the deal soon.*

abschminken — *to remove makeup; get something out of one's head*
Sie hat sich die Augen abgeschminkt. *She removed her eye makeup.*
Ich soll die Verantwortung dafür übernehmen? Das kannst du dir abschminken. *Me take responsibility for that? You can put that out of your mind.*

abschnallen — *to unfasten; unbuckle; be flabbergasted*
Was uns die Arbeit an Mühe gekostet hat, da schnallst du ab. *You'd be flabbergasted at how much trouble the job caused us.*

absehen — *to foresee; predict*
In absehbarer Zeit lässt sich das nicht machen. *In the foreseeable future it won't be possible to do that.*

es abgesehen haben — *to be out for.*
Der Geizhals erklärte, alle hätten es auf sein Geld abgesehen. *The miser declared that everyone was after his money.*

es abgesehen haben — *to have it in for*
Der Gefreite glaubte, dass der Feldwebel es auf ihn abgesehen hatte. *The private thought the sergeant had it in for him.*

die Absicht — *intention*
sich mit der Absicht tragen — *to be thinking about.*
Seit Jahren trägt er sich mit der Absicht, sein Geschäft auszubauen. *For years he's been thinking about expanding his business.*

absitzen — *to serve out a prison sentence*
Nachdem er seine Strafe abgesessen hat, will er nie wieder auf die schiefe Bahn. *After serving his sentence, he never wants to stray from the straight and narrow again.*

abhören — *to eavesdrop; to tap (telephone, etc.)*
Nachdem die Gespräche des Gangsters abgehört wurden, verhaftete man
ihn. *After the gangster's conversations were tapped, he was arrested.*

ablaufen — *to flow away (out); empty*
　ablaufen lassen — *to send packing.*
Er versuchte wieder freundlich zu sein, aber sie ließ ihn ablaufen. *He tried
to be friendly again, but she sent him packing.*

abmalen — *to paint a picture*
Da möchte ich nicht abgemalt sein! *I wouldn't be caught dead there!*

abnehmen — *to take off; to take from*

　abnehmen — *to buy*
Eine solche Geschichte nehm ich euch nicht ab. *I'm not buying your story.*

　abnehmen — *to review*
Die Königin nahm die Parade ab. *The queen reviewed the parade.*

　abnehmen — *to lose weight*
Sie hat viel abgenommen. *She's lost a lot of weight.*

　die Beichte abnehmen — *to hear confession.*
Anglikanische Priesterinnen können auch die Beichte abnehmen. *Anglican
priestesses can also hear confessions.*

　abnehmend — *waning*
Bei abnehmendem Mond will die Isispriesterin nichts unternehmen. *When
the moon is waning the priestess of Isis won't undertake anything.*

abreißen — *to tear down; tear off*
　nicht abreißen — *to continue unabated.*
Der Streit um das Bauvorhaben reißt nicht ab. *The dispute concerning
building project continues unabated.*

der Absatz — *heel*
　auf dem Absatz kehrtmachen — *to turn on one's heels.*
Zutiefst beleidigt, machte die Diva auf dem Absatz kehrt und verlie
Bühne. *Deeply insulted, the diva turned on her heels and left th*

abspielen — *to play*

vom Blatt abspielen —*to play at sight.*

Die Pianistin spielte die Beethoven-Sonate vom Blatt ab. *The pianist played the Beethoven Sonata at sight.*

sich abspielen — *to happen; be set.*

Das alles soll sich gestern abgespielt haben? *All that is supposed to have happened yesterday?*

Wo spielt sich die Szene ab? *Where is the scene set?*

---

der Abstand — *distance*

Abstand nehmen — *to refrain from; give up (on).*

Die Senatorin hat von ihrem Plan Abstand genommen. *The senator gave up on her plan.*

auf Abstand gehen — *to back out.*

Sie erklärten sich zum Kauf bereit aber jetzt gehen sie auf Abstand. *They declared they were ready to buy, but now they're backing out.*

mit Abstand — *by far.*

Sie ist mit Abstand die beste Kandidatin. *She is by far the best candidate.*

---

absteigen — *to get off; come down*

Die Gräfin stieg von ihrem Pferd ab. *The countess got off her horse.*

gesellschaftlich absteigen — *to decline in social status; to come down in the world.*

Wegen vieler Skandale ist sie gesellschaftlich abgestiegen. *Because of many scandals her social status has declined.*

absteigen — *to stay at an inn/hotel.*

Trotzdem steigt sie nur noch in Nobelhotels ab. *But she still stays only at ritzy hotels.*

---

abtun — *to dismiss*

Der Roman wurde von einigen Kritikern als Schund abgetan. *The novel was dismissed as trash by some critics.*

abgetan sein — *to be finished, over.*

Für sie war die Sache damit abgetan. *For them that was the end of the matter.*

---

abwarten — *to wait and see*

Sie wollen die Entwicklung der Dinge abwarten. *They want to wait and see how things develop.*

abwarten und Tee trinken — *to wait patiently and see what happens.*

Wir können nur abwarten und Tee trinken. *We can only wait patiently and see what happens.*

die Abwesenheit — *absence*

durch Abwesenheit glänzen — *to be conspicuous by one's absence.*

Bei der Sitzung glänzte er durch Abwesenheit. *At the meeting he was conspicuous by his absence.*

abwinken — *to wave aside; flag down*

bis zum Abwinken — *in great profusion; galore.*

Auf dem Fest gab es Champagner bis zum Abwinken. *At the feast there was champagne galore.*

ach — *oh (dear)*

mit Ach und Krach — *by the skin of one's teeth.*

Mit Ach und Krach hat die Partei die Wahl gewonnen. *The party won the election by the skin of its teeth.*

mit Ach und Weh — *moaning and groaning.*

Mit vielem Ach und Weh gab er endlich nach. *With much moaning and groaning he finally gave in.*

die Achse — *axis; axle*

auf (der) Achse sein — *to be on the move/go.*

Ich bin den ganzen Tag auf Achse gewesen und möchte mich jetzt ausruhen. *I've been on the go all day and want to rest now.*

die Achsel — *shoulder*

die Achsel zucken — *to shrug one's shoulders.*

Er hat nur die Achsel gezuckt. *He just shrugged his shoulders.*

auf die leichte Achsel nehmen — *to underestimate; minimize.*

Ihr seelisches Leiden sollten Sie nicht auf die leichte Achsel nehmen. *You shouldn't minimize her psychic suffering.*

über die Achsel ansehen — *to look down on.*

Jetzt ist sie reich und sieht die alten Schulfreunde über die Achsel an. *Now she's rich and looks down on her old school friends.*

die Achterbahn — *roller coaster*

Achterbahn fahren — *to ride the roller coaster; be unstable.*

Der Aktienmarkt fährt noch Achterbahn. *The stock market is still unstable.*

die Achtung — *respect; attention*

Alle Achtung! — *Well done!*

Keiner glaubte, dass unsere Kandidatin so viele Stimmen erhalten würde. Alle Achtung! *Nobody thought our candidate would get so many votes. Well done!*

der Acker — *field*

sich vom Acker machen — *to scram, clear off*

Die Polizei kam und er machte sich schnell vom Acker. *The police came and he cleared off fast.*

die Adresse — *address*

Diese Warnung/der Vorwurf geht an Ihre eigene Adresse. *This warning/reproach is directed to you personally.*

an der richtigen/falschen Adresse sein — *to have come to the right/wrong place.*

Wenn Sie Geld von uns erwarten, dann sind Sie an der falschen Adresse. *If you expect money from us, you've come to the wrong place.*

der Affe — *monkey*

einen Affen gefressen haben — *to be nuts about.*

Er hat an seiner neuen Freundin einen Affen gefressen. *He's nuts about his new girlfriend.*

seinem Affen Zucker geben — *to indulge in one's hobby; to talk to please oneself.*

Ich hörte nicht mehr zu, denn jeder wollte nur seinem Affen Zucker geben. *I stopped listening because all were talking just to please themselves.*

sich einen Affen kaufen — *to get drunk.*
Gestern abend hat er sich wieder einen Affen gekauft. *He got drunk again last night.*

vom wilden Affen gebissen sein — *to be off one's rocker.*
Wenn du das glaubst, bist du vom wilden Affen gebissen. *If you believe that, you're off your rocker.*

zum Affen halten — *to make a monkey out of*
Er versuchte, mich zum Affen zu halten. *He tried to make a monkey out of me.*

die Affenschande — *a crying shame*
Es wäre eine Affenschande, ihre Dichtungen zu vernachlässigen. *It would be a crying shame to neglect her literary works.*

der Affenzahn — *monkey tooth*
mit einem Affenzahn — *extremely fast.*
Mit der Magnetschwebebahn fährt man mit einem Affenzahn. *With the magnetic levitation train one travels extremely fast.*

die Aktie — *stock*
Seine Aktien steigen. *His prospects are improving.*
Wie stehen die Aktien? *How are things?*

der Akzent — *accent*
Akzente setzen — *to set a course; to indicate directions.*
Gleich nach Amtsantritt wollte die Präsidentin Akzente setzen. *Right after taking office the president wanted to set a course.*

der Alarm — *alarm*
Alarm schlagen — *to raise (sound) an alarm.*
Zum Glück hatten Umweltschützer rechtzeitig Alarm geschlagen. *Fortunately, environmentalists had sounded the alarm in time.*

das Alibi — *alibi*
eine Alibifunktion haben — *to serve as an excuse, be token*

Die paar Frauen unter den Konferenzteilnehmern hätten nur eine Alibifunktion, behauptete sie. *The few women attending the conference were only tokens, she claimed.*

das All — *the universe; space*
Isolde hoffte, Tristan im All wiederzufinden. *Isolde hoped to find Tristan again in the universe.*

der/die Alleinerziehende — *single parent*
Es gibt immer mehr Alleinerziehende. *There are more and more single parents.*

der Alleingang — *independent initiative*
etwas im Alleingang tun — *to do something on one's own.*
Wenn ich jünger wäre, würde ich's im Alleingang tun. *If I were younger I'd do it on my own.*

die Alleinherrschaft — *dictatorship*
Obwohl das Land eine Alleinherrschaft ist, gibt's auch ein Parlament. *Although the country is a dictatorship, there is also a Parliament.*

der/die Alleinstehende — *person living on his/her own*
Für viele ältere Alleinstehende ist das Fernsehen ein Trost. *For many elderly people who live alone, television is a consolation.*

all — *every; all*
alle zwei Tage — *every other day.*
Sie besucht uns alle zwei Tage. *She visits us every other day.*

allemal — *any time; every time*
Alles, was er kann, das kann doch Annie allemal. *Anything he can do, Annie can do too.*

allenfalls — *at most; at the outside*
Es waren allenfalls fünfzig Leute im Konzertsaal. *There were at most 50 people in the concert hall.*

allenfalls — *if necessary; if need be.*
Allenfalls könnten wir's im Alleingang machen. *If necessary, we could do it on our own.*

alt — *old*
beim Alten bleiben — *to stay the same.*
Seine Versprechen klangen nach Fortschritt, aber es blieb alles beim Alten. *His promises sounded like progress, but everything stayed the same.*

es/alles beim Alten lassen — *to leave things as they were.*
Es wäre besser, wenn Sie alles beim Alten gelassen hätten. *It would have been better if you'd left everything alone.*

alt — *used*
Altöl und Altpapier können wieder verwertet werden. *Used oil and (waste) paper can be recycled.*

der Alltag — *everyday life; a typical day*
Ich will Ihnen sagen, wie mein Alltag aussieht. *I'll tell you what a typical day in my life is like.*

alltäglich — *commonplace; ordinary*
Alltägliches interessiert uns nicht. *The commonplace doesn't interest us.*

das Amt — *office; official agency*
von Amts wegen — *in an official capacity.*
"Ich bin von Amts wegen hier," erklärte der Polizeibeamte. *"I'm here in an official capacity," declared the policeman.*

der Amtsschimmel — *bureaucracy; red tape*
den Amtsschimmel reiten — *to be a stickler for red tape; to do everything by the book.*
Wir mussten warten, weil die Beamten den Amtsschimmel reiten wollten. *We had to wait because the officials wanted to do everything by the book.*

Der Amtsschimmel wiehert — *Bureacracy reigns.*
In seiner Abteilung wiehert laut der Amtsschimmel. *In his department bureaucracy reigns supreme.*

an — *at; on; to*
   an (und für) sich — *basically.*
   An und für sich habe ich nichts dagegen. *Basically I have nothing against it.*

   an sich — *in itself/themselves.*
   Einige von Kants Ideen sind an sich nicht schlecht. *Some of Kant's ideas aren't bad in themselves.*

anbeißen — *to bite into; to take a bite of*
   Schneewittchen biss den Apfel an. *Snow White bit into the apple.*

   zum Anbeißen sein — *to look good enough to eat.*
   Die Zwerge fanden sie zum Anbeißen schön. *The dwarves thought she looked good enough to eat.*

anbinden — *to tie up*
   kurz angebunden — *curt, abrupt(ly).*
   Er antwortete kurz angebunden auf alle Fragen. *He answered all questions abruptly.*

   anbinden — *to pick a quarrel.*
   Der Matrose war betrunken und wollte mit allen anbinden. *The sailor was drunk and wanted to pick a quarrel with everyone.*

anbringen — *to put up*
   In der Wohnung brachten wir viele Plakate von Toulouse-Lautrec an. *We put up many Toulouse-Lautrec posters in the apartment.*

der Anfang — *beginning*
   den Anfang machen — *to be the first to begin.*
   Keiner wagte, den Anfang zu machen. *No one dared to be the first to begin.*

   den Anfang nehmen — *to begin; have its beginning.*
   Ihrer Theorie nach nahm die Sprache ihren Anfang in der Musik. *According to her theory language began in music.*

anfangen — *to begin*
   anfangen mit — *to do with; to make of.*
   Was sollen wir damit anfangen? *What are we supposed to do with that?*

die Angel — *hinge; fishing rod and line*

jmdm. an die Angel gehen — *to swallow bait/fall for s.o.'s line.*

Viele sind dem Schwindler an die Angel gegangen. *Many fell for the con man's line.*

aus den Angeln gehen — *to fall apart at the seams.*

Das Wirtschaftssystem ist aus den Angeln gegangen. *The economic system fell apart at the seams.*

aus den Angeln heben — *to turn upside down.*

Durch den Krieg wurde ihr Leben aus den Angeln gehoben. *Their life was turned upside down by the war.*

aus den Angeln sein — *to be out of joint.*

Hamlet fand, dass die Welt aus den Angeln war. *Hamlet thought the world was out of joint.*

die Angst — *fear*

Angst haben — *to be afraid.*

Zuerst hatte das Mädchen große Angst vor dem Tod. *At first the girl was very afraid of death.*

Angst und Bange haben — *to be very afraid.*

Er hatte Angst und Bange vor der Wurzelbehandlung, aber es war nicht so schlimm. *He was terrified of the root canal, but it wasn't so bad.*

die Angstmacherei — *scare tactics*

Die Senatorin bezeichnete die Argumente ihres Gegners als Angstmacherei. *The senator called her opponent's arguments scare tactics.*

anhaben — *to have on*

Nur der Junge wagte zu sagen, dass der Kaiser nichts anhatte. *Only the boy dared to say that the emperor had nothing on.*

anhaben — *to harm.*

Sie glaubten, dass in der Kirche niemand ihnen etwas anhaben könnte. *They thought that no one could harm them in the church.*

der Anhieb — *thrust*
  auf Anhieb — *right away; at first go.*
  Auf Anhieb verstand ich nicht, was sie wollten. *I didn't understand right away what they wanted.*

der Anker — *anchor*
  vor Anker gehen — *to drop anchor; get married; settle down.*
  Der alte Frauenheld will endlich vor Anker gehen. *That old womanizer finally wants to settle down.*

ankommen — *to arrive*
  ankommen — *to find acceptance; to be popular.*
  Ihre Gemälde kommen beim Publikum gut an. *Her paintings are popular with the public.*

  ankommen — *to get somewhere.*
  Ohne Beziehungen wäre er nicht angekommen. *Without connections he wouldn't have gotten anywhere.*

  auf etwas ankommen — *to depend on.*
  Es kommt darauf an, ob wir genug Zeit haben. *It depends on whether we have enough time.*

  auf etwas ankommen — *to matter, count.*
  Beim Sport kommt es auf jede Sekunde an. *In sports every second counts.*

  es auf etwas ankommen lassen — *to take a chance on s.t.*
  Obwohl er an Popularität verloren hat, will der Präsident es auf neue Wahlen ankommen lassen. *Although his popularity has declined, the president is willing to risk new elections.*

  gegen etwas nicht ankommen — *to fight a losing battle against s.t.*
  Seit den Umbauarbeiten kommen wir gegen den Schmutz nicht mehr an. *Ever since the renovation work began, we've been fighting a losing battle against the dirt.*

anlegen — *to invest*
  sich etwas angelegen sein lassen — *to make it one's business; to see to it that.*
  Ich werde es mir angelegen sein lassen, ihrem Freund behilflich zu sein. *I'll make it my business to help your friend.*

anmachen — *to turn on*
Es wird schon dunkel; mach's Licht an! *It's getting dark already; turn the light on.*
Diese Rockgruppe macht viele Jugendliche ungeheuer an. *This rock group really turns on many young people.*

anmachen — *to dress a salad.*
Hast du den Salat schon angemacht? *Have you dressed the salad yet?*

der Anmarsch — *marching up; advance*
im Anmarsch sein — *to be on the way.*
Durchgreifende Veränderungen sind im Anmarsch. *Drastic changes are on the way.*

anschreiben — *to write up; to write to; give credit*
Der Wirt wollte ihm nichts mehr anschreiben. *The innkeeper didn't want to give him any more credit.*

gut/schlecht angeschrieben sein — *to be in someone's good/bad books.*
Sie ist bei ihren Vorgesetzten gut angeschrieben. *She is in her superior's good books.*

der Anschluss — *connection*
im Anschluss an — *immediately following.*
Im Anschluss an die Pressekonferenz fand eine Diskussion statt. *Immediately following the press conference a discussion took place.*

der Anspruch — *claim*
Anspruch erheben — *to make a claim.*
Zuerst wollte sie keinen Anspruch auf das Geld erheben. *At first she didn't want to make a claim on the money.*

Ansprüche stellen — *to make demands; be demanding.*
In dieser Schule werden die höchsten Ansprüche an Studenten und Lehrer gestellt. *In that school the greatest demands are made of teachers and students.*

in Anspruch genommen sein — *to be too busy.*
Besprechen Sie das mit meinen Kollegen — ich bin zu sehr in Anspruch genommen. *Discuss that with my colleagues — my time is all taken up.*

die Anstalt — *institution*
Anstalten treffen — *to make a move to do.*
Trotz der späten Stunde machte er keine Anstalten nach Hause zu gehen.
Despite the late hour he made no move to go home.

der Anstand — *decency; objection*
Anstand nehmen — *to object; to take offense.*
Die Senatorin nahm an der Gesetzesvorlage keinen Anstand. *The senator
didn't object to the proposed bill.*
Oma nahm an den Kraftausdrücken im Stück keinen Anstand. *Grannie
took no offense at the strong language in the play.*

der Anteil — *share*
Anteil nehmen — *to be interested in.*
Sie hat stets großen Anteil am Theater gehabt. *She's always been very
interested in the theater.*

der Antrieb — *drive (vehicle)*
neuen Antrieb geben — *to give fresh impetus.*
Ihre Gegenwart hat uns neuen Antrieb gegeben. *Her presence has given
us fresh impetus.*

aus eigenem Antrieb — *of one's own accord.*
Er hat es aus eigenem Antrieb getan. *He did it of his own accord.*

antun — *to do to*
es angetan haben — *to be captivated; taken with.*
Die Schauspielerin hat es ihm sehr angetan. *He is entirely taken with the
actress.*

die Antwort — *answer*
keine Antwort schuldig bleiben — *to be quick to reply.*
Die Senatorin blieb ihren Gegnern keine Antwort schuldig. *The senator
was quick to reply to her opponents.*

anwurzeln — *to take root*
wie angewurzelt stehenbleiben — *to be rooted to the spot.*
Statt zu fliehen, blieben sie wie angewurzelt stehen, als sie das Ungeheuer erblickten. *Instead of fleeing, they stood rooted to the spot when they saw the monster.*

der Anzug — *suit*
aus dem Anzug fallen — *to be extremely thin.*
Der Milliardär aß kaum mehr und fiel aus dem Anzug. *The billionaire rarely ate any more and was extremely thin.*

aus dem Anzug springen — *to fly off the handle.*
Spring doch nicht gleich aus dem Anzug, wir kommen bald. *Keep your shirt on, we're coming soon.*

der Apfel — *apple*
für einen Apfel und ein Ei — *for very little money.*
Sie haben das Grundstück für einen Apfel und ein Ei gekauft. *They bought the land for very little money.*

in den sauren Apfel beißen — *to bite the bullet.*
Auch ich hab keine Lust dazu, aber einer muss doch in den sauren Apfel beißen. *I don't feel like it either, but someone's got to bite the bullet.*

der Apparat — *apparatus; appliance; telephone*
am Apparat bleiben — *to hold the line.*
Bleiben Sie bitte am Apparat! *Please hold the line.*

der April — *April*
in den April schicken — *to play an April Fool's joke on; to send on an April Fool's errand.*
Die Büroangestellten schickten ihren neuen Kollegen in den April. *The office workers sent their new colleague on an April Fool's errand.*

das Arbeiterdenkmal — *workers' monument*
ein Arbeiterdenkmal machen — *to lean idly on a shovel.*
Einer von ihnen arbeitete wie ein Pferd, während die anderen ein Arbeiterdenkmal machten. *One of them worked like a horse, while the others stood by idly.*

die Arbeitgeber — *employers; management*
  die Arbeitnehmer — *employees; labor*
  Arbeitgeber und Arbeitnehmer waren mit dem Tarifvertrag zufrieden.
  Management and labor were satisfied with the union contract.

arg — *bad*
  im Argen liegen — *to be in disorder.*
  In seiner Abteilung liegt noch vieles im Argen. *There is still much that's*
  not in order in his department.

  sich ärgern — *to get angry.*
  Mensch, ärgere dich nicht so darüber — es ist nur ein Spiel! *Man, don't*
  get angry about it — it's only a game.

der Arm — *arm*
  der verlängerte Arm — *tool.*
  Die Reporterin behauptete, der Bürgermeister sei nur der verlängerte
  Arm der Mafia. *The reporter asserted the mayor was merely the tool of*
  the Mafia.

  einen langen Arm haben — *to be very influential.*
  In der Stadt hat die Mafia einen langen Arm. *The Mafia is very influential*
  in the city.

  jmdn. auf den Arm nehmen — *to take s.o. onto one's arm; to pull s.o.'s*
  leg/put on.
  Ich glaube, du nimmst mich wieder auf den Arm. *I think you're putting*
  me on again.

  in die Arme laufen — *to run into.*
  Beim Einkaufen bin ich gestern meinem alten Schulkameraden in die
  Arme gelaufen. *While shopping yesterday I ran into my old school*
  friend.

  unter die Arme greifen — *to come to the aid of.*
  Sie hat den Kriegsopfern unter die Arme gegriffen. *She came to the aid of*
  the war victims.

arm — *poor*
  arm dran sein — *to be in a bad way.*
  Menschen, die nicht lieben können, sind arm dran. *People who can't love are in a bad way.*

der Ärmel — *sleeve*
  aus dem Ärmel schütteln — *to come up with just like that.*
  Frank L. Wright sagte, er könnte seine vielen Bauprojekte nur so aus dem Ärmel schütteln. *Frank L. Wright said he could come up with his many building projects just like that.*

  die Ärmel aufkrempeln — *to roll up one's sleeves.*
  Die Ingenieure krempelten die Ärmel auf und planten den Tunnel unter dem Ärmelkanal. *The engineers rolled up their sleeves and planned the tunnel under the English Channel.*

  im Ärmel haben — *to have up one's sleeve.*
  Der Zocker hatte noch mehr Asse im Ärmel. *The professional gambler had still more aces up his sleeve.*

die Armut — *poverty*
  sich ein Armutszeugnis ausstellen — *to proclaim one's ignorance/ inadequacy.*
  Durch ihre dumme Kritik hat sie sich nur ein Armutszeugnis ausgestellt. *She merely proclaimed her own ignorance with her stupid review.*

das As — *ace*
  ein As auf der Bassgeige sein — *to be an ace on the bass fiddle; to be a clever devil.*
  Selbst Sherlock Holmes hat er überlistet; er ist ein As auf der Bassgeige. *He outsmarted even Sherlock Holmes; he's a clever devil.*

aufbringen — *to summon up*
  Ich weiß nicht, wie ich den Mut dazu aufbringen werde. *I don't know how I'll summon up the courage for it.*

  aufbringen — *to infuriate.*
  Nachdem die Königin erfuhr, dass Schneewittchen noch lebte, war sie sehr aufgebracht. *After the queen heard the news that Snow White still lived, she was infuriated.*

aufbringen — *to set against.*

Er tat alles, um sie gegen einander aufzubringen. *He did everything to set them against each other.*

der Aufbruch — *departure, setting out on a journey*

die Aufbruchstimmung — *spirit of optimism/get up and go.*

Nach dem letzten Wahlsieg herrscht Aufbruchstimmung in der Partei. *After the last electoral victory, the party's optimistic.*

auffliegen — *to fly up; to expose, bust*

Die Reporterin ließ den Schwindler auffliegen. *The reporter exposed the swindler.*

aufgeben — *to give up*

eine Anzeige aufgeben — *to take an ad.*

Sie hat eine Zeitungsanzeige aufgegeben. *She took an ad in the newspaper.*

aufgehen — *to rise*

Um wieviel Uhr ist die Sonne aufgegangen? *At what time did the sun rise?*

aufgehen — *to work out.*

Minnie mogelt, wenn die Patience nicht aufgeht. *Minnie cheats when the game of patience doesn't work out.*

aufgehen — *to realize.*

Die Bedeutung dieser Ereignisse ist mir erst später aufgegangen. *Only later did I realize the meaning of these events.*

aufgehen in — *to be completely absorbed in.*

Die Botanikerin geht ganz in ihrer Arbeit auf. *The botanist is completely absorbed in her work.*

aufheben — *to pick up*

Sie hob die bunten Herbstblätter auf. *She picked up the colorful autumn leaves.*

viel Aufheben(s) machen — *to make a fuss.*

Mach doch nicht immer so viel Aufheben! *Don't always make such a fuss.*

aufheben — *to store.*

Sie hob die Blätter in einem Buch auf. *She stored the leaves in a book.*

gut aufgehoben sein — *to be in good hands.*

Bei ihnen sind Sie gut aufgehoben. *You're in good hands with them.*

aufheben — *to cancel; supersede.*

Die neuen Vorschriften heben die alten auf. *The new regulations supersede the old ones.*

---

aufreißen — *to tear open*

Der schüchterne Junge versuchte, bei der Party aufzureißen. *The shy boy tried to open up to people at the party.*

---

aufschieben — *to postpone*

Aufgeschoben ist nicht aufgehoben. *Deferred doesn't mean defunct. (There'll always be another opportunity.)*

---

auftreiben — *to get together*

Wir haben endlich das dafür nötige Geld aufgetrieben. *We finally got together the money necessary for it.*

auftreiben — *to stir up.*

Der Wind hat die Blätter aufgetrieben. *The wind stirred up the leaves.*

---

das Auge — *eye*

In meinen Augen ist das ein böses Zeichen. *To my mind that's a bad sign.*

sehenden Auges — *with full awareness.*

Sehenden Auges hat die Firma die Folgen wahrgenommen, aber nichts dagegen getan. *The company was completely aware of the consequences, but did nothing about it.*

aufs Auge drücken — *to compel.*

Der Präsidentin wurde die Steuerreform aufs Auge gedrückt. *The tax reform was forced on the president.*

ins Auge fallen — *to catch someone's eye.*

Im Schaufenster ist ihr ein Kollier besonders ins Auge gefallen. *In the shop window a necklace caught her eye.*

mit einem blauen Auge davonkommen — *to get off easy.*

Der gedopte Sportler kam mit einem blauen Auge davon; ihm wurde nur der Titel aberkannt. *The drug-taking athlete got off lightly; they just took away his title.*

mit einem lachenden und einem weinenden Auge — *with mixed emotions.*

Mit einem lachenden und einem weinenden Auge legte er sein Amt nieder. *He had mixed feelings about resigning from his office.*

unter vier Augen — *privately.*

Das müssen wir unter vier Augen besprechen. *We'll have to discuss that privately.*

Aus den Augen aus dem Sinn. *Out of sight out of mind.*

das Augenmaß — *sense of proportion.*

Augenmaß haben — *to be able to size up/gauge situations.*

Wir müssen die Lage mit viel Augenmaß betrachten. *We'll have to take a long and careful look at the situation.*

---

ausbaden — *to take the rap for/carry the can for (Brit.)*

Was du getan hast, muss ich jetzt ausbaden. *Now I've got to take the rap for what you did.*

---

das Ausbleiben — *absence*

Ich konnte mir sein Ausbleiben nicht erklären. *I couldn't understand his absence.*

ausbleiben — *to fail to materialize; not happen.*

Der erhoffte Sieg blieb aus. *The hoped for victory didn't happen.*

---

ausgehen — *to go out*

von etwas ausgehen — *to think; act on the assumption.*

Ich gehe davon aus, dass er die Wahrheit gesagt hat. *I'm acting on the assumption that he told the truth.*

---

auskommen — *to get by on*

Mit einem so niedrigen Gehalt kommt er kaum aus. *He scarcely gets by on such a low salary.*

auskommen — *to get on with.*
Es ist nicht leicht, mit ihm auszukommen. *It's not easy to get on with him.*

das Ausland — *foreign countries; abroad*
Sie lebten lange im Ausland. *They lived abroad for a long time.*

auslasten — *to load fully; to operate/use at full capacity*
Die Fabrik ist nur zur Hälfte ausgelastet. *The factory is operating only at half capacity.*

auslernen — *to finish one's apprenticeship*
Man lernt nie aus. *One is never done learning.*

auslöffeln — *to spoon out*
die Suppe/etwas auslöffeln. *To take the consequences.*
Du hast alles verkehrt gemacht und musst jetzt die Suppe auslöffeln. *You messed up everything and have to take the consequences now.*

ausrutschen — *to slip and fall*
Der Eiskunstläufer rutschte auf dem Glatteis aus. *The figure skater slipped and fell on the ice.*

ausrutschen — *to put one's foot into it.*
Beim Empfang auf der Botschaft rutschte sie wieder aus. *At the embassy reception she put her foot in it again.*

ausschildern — *to put up signs*
ausgeschildert sein — *to have signs; be marked.*
Die Straße ist gut ausgeschildert. *The road is well marked.*

der Bach — *brook*
den Bach heruntergehen — *to go down the drain.*
Wir wollen nicht, dass das Errungene den Bach heruntergeht. *We don't want everything we've achieved to go down the drain.*

die Bahn — *road*

auf die schiefe Bahn geraten — *to go wrong.*
Sein Sohn ist auf die schiefe Bahn geraten. *His son went wrong.*

freie Bahn — *a clear track.*
Alle Schwierigkeiten sind beseitigt, und wir haben jetzt freie Bahn. *All difficulties are resolved and we now have a clear track.*

Bahn frei! — *Get out of the way! Make way! Coming through!*

die (Eisen)Bahn — *railroad.*
Wir sind mit der Bahn gefahren. *We went by train.*

sich Bahn brechen — *to become established; to open up.*
Neue Verfahren in der Mikrotechnik brechen sich Bahn. *New procedures in microtechnology are opening up.*

sich in neuen Bahnen bewegen — *to break new ground.*
Mit seiner Erfindung gelang es Roebling, im Brückenbau neue Bahnen zu bewegen. *Roebling's invention broke new ground in bridge building.*

der Bahnhof — *railroad station*

Bahnhof verstehen — *to be "all Greek" or "double Dutch."*
Ich verstand nur Bahnhof. *It was all Greek to me.*

einen großen Bahnhof bereiten — *to roll out the red carpet.*
Man bereitete der Mannschaft einen großen Bahnhof. *They rolled out the red carpet for the team.*

der Balken — *beam*

dass sich die Balken biegen — *like crazy, like all get out.*
Im Haushalt wird so viel gestrichen, dass sich die Balken biegen. *They're making budget cuts like crazy.*

der Ball — *ball*

am Ball bleiben — *to keep at it.*
Die Reporterin blieb für ihre Zeitung am Ball. *The reporter kept at it for her newspaper.*

am Ball sein — *to be on the ball.*
Sie ist immer am Ball. *She's always on the ball.*

den Ball wieder rund machen — *to sort things out.*
Bei den Verhandlungen versuchen wir den Ball wieder rund zu machen.
We're trying to sort things out during the negotiations.

die Bandage — *bandage*
mit harten Bandagen kämpfen — *to pull no punches.*
Du musst lernen, mit harten Bandagen zu kämpfen. *You must learn to pull
no punches.*

die Bank — *bench*
auf die lange Bank schieben — *to put off.*
Schieben Sie das nicht auf die lange Bank! *Don't put that off.*

durch die Bank — *every single one; the whole lot.*
Sie stimmten durch die Bank gegen seine Bestätigung. *Every single one of
them voted against his confirmation.*

vor leeren Bänken spielen — *to play to an empty house.*
Wegen Angst vor Terroristen mussten wir gestern abend vor leeren
Bänken spielen. *Because of fear of terrorists we had to play to an empty
house last night.*

der Bär — *bear*
jemandem einen Bären aufbinden — *to pull someone's leg.*
Willst du mir damit einen Bären aufbinden? *Are you trying to pull my leg?*

einen Bärendienst erweisen — *to do a disservice.*
Er wollte helfen, aber er hat uns einen Bärendienst erwiesen. *He wanted
to help, but he did us a disservice.*

auf der Bärenhaut liegen — *to laze, lounge about.*
Den ganzen Tag liegt er auf der Bärenhaut, trotzdem hat er immer einen
Bärenhunger. *He lazes about all day, yet he's always ravenous.*

eine Bärenruhe haben — *to be completely unflappable.*
Trotz aller Krisen hat er immer eine Bärenruhe. *Despite all crises he
remains completely unflappable.*

bärbeißig — *grouchy.*
Sind Sie immer so bärbeißig? *Are you always so grouchy?*

der Bart — *beard*

um des Kaisers Bart streiten — *to quarrel about trifles.*
Statt um des Kaisers Bart zu streiten, solltet ihr euch mit den wirklichen
Streitfragen beschäftigen. *Instead of squabbling about petty details, you
should deal with the real issues.*

der Bauch — *belly*

aus dem hohlen Bauch — *instinctively, with a gut feeling.*
Aus dem hohlen Bauch scheint mir der Plan fragwürdig. *My gut feeling is
that the plan is questionable.*

den Bauch voll schlagen — *to overeat, stuff oneself.*
Jeden Tag kommt sein Onkel und schlägt sich bei uns den Bauch voll.
Every day his uncle comes and stuffs his belly (face) at our place.

die Beine in den Bauch stehen — *to be on one's feet for a long time.*
Stühle gab's nicht; wir mussten uns die Beine in den Bauch stehen.
There were no chairs and we had to stand for a long time.

mit etwas auf den Bauch fallen — *to fall flat on one's face.*
Mit den neuen Plan sind wir auf den Bauch gefallen. *We fell flat on our
face with that new plan.*

sich vor Lachen den Bauch halten — *to split one's sides laughing.*
Die Komikerin war hinwerfend; wir hielten uns den Bauch. *The comic
was a scream. We split our sides laughing.*

bauen — *to build*

bauen auf — *to build on; to count on.*
Als Optimist baut er trotzdem auf bessere Zeiten. *As an optimist, he's
counting on better times.*

der Bauklotz — *building brick*

Bauklötze staunen — *to be staggered, flabbergasted.*
Die Chemikerin staunte Bauklötze, als sie die Mutation beobachtete. *The
chemist was flabbergasted when she saw the mutation.*

der Baum — *tree*

Bäume ausreißen können — *to feel ready to take on anything.*
Zuerst glaubte er, Bäume ausreißen zu können. *At first he felt ready to
take on anything.*

zwischen Baum und Borke sitzen — *to be on the horns of a dilemma.*
Die Präsidentin sitzt zwischen Baum und Borke. *The president is on the horns of a dilemma.*

Bäume wachsen nicht in den Himmel — in der Beschränkung zeigt sich der Meister. — *There are limits to everything. It's limitations that test a master's mettle.*

---

baumeln — *to dangle; to swing (hang)*
Der Scheriff schwor, dass er den Räuber baumeln lassen würde. *The sheriff swore he'd see the bandit hang.*

---

bedienen — *to wait on*
vorn und hinten bedienen — *to wait on hand and foot.*
Der braucht jemand, der ihn vorn und hinten bedient. *He needs someone who'll wait on him hand and foot.*

bedienen — *to serve.*
Wer bedient in diesem Restaurant? *Who is serving in this restaurant?*

sich bedienen — *to help oneself.*
Hier gibt's keine Bedienung; Sie müssen sich selbst bedienen. *There's no service here; you have to help yourself.*

---

der Begriff — *concept*
Für meine Begriffe ist das eine veraltete Methode. *To my way of thinking, that's an outmoded method.*

ein Begriff sein — *to be well known.*
Diese Marke ist ein Begriff für Qualität. *This brand is well known for quality.*

schwer von Begriff sein — *to be slow on the uptake.*
Sag's ihm wieder; er ist schwer von Begriff. *Tell him again; he's slow on the uptake.*

im Begriff sein etwas zu tun — *to be about to do something.*
Die Gräfin war im Begriff auszugehen, als das Telefon klingelte. *The countess was about to go out when the phone rang.*

---

bei — *near; at; with; in*

bei — *care of.*

Schreiben Sie ihm bei Müller & Sohn! *Write him c/o Müller & Son.*

bei — *at someone's home.*

Gestern waren wir bei ihnen. *We were at their place yesterday.*

bei — *in the work of.*

Sie schrieb über das Persische bei Goethe. *She wrote on Persian elements in Goethe's work.*

bei — *over.*

Bei einer Tasse Kaffee sprachen wir über Goethe. *We talked about Goethe over a cup of coffee.*

bei — *in case of.*

Bei Feuer Scheibe einschlagen. *In case of fire, break glass.*

---

beilegen — *to enclose with*

Meinem Brief lege ich einen Zeitungsartikel bei. *With my letter I enclose a newspaper article.*

beilegen — *to attach.*

Legen Sie der Sache viel Bedeutung bei? *Do you attach much importance to the matter?*

---

das Bein — *leg*

auf den Beinen sein — *to be on one's feet.*

Ich bin seit sieben Uhr auf den Beinen. *I've been on my feet since seven o'clock.*

auf die Beine bringen — *to launch.*

Es ist schwer, ein solches Unternehmen auf die Beine zu bringen. *It's difficult to launch an enterprise like that.*

ein Bein stellen — *to trip (up).*

Er hat sich selbst ein Bein gestellt. *He tripped himself up.*

jmdm./etwas Beine machen — *to make s.o./s.t. get going/get a move on.*

Die Präsidentin will der flauen Wirtschaft Beine machen. *The president wants to get the sluggish economy moving.*

sich die Beine in die Hand nehmen — *to take off fast.*
Der Junge warf den Schneeball und nahm dann die Beine in die Hand.
The boy threw the snowball and then took off fast.

wieder auf die Beine kommen — *to get back on one's feet.*
Wir hoffen, dass Adeles Tante bald wieder auf die Beine kommt. *We hope
Adele's aunt gets back on her feet soon.*

wieder auf den Beinen sein — *to be back on one's feet.*
Sie ist wieder auf den Beinen. *She's back on her feet again.*

---

bekommen — *to receive*
es über sich bekommen — *to bring oneself to do something.*
Ich konnte es nicht über mich bekommen, ihnen sofort die ganze Wahrheit
zu sagen. *I couldn't bring myself to tell them the whole truth right away.*

bekommen — *to agree with.*
Die makrobiotische Kochkunst bekam uns nicht ganz. *Macrobiotic
cooking didn't entirely agree with us.*
Wohl bekomm's! *To your good health! (Enjoy!)*

---

bereiten — *to prepare*
Freude bereiten — *to give pleasure.*
Mit eurem Geschenk habt ihr mir viel Freude bereitet. *With your gift
you've given me much pleasure.*

---

der Berg — *mountain; hill*
goldene Berge versprechen — *to promise the moon.*
Er versprach ihr goldene Berge. *He promised her the moon.*

nicht hinter dem Berg halten — *to be unhesitating.*
Mit Kritik hielt die Opposition nicht hinter dem Berg. *The opposition did
not hesitate to criticize.*

über alle Berge sein — *to be miles away.*
Der Dieb war schon über alle Berge. *The thief was already miles away.*

über den Berg sein — *to be out of the woods.*
Es geht ihr besser, aber sie ist noch nicht über den Berg. *She's feeling
better, but she's not yet out of the woods.*

bergab — *downhill*

"Es geht bergab mit uns," behauptete der Pessimist. *"Things are going downhill for us," asserted the pessimist.*

bergauf — *uphill*

"Es geht bergauf mit uns," erklärte der Optimist. *"Things are looking up for us," declared the optimist.*

der Beruf — *occupation, profession*

den Beruf verfehlt haben — *to have missed one's calling.*

Er glaubt, seinen Beruf verfehlt zu haben. *He thinks he's missed his calling.*

von Beruf sein — *to do, exercise a profession.*

Ich bin Bauarbeiter von Beruf. Was sind Sie von Beruf? *I'm a construction worker. What do you do?*

der Bescheid — *information*

Bescheid geben/sagen — *to inform; tell.*

Sagen Sie ihr Bescheid, dass wir spät kommen. *Tell her that we'll be late.*

Bescheid stoßen — *to tell off.*

Wenn er wieder versucht, mir 'was vorzumachen, stoß ich ihm gehörig Bescheid. *If he tries to fool me again, I'll tell him off.*

Bescheid wissen — *to be informed; to know one's way around or with.*

Entschuldigung, wissen Sie hier Bescheid? *Pardon me, do you know your way around here?*

der Bescheid — *decision.*

Wir erhielten einen abschlägigen Bescheid. *We received a refusal (negative decision).*

der Besen — *broom*

einen Besen fressen — *to eat one's hat.*

Wenn dem wirklich so ist, fress ich einen Besen. *If that's really the case, I'll eat my hat.*

Neue Besen kehren gut. *A new broom sweeps clean.*

die Besserung — *improvement*
Gute Besserung! *Get well soon!*
auf dem Wege der Besserung sein — *to be on the road to recovery.*
Sie war schwer krank, jetzt ist sie aber auf dem Wege der Besserung. *She
was very sick, but now she's getting better.*

best — *best*
Am besten nehmen wir die Autobahn. *We'd best take the freeway.*
Besten Dank für das Paket! *Many thanks for the package.*
in den besten Jahren sein — *to be in one's prime.*
Fräulein Brodie war in den besten Jahren. *Miss Brodie was in her prime.*
zum Besten haben/halten — *to put one over on.*
Er versuchte, uns zum Besten zu haben. *He tried to put one over on us.*

der Betreuer — *social worker*
Der Betreuer macht zweimal die Woche die Hausarbeiten für sie. *The
social worker does the housework for them twice a week.*

die Betreuung — *looking after*
Wir haben eine Krankenpflegerin zur Betreuung der Großeltern
eingestellt. *We hired a nurse to look after our grandparents.*

der Betrieb — *business*
außer Betrieb sein — *to be out of order.*
Die Rolltreppe im Kaufhaus war außer Betrieb. *The escalator in the
department store was out of order.*
Betrieb herrschen — *to be busy.*
Nachmittags bei uns im Laden herrscht viel Betrieb. *Afternoons it's
always very busy in our store.*
den ganzen Betrieb aufhalten — *to hold everyone up.*
Vielleicht hast du recht, aber du brauchst nicht den ganzen Betrieb
aufzuhalten. *Maybe you're right but you don't have to hold everyone up.*
in Betrieb nehmen — *to put into service, operation.*
Wann wird die neue Bahnlinie in Betrieb genommen? *When will the new
rail line be put into service?*

betucht — *well-heeled, well off*
Nur (gut) betuchte Leute gehören diesem Verein an. *Only wellheeled people belong to this club.*

sich bewahrheiten — *to come true; turn out to be true*
Einige ihrer Prophezeiungen haben sich schon bewahrheitet. *Some of her prophecies have already come true.*

der Beweis — *proof*
unter Beweis stellen — *to give proof of.*
Sie hat ihre Kochkünste unter Beweis gestellt. *She has given proof of her culinary skills.*

die Biege — *bend*
eine Biege fahren — *to go for a spin.*
Er wollte eine Biege fahren, aber wegen der Umweltverschmutzung sagten wir nein. *He wanted to go for a spin, but we said no because of environmental pollution.*

biegen — *to bend*
auf Biegen oder Brechen — *by hook or by crook, one way or another.*
Auf Biegen oder Brechen werden wir's schon schaffen. *One way or another we'll manage it.*

das Bier — *beer*
jemands Bier sein — *to be someone's business.*
Das ist weder mein noch dein Bier. *That's not your business or mine.*

bierernst — *deadly serious.*
Nimm's nicht so bierernst! *Don't take it with such deadly seriousness.*

das Bild — *picture*
sich ein Bild machen — *to form an impression.*
Durch archäologische Funde können wir uns ein Bild von der Kultur der alten Mayas machen. *Through archaeological finds we can form an impression of ancient Mayan culture.*

die Bildung — *education*

die Leute von Besitz und Bildung — *the propertied and educated classes.*

Die Partei versuchte, die Leute von Besitz und Bildung anzusprechen. *The party tried to appeal to the propertied and educated classes.*

Einbildung ist auch eine Bildung! — *Such (your) conceit knows no bounds.*

Du wärst für den Posten geeigneter gewesen? *Na, Einbildung ist auch eine Bildung! You would have been more suited for the post? Your conceit knows no bounds.*

der Bildungsroman — *novel of character formation/development.*

Wir haben Bildungsromane von Goethe, Keller und Hesse gelesen. *We read novels of character formation by Goethe, Keller, and Hesse.*

---

die Binse — *reed; marsh grass*

in die Binsen gehen — *to go down the drain; fall apart.*

Er tröstete sich mit Binsenwahrheiten, nachdem seine Ehe in die Binsen gegangen war. *He consoled himself with truisms after his marriage fell apart.*

die Binsenwahrheit — *truism.*

Er sammelt Binsenwahrheiten für sein Buch. *He's collecting truisms for his book.*

---

die Birne — *pear; head; light bulb*

eine weiche Birne haben — *to be dimwitted, soft in the head.*

Der hat ein gutes Herz aber 'ne weiche Birne. *He's got a good heart but he's a bit dimwitted.*

---

blasen — *to blow*

jemandem den Marsch blasen — *to give someone a bawling out.*

Wenn's der Chef erfährt, wird er dir den Marsch blasen. *If the boss finds out he'll give you a bawling out.*

Trübsal blasen — *to lament, sing the blues.*

Man vermeidet ihn, weil er immer nur Trübsal bläst. *People avoid him because he's always singing the blues.*

---

das Blatt — *leaf*

Das Blatt hat sich endlich gewendet — *Things have finally taken a different turn.*

ein unbeschriebenes Blatt sein — *to be an unknown quantity.*
Diese Kandidatin ist noch ein unbeschriebenes Blatt. *This candidate is still an unknown quantity.*

---

blau — *blue*

blau machen — *to skip school, work (call in sick without being sick).*
Er macht oft blau, weil er auch schwarzarbeitet. *He often calls in sick because he's got another undeclared job.*

blau sein — *to be drunk, plastered.*
Er war wieder völlig blau. *He was completely plastered again.*

blauer Dunst — *rubbish.*
Alles, was er sagte, war nur blauer Dunst. *Everything he said was just rubbish.*

sein blaues Wunder erleben — *to get a nasty surprise.*
Wenn sich das doch bewahrheitet, werden Sie ihr blaues Wunder erleben. *But if that turns out to be true, you'll get a nasty surprise.*

---

das Blaue — *the blue*

das Blaue vom Himmel herunterlügen — *to lie through one's teeth.*
Um Geschäfte zu machen, lügt er das Blaue vom Himmel herunter. *To make business deals, he lies through his teeth.*

ins Blaue hineinreden — *to engage in idle chatter, talk aimlessly.*
Glaub ihm nicht; er redet nur ins Blaue hinein. *Don't believe him; he's just talking so he can hear himself talk.*

ins Blaue schießen — *to fire a shot in the dark, fire at random.*
Der Detektiv hatte ins Blaue geschossen und ins Schwarze getroffen. *The detective fired a shot in the dark and hit the mark (bullseye).*

blauäugig — *blue-eyed; naïve, starry-eyed.*
Blauäugiger Optimismus nützt uns jetzt nichts. *Naïve optimism is of no use to us now.*

---

das Blech — *sheet metal*
Blech reden — *to talk nonsense.*
Red kein Blech. *Don't talk rubbish.*

---

bleiben — *to remain; be*
Wir warten schon lange. *Wo bleibt das Essen? We've been waiting for
some time. Where's the food?*

außen vor bleiben — *to be excluded, ignored.*
Solche radikalen Begriffe bleiben noch in der großen Gesellschaft außen
vor. *Such radical concepts are still ignored in society at large.*

dabei bleiben — *to stick to.*
Ich hab's versprochen und ich bleibe dabei. *I promised it and I'm sticking
to it.*

vom Leibe bleiben — *to keep away.*
Bleib mir vom Leibe mit solch skandalösen Geschichten! *Keep away from
me with such scandalous stories.*

---

blind — *blind*
blinden Alarm schlagen — *to turn in a false alarm; to cry wolf.*
Der Junge hat wieder blinden Alarm geschlagen. *The boy turned in a false
alarm again.*

blinder Passagier — *stowaway.*
Sie versuchten als blinde Passagiere, das Land zu verlassen. *They tried to
leave the country as stowaways.*

---

das Blümchen — *little flower*
der Blümchenkaffee — *weak coffee; coffee substitute.*
Heimlich goss er Rum in seinen Blümchenkaffee. *Furtively, he poured
rum into his weak coffee.*

die Blume — *flower*

durch die Blume sagen — *to say in a roundabout way.*
Sie hat es nicht direkt sondern durch die Blume gesagt. *She didn't say so
directly but in a roundabout way.*

---

der Bock — *billy goat; buck; fun, inclination*

Ihn stößt wieder der Bock. *He's being ornery/contrary again.*

einen Bock schießen. *To make a blunder/blooper/howler.*

Er hat wieder einen großen Bock geschossen. *He made another whale of a blunder.*

Bock/Lust haben auf — *to feel like.*

Sie sagt, sie hätte es nur aus Bock getan; das ist aber keine Entschuldigung. *She says she did it just because she felt like it; but that's no excuse.*

---

der Boden — *ground; soil*

am Boden liegen — *to be in a sorry state.*

In der Gegend liegt die Stahlindustrie total am Boden. *In that area the steel industry is in a very sorry state.*

den Boden unter den Füßen wegziehen — *to pull the rug out from under.*

Sie entzogen ihre Hilfe, und damit zogen sie mir den Boden unter den Füßen weg. *They withdrew their aid and thus pulled the rug out from under me.*

---

der Bogen — *arc; curve; detour*

den Bogen heraushaben — *to have gotten the hang of it.*

Endlich hab ich den Bogen heraus! *I've finally gotten the hang of it!*

den Bogen überspannen — *to overstep the mark, go too far.*

Schau zu, dass du den Bogen nicht wieder überspannst! *Be careful you don't go too far again.*

einen großen Bogen machen — *to go out of one's way to avoid.*

Viele machen einen großen Bogen um die Zahl 13. *Many go out of their way to avoid the number 13.*

---

die Bohne — *bean*

Bohnen in den Ohren haben — *to play deaf.*

Der Kellner hat mich gehört und gesehen, kommt aber nicht. Hat wohl Bohnen in den Ohren. *The waiter saw and heard me, but he doesn't come. He must be playing deaf.*

Jede Bohn' hat ihren Ton or **Jedes Böhnchen hat sein Tönchen/Jedes Böhnchen gibt sein Tönchen.** *Beans produce flatulence.*

Iss nicht zu viele Bohnen; du weißt ja, jede Bohn' hat ihren Ton. *Don't eat too many beans; you know each bean has its own tone.*

nicht die Bohne — *not a scrap/whit/bit.*

Die Kritiker haben nicht die Bohne von ihrem Roman verstanden. *The critics didn't understand her novel at all.*

---

bombensicher — *absolutely safe*

Der Finanzberater meint, es sei eine bombensichere Sache und werde einen Bombenerfolg haben. *The financial advisor says it's absolutely safe and will be a smash hit.*

---

das Boot — *boat*

jmdn. mit ins Boot holen — *to make s.o. part of a group, firm etc.*

Statt sie anzufeinden, sollten wir sie vielleicht lieber ins Boot holen. *Instead of making enemies of them, maybe we should get them to come on board.*

im selben Boot/in einem Boot sitzen — *to be in the same boat.*

Schließlich sitzen wir alle in einem Boot. *After all, we're all in the same boat.*

---

der Braten — *roast*

den Braten riechen — *to smell a rat.*

Der Gangster hatte den Braten gerochen und ging nicht in die Falle. *The gangster smelled a rat and didn't fall into the trap.*

---

braun — *brown; Nazi*

Schnell verdrängte er seine braune Vergangenheit, schloss sich eifrig den Roten an, und paktierte auch mit den Schwarzen und Grünen.

He quickly supressed his Nazi past, enthusiastically joined the Reds, and dealt with the Blacks (conservatives, clerics) and Greens (ecologists) too.

braungebrannt — *suntanned.*

Nick kam braungebrannt aus Afrika zurück. *Nick came back from Africa with a suntan.*

---

der Brei — *porridge*

um den heißen Brei herumreden — *to beat about the bush.*

Hör doch auf, um den heißen Brei herumzureden, und sag mir alles
  sofort! *Stop beating about the bush and tell me everything right away.*

zu Brei schlagen — *to beat to a pulp.*

Die Hooligans haben ihn zu Brei geschlagen. *The hooligans beat him to
  a pulp.*

breit — *wide*

sich breit machen — *to spread.*

Unruhe macht sich in vielen Schichten der Bevölkerung breit. *Unrest is
  spreading in many groups in the population.*

in die Breite gehen — *to get fat.*

Iss nicht so viele Torten oder du gehst in die Breite. *Don't eat so many
  tarts or you'll get fat.*

in die Breite wirken — *to reach a large audience.*

Mit ihrem neuen Buch will die Professorin mehr in die Breite wirken.
  With her new book the professor wants to reach a larger audience.

brennen — *to burn*

Gebranntes Kind scheut das Feuer. *Once bitten, twice shy.*

darauf brennen, etwas zu tun — *to be dying (longing) to do something.*

Wir brennen darauf, die ganze Geschichte zu hören. *We're dying to hear
  the whole story.*

die Bresche — *breech, gap*

sich in die Bresche schlagen für — *to go to bat for, stand up for.*

Seine Frau hat sich für ihn in die Bresche geschlagen. *His wife stood up
  for him.*

das Brett — *board*

das Brett/Holz bohren, wo es am dünnsten ist — *to look for a too-
  simple solution.*

Dieser Faulpelz will immer das Holz bohren, wo es am dünnsten ist.
  That lazybones is always looking for an easy way out.

ein dickes Brett bohren — *to cope with a difficult problem.*

Die Verhandlungen laufen — es gibt noch viele dicke Bretter zu bohren.
Negotiations are continuing — there are still many thorny problems to deal with.

ein Brett vor dem Kopf haben — *to be slow on the uptake; have a mental block.*

Heute habe ich ein Brett vor dem Kopf. *My head isn't on straight today.*

der Brief — *letter*
blauer Brief — *warning letter; pink slip.*

Es heißt, fast die Hälfte der Belegschaft soll einen blauen Brief bekommen soll. *They're saying half the workforce is going to get pink slips.*

bringen — *to bring*
es auf etwas bringen — *to get as far as.*

Die Splitterpartei brachte es nur auf fünftausend Stimmen. *The splinter party only got (as far as) 5,000 votes.*

es weit bringen — *to amount to much.*

Sie glaubten, Hans würde es nie weit bringen. *They thought Hans would never amount to much.*

das Brot — *bread*
Das ist eine brotlose Kunst. *There's no money in that.*

brotlos machen — *to put out of work.*

Die Arbeiter hatten Angst, dass die Roboter sie brotlos machen würden. *The workers were afraid the robots would put them out of work.*

die Brotzeit — *coffee/lunch break.*

Während der Dreharbeiten in München freuten wir uns auf die Brotzeit. *While making a movie in Munich we looked forward to the lunch break.*

das Brötchen — *roll*
kleine Brötchen backen — *to operate on a small scale.*

Wir backen noch kleine Brötchen aber wir haben große Pläne. *We're still small potatoes but we have great plans.*

kleinere Brötchen backen — *to limit operations, downsize.*
Wegen der Kürzungen müssen wir leider noch kleinere Brötchen backen.
Because of cutbacks we'll have to downsize even more.

der Bruch — *fracture*
Deutschsprachigen Schauspielern sagt man: "Hals- und Beinbruch!" *One says "break a leg and your neck" to German-speaking actors.*

in die Brüche gehen — *to collapse.*
Ihre Ehe droht, in die Brüche zu gehen. *Their marriage is in danger of collapsing.*

bruchlanden — *to crash-land.*
Die Pilotin musste bruchlanden. *The pilot had to crash-land.*

die Brücke — *bridge*
alle Brücken hinter sich abbrechen — *to burn one's bridges behind one.*
Jetzt bereuen wir's, alle Brücken hinter uns abgebrochen zu haben. *Now we're sorry we burned all our bridges behind us.*

Brücken schlagen — *to build bridges; establish ties.*
Die ehemaligen Feinde versuchen jetzt, Brücken zu einander zu schlagen. *The former enemies are now trying to build bridges to each other.*

eine goldene Brücke bauen — to smooth the way for.
Er meinte, sein Onkel würde ihm im Geschäft eine goldene Brücke bauen. *He thought his uncle would smooth the way for him in the business.*

bügeln — *to iron*
geschniegelt und gebügelt — *all spruced up.*
Für den Staatsbesuch war die Stadt geschniegelt und gebügelt. *The city was all spruced up for the state visit.*

der Buhmann — *whipping boy; bogeyman*
Nach den Enthüllungen in der Zeitung wurde er zum Buhmann der Nation. *After the revelations in the newspaper, he became the nation's scapegoat.*

die Bühne — *stage*

reibungslos über die Bühne gehen — *to go off without a hitch.*
Es ist alles reibunglos über die Bühne gegangen. *Everything went off without a hitch.*

bunt — *multicolored*

Ein bunt gemischtes Publikum verkehrt in dem Lokal. *A very mixed clientele patronizes that place.*

bunter Abend — *evening of music and entertainment.*
Nächste Woche veranstaltet das Hotel einen bunten Abend. *Next week the hotel is arranging for an evening of music and entertainment.*

es zu bunt treiben — *to go too far.*
Diesmal hat er es zu bunt getrieben. *This time he went too far.*

zu bunt werden — *to get to be too much for.*
Es wurde mir zu bunt, und ich ging nach Hause. *Things got to be too much for me and I went home.*

der Busch — *bush*

auf den Busch klopfen — *to sound out.*
Er klopfte bei mir auf den Busch, ob ich ihn unterstützen würde. *He sounded me out as to whether I'd support him.*

im Busch sein — *to be brewing.*
Ich weiß nicht genau, was sie vorhaben, aber etwas ist im Busch. *I don't know for sure what they're planning, but something's brewing.*

sich in die Büsche schlagen — *to slip away; to go underground.*
Kafkas Affe dachte daran, seinem Käfig zu entkommen, und sich in die Büsche zu schlagen. *Kafka's monkey thought of escaping its cage and slipping away.*
Man gab ihm eine neue Identität und er schlug sich in die Büsche. *They gave him a new identity and he went underground.*

die Butter — *butter*

in (bester) Butter sein — *to be going smoothly.*
Sie hatten einige Schwierigkeiten, aber jetzt ist alles in bester Butter. *They had some difficulties, but everything is going smoothly now.*

der Chaot — *anarchist; violent demonstrator*
   ein Chaot sein — *to be terribly disorganized.*
   Jetzt ist er sehr scharf auf Ordnung, aber in jungen Jahren war er ein
      furchtbarer Chaot. *Now he's keen on order, but when he was young he
      was terribly disorganized.*

das Dach — *roof*
   unter Dach und Fach bringen — *to complete successfully; wrap up*
   Sie hat jetzt ihre Dissertation unter Dach und Fach. *She's now successfully
      completed her dissertation.*

der Damm — *levee; embankment; roadway*
   wieder auf dem Damm sein — *to be feeling fit again.*
   Onkel Otto war krank, aber jetzt ist er wieder auf dem Damm. *Uncle Otto
      was sick, but now he's feeling fit again.*

der Dampfer — *steam ship*
   auf dem falschen Dampfer sitzen — *to be barking up the wrong tree.*
   Der Detektiv saß wieder auf dem falschen Dampfer. *The detective was
      barking up the wrong tree again.*

der Dämpfer — *mute; damper*
   einen Dämpfer aufsetzen — *to dampen enthusiasm.*
   Er versuchte, mir einen Dämpfer aufzusetzen, aber ich ließ mich nicht
      kleinkriegen. *He tried to dampen my enthusiasm, but I wouldn't be
      intimidated.*

dauern — *to last*
der Dauerbrenner — *slow-burning oven; long-lasting success.*
Einige ihrer Lieder sind zu Dauerbrennern geworden. *Some of her songs have become long-lasting successes.*

der Daumen/das Däumchen — *thumb*
den Daumen aufs Auge halten — *to pressure; put the screws on.*
Du brauchst mir nicht den Daumen aufs Auge zu halten, ich beuge mich dem allgemeinen Willen. *You don't have to pressure me, I yield to the general will.*

den (die) Daumen drücken — *to keep one's fingers crossed for.*
Ich werde dir den Daumen drücken, dass alles gut klappt. *I'll keep my fingers crossed for you that everything goes right.*

die Daumen drehen/Däumchen drehen — *to twiddle one's thumbs.*
Jetzt musst du handeln, statt nur die Daumen zu drehen. *You've got to take action now instead of just twiddling your thumbs.*

über den Daumen peilen — *to make a rough estimate.*
Über den Daumen gepeilt, dürfte die Oase nicht mehr weit weg sein. *At a rough estimate, the oasis shouldn't be too far off now.*

die Decke — *cover, blanket; ceiling, roof*
Mir fällt die Decke auf den Kopf; ich brauche Tapetenwechsel. *I'm going stir-crazy; I need a change of scenery.*

an die Decke gehen — *to hit the ceiling.*
Geh nicht gleich an die Decke! *Don't fly off the handle right away.*

sich nach der Decke strecken — *to make do with what's available, cut one's coat according to one's cloth.*
Dein Vater ist arbeitslos und wir müssen uns jetzt nach der Decke strecken. *Your father's unemployed and we have to make do with less now.*

denken — *to think*
Das hätte ich mir denken können! *I might have known!*
Denken ist Glückssache — *thinking is a matter of chance, and you weren't lucky.*

Gedacht, getan! *No sooner said than done.*

zu denken geben — *to make suspicious.*
Sein Verhalten gab mir zu denken. *His behavior made me suspicious.*

denken an — *to think of.*
Goethe dachte an das Röslein und später an die Urpflanze. *Goethe thought of the little rose and later of the primordial plant.*

nicht im Traum an etwas denken — *to not dream of, have no intention of.*
Ich denke nicht im Traum daran, ihn einzuladen. *I wouldn't dream of inviting him.*

denken über — *to think about.*
Sie weiß nicht, wie sie über seinen Brief denken soll. *She doesn't know what to think about his letter.*

deutsch — *German*
der deutsche Michel — *simple, honest, provincial German.*
Sie war den Wählern zu dynamisch, die eher einen deutschen Michel, eine Zipfelmütze, wollten.
She was too dynamic for the voters, who preferred a simple, colorless guy from Dullsville.

die Diät — *diet*
Diät machen — *to be on a diet.*
Er macht wieder Diät. *He's on a diet again.*

diät essen/kochen/leben — *to eat/cook/live according to a diet.*
Er isst diät, und seine Frau kocht diät für ihn. *He eats according to a diet, and his wife prepares diet meals for him.*

dicht — *thick; sealed*
nicht ganz dicht sein — *to be a little cracked/crazy.*
Franz ist nett aber nicht ganz dicht. *Franz is nice but a little cracked.*

dichtmachen — *to close; to shut up shop.*
Wir haben heute den Laden etwas früher dichtgemacht. *We closed the store a little earlier today.*

dichten — *to write poetry*

In seiner Jugend dichtete er Tag und Nacht. *In his youth he wrote poetry day and night.*

sein Dichten und Trachten — *all one's thoughts.*

Jetzt ist sein Dichten und Trachten nur auf Geld gerichtet. *Now all he thinks about is money.*

dick — *thick; fat*

dick machen — *to make pregnant.*

Er hat seine Freundin dick gemacht. *He got his girlfriend pregnant.*

dick werden — *to get fat.*

Sie isst viel Schlagsahne, wird aber nicht dick. *She eats lots of whipped cream, but she doesn't get fat.*

durch dick und dünn gehen — *to go through thick and thin.*

Wir sind mit einander durch dick und dünn gegangen. *We've been through thick and thin together.*

es dick haben — *to be well off.*

Er ließ uns zahlen, obwohl wir es gar nicht so dick haben. *He let us pay even though we're not well off at all.*

dicke Luft — *pessimistic atmosphere.*

Wegen des Übernahmeversuchs herrscht dicke Luft auf der Chefetage. *The atmosphere on the executive floor is pretty bleak because of the takeover attempt.*

sich dicke tun — *to show off.*

Auf dem Rummelplatz tat er sich mit seiner Kraft dicke. *At the fair he showed off his strength.*

dienen — *to serve*

ausgedient haben — *to be history, be passé.*

In den diesjährigen Modekollektionen haben Extreme ausgedient. *In this year's fashion collections, extremes are passé.*

der Dienst — *service*

Dienst ist Dienst, und Schnaps ist Schnaps. *Work is one thing and pleasure is another/you shouldn't mix business and pleasure.*

vom Dienst — *on (official) duty; stock, constant.*

Die Rolle hab ich abgelehnt; ich bin es satt, immer den Bösewicht vom Dienst zu spielen. *I turned down the role; I'm fed up with always playing the stock villain.*

das Ding — *thing*

Es geht nicht mit rechten Dingen zu. *There's something crooked going on.*
Gut Ding will Weile haben. *It takes time to do things right.*

vor allen Dingen — *above all.*

Vor allen Dingen müssen die Kriegsopfer betreut werden. *Above all, the victims of the war need to be looked after.*

Aller guten Dinge sind drei! — *All good things come in threes!/The third try will be lucky.*

"Aller guten Dinge sind drei," sagten das Ehepaar und ihr Hausfreund. *"All good things come in threes," said the married couple and their friend.*

dingfest machen — *to arrest; apprehend.*

Bislang hat ihn die Polizei nicht dingfest machen können. *Up to now the police haven't been able to apprehend him.*

donnern — *to thunder*

Es donnerte. *There was thunder.*

eine donnern — *to give a good whack.*

Es riss ihm die Geduld, und er donnerte dem Jungen eine. *His patience ran out and he gave the boy a good whack.*

doppelt — *double*

doppelt gemoppelt — *to repeat unnecessarily.*

Das ist wieder doppelt gemoppelt. *That's more unnecessary repetition.*

doppelter Boden — *false bottom.*

Der Dieb versteckte den Schmuck in einer Kiste mit doppeltem Boden. *The thief hid the jewels in a box with a false bottom.*

das Dornröschen — *Sleeping Beauty*
   aus seinem Dornröschenschlaf erwachen — *to become active after a period of torpor.*
   Mir wär's lieber, wenn unser einst so beschauliches Dörfchen nicht aus seinem Dornröschenschlaf erwacht wäre. *I'd rather our once picturesque little village had stayed a sleepy hamlet.*

der Draht — *wire*
   auf Draht bringen — *to get into shape; bring up to scratch/speed.*
   Die neue Chefin versucht das Unternehmen auf Draht zu bringen. *The new boss is trying to get the company into shape.*

   auf Draht sein — *to be a live wire; be on the ball.*
   Sie wird Erfolg haben, denn sie ist immer auf Draht. *She will be successful for she's always on the ball.*

   einen Draht haben — *to be well in with, have a connection with/line to.*
   Er glaubt einen Draht zum Herrgott zu haben. *He thinks he has a direct line to God Almighty.*
   Unsere Partei hat einen besseren Draht zu den Wählern. *Our party is more in touch with the voters.*

der Drahtesel — *bicycle*
   In Münster sieht man viele Drahtesel. *One sees many bikes in Münster.*

der Dreck — *dirt*
   den Karren aus dem Dreck ziehen — *to get out of/clean up a mess.*
   Wir stecken noch im Dreck aber vielleicht wird der neue Präsident den Karren aus dem Dreck ziehen. *We're still in the muck, but maybe the new president will clean up the mess.*

   Dreck am Stecken haben — *to have a shady past/skeletons in the closet.*
   Es hat sich herausgestellt, dass der große Moralapostel selber Dreck am Stecken hat. *It turned out that the great moral crusader had skeletons in his closet.*

drehen — *to turn*
   es drehen und wenden, wie man will — *to examine from every possible angle.*

Du kannst es drehen und wenden, wie die willst, es läuft alles auf dasselbe hinaus. *You can examine it from every possible angle, it still amounts to the same thing.*

Filme drehen — *to make movies.*
Sie träumt davon, Filme zu drehen. *She's dreaming of making movies.*

dreizehn — *thirteen*
Jetzt schlägt's (aber) dreizehn! — *That's too much!*
Sie verlangen wieder Geld? Jetzt schlägt's aber dreizehn! They're asking for money again? That's going too far!

dreschen — *to thresh*
mit der Faust auf den Tisch dreschen — *to pound the table with one's fist.*
Um seinen Worten Nachdruck zu verleihen, drischt er oft mit der Faust auf den Tisch. *To lend emphasis to his words, he often pounds the table with his fist.*

Phrasen dreschen — *to mouth trite phrases.*
In seiner Rede hat er aber nur Phrasen gedroschen. *But all he did in his speech was mouth trite phrases.*

drücken — *to press; push*
Die drückende Hitze drückte auf die Stimmung. *The oppressive heat dampened the mood.*

die Oppositionsbank drücken — *to be in the opposition.*
Früher bildeten sie die Regierung; jetzt drücken sie die Oppositionsbank. *Formerly they formed the government; now they're in the opposition.*

die Schulbank drücken — *to go to school.*
Er war schon 15 Jahre alt und wollte nicht mehr die Schulbank drücken. *He was already 15 years old and didn't want to go to school any more.*

ans Herz drücken — *to hug close.*
Nach der langen Trennung drückte er sie ans Herz. *After the long separation, he hugged her close.*

sich drücken — *to shirk; avoid.*
Er drückte sich vor jeder Arbeit. *He avoided any kind of work.*

drum — *around*
mit allem Drum und Dran — *with all the trimmings.*
Wenn Ulla heiratet, muss es mit allem Drum und Dran sein. *When Ulla gets married, it'll have to be with all the trimmings.*

drunter — *underneath*
drunter und drüber — *topsy-turvy.*
Es ist jetzt alles drunter und drüber. *Everything is topsy-turvy now.*

du — *you*
auf du und du sein — *to be very familiar with.*
"Die Bürger unserer Stadt leben mit der Kunst auf du und du," sagte stolz die Bürgermeisterin. *"The citizens of our town are very familiar with the arts," said the mayor proudly.*

dumm — *stupid*
Das ist mir einfach zu dumm! *I've had enough of that!*
Mir ist ganz dumm im Kopf. *My head is swimming.*
Man nennt sie eine dumme Gans, aber sie ist eigentlich sehr gescheit. *They call her a silly goose, but she's really very astute.*

für dumm verkaufen — *to put one over on.*
Er versuchte, mich für dumm zu verkaufen. *He tried to put one over on me.*

aus Dummsdorf sein — *to be born yesterday.*
Er glaubt, wir sind aus Dummsdorf. *He thinks we were born yesterday.*

das Dunkel — *darkness; mystery*
Das Dunkel um den Schatz des Priamos hat sich gelichtet. *The mystery surrounding Priam's treasure has been cleared up.*

im Dunkeln liegen — *to be unknown.*
Das Motiv der Täter liegt noch im Dunkeln. *The perpetrators' motives are still unknown.*

der Dünkel — *arrogance, conceit*
einen ungeheuren Dünkel haben — *to be very conceited.*

Ohne jede Berechtigung dazu, hat er einen ungeheuren Dünkel. *Without any justification at all for it, he is immensely conceited.*
In einigen Kreisen gibt es noch Standesdünkel. *In some circles there is still class snobbery.*

der Dunkelmann — *shady character*
Auch im Zeitalter der Aufklärung hat es Dunkelmänner gegeben. *In the Age of Enlightenment too, there were shady characters.*

die Dunkelziffer — *unreported number*
Tausende erkranten am neuen Medikament und die Dunkelziffer dürfte noch größer sein. *The new drug made thousands sick, and the number of unreported cases is probably even greater.*

durch — *through*
durchbeißen — *to bite through.*
Ohne sein Gebiss konnte er das Brot nicht durchbeißen. *Without his false teeth he couldn't bite through the bread.*

sich durchbeißen — *to get out of a tight spot.*
Am Ende konnten sich Max und Moritz nicht mehr durchbeißen. *At the end Max and Moritz couldn't get out of a tight spot any more.*

durchdrehen — *to grind, chop; to crack up.*
Auf der Tropeninsel war es so heiß, dass der Missionar durchdrehte. *It was so hot on the tropical island that the missionary cracked up.*

durchgehen — *to walk through; to run off and leave.*
Gauguin ist seiner Familie durchgegangen. *Gauguin ran off and left his family.*

durchgreifen — *to take drastic measures.*
Die Senatorin versprach, gegen die Kriminalität hart durchzugreifen. *The senator promised to take drastic measures against crime.*

durchnehmen — *to go through (a text); gossip about.*
In der Schule haben wir alle Dramen Grillparzers durchgenommen. *In school we went through all of Grillparzer's plays.*
Sie nehmen noch die neue Nachbarin durch. *They're still gossiping about the new neighbor.*

sich durchschlagen — *to fight (make) one's way through.*
Trotz aller Hindernisse schlug sie sich erfolgreich durch. *Despite all obstacles, she fought her way through successfully.*

durchschneiden — *to cut through.*
Einst glaubte man, dass der Mars von Kanälen durchschnitten war. *Once it was believed that Mars was crisscrossed by canals.*

der Durst — *thirst*
Durst haben — *to be thirsty.*
Er hat immer Durst. *He's always thirsty.*

Durst haben auf — *to be thirsty for.*
Er hatte großen Durst auf ein Bier. *He was very thirsty for a beer.*

einen über den Durst trinken — *to have a drink beyond one's limit.*
Das ist nicht das erste Mal, das er einen über den Durst trinkt. *This is not the first time that he drinks beyond his limit.*

die Ebbe — *low tide*
Ebbe in der Kasse/im Geldbeutel/im Portemonnaie — *short on funds.*
Nach der Renovierung is nun Ebbe in der Kasse. *We're low on funds now, after the renovation work.*

die Ecke — *corner*
an allen Ecken und Enden — *all over the place; everywhere.*
An allen Ecken und Enden gab es Unzufriedenheit. *There was dissatisfaction everywhere.*

Ecken und Kanten haben — *to have rough edges; be idiosyncratic, difficult to get along with.*
Er hat seine Ecken und Kanten aber ich mag ihn doch gern. *He's not easy to get along with but I'm still quite fond of him.*

eine Ecke sein — *to be at some distance.*
Bis dahin ist es noch eine ganze Ecke. *That's still quite a way off.*

um die Ecke bringen — *to bump off, rub out, kill.*

Der Mafiachef ließ seinen Rivalen umbringen. *The Mafia boss had his rival rubbed out.*

ben Ecken verwandt sein — *to be distantly related.*

Sie ist mit meiner Frau um sieben Ecken verwandt sein. *She's distantly related to my wife.*

---

edel — *noble; fine*

Die Winzer kosteten den edlen Wein und sprachen von der Edelfäule. *The vintners tasted the fine wine and spoke of noble rot.*

die Edelschnulze — *pretentious schmaltz.*

Elsa liebte den Roman, obwohl die Professorin ihn als Edelschnulze abgetan hatte. *Elsa loved the novel even though the professor had dismissed it as pretentious schmaltz.*

der Edelstahl — *stainless steel.*

Einige Winzer sprachen von den Vorteilen des Edelstahls. *Some vintners spoke of the advantages of stainless steel.*

der Edelstein — *precious stone; gem.*

Der ästhetische Edelmann sammelte Edelsteine aller Farben. *The aesthetic nobleman collected gems in all colors.*

Effeff (aus dem Effeff verstehen) — *to know thoroughly*

Sie versteht ihr Fach aus dem Effeff. *She knows her subject thoroughly.*

---

die Ehe — *marriage*

in wilder Ehe leben — *to live together without benefit of clergy, without being officially married.*

Vor der Trauung hatten sie schon lange Jahre in wilder Ehe gelebt. *Before the marriage ceremony they had already lived together for a long time.*

---

die Ehre — *honor*

der Wahrheit die Ehre geben — *to tell the truth.*

Um der Wahrheit die Ehre zu geben, möchte ich lieber nichts damit zu tun haben. *To tell the truth, I'd prefer to have nothing to do with it.*

sich die Ehre geben — *to have the honor of inviting.*

Wir geben uns die Ehre, Sie zu unserem Julfest einzuladen. *We have the honor of inviting you to our Yuletide celebration.*

ehrenamtlich — *honorary; voluntary.*

Viele ehrenamtliche Mitarbeiter helfen uns, die Armen zu ernähren. *Many volunteer co-workers help us to feed the poor.*

---

das Ei — *egg*

das Ei des Kolumbus — *simple, obvious solution.*

Zuerst lehnten sie seine Erfindung ab, aber später sahen sie ein, dass sie das Ei des Kolumbus war. *At first they rejected his invention, but later they realized that it was the obvious solution.*

sich gleichen wie ein Ei dem anderen — *to be as alike as two peas in a pod.*

Sie gleichen sich wie ein Ei dem anderen. *They are as alike as two peas in a pod.*

sich um ungelegte Eier kümmern — *to worry in advance.*

Kümmere dich nicht um ungelegte Eier. *Don't cross that bridge before you come to it.*

wie aus dem Ei gepellt — *neat as a pin, spick and span, dressed to the nines.*

Warum läuft er heute herum wie aus dem Ei gepellt? *Why's he walking around dressed to the nines today?*

---

die Eile — *haste*

Eile haben — *to be urgent.*

Die Sache hat Eile. *The matter is urgent.*

---

eilen — *to hasten*

Eile mit Weile. *Make haste slowly.*

es eilig haben — *to be in a hurry.*

Sie haben's immer eilig. *They're always in a hurry.*

---

der Eimer — *pail, bucket*

im Eimer sein — *to be down the drain.*

Alles wofür wir jahrelang gearbeitet haben, ist jetzt im Eimer. *Everything we worked for years is now down the drain.*

ein — *one*
ein für allemal — *once and for all.*
Ein für allemal sag ich dir, ich will nichts damit zu tun haben. *Once and for all I'm telling you I want nothing to do with it.*

einfallen — *to occur to; think*
Es fiel ihm nichts Neues ein. *He couldn't think of anything new.*
Lass dir so etwas ja nicht einfallen! *Don't even think of doing anything like that!*

der Eingang — *entrance*
Eingang finden — *to become established.*
Sie hat im Fernsehen Eingang gefunden. *She's become established in television.*

eingängig — *easily accessible; catchy.*
Sie schrieb die eingängige Musik zu dieser Fernsehwerbung. *She wrote the catchy music to this TV ad.*

eingängig erklären — *to explain simply and clearly.*
Könnten Sie mir das vielleicht eingängiger erklären? *Could you explain that to me more simply and clearly?*

eingehen — *to enter*
Elisabeth hoffte, dass Tannhäuser mit ihr in das ewige Reich eingehen würde. *Elisabeth hoped that Tannhäuser would enter the Kingdom of Heaven with her.*

das Risiko eingehen — *to take/run the risk.*
Trotzt genetischer Belastung will sie das Risiko eingehen und das Kind austragen. *Despite genetic defects she wants to take the risk and carry the baby to term.*

eingehen — *to arrive*
Der Brief ist bei uns noch nicht eingegangen. *We haven't received the letter yet.*

in die Geschichte eingehen — *to go down in history.*
Der General hoffte, in die Geschichte einzugehen. *The general hoped to go down in history.*

Kompromisse eingehen — *to make compromises.*
Er erklärte sich bereit, Kompromisse einzugehen. *He declared that he was ready to make compromises.*

einhaken — *to hook in*
eingehakt — *arm in arm.*
Eingehakt betraten sie den Ballsaal. *Arm in arm they entered the ballroom.*

einhergehen — *to walk around; be accompanied by*
Alter geht nicht immer mit Krankheit einher. *Old age isn't always accompanied by illness.*

einmal — *once*
auf einmal — *suddenly; at once.*
Auf einmal stand er auf und ging weg. *He suddenly stood up and went away.*

einmal ist keinmal — *trying something once doesn't count.*
Du hast's nur einmal versucht? Einmal ist keinmal. Versuch's doch noch einmal! *You tried it only once? Once isn't enough. Try it again.*

nicht einmal — *not even.*
Er hat nicht geschrieben, nicht einmal angerufen. *He didn't write, didn't even telephone.*

Versuch nicht, alles auf einmal zu tun. *Don't try to do everything at once.*

einschlagen — *to bash in*
Und willst du nicht mein Bruder sein, so schlag ich dir den Schädel ein. *If you won't be my buddy I'll bash your head in.*

einen Weg einschlagen — *to take a path.*
Sie dachte an das Gedicht von Frost über den nicht eingeschlagenen Weg. *She thought of the poem by Frost about the road not taken.*

einsetzen — *to put in; appoint*

Wir setzten Karpfen in den Teich ein. *We put carp into the pond.*

Sie hat ihn als Testamentsvollstrecker eingesetzt. *She appointed him executor of the will.*

sich einsetzen — *to work for.*

Seit Jahren setzt sie sich für die soziale Gerechtigkeit ein. *For years she's worked for social justice.*

einsitzen — *to serve a prison sentence*

Er sitzt für vier Jahre ein. *He's serving a four-year prison sentence.*

einstecken — *to put in; plug in*

eine Niederlage einstecken — *to swallow (endure) a defeat.*

Sie hat gesiegt, aber ihre Partei hat eine Niederlage einstecken müssen. *She won, but her party had to swallow a defeat.*

das Eisen — *iron*

ein heißes Eisen — *a controversial issue; a hot potato.*

Ein so heißes Eisen will kein Politiker jetzt anfassen. *No politician wants to touch a hot potato like that now.*

Man muss das Eisen schmieden, solange es heiß ist. *You've got to strike while the iron is hot.*

zum alten Eisen zählen — *to write off as too old.*

Er fühlte sich noch stark, und wollte sich nicht zum alten Eisen zählen lassen. *He still felt strong and didn't want to be written off as too old.*

die Eisenbahn — *railroad*

(die) höchste Eisenbahn sein — *to be high time.*

Es ist die höchste Eisenbahn, dass wir nach Hause fahren. *It's high time for us to go home.*

der Elefant — *elephant*

sich wie ein Elefant im Porzellanladen benehmen — *to behave like a bull in a china shop.*

Ich weiß, er ist noch jung, aber er braucht sich nicht wie ein Elefant im Porzellanladen zu benehmen. *I know he's still young, but he doesn't have to behave like a bull in a china shop.*

der Ellbogen — *elbow*

seine Ellbogen gebrauchen — *to elbow one's way; to be pushy.*

Richard weiß, seine Ellbogen zu gebrauchen. *Richard knows how to be pushy.*

keine Ellbogen haben — *to lack drive.*

Robert ist intelligenter, aber er hat keine Ellbogen. *Robert is more intelligent, but he lacks drive.*

---

die Eltern — *parents*

nicht von schlechten Eltern sein — *to be not bad at all.*

Obwohl sie nicht gewonnen hat, war ihr Sprung nicht von schlechten Eltern. *Although she didn't win, her jump wasn't bad at all.*

---

der Empfang — *receipt; reception*

in Empfang nehmen — *to accept.*

Voll Freude nahm sie den Preis in Empfang. *Full of joy, she accepted the prize.*

---

das Ende — *end*

am Ende — *at the end; after all's said and done.*

Am Ende musste er's doch machen. *After all was said and done he had to do it anyway.*

am Ende sein — *to be exhausted.*

Nach dem Rennen war ich am Ende. *After the race I was exhausted.*

am falschen/richtigen Ende anfassen — *to go about in the wrong/right way.*

Er hat die Sache am falschen Ende angefasst. *He went about the matter in the wrong way.*

das bessere Ende haben — *to win, come out ahead.*

Unsere Mannschaft hat endlich das bessere Ende gehabt. *Our team finally won.*

das dicke Ende — *The worst is yet to come; the time when the piper will have to be paid.*

Später kommt das dicke Ende noch. *Later the piper will have to be paid.*

das Ende vom Lied — *the (unpleasant) end of the story.*
Das Ende vom Lied war dann, dass sie ihn sitzen ließ. *The end of the story was that she then jilted him.*

ein Ende machen — *to put an end to; stop.*
Mit ihrem Zeit- und Geldverschwenden muss ein Ende gemacht werden. *Their waste of time and money must be stopped.*

Ende gut, alles gut. All's well that ends well.

kein Ende nehmen — *to not come to an end.*
Der Film schien kein Ende nehmen zu wollen. *It seemed the movie would never (come to an) end.*

letzten Endes — *finally; after all.*
Letzten Endes ist er doch auch ein Mensch. *After all, he's a human being too.*

zu Ende führen — *to complete.*
Hat sie das Projekt zu Ende geführt? *Did she complete the project?*

---

die Entwicklung — *development*
in der Entwicklung sein — *to be an adolescent.*
Er ist noch in der Entwicklung. *He's still an adolescent.*

das Entwicklungsland — *developing country.*
Die Regierung plant, mehr Entwicklungshelfer in die Entwicklungsländer zu schicken. *The government plans to send more volunteer workers to the developing countries.*

---

der Erfolg — *success*
Erfolg haben — *to be successful.*
T. Williams letzte Stücke hatten keinen Erfolg. *T. Williams' last plays weren't successful.*

der Erfolg hat viele Väter. *Nothing succeeds like success.*
Viele wollten das Telefon, das Auto, die Glühbirne erfunden haben. Der Erfolg hat viele Väter. *Many claimed to have invented the telephone, the automobile, the light bulb. Nothing succeeds like success.*

---

sich erfreuen — *to enjoy oneself*

sich großer Beliebtheit erfreuen — *to be popular.*

Die Schauspielerin erfreut sich noch großer Beliebtheit. *The actress is still very popular.*

ernähren — *to feed*

Wird das Kind mit der Flasche ernährt? *Is the child being bottlefed?*

seinen Mann ernähren — *to make a good living.*

Ihr Geschäft geht gut und ernährt seinen Mann. *Their business is doing well and making them a good living.*

sich ernähren — *to live on; to eat.*

Sie ernährt sich nur von Biokost. *She eats only organically grown foods.*

der Ernst — *seriousness*

Ist das Ihr Ernst? *Do you really mean that?*

der Ernst des Lebens — *the serious side of life.*

Für die Kinder beginnt bald genug der Ernst des Lebens. *The serious side of life will begin soon enough for the children.*

tierischer Ernst — *deadly seriousness.*

Von seinem tierischen Ernst habe ich genug. *I've had enough of his deadly seriousness.*

erst — *first*

fürs Erste — *for the present.*

Die neue Chefin sagte, sie wolle fürs Erste nichts ändern. *The new boss said she didn't want to change anything for the present.*

zum Ersten, zum Zweiten, zum Dritten. *Going once, going twice, sold!* (*auction*).

Ich wollte mehr für das Gemälde bieten, aber der Versteigerer hatte schon "Zum ersten, zum Zweiten, zum Dritten" ausgerufen. *I wanted to bid more for the painting, but the auctioneer had already announced, "Going once, going twice, sold!"*

das Erstaunen — *amazement*

in Erstaunen setzen — *to amaze.*

Das plötzliche Erscheinen des Engels setzte uns in Erstaunen. *The angel's sudden appearance amazed us.*

der Esel — *donkey*

Wenn man den Esel nennt, kommt er gerennt. *Speak of the devil and there he is.*

den Sack schlagen, und den Esel meinen — *to accuse an (innocent) subordinate because one is afraid to go after the boss.*

Sie beschuldigten den Sekretär, nicht den Präsidenten—man schlägt den Sack, meint aber den Esel. *They accused the secretary not the president—it's the little fellow who always gets it.*

die Eselei — *a stupid, foolish thing.*

Das war aber eine Eselei! *That was a stupid thing to do!*

die Eselsbrücke — *mnemonic device.*

Trotz der Eselsbrücken vergaß er alles. *Despite the mnemonic devices, he forgot everything.*

der Eskimo — *eskimo*

Das haut den stärksten Eskimo vom Schlitten! *That's too much for anybody!*

essen — *to eat*

zu Abend essen/Abendbrot essen — *to have dinner/supper.*

Ich möchte mit dir zu Abend essen. *I'd like to have dinner with you.*

zu Mittag essen — *to eat lunch.*

Wo sollen wir zu Mittag essen? *Where shall we have lunch?*

die Eule — *owl*

Eulen nach Athen tragen — *to carry coals to Newcastle.*

Da sein Onkel Winzer ist, hieße es Eulen nach Athen tragen, ihm eine Flasche Wein zu schenken. *Since his uncle's a vintner, it would be like carrying coals to Newcastle to give him a bottle of wine.*

die Eulenspiegelei — *practical joke; tomfoolery.*

Seine Eulenspiegeleien waren nicht immer harmlos. *His practical jokes weren't always harmless.*

das Fach — *subject; trade*
  vom Fach sein — *to be a professional, an expert.*
  Wir sind nicht vom Fach aber wir wissen, was wir wollen. *We're not experts, but we know what we want.*

  das Fachchinesisch — *technical jargon; mumbo-jumbo, gobbledygook.*
  Hast du was vom Fachchinesisch der Rechtsanwälte verstanden? *Do you catch any of the lawyers' legalese?*

  fachsimpeln — *to talk shop.*
  Wenn ihr weiter so fachsimpelt, hau ich ab. *If you persist in talking shop, I'm taking off.*

  in der Fachwelt — *among experts.*
  In der Fachwelt wird sie sehr hochgeschätzt. *She's very highly thought of among experts.*

der Faden — *thread*
  alle Fäden fest in der Hand halten — *to keep a tight rein on.*
  Die Chefin hält alle Fäden fest in der Hand. *The boss keeps a tight rein on everything.*

  Fäden spinnen — *to weave a web of intrigue.*
  Iago wurde nie müde, seine Fäden zu spinnen. *Iago never tired of weaving his web of intrigues.*

  keinen trockenen Faden mehr am Leib haben — *to be soaked to the skin.*
  Es goss in Strömen und ich hatte keinen trockenen Faden mehr am Leibe. *It was pouring rain and I was soaked to the skin.*

die Fahne — *flag*
  eine Fahne haben — *to reek of alcohol.*
  Obwohl er eine Fahne hatte, beteuerte er, nicht betrunken zu sein. *Although he reeked of alcohol, he insisted that he wasn't drunk.*

  sich auf die Fahnen schreiben — *to espouse; to make part of one's platform, program.*

Nach der Niederlage muss sich die Partei jetzt neue Ideale auf die Fahnen schreiben. *After the defeat, the party must now espouse new ideals.*

fahnenflüchtig werden — *to desert*
Die Soldaten wurden fahnenflüchtig. *The soldiers deserted.*

fahren — *to travel; drive*
Was ist in dich gefahren? Fahr zum Teufel! *What's gotten into you? The devil take you!*

aus der Haut fahren — *to blow one's top.*
Du brauchst nicht gleich aus der Haut zu fahren. *You needn't blow your top right away.*

über den Mund fahren — *interrupt; cut off.*
Die Journalisten fuhren einander dauernd über den Mund. *The journalists kept interrupting each other.*

fallen — *to fall*
Ihre beiden Söhne sind im Krieg gefallen. *Her two sons died in the war.*
Kein einziges Wort ist über unsere Ansprüche gefallen. *Not a single word was said about our claims.*
Manchmal fällt sie in ihren scharmanten Dialekt. *Sometimes she lapses into her charming dialect.*

falsch — *false*
ein falscher Fünfziger (Fuffziger) sein — *to be dishonest; be phony as a three-dollar bill.*
Sie hielt ihre Anwältin für einen falschen Fünfziger. *She thought her lawyer was dishonest.*

Farbe — *color*
Farbe bekennen — *to show one's colors, take a stand.*
Wenn ein Schwarz-Weiß-Denker Farbe bekennen muss, sieht er meistens Rot. *When those who think in black and white are forced to show their true colors, they usually see red.*

das Fass — *barrel*

das Fass zum überlaufen bringen — *to be the last straw.*
Diese Beleidigung brachte das Fass zum überlaufen. *That insult was the last straw.*

dem Fass den Boden ausschlagen — *to take the cake.*
Das schlug dem Fass den Boden aus. *That took the cake.*

ein Fass ohne Boden — *a bottomless pit.*
Noch mehr Geld for das Bauprojekt? Das ist ein Fass ohne Boden. *Still more money for the building project? That's a bottomless pit.*

vom Fass — *from the barrel.*
Er trinkt gerne Bier vom Fass. *He likes draft beer.*

die Faust — *fist*

auf eigene Faust — *on one's own initiative.*
Haben Sie es auf eigene Faust unternommen? *Did you undertake it on your own initiative?*

sich ins Fäustchen lachen — *to laugh up one's sleeve.*
Der Schwindler lachte sich ins Fäustchen. *The swindler laughed up his sleeve.*

faustdick — *fist thick.*
Das war eine faustdicke Lüge. *That was a barefaced lie.*

es faustdick hinter den Ohren haben — *to be crafty, sly.*
Sie spielt gern die Unschuld vom Lande, doch hat sie es faustdick hinter den Ohren. *She likes to play the innocent country girl, but she's sly.*

die Feder — *feather*

sich mit fremden Federn schmücken — *to take credit for another's work.*
Dieser Dümmling machte einen lächerlichen Versuch, sich mit fremden Federn zu schmücken. *That dummy made a ridiculous attempt to pass that off as his own.*

fein — *fine*

das Feinste vom Feinen — *the best of the best.*
Sie ist Feinschmeckerin und isst nur das Feinste vom Feinen. *She is a gourmet and eats only the best of the best.*

sich zu fein sein — *to feel above, think o.s. too good for.*
Der Chef war sich nicht zu fein, mit anzupacken. *The boss didn't feel above lending us a helping hand.*

klein aber fein — *small but good.*
Unser Laden ist klein aber fein. *Our store is small but good.*

vom Feinsten sein — *to exemplify the best.*
Dieser Tempel ist buddhistische Architektur vom Feinsten. *This temple is one of the finest examples of Buddhist architecture.*

die Feier — *party; celebration*
Keine Feier ohne Meier. *He never misses a party.*
Man muss die Feste feiern, wie sie fallen. *You've got to make hay while the sun shines.*
Machen wir noch 'ne Flasche auf. Man muss die Feste feiern, wie sie fallen. *Let's open another bottle. There's always a reason to party.*

der Feierabend — *evening time after work; retirement.*

Feierabend machen — *to knock off from work.*
Jetzt mach ich Feierabend und geh nach Hause. *I'm going to knock off from work now and go home.*

die Feierabendbeschäftigung — *leisure time activity.*
Sie widmet sich immer mehr ihren Feierabendbeschäftigungen. *She spends more and more time on leisure time activities.*

das Feld — *field*
aus dem Feld schlagen — *to get rid of; to beat out.*
Es ist ihrer Firma gelungen, die Konkurrenz aus dem Felde zu schlagen. *Their firm succeeded in beating out the competition.*

zu Felde ziehen — *to crusade, campaign*
Er zog zu Felde gegen seine Feinde. *He campaigned against his enemies.*

ferner — *furthermore; in addition*
ferner liefen — *also ran.*
Er strengte sich an, um nicht wieder unter: "ferner liefen" eingestuft zu werden. *He made a great effort not to be classified as an also ran again.*

fernsehen — *to watch television*
Die Kinder wollten fernsehen. *The children wanted to watch television.*

fertig — *finished*
   fertig machen — *to finish up; to ruin.*
Dieser Klatschreporter hat schon viele Prominente fertig gemacht. *This gossip columnist has already ruined many prominent people.*

   fertig werden — *to cope/deal with.*
Verschiedene Religionen halfen ihm, mit seinen inneren Ängsten fertig zu werden. *Various religions helped him to deal with his inner anxieties.*

   völlig fertig sein — *to be thoroughly exhausted.*
Nach der langen Reise waren wir völlig fertig. *After the long trip, we were thoroughly exhausted.*

fest — *solid; firm*
   fest befreundet sein — *to be close friends; to go steady.*
Sie sind mit einander fest befreundet. *They're going steady.*

   festfahren — *to get stuck; to be bogged down, stalled,*
Die festgefahrenen Tarifverhandlungen sollen wieder aufgenommen werden. *The stalled wage negotiations are to be resumed.*

   festsitzen — *to be stranded.*
Wegen des Streiks sitzen viele Passagiere im Flughafen fest. *Because of the strike, many passengers are stranded at the airport.*

die Festbeleuchtung — *festive lights; all the lights blazing*
Was soll diese Festbeleuchtung? Ich hab keine Elekrizitätsaktien. *Why is this place all lit up? I haven't got any stocks in the electric company.*

das Fett — *fat*
   das Fett abschöpfen — *to skim off the cream.*
Das Fett hat der Senator für sich abgeschöpft. *The senator skimmed off the cream for himself.*

   sein Fett kriegen — *to get it.*
Wenn Mutti dich erwischt, wirst du dein Fett kriegen. *If mother catches you, you're going to get it.*

ins Fettnäpfchen treten — *to put one's foot in it/put one's foot in one's mouth.*

Da bist du wieder ins Fettnäpfchen getreten. *There you've gone and put your foot in it again.*

die fetten Jahre — *the good times.*

In den fetten Jahren lebten sie auf großem Fuß. *In the good times they lived in great style.*

fettgedruckt — *in boldface type.*

Er hat nur die fettgedruckten Stellen gelesen. *He just read the passages in boldface.*

---

der Fetzen — *rag, scrap, tatter, shred*

dass die Fetzen fliegen — *like all get out.*

Wir wollen feiern, dass die Fetzen fliegen. *We want to celebrate like mad.*

in Fetzen gehen — *to fall to pieces, to tatter.*

Beim Rave hab ich so viel getanzt, dass mein Kleid fast in Fetzen ging. I danced so much at the rave that my dress almost fell to pieces.

---

das Feuer — *fire*

Feuer geben/haben — *to give/have a light.*

Können Sie mir bitte Feuer geben? *Can you give me a light, please?*

Feuer haben — *to be spirited.*

Die Weine und die Pferde der ungarischen Gräfin haben Feuer. *The Hungarian countess' wines and horses are spirited.*

das Feuer vom Himmel holen — *to be very bright.*

Er hat das Feuer vom Himmel nicht geholt. *He's not very bright.*

Feuer und Flamme sein — *to be full of enthusiasm.*

Zuerst war er ganz Feuer und Flamme für die Ideale der Revolution. *At first he was full of enthusiasm for the ideals of the revolution.*

zwischen zwei Feuer geraten — *to get caught in the crossfire of opposing camps.*

Indem sie versuchte, beiden Seiten gerecht zu werden, geriet sie zwischen zwei Feuer. *By trying to be fair to both sides she got caught in he crossfire.*

65

die Feuerprobe — *acid test.*
Ihre Liebe hat die Feuerprobe der Trennung bestanden. *Their love has passed the acid test of separation.*

finden — *to find*
Niemand weiß, was sie an ihm findet. *No one know what she sees in him.*

sich finden — *to work out all right.*
Später wird sich schon alles finden. *Everything will work out all right later.*

der Finger — *finger*
  die Finger lassen — *to keep hands off; stay away from.*
  Lass die Finger von einer solchen Person! *Stay away from a person like that!*

  lange Finger machen — *to steal; to have sticky fingers.*
  Jemand unter ihnen hat lange Finger gemacht. *One among them did some stealing.*
  Wenn man ihm den kleinen Finger reicht, nimmt er gleich die ganze Hand. *Give him an inch and he'll take a mile.*

  fingerfertig — *nimble fingered.*
  Nimm dich in acht vor fingerfertigen Taschendieben. *Watch out for nimble-fingered pickpockets.*

die Fingersprache — *sign language*
Jane sprach und benutzte gleichzeitig die Fingersprache. *Jane spoke and simultaneously used sign language.*

  das Fingerspitzengefühl — *a special feeling for; tact.*
  Dafür muss man Fingerspitzengefühl haben. *You have to have a special feeling for that.*

der Fisch — *fish*
Kennen Sie den Zungenbrecher: "Fischers Fritz fischt frische Fische, frische Fische fischt Fischers Fritz". *Do you know the tongue-twister: "Fisher's Fritz fishes fresh fish, fresh fish fishes Fisher's Fritz."*

ein dicker/großer Fisch — *crime boss, kingpin, big fish.*

Der Polizei ging ein dicker Fisch ins Netz. *The police caught a big fish in their net.*

faule Fische — *lame excuses.*

Das sind alles nur faule Fische und die nehm ich dir nicht ab. *All that is just lame excuses and I'm not buying them.*

weder Fisch noch Fleisch/weder Fisch noch Vogel. *Neither fish nor fowl.*

Das ist so ein Zwitterding. Weder Fisch noch Fleisch. *That's a kind of hybrid, a crossbreed. Neither fish nor fowl.*

Der Gast ist wie der Fisch, er bleibt nicht lange frisch. *Guests and fish stink after three days.*

---

der Flachs — *flax; kidding.*

Ich glaube, er hat nur Flachs gemacht, aber bei ihm weiß man nie. *I think he was just kidding, but you never know with him.*

---

die Flagge — *flag*

Flagge zeigen — *to show one's true colors, take a stand.*

Du musst jetzt Flagge zeigen, Farbe bekennen. *You've got to take a stand now, show your true colors.*

---

die Flasche — *bottle*

die Einwegflasche — *nondeposit (disposable) bottle.*

die Mehrwegflasche — *deposit (returnable, recyclable) bottle.*

Sind diese Ein- oder Mehrwegflaschen? *Are these disposable or returnable bottles?*

---

das Fleisch — *flesh; meat*

sich ins eigene Fleisch schneiden — *to cut off one's nose to spite one's face.*

Er wusste, dass er sich dabei ins eigene Fleisch schnitt, aber er tat es trotzdem. *He knew that he was cutting off his nose to spite his face, but he did it anyway.*

---

der Fleiß — *diligence*
Ohne Fleiß, keinen Preis. *If you want rewards, you've got to work for them.*

die Fliege — *fly*
Ihn stört die Fliege an der Wand. *Every little thing upsets him.*
die Fliege/'ne Fliege machen — *to scram, buzz off.*
Du gehst mir auf den Keks; mach jetzt 'ne Fliege! *You're getting on my nerves; buzz off!*
zwei Fliegen mit einer Klappe schlagen — *to kill two birds with one stone.*
Es gelang ihr, zwei Fliegen mit einer Klappe zu schlagen. *She succeeded in killing two birds with one stone.*
fliegen — *to fly; be fired.*
"Du musst einlenken oder du fliegst," drohte der Chef. *"You must compromise or you'll be fired," threatened the boss.*

die Flinte — *shotgun*
die Flinte ins Korn werfen — *to throw in the towel.*
Jetzt ist nicht die Zeit, die Flinte ins Korn zu werfen. *Now is not the time to throw in the towel.*
vor die Flinte kommen — *to get into one's gun sights; to get one's hands on.*
Der soll mir nur vor die Flinte kommen! *Just let me get my hands on him!*

der Floh — *flea*
die Flöhe husten (niesen) hören — *to know it all before it happens.*
Dein Onkel meint immer, die Flöhe husten zu hören. *Your uncle always thinks he knows everything before it happens.*
jmdm. einen Floh ins Ohr setzen — *to put a bee in someone's bonnet.*
Ich will aber gar nicht nach Australien auswandern. Wer hat dir diesen Floh ins Ohr gesetzt? *I have no intention of emigrating to Australia. Who put that bee in your bonnet?*
Angenehmes Flohbeißen! *Good night. Sleep tight. Don't let the bedbugs bite!*

flöten — *to flute*

flöten gehen — *to go down the drain; be wasted.*
Unsere Pläne gingen flöten. *Our plans went down the drain.*

Flötentöne beibringen — *to teach a thing or two.*
Diesem Besserwisser werde ich schon die Flötentöne beibringen. *I'll teach that smart aleck a thing or two.*

die Flucht — *flight*

die Flucht noch vorne greifen/antreten — *to make offense the best defense, make counter-charges; take the bull by the horns.*
Der Senator beantwortete keine Frage der Reporter, griff aber die Flucht nach vorne. *The senator answered none of the reporters' questions but made countercharges instead.*

der Fluss — *river*

in Fluss bringen — *to get going.*
Sie brachte das Gespräch wieder in Fluss. *She got the conversation going again.*

im Fluss sein — *to be in a state of flux; to be in progress.*
Die Verhandlungen sind noch im Fluss. *The negotiations are still in progress.*

die Folge — *consequence*

Folge leisten — *to accept.*
Gerne leiste ich Ihrer Einladung Folge. *I gladly accept your invitation.*

der Fön/Föhn — *Alpine wind; electric hair dryer*

Der Fön ist kaputt. *The hair dryer is broken.*

fönen — *to blow-dry.*
Der Umwelt zuliebe fönt sie ihre Haare nicht mehr. *For the sake of the environment she doesn't blow-dry her hair any more.*

die Frage — *question*

außer Frage stehen — *to be certain.*
Natürlich steht meine Unterstützung außer Frage. *Of course my support is certain.*

in Frage kommen — *to be a possibility.*

Wie kann ein solcher Mensch für einen so hohen Posten in Frage kommen? *How can someone like that be a possibility for such a high position?*

nicht in Frage kommen — *to be out of the question.*

Keine Bange, seine Ernennung kommt gar nicht in Frage. *Don't worry, his appointment is out of the question.*

in Frage stellen — *to cast doubt on.*

Die Journalistin stellte die Glaubwürdigkeit des Senators in Frage. *The journalist cast doubt on the senator's credibility.*

eine Frage stellen — *to put (ask) a question.*

Die Priester stellten ihm drei Fragen. *The priests asked him three questions.*

gefragt sein — *to be in demand.*

Karten für dieses Stück sind sehr gefragt. *Tickets for this play are much in demand.*

überfragt sein — *to be asked too much; to not know the answer.*

Als man mich bat, die Relativitätstheorie zu erklären, da war ich überfragt. *They asked too much of me when they asked me to explain the theory of relativity.*

sich fragen — *to wonder.*

Ich frage mich, ob er es wirklich so machen sollte. *I wonder if he should really do it that way.*

frei — *free*

Ist hier noch frei? *Is this seat taken?*

ein Zimmer frei haben — *to have a room available.*

Haben Sie noch ein Doppelzimmer frei? *Do you still have a double room available?*

die Freiberufler — *freelance professionals.*

Viele Freiberufler können zu Hause arbeiten. *Many freelance professionals can work at home.*

das Fressen — *food for animals; grub*
  ein gefundenes Fressen — *a real gift/feeding frenzy.*
  Der letzte Skandal über den Senator war für die Medien ein gefundenes
  Fressen. *The last scandal concerning the senator was a real gift to the
  media.*

  fressen — *to eat (animals); to eat ravenously.*
  Friß, Vogel, oder stirb! *Take it or leave it!/Root hog or die!/Do or die!*
  Wir mussten die schlechten Bedingungen annehmen, friss, Vogel, oder
  stirb! *We had to accept the poor terms, we had no choice.*

Friedrich Wilhelm — *John Hancock (signature)*
  Setz deinen Friedrich Wilhelm hier unten, dann ist alles in Ordnung. *Put
  your John Hancock here and everything will be in order.*

frisch — *fresh*
  auf frischer Tat ertappen — *to catch red-handed.*
  Die Panzerknacker wurden auf frischer Tat ertappt. *The safe crackers
  were caught red-handed.*

der Fuchs — *fox*
  wohnen, wo sich die Füchse gute Nacht sagen — *to live in a remote
  area, "the sticks."*
  Wir würden gerne wohnen, wo sich die Füchse gute Nacht sagen. *We'd
  like to live in a remote area.*

führen — *to lead*
  ein Gespräch führen — *to carry on a conversation.*
  Sie hatte keine Zeit, ein langes Gespräch mit ihnen zu führen. *She had no
  time to carry on a long conversation with them.*

der Führerschein — *driver's license*
  den Führerschein machen — *to learn to drive; take the driving test.*
  Sie hat den Führerschein noch nicht gemacht. *She hasn't learned how to
  drive yet.*

fünf — *five*

fünf gerade sein lassen — *to turn a blind eye; bend the rules a little.*
Die Lehrerin ist sehr streng, aber manchmal lässt sie fünf gerade sein. *The teacher is very strict but sometimes she bends the rules a little.*

fünf Minuten vor zwölf — *the eleventh hour; the last minute.*
Es ist fünf Minuten vor zwölf; wir müssen handeln! *It is the eleventh hour; we must act!*

funkeln — *to sparkle*

funkelnagelneu — *brand new.*
Das Dorfmuseum ist funkelnagelneu. *The village museum is brand new.*

das Fürchten — *fear*

jmdn. das Fürchten lehren — *to put the fear of God into s.o.*

das Fürchten lernen — *to find out what fear really is.*
Wenn die Fusion klappt wird die Konkurrenz das Fürchten lernen. *If the merger comes off, the competition will learn the meaning of fear.*

für sich — *alone*
Greta wollte für sich sein. *Greta wanted to be alone.*

der Fuß — *foot*

auf freien Fuß setzten — *to set free; release.*
Die Gefangenen wurden auf freien Fuß gesetzt. *The prisoners were released.*

auf großem Fuß leben — *to live in grand style.*
Trotz, oder vielmehr dank ihrer Schulden, leben sie noch auf großem Fuß. *Despite, or rather thanks to their debts, they still live in great style.*

auf Kriegsfuß stehen — *to be on a hostile footing.*
Der Senator steht jetzt mit seinen ehemaligen Freunden auf Kriegsfuß. *The senator is now on a hostile footing with his former friends.*

Fuß fassen — *to gain a foothold; become established; take root.*
In dem Land hat die Demokratie nie richtig Fuß gefaßt. *Democracy never really took root in that country.*

der Gang — *movement; course; walk*

der Fleischergang/Metzgergang/Schneidergang — *fool's errand.*

Hoffentlich lohnt es sich diesmal; ich will wieder keinen Metzgergang machen. *I hope it'll be worthwhile this time; I don't want to go on another fool's errand.*

einen Gang nach Kanossa machen/einen Kanossagang machen — *to eat humble pie, apologize profusely.*

Ich hatte eigentlich recht, musste aber einen Kanossagang machen. *I really was right; nevertheless I had to eat humble pie.*

einen Gang zurückschalten — *to take things easier.*

Der Arzt riet ihm, einen Gang zurückzuschalten. *The doctor advised him to take things easier.*

Gänge machen — *to do errands.*

Wir haben noch einige Gänge zu machen. *We still have some errands to do.*

im Gang sein — *to be going on.*

Die Verhandlungen sind noch im Gang. *The negotiations are still going on.*

in Gang bringen — *to get going; start up.*

Er brachte die Maschine in Gang. *He got the machine going.*

gang und gäbe sein — *to be usual, customary.*

In anderen Ländern sind solche Prüfungen gang und gäbe. *In other countries such exams are customary.*

---

ganz — *whole(ly)*

ganz und gar — *totally, absolutely.*

Das ist ganz und gar unmöglich. *That's absolutely impossible.*

im Ganzen/im großen Ganzen/im Großen und Ganzen — *on the whole/by and large/in general.*

Im Großen und Ganzen sind wir damit einverstanden. *In general, we agree.*

Im Ganzen hat sie's gut gemacht. *On the whole she did well.*

---

das Garn — *yarn*

ein Garn spinnen — *to spin a yarn, tell tales.*

Abends in der Kneipe spinnt der alte Seemann sein Garn. *Evenings in the tavern the old sailor tells his tales.*

ins Garn gehen — *to fall into a trap.*

Die Schwerverbrecher gingen der Polizei ins Garn. *The dangerous criminals fell into the police's trap.*

---

die Gasse — *lane; alley*

mit dem Hund Gassi gehen — *to take the dog for a walk.*

Mit dem Hund geh ich gern Gassi. *I like to take the dog for a walk.*

---

der Gaul — *horse, nag*

Einem geschenkten Gaul schaut man nicht ins Maul. *You don't look a gift horse in the mouth.*

Auch der beste Gaul strauchelt einmal. *Even the best horse can stumble./We all have our off days.*

---

geben — *to give*

Einstand geben — *to play one's first match; to celebrate starting a new job.*

Gestern hat sie Einstand gegeben. *Yesterday she played her first match.*

es gibt — *there is, there are.*

Da gibt's nichts, du musst dich wehren. *There is nothing else to do about it, you must defend yourself.*

sich geben — *to declare.*

Die Senatorin gab sich mit dem Ergebnis zufrieden. *The senator declared she was satisfied with the result.*

sich geben — *behave.*

In diesem Stadtviertel kann sich jeder geben, wie er will. *In this section of the city all can behave as they please.*

von sich geben — *to utter.*

Sie gab einen Seufzer von sich, und vergab ihm wieder. *She uttered a sigh and forgave him again.*

---

das Gebet — *prayer*

sein Gebet verrichten — *to say prayers.*

Mehrmals täglich verrichtete der Brahmane sein Gebet. *Several times a day the Brahmin said his prayers.*

ins Gebet nehmen — *to give a good talking to.*

Er hatte die Absicht, seinen Sohn ins Gebet zu nehmen. *He had the intention of giving his son a good talking to.*

---

der Geburtstag — *birthday*

Geburtstag haben — *to be one's birthday.*

Marlene war bei Johnny, als er Geburtstag hatte; sie wünschte ihm mehrmals alles Gute zum Geburtstag. *Marlene was with Johnny on his birthday; she repeatedly wished him all the best for his birthday.*

---

die Geduld — *patience*

die Geduld reißen — *to run out of patience.*

Ihr riss die Geduld und sie ging nach Hause. *She ran out of patience and went home.*

Geduld bringt Rosen. *Patience brings success.*

Mit Geduld und Spucke fängt man eine Mucke. *With a little patience and ingenuity, you'll (we'll) make it.*

---

das Gefallen — *pleasure*

Gefallen finden — *to find acceptance; to be appreciated.*

Zuerst fand sie nirgends Gefallen mit ihren Gemälden und Skulpturen. *At first her paintings and sculptures weren't appreciated anywhere.*

Gefallen finden an — *to take pleasure in.*

Jetzt finden alle Gefallen an ihren Werken. *Now all take pleasure in her works.*

gefallen — *to be pleasing; like.*

Die ganze Sache gefällt uns nicht. *We don't like the whole affair.*

sich etwas gefallen lassen — *to put up with.*
Seine Überheblichkeit lassen wir uns nicht länger gefallen. *We won't put up with his arrogance any more.*

---

geheim — *secret*
im Geheimen — *in secret; privately.*
Im Geheimen freute sie sich darüber. *Privately she was pleased about it.*
streng geheim — *top secret.*
Die Sache ist streng geheim. *The matter is top secret.*
der Geheimtipp — *insider's secret.*
Dieses Strandhotel ist nicht mehr ein Geheimtipp; jetzt ist es von Touristen überrannt. *That seashore hotel isn't an insider's secret anymore; it's overrun with tourists now.*

---

gehen — *to go*
auf ein Konto gehen — *to be credited to an account; to be responsible for.*
Die Polizei glaubt, auch andere Verbrechen gehen auf sein Konto. *The police think he is responsible for other crimes too.*

nach Kanossa gehen — *to capitulate, give in.*
"Nach Kanossa gehen wir nicht," sagte der antiklerikale Bismarck. *"We won't go to Canossa (give in)," said anticlerical Bismarck.*

vor die Tür gehen — *to set foot out of the house.*
Bei dieser Kälte gehen wir nicht vor die Tür. *In this cold we're not setting foot out of the house.*

gehen — *to do.*
Das geht nicht! *That won't do!*
Persönlich geht es uns gut, aber finanziell geht es uns schlecht. *Things are going well for us personally, but we're doing badly financially.*

gehen — *to be possible.*
Ohne ihre Erlaubnis geht's nicht. *It's not possible without her permission.*

gehen — *to feel.*
Gestern ging es ihm schlecht; heute geht es ihm besser. *He wasn't feeling well yesterday; today he's feeling better.*

gehen — *to face.*
Unsere Fenster gehen auf den Hof. *Our windows face the courtyard.*

gehen um — *to be a matter of,*

Es geht um Leben und Tod. *It's a matter of life and death.*

gehen um — *to be at issue, at stake; to be about.*

In den meisten Kriegen geht es mehr um Macht und Ausdehnungslust als um Gerechtigkeit. *Most wars are more about power and expansionism than justice.*

---

die Geige — *violin*

die erste/große Geige spielen — *to play first violin; to call the tune, be the star.*

Bei der Konferenz will der Chef die große Geige spielen. *The boss wants to be the star of the conference.*

Der Himmel hängt voller Geigen — *to be ecstatically happy.*

Sie verliebten sich auf den ersten Blick, und der Himmel hing ihnen voller Geigen. *They fell in love at first sight and were ecstatically happy.*

nach jemands Geige tanzen — *to dance to someone's tune.*

Er will, dass alle nach seiner Geige tanzen. *He wants everyone to dance to his tune.*

---

der Geist — *spirit*

auf den Geist gehen — *to get on one's nerves.*

Mit seinen ewigen Nörgeleien geht er mir auf den Geist. *He gets on my nerves with his constant grumbling.*

von allen guten Geistern verlassen — *to have taken leave of one's senses.*

Die Schauspielerin schien, von allen guten Geistern verlassen zu sein. *The actress seemed to have taken leave of her senses.*

der Geisterfahrer — *s.o. driving in the wrong lane.*

Die Verkehrspolizei verhaftete den Geisterfahrer. *The traffic cops arrested the delinquent driver.*

wie von/durch Geisterhand — *as if by magic/an invisible hand.*

Wie von Geisterhand öffnete sich die Tür. *The door opened as if by magic.*

geistern — *to wander like a ghost, haunt.*

Im Schloss soll's geistern. *They say the castle's haunted.*

---

das Geld — *money*

Geld regiert die Welt. *Money makes the world go round.*

Geld stinkt nicht. *Money has no smell.*

ins Geld gehen — *to prove costly; to get expensive.*
Seine Sammelwut geht ins Geld. *His collecting mania is getting expensive.*

nach Geld stinken — *to be filthy rich.*
Offenkundig stinkt er nach Geld. *He's obviously filthy rich.*

die Gelegenheit — *opportunity, possibility*

Gelegenheit macht Diebe. *Opportunity makes the thief. (People will break the law if they think they can get away with it.)*
Der Senator sagte er sei Opfer der Polizei, die ihn in eine Falle gelockt hätte. Ja, Gelegenheit macht Diebe. *The senator said he was a victim of police entrapment. Even saints aren't strangers to temptation.*

gelingen — *to succeed*
Es ist ihnen gelungen, die Überlebenden zu bergen. *They succeeded in rescuing the survivors.*
Mit diesem Roman gelang ihr der große Durchbruch. *This novel was her big breakthrough.*

nicht gelingen wollen — *not to work out.*
Das wollte ihm nicht gelingen. *That just didn't work out for him.*

gelten — *to be essential*
Es gilt, rasch zu handeln. *It is essential to act quickly.*

gelten — *to be meant for.*
Die Kugel galt dem Gangster, aber sie traf seine Frau. *The bullet was meant for the gangster, but it hit his wife.*

geltend machen — *to assert influence/rights.*
Der Senator versuchte, seinen Einfluss geltend zu machen. *The senator tried to assert his influence.*

genießbar — *edible; potable; bearable*

Nach zwei Wochen in der Wüste waren Essen und Trinken nicht mehr genießbar. *After two weeks in the desert, our food and drink were no longer fit for consumption.*

Der alte Herr ist heute ungenießbar. *The old gentleman is unbearable today.*

nicht zu genießen sein — *to be unbearable.*

Herr Weintraub ist Genussmensch, aber gestern war er gar nicht zu genießen. *Mr. Weintraub is a hedonist, but yesterday he was quite unbearable.*

---

gerade — *straight*

gerade dabei sein — *to be about to.*

Ich war gerade dabei, zu Abend zu essen, als das Telefon klingelte. *I was just about to eat dinner when the telephone rang.*

gerade recht kommen — *to be opportune.*

Das gefundene Geld kam mir gerade recht. *The money I found was just what I needed.*

geradeaus — *straight ahead.*

Immer geradeaus fahren, dann an der dritten Ampel links abbiegen. *Keep on driving straight ahead then turn left at the third traffic light.*

---

geraten — *to get into*

Sie sind in ein Unwetter geraten. *They got caught in a storm.*

ins Stocken geraten — *to get bogged down.*

Die Verhandlungen sind ins Stocken geraten. *The negotiations have bogged down.*

geraten — *to turn out.*

Ihnen sind die Kinder schlecht geraten. *Their children turned out badly.*

---

das Gerede — *gossip*

ins Gerede kommen — *to get a bad reputation.*

Sein Benehmen und sein Unternehmen sind ins Gerede gekommen. *His behavior and his business have gotten a bad reputation.*

---

das Gericht — *court*

das Jüngste Gericht — *the Last Judgement.*

Die Theologen sprachen über den Begriff eines Jüngsten Gerichtes bei verschiedenen Religionen. *The theologians spoke of the concept of a Last Judgment in various religions.*

ins Gericht gehen — *to rebuke; to take to task.*

Die Senatorin ging mit ihren Gegnern besonders scharf ins Gericht. *The senator severely rebuked her opponents.*

vor Gericht stellen — *to put on trial.*

Die Verbrecher sollten vor Gericht gestellt werden. *The criminals were to be put on trial.*

---

gern — *gladly*

Danke für Ihre Hilfe. — Gern geschehen. *Thank you for your help. — You're welcome.*

gern haben — *to be fond of; like.*

Wir haben den Alten trotzdem gern. — *We're fond of the old man anyway.*

Ulla singt gern. — Ja, sie spielt, tanzt, und feiert auch gern. — *Ulla likes to sing. — Yes, she likes to play, dance, and celebrate too.*

---

das Gesicht — *face*

das Gesicht wahren — *to save face.*

Der Senator bemühte sich trotz allem, das Gesicht zu wahren. *The senator tried to save face despite everything.*

ein anderes Gesicht bekommen — *to take on a new character.*

Mit den letzten Enthüllungen hat die Sache ein neues Gesicht bekommen. *With the latest revelations the matter has taken on a new character.*

sein wahres Gesicht zeigen — *to show one's true colors.*

Er geriet unter Druck und zeigte sein wahres Gesicht. *He came under pressure and showed his true colors.*

---

das Gespräch — *conversation*

im Gespräch sein — *to be under discussion, consideration.*

Sie ist als mögliche Kandidatin im Gespräch. *She is under discussion as a possible candidate.*

---

gesund — healthy

gesund und munter — *hale and hearty, alive and kicking.*

Die ganze Familie ist gesund und munter. *The whole family's in good health and good spirits.*

gesundbeten — *to heal by faith.*

Der Gesundbeter versucht ihn jetzt gesundzubeten. *Now the faith healer's trying to cure him.*

die Gewalt — *power; force*

höhere Gewalt — *an act of God.*

Gibt es eine höhere Gewalt Klausel in dem Vertrag? *Is there an act of God clause in the contract?*

gewinnen — *to win*

"Wie gewonnen, so zerronnen," war die Devise des Fachspielers. *"Easy come, easy go" was the professional gambler's motto.*

gießen — *to pour*

in Strömen gießen — *to pour (rain).*

Heute gießt es wieder in Strömen. *It's pouring again today.*

sich einen hinter die Binde gießen — *to belt one down.*

Er stand an der Theke und goss sich einen nach dem anderen hinter die Binde. *He stood at the bar and belted down one after another.*

das Gift — *poison*

auf etwas Gift nehmen können — *to be able to bet one's life on.*

Sie ist unschuldig, darauf kannst du Gift nehmen. *She's innocent; you can bet your life on that.*

Gift und Galle spucken — *to spew venom; to be boiling mad.*

Er spuckte Gift und Galle, als er die Wahrheit erfuhr. *He was boiling mad when he found out the truth.*

das Glas — *glass*

zu tief ins Glas schauen — *to have a few too many.*

Gestern abend hat er wieder zu tief ins Glas geschaut. *He had a few too many again last night.*

das Glashaus — *glass house; greenhouse.*
Wer im Glashaus sitzt, soll nicht mit Steinen werfen. *People who live in glass houses shouldn't throw stones.*

die Glocke — *bell*
    etwas an die große Glocke hängen — *to tell the whole world; broadcast.*
    Ja, er ist vorbestraft; das brauchst du aber nicht an die große Glocke zu hängen. *Yes, he has a criminal record; but you don't have to broadcast it.*

    wissen, was die Glocke geschlagen hat — *to know what's in store for.*
    Du weißt, was du getan hast, und was die Glocke geschlagen hat. *You know what you've done and what's in store for you.*

das Glück — *luck*
    auf gut Glück — *trusting to luck; at random.*
    Er wählte eine Farbe auf gut Glück. *He selected a color at random.*

    bei den Frauen Glück haben — *to be popular with women.*
    Trotz seines hohen Alters hat Herr Bellamy noch Glück bei den Frauen. *Despite his advanced age, Mr. Bellamy is still popular with women.*

    ein Glück sein — *to be a lucky/good thing.*
    Es war ein Glück, dass wir sie rechtzeitig warnen konnten. *It was a good thing that we could warn them in time.*

    Glück haben — *to be lucky.*
    In Las Vegas hat er kein Glück gehabt. *He wasn't lucky in Las Vegas.*
    Jeder ist seines Glückes Schmied. *Life is what you make it.*

    sein Glück machen — *to become successful; to make it.*
    Sie hoffte, in der Großstadt ihr Glück zu machen. *She hoped to become successful in the big city.*

    zum Glück — *luckily, fortunately.*
    Zum Glück konnte ich sie noch erreichen. *Fortunately I was still able to reach them.*

    glücken — *to succeed.*
    Es glückte ihnen, dem Gefängnis zu entfliehen. *They succeeded in escaping from prison.*

glücklich — *happy.*

Die beiden haben die ganze Nacht getanzt und gefeiert—den Glücklichen schlägt keine Stunde. *They danced and celebrated all night—time means nothing when you're happy.*

die Gnade — *grace*

das Gnadenbrot geben — *to treat the old charitably.*

Wir lieben unseren alten VW Käfer und geben ihm das Gnadenbrot. *We love our old VW beetle and look after it in its old age.*

der Gnadenstoß — *death blow, finishing stroke, coup de grâce.*

Die Firma kränkelt und die Konkurrenz versucht ihr den Gnadenstoß zu geben. *The firm's in a bad way and the competition is trying to finish it off.*

das Gold — *gold*

Es ist nicht alles Gold, was glänzt. *All that glitters is not gold.*

Gold in der Kehle haben — *to have a golden voice.*

Die neue Sopranistin hat Gold in der Kehle. *The new soprano has a golden voice.*

nicht mit Gold aufzuwiegen sein — *to be worth (more than) one's weight in gold.*

Omas Erfahrung und Hilfe sind nicht mit Gold aufzuwiegen. *Grandma's experience and help are worth (more than) their weight in gold.*

die Goldgräberstimmung — *a spirit of unbridled optimism.*

Goldgräberstimmung macht sich unter den Anlegern breit. *A spirit of unbridled optimism is spreading among investors.*

das Goldkind — *darling, precious child*

Sie halten ihren Lausbuben für ein Goldkind. *They think their little rascal is a darling.*

goldrichtig — *absolutely on the mark*

Sie suchen Erholung und Entspannung? In unserem Hotel wären Sie goldrichtig. *You're looking for rest and relaxation? Our hotel is just the place for you.*

die Goldwaage — *gold balance (scale)*
  auf die Goldwaage legen — *to take too literally.*
  Du brauchst nicht alles, was er sagt, auf die Goldwaage zu legen. *You don't have to take everything he says too (so) literally.*

der Gott — *God*
  Ach du lieber Gott! *Oh my goodness!*

  dem lieben Gott den Tag stehlen — *to laze away the day.*
  Er hält es für Sünde, dem lieben Gott den Tag zu stehlen. *He thinks it a sin to laze away the day.*

  den lieben Gott einen guten Mann sein lassen — *to take things as they come; to keep one's cool.*
  Während die anderen sich aufregten, ließ er den lieben Gott einen guten Mann sein. *While the others got upset, he kept his cool.*

  über Gott und die Welt reden — *to talk about this, that, and everything.*
  Wir redeten über Gott und die Welt. *We talked about this, that, and everything.*

  wie Gott in Frankreich leben — *to live in the lap of luxury; to live the life of Riley.*
  Vor der Revolution lebten sie, wie Gott in Frankreich. *Before the revolution they lived in the lap of luxury.*

das Gras — *grass*
  das Gras wachsen hören — *to read too much into things; to be a know-it-all.*
  Du hörst wieder das Gras wachsen. *You're reading too much into things again.*

  das Gras wachsen lassen — *to let the dust settle.*
  Darüber soll man erst das Gras wachsen lassen. *We should first let the dust settle on that.*

  ins Gras beißen — *to bite the dust; to die.*
  Die Soldaten hatten keine Lust, ins Gras zu beißen. *The soldiers had no desire to bite the dust.*

grau — *gray*

  alles grau in grau sehen — to take a pessimistic view.

  Ihr Man sieht alles grau in grau. *Her husband takes a pessimistic view of everything.*

greifen — *to grip, grasp*

  Sie griff zur Flasche, ihr Bruder zu Drogen. *She turned to the bottle, her brother to drugs.*

  Der General griff nach der Macht. *The general tried to seize power.*

  um sich greifen — *to spread.*

  In der Stadt griff die Panik um sich. *Panic spread in the city.*

die Grenze — *border, frontier; limit*

  Alles hat seine Grenzen. *Everything has its limits.*

  über die grüne Grenze gehen — *to cross a border illegally.*

  Sie versuchten, über die grüne Grenze zu gehen. *They tried to cross the border illegally.*

  grenzüberschreitend — *across borders.*

  Neue grenzüberschreitende Bahnstrecken wurden geöffnet. *New international rail lines were opened.*

der Griff — *grip*

  im Griff haben — *to have the hang of; to have under control.*

  Die Ärzte sagten, sie hätten die Krankheit im Griff. *The doctors said they had the disease under control.*

  in den Griff bekommen — *to get the hang of; to get under control.*

  Es dauerte eine Weile, bevor ich das Gerät in den Griff bekommen konnte. *It took a while before I could get the hang of the apparatus.*

der Groschen — *coin, penny*

  Bei mir ist jetzt endlich der Groschen gefallen. *I've finally caught on now.*

  der Groschen fällt pfennigweise — *not to understand readily.*

  Du darfst nicht zu viel von ihm erwarten; bei ihm fällt der Groschen nur pfennigweise. *You mustn't expect too much from him; he's slow on the uptake.*

nicht (ganz) bei Groschen sein — *to be crazy, not to have all one's marbles.*

Onkel Otto ist nicht mehr ganz bei Groschen; wir haben ihn aber doch lieb. *Uncle Otto isn't quite all there anymore, but we're fond of him anyway.*

groß — *big*

Groß und Klein — *young and old, children and adults, everyone.*

Ihre Erzählungen sind immer noch bei Groß und Klein beliebt. *Her stories are still universally popular.*

Was ist das schon groß? *Big deal!/So what?*

"Unser Sohn hat wieder einen Preis gewonnen."—"Was ist das schon groß? Er bleibt ein Idiot." *"Our son won a prize again."—"So what? He's still an idiot."*

grün — *green*

im grünen Bereich sein — *to be normal, under control; in the safety zone.*

Es ist alles noch im grünen Bereich. *Everything is still normal.*

nicht grün sein — *to dislike.*

Die Nachbarn sind sich nicht grün. *The neighbors dislike each other.*

dasselbe in Grün sein — *to make no real difference.*

Stell den Tisch da oder da drüben, das ist dasselbe in Grün. *Put the table here or there, it makes no real difference.*

der Grund — *ground; basis*

auf Grund — *on the basis of.*

Auf Grund der neusten Beobachtungen wurde ihre Theorie bestätigt. *On the basis of the latest observations, her theory was confirmed.*

den Grund legen — *to lay the groundwork.*

Ich sag's ihm schon, aber zuerst muss ich den Grund dazu legen. *I'll tell him, but first I have to lay the groundwork for it.*

einer Sache auf den Grund gehen — *to investigate thoroughly; to get to the bottom of.*

Wir sind der Sache auf den Grund gegangen. *We investigated the matter thoroughly.*

in Grund und Boden — *utterly; totally; thoroughly.*
Er schämte sich in Grund und Boden. *He was thoroughly ashamed.*

---

gut — *good*

es gut sein lassen — *to leave it at that.*
Damit lassen wir's gut sein. *Let's leave it at that.*

gut sein — *to be fond of.*
Du weißt, ich bin dir gut. *You know I'm fond of you.*

gutachten — *to give an expert opinion.*
Der gutachtende Arzt trat als Zeuge der Anklage auf. *The medical expert appeared as a witness for the prosecution.*

gutheißen — *to approve of.*
Gewalttaten können wir nicht gutheißen. *We can't approve of violence.*

---

das Haar — *hair*

die Haare vom Kopf fressen — *to eat out of house and home.*
Dein Bruder frisst uns die Haare vom Kopf. *Your brother is eating us out of house and home.*

ein Haar in der Suppe finden — *to find fault; to quibble.*
Erstaunlich, dass er diesmal kein Haar in der Suppe fand. *Amazing, he found nothing to quibble about this time.*

Haare auf den Zähnen haben — *to be a tough customer.*
Die neue Chefin hat Haare auf den Zähnen. *The new boss is one tough customer.*

kein gutes Haar lassen — *to pull to pieces; to find nothing commendable in.*
An unseren Vorschlägen ließ sie kein gutes Haar. *She pulled our suggestions to pieces.*

kein Haar krümmen — *not to hurt a hair on someone's head.*
Sie wird dir kein Haar krümmen. *She won't hurt a hair on your head.*

sich in den Haaren liegen — *to bicker, be at odds with.*
Sie liegen sich dauernd in den Haaren. *They're constantly bickering.*

um ein Haar — *by a hair; almost.*
Um ein Haar hätte ihn der Blitz getroffen. *He was almost struck by lightning.*

---

haben — *to have*
es in sich haben — *to be a potent drink; to be difficult, complicated*
Dein hausgebranntes Elixir hat's in sich! *Your home-brewed elixir is potent!*

es mit etwas haben — *to have problems with.*
Jahrelang hat er geraucht; jetzt hat er es mit der Lunge. *He smoked for years; now he's having trouble with his lungs.*

für etwas zu haben sein — *to be game for; be one's sort of thing*
Für ein Glas Bier ist er immer zu haben. *He's always game for a glass of beer.*
Für so etwas sind wir nicht zu haben. *Something like that isn't our sort of thing.*

noch zu haben sein — *to be unattached, unmarried.*
Er wollte wissen, ob die Milliardärin noch zu haben war. *He wanted to know whether the billionairess was still unattached.*

wie gehabt — *as before; as it was.*
Sie wollte nicht mehr weitermachen wie gehabt. *She didn't want to continue as before.*

zu haben sein — *to be available.*
Seidenteppiche wie diese sind selten und nur für viel Geld zu haben. *Silk rugs like these are rare and available only for a lot of money.*

---

der Hahn — *rooster*
Danach kräht kein Hahn. *Nobody gives a hoot about that.*

der Hahn im Korb sein — *to be cock of the walk.*
Auf der Fete war der neue Millionär der Hahn im Korb. *At the party the new millionaire was cock of the walk.*

---

der Haken — *hook*

einen Haken haben — *to have a catch, disadvantage.*
Der technische Fortschritt hat so manchen Haken. *Technical progress has many a disadvantage.*

Haken schlagen — *to dart sideways; be evasive.*
Sie warf dem Präsidenten vor, Haken zu schlagen. *She accused the president of being evasive.*

mit Haken und Ösen — *with no holds barred.*
Die Mannschaften spielten mit Haken und Ösen. *The teams played with no holds barred.*

halb — *half*

ein halbes Hemd — *a weakling, half-pint.*
Alle hielten Kasper für ein halbes Hemd, bis er sie überraschte. *Everyone thought Kasper was a weakling, until he surprised them.*

halbwegs — *to some extent, more or less; a bit.*
Vorm Krieg lebten die verschiedenen Völker halbwegs friedlich zusammen. *Before the war the various ethnicities lived more or less peacefully together.*
Jetzt geht's ihnen halbwegs besser. *They're doing a bit better now.*

der Halbstarke — *young hooligan*

Er begann als Halbstarker; jetzt ist er Schwerverbrecher. *He started as a young hooligan; now he's a dangerous criminal.*

der Hals — *neck*

den Hals nicht voll genug kriegen — *to be greedy.*
Die Eroberer der Neuen Welt konnten den Hals nicht voll genug kriegen. *The conquerors of the New World were greedy.*

einen langen Hals (lange Hälse) machen — *to crane one's (their) neck(s).*
Alle machten lange Hälse, um die Königin zu sehen. *All craned their necks to see the queen.*

sich auf den Hals laden — *to take on.*
Sie wollte sich keine neuen Verpflichtungen auf den Hals laden. *She didn't want to take on any new obligations.*

sich Hals über Kopf verlieben — *to fall head over heels in love.*
König Ludwig verliebte sich Hals über Kopf in Lola. *King Ludwig fell head over heels in love with Lola.*

zum Halse heraushängen — *to be sick and tired of.*
Das Treiben der Politiker hing Lola zum Halse raus. *Lola was sick and tired of the doings of the politicians.*

halten — *to hold*
eine Rede halten — *to make/deliver a speech.*
Die Botschafterin hielt eine Rede vor der Vollversammlung der Vereinten Nationen. *The ambassador delivered a speech to the United Nations General Assembly.*

halten auf — *to attach importance to; think highly of.*
Dieser Kritiker hält viel auf moralisierende Stücke. *This critic thinks highly of moralizing plays.*

halten mit — *to stick to; stay with.*
"Halten Sie es mit den altbewährten Wahrheiten," riet er. *"Stick to the tried and true verities," he advised.*
halten von — *to consider; think.*
Viele hielten aber diesen Kritiker für einen Heuchler. *But many thought that critic was a hypocrite.*

zum Narren halten — *to make a fool of.*
Er hat uns lange genug zum Narren gehalten. *He's made a fool of us long enough.*

der Hammer — *hammer*
ein dicker Hammer — *an awful blunder, mistake.*
Die Lehrerin sammelte die in den Schulaufgaben vorgekommenen dicken Hämmer. *The teacher collected the awful mistakes in her students' homework assignments.*

ein Hammer sein — *to be staggering (in a positive or negative way).*
Das ist ein Hammer! *That's terrific, fantastic! (That's totally outrageous!)*

einen Hammer haben — *to be around the bend.*
Dass er noch an Thor glaubt, heisst keineswegs, dass er einen Hammer hat. *The fact that he still believes in Thor doesn't mean that he's around the bend.*

die Hand — *hand*

"Hände hoch, oder wir schießen," riefen die Räuber. *"Hands up or we'll shoot," cried the robbers.*

aus einer Hand — *from one source/supplier.*

Dank den neuen Fusionen können wir jetzt alles aus einer Hand bekommen. *Thanks to the new mergers we can now get everything from one supplier.*

eine grüne Hand haben — *to have a green thumb.*

Seine Frau hat eine grüne Hand. *His wife has a green thumb.*

Hand und Fuß haben — *to make sense, be well grounded.*

Ihre Argumente haben Hand und Fuß. *Her arguments make sense.*

in der Hinterhand haben — *to have in reserve.*

Einige chemische Unternehmen haben bereits umweltfreundlichere Alternativen in der Hinterhand. *Some chemical companies already have more environmentally friendly alternatives in reserve.*

leicht von der Hand gehen — *to have a knack for.*

Das Restaurieren alter Möbel geht ihr leicht von der Hand. *She has a knack for restoring old furniture.*

mit Hand anlegen — *to pitch in.*

Alle wollten mit Hand anlegen. *Everybody wanted to pitch in.*

unter der Hand — *in secret.*

Das verbotene Buch kursierte unter der Hand. *The banned book circulated in secret.*

von der Hand weisen — *to reject out of hand.*

Nicht alle sogenannten Altweibergeschichten sind von der Hand zu weisen. *Not all so-called old wives' tales are to be rejected out of hand.*

von langer Hand vorbereiten — *to plan well in advance.*

Sie hatte die Geburtstagsfeier von langer Hand vorbereitet. *She planned the birthday party well in advance.*

zu Händen von — *to the attention of.*

Ich hab's zu Händen von Frau Meyer geschickt. *I sent it to the attention of Mrs. Meyer.*

zur Hand haben — *to have handy.*

Ich hatte kein Kleingeld zur Hand. *I had no change handy.*

der Handel — *trade, commerce*
Handel und Wandel — *commercial and social life.*
Durch den Krieg wurden Handel und Wandel beeinträchtigt. *Because of the war, commercial and social activities were restricted.*

handeln — *to trade; to do business*
Mit ihm lässt sich nicht handeln. *There's no doing business with him.*
handeln mit — *to deal in.*
Diese fliegenden Händler handeln mit allem. *These peddlers deal in everything.*

handeln über; handeln von — *to be about.*
Worüber handelt der Roman? *What's the novel about?*
Er handelt von betrogener Liebe. *It's about love betrayed.*

sich handeln um — *to be a matter of, to concern.*
Es handelt sich wieder um einen Spionagefall. *It's (a matter of) another case of espionage.*
Es handelt sich um viel Geld. *Much money is involved.*

das Handgelenk — *wrist*
aus dem Handgelenk — *offhand; off the cuff.*
Aus dem Handgelenk konnte sie es nicht sagen. *She couldn't say offhand.*

ein lockeres Handgelenk haben — *to be quick to slap.*
Bleib ihm vom Leibe; er hat ein lockeres Handgelenk. *Stay away from him; he's slaphappy.*

der Handkuss — *kiss on the hand*
mit Handkuss — *with the greatest pleasure.*
Weil sie intelligent, kompetent und scharmant ist, stellte man sie mit Handkuss ein. *Because she's intelligent, competent, and charming, they were delighted to hire her.*

der Händler — *dealer*
Einst war er Lebensmittelhändler; jetzt arbeitet er im Supermarkt. *Once he was a grocer; now he works in the supermarket.*

fliegender Händler — *peddler*
In der Stadt gibt es viele fliegende Händler. *In the city there are many peddlers.*

im Handumdrehen — *in no time at all*
Im Handumdrehen war sie wieder da. *She returned in no time at all.*

das Handwerk — *craft; trade*
das Handwerk legen — *to put a stop to wrongdoing.*
Die Regierung versucht, der internationalen Müll Mafia das Handwerk zu legen. *The government is trying to put a stop to the activities of the international garbage mafia.*
Handwerk hat einen goldenen Boden. *Learning a trade assures a solid future.*

ins Handwerk pfuschen — *to try to do someone else's job; to mind someone else's business.*
Einige Polizeibeamte klagten, dass Fräulein Marple ihnen ins Handwerk pfuschte. *Some police officials complained that Miss Marple was trying to do their job.*

hängen — *to hang*
an etwas hängen — *to be attached to s.t.*
Die Parkwächter hängen an ihren Wäldern mit ihrem Herzblut. *The park rangers are deeply attached to their forests.*

Hans — *Johnny*
Hans im Glück sein — *to be a lucky devil.*
Sein Bruder ist ein richtiger Hans im Glück. *His brother is a real lucky devil.*

Hans Guckindieluft — *a dreamer.*
Sie nannte ihn Hans Guckindieluft und heiratete ihn nicht. *She called him a dreamer and didn't marry him.*

Hansdampf in allen Gassen sein — *to be a Jack of all trades.*
Der Schuster blieb nicht bei seinem Leisten und wurde Hansdampf in allen Gassen. *The cobbler didn't stick to his last and became a Jack of all trades.*

der Harnisch — *armor*
in Harnisch bringen — *to infuriate.*
Jeden Abend bringen ihn die Nachrichten im Fernsehen in Harnisch.
Every evening the news on TV infuriates him.

hart — *hard*
hart auf hart kommen/gehen — *to come down to the crunch/nitty gritty.*
Wenn es hart auf hart kommt, wird man nicht auf ihn bauen können. *We won't be able to count on him in a tight spot.*

hart im Nehmen sein — *to be tough, hardy.*
Das schlechte Wetter machte ihm nichts aus; er ist hart im Nehmen. *The bad weather didn't bother him; he's tough.*

der Hase — *hare*
ein alter Hase — *an old hand.*
Lass dir alles von den alten Hasen erklären. *Get the old hands to explain everything to you.*
Mein Name ist Hase. *I know nothing about the matter and want nothing to do with it. (I'm giving name, rank, and serial number and nothing more.)*

wissen, wie der Hase läuft — *to know which way the wind is blowing.*
Jetzt weiß er, wie der Hase läuft. *Now he knows which way the wind is blowing.*

(nicht ganz) hasenrein sein — *to be suspect, fishy.*
Sein Verhalten schien uns, nicht ganz hasenrein zu sein. *His behavior seemed suspect to us.*

die Haube — *bonnet*
unter der Haube sein — *to be married.*
Er war froh, dass die meisten seiner Töchter unter der Haube waren. *He was glad that most of his daughters were married.*

hauen — *to beat*
aus dem Anzug hauen — *to knock for a loop.*

Der bloße Anblick hat mich aus dem Anzug gehauen. *The mere sight knocked me for a loop.*

---

der Haufen — *heap, pile*
über den Haufen werden — *to mess/screw up.*
Die letzten Ereignisse haben unsere Pläne über den Haufen geworfen. *The latest events have disrupted our plans.*

---

das Hauruck-Verfahren — *heave-ho/slam dunk approach*
Schwere Umweltprobleme wie diese lassen sich nicht im Hauruck-Verfahren lösen. *A slam-dunk approach won't solve such difficult environmental problems.*

---

das Haus — *house*
auf etwas zu Hause sein — *to be well informed.*
Auch auf diesem Gebiet ist sie zu Hause. *She's well informed in this area too.*

Haus an Haus wohnen — *to live next door.*
Wir wohnen Haus an Haus mit ihnen. *We live right next door to them.*

ins Haus stehen — *to be in store for.*
Du wirst bald erfahren, was dir ins Haus steht. *You'll soon find out what's in store for you.*

nach Hause gehen/fahren — *to go/drive home.*
Sie gingen spät nach Hause. *They went home late.*

von Haus zu Haus — *from all of us to all of you.*
Herzlichste Grüße von Haus zu Haus. *Warmest greetings from all of us to all of you.*

von Haus(e) aus — *originally, really.*
Von Hause aus ist sie Malerin. *She is really a painter.*

zu Hause — *at home.*
Er ist jetzt nicht zu Hause. *He's not home now.*
Dieser Brauch ist in Bayern zu Hause. *This custom comes from Bavaria.*

aus dem Häuschen geraten — *to go wild with excitement.*
Die Menge geriet ganz aus dem Häuschen. *The crowd went wild with excitement.*

---

haushoch — *high as a house*
haushoch gewinnen — *to win hands down.*
Sie hat haushoch gewonnen. *She won hands down.*

haushoch überlegen sein — *to be vastly superior to.*
Sie war ihren Gegnern haushoch überlegen. *She was vastly superior to her opponents.*

die Haut — *skin, hide*
nicht in jemands Haut stecken mögen — *not to want to be in someone's shoes.*
Überall sucht ihn die Polizei; ich möchte nicht in seiner Haut stecken. *The police are looking for him everywhere; I wouldn't want to be in his shoes.*

nicht wohl in seiner Haut sein — *to be existentially ill at ease; to be discontent with one's lot.*
Bevor sie Priesterin Gaias wurde, war ihr in ihrer Haut nicht wohl. *She was discontent before she became a priestess of Gaia.*

hautnah — *up close.*
In dem Tierpark kann man die Tiere hautnah erleben. *One can experience the animals up close in that zoo.*
Sie tanzten hautnah. *They danced cheek to cheek.*

der Hebel — *lever*
am längeren Hebel sitzen — *to have the upper hand; to have more leverage, clout.*
Diesmal sitzt er leider am längeren Hebel. *This time, unfortunately, he has the upper hand,.*

alle Hebel in Bewegung setzen — *to do everything possible.*
Die Bürgermeisterin will alle Hebel in Bewegung setzen, um den Tourismus zu fördern. *The mayor wants to do everything possible to promote tourism.*

heben — *to lift*
einen heben — *to drink alcohol.*
Dann und wann hebt sie gern einen. *Occasionally she likes to take a drink.*

der Heide — *pagan, heathen*

Gläubige, fromme Heiden gibt's heute überall, nicht nur auf der Heide. *There are pious, practicing heathens everywhere today, not just on the heath.*

das Heidengeld — *a pile of money.*

Er hatte verteufelt viel Glück und gewann ein Heidengeld. *He was extremely lucky and won a pile.*

der Heidenrespekt — *a healthy respect.*

Sie hat einen Heidenrespekt vor Schlangen. *She has a healthy respect for snakes.*

der Hecht — *pike*

der Hecht im Karpfenteich sein — *to be a big fish in a small pond; to be a real live wire.*

In unserem einst friedlichen Büro ist er jetzt der Hecht im Karpfenteich. *He's a real live wire in our formerly peaceful office.*

ein toller Hecht — *an incredible fellow; a hotshot.*

Er glaubt, er sei ein toller Hecht. *He thinks he's a real hotshot.*

der Hehler — *receiver of stolen goods; fence*

Der Hehler ist so schlimm wie der Stehler. *The fence is as bad as the thief.*

die Hehlerei — *receiving stolen goods.*

Er machte kein(en) Hehl daraus, dass er wegen Hehlerei schon eingesessen hatte. *He made no secret of having already served a prison sentence for receiving stolen goods.*

das Heimchen — *cricket*

das Heimchen am Herd — *submissive little wife; homebody, hausfrau.*

Wenn du dir ein Heimchen am Herd gewünscht hast, dann hättest du eine andere heiraten sollen. *If you wanted a submissive little hausfrau then you should have married somebody else.*

der/die Heilige — *saint*

ein sonderbarer Heiliger — *a strange type; a queer fish.*

Der war ein sonderbarer Heiliger. *He was a strange type.*

der Heiligenschein — *halo*
mit einem Heiligenschein umgeben — *to be blind to faults.*
Du bist in ihn verliebt, aber du musst ihn nicht mit einem Heiligenschein umgeben. *You're in love with him, but you mustn't be blind to his faults.*

heiligsprechen — *to canonize*
Jahrhunderte nach ihrer Verbrennung wurde die Jungfrau von Orleans heiliggesprochen. *Centuries after her burning the Maid of Orleans was canonized.*

das Heimspiel — *home game; a sure thing, easy victory*
Das Durchsetzen des neuen Konzepts ist keineswegs ein Heimspiel. *Implementing the new concept is anything but easy.*

heiß — *hot*
Es wird nie so heiß gegessen wie gekocht. *Food on the plate is never as hot as food in the pot. (There's more heat than light there. Wait till the shouting's over.)*
Zuerst nahmen viele den Diktator nicht ernst und sagten: Es wird nie so heiß gegessen wie gekocht. *At first many thought the dictator would simmer down and they didn't take him seriously.*

der Held — *hero*
kein Held in etwas sein — *to be no great shakes at; not to be very good at.*
Er war kein Held in der Schule. *He was no star pupil.*

helfen — *to help*
Da hilft kein Jammer und kein Klagen. *It's no use moaning and groaning.*
Hilf dir selbst, so hilft dir Gott. *God helps those who help themselves.*
Ihnen ist nicht mehr zu helfen. *They're beyond all help.*
Mit schönen Worten ist uns nicht geholfen. *Pretty words won't do us any good.*

hell — *light*
am hellichten Tag — *in broad daylight.*

Am hellichten Tag wurde das Mordattentat verübt. *The attempted assasination was carried out in broad daylight.*

das Hemd — *shirt*

Das Hemd ist näher als der Rock. *Charity begins at home.*

bis aufs Hemd ausziehen — *to fleece.*

Beim Kartenspielen hatten sie ihn bis aufs Hemd ausgezogen. *They really fleeced him playing cards.*

der Hengst — *stallion; virile male*

der Schreibtischhengst/Verwaltungshengst — *Nasty bureaucrat (lit. "writing desk/administration stallion").*

Von diesem Schreibtischhengst am grünen Tisch lass ich mir nichts vorsagen. *I'm not going to be dictated to by that nasty bureaucrat.*

der Tastenhengst — *keyboard whiz (computer, piano).*

Kai ist echt ein Tastenhengst auf dem Tastenkasten. *Kai sure knows how to tickle the ivories.*

der Herr — *Mr.; master*

aus aller Herren Länder(n) — *from all over.*

"Unsere Gäste kommen aus aller Herren Länder," sagte stolz die Hotelbesitzerin. *"Our guests come from all over," said the hotel owner proudly.*

einer Sache Herr werden — *to get under control.*

Er versucht, seiner Spielleidenschaft Herr zu werden. *He's trying to get his passion for gambling under control.*

in aller Herrgottsfrühe — *at the crack of dawn.*

Wir mussten in aller Herrgottsfrühe aufstehen. *We had to get up at the crack of dawn.*

herrschen — *to rule; to be prevalent*

In Regierungskreisen herrscht die Ansicht, dass es zu spät ist. *The prevailing opinion in government circles is that it's too late.*

herrschen — *to be.*

Es herrschte richtiges Kaiserwetter, als wir in Rom ankamen. *The weather was really splendid when we arrived in Rome.*

herum — *around*

herumlungern — *to loaf/hang around.*

Statt herumzulungern, sollte der Junge lernen, Sport treiben, oder arbeiten. *Instead of loafing around, the boy should study, play sports, or work.*

sich herumsprechen — *to get around by word of mouth.*

Es hat sich unter den Studenten schnell herumgesprochen, dass die neue Professorin sehr streng ist. *Word got around fast among the students that the new professor is very strict.*

---

herunterfahren — *to drive down*

Er möchte lieber auf seinem Motorrad herunterfahren. *He'd rather drive down on his motorcycle.*

herunterfahren — *to play down, to deescalate.*

Man muss versuchen, den Konflikt herunterzufahren. *One must try to deescalate the conflict.*

---

sich hervortun — *to distinguish oneself*

Hermann Hesse hat sich auch als Maler hervorgetan. *Hermann Hesse also distinguished himself as a painter.*

---

das Herz — *heart*

am Herzen liegen — *to really care about.*

Jetzt ist sie ein großer Star und will nur Rollen spielen, die ihr am Herzen liegen. *Now that she's a big star, she just wants to play roles she cares about.*

auf Herz und Nieren prüfen — *to give a good going over; to grill.*

Er wurde vom Senatsausschuss auf Herz und Nieren geprüft. *He was grilled by the Senate committee.*

das Herz auf dem rechten Fleck haben — *to have one's heart in the right place.*

Er hilft uns wenig, doch hat er das Herz auf dem rechten Fleck. *He doesn't help us much, but his heart is in the right place.*

ein Herz und eine Seele sein — *to be inseparable; to be bosom friends*

Lange Zeit waren sie ein Herz und eine Seele. *For a long time they were inseparable.*

es nicht übers Herz bringen — *not have the heart to.*

Sie konnte es nicht übers Herz bringen, ihm alles zu sagen. *She didn't have the heart to tell him everything.*

etwas auf dem Herzen haben — *to have on one's mind.*

Hast du noch etwas auf dem Herzen, mein Sohn? *Do you still have something on your mind, my son?*

im Grunde seines Herzens — *in one's heart of hearts.*

Im Grunde ihres Herzens wusste sie, dass sie recht hatte. *In her heart of hearts she knew she was right.*

seinem Herzen Luft machen — *to give vent to one's feelings; to tell off.*

Endlich konnte sie ihrem Herzen Luft machen. *At last she could give vent to her feelings.*

Wes das Herz voll ist, des geht ihm der Mund über. *When you're excited about something, you can't help but talk about it constantly.*

heute — *today*

heute Morgen — *this morning.*

Heute Morgen können wir nicht. *We can't this morning.*

heute Nacht — *tonight.*

Heute Nacht will ich nicht singen. *I won't sing tonight.*

heute oder morgen — *at any time; at a moment's notice .*

Heute oder morgen kann sich alles ändern. *Everything can change at a moment's notice.*

von heute auf morgen — *very rapidly; on short notice.*

Das geht nicht von heute auf morgen. *That can't be done on such short notice.*

das Hickhack — *squabbling, wrangling*

Nach langem Hickhack ist das Abkommen jetzt endlich unter Dach und Fach. *After much wrangling, the agreement is finally all wrapped up.*

der Hieb — *blow*

hieb- und stichfest — *cast-iron, airtight*

Die Staatsanwältin glaubt nicht an sein hieb- und stichfestes Alibi. *The district attorney doesn't believe in his castiron alibi.*

hinter — *behind*
hinter her sein — *to pursue.*
Lange Jahre war Javert hinter ihm her. *Javert pursued him for many years.*

hobeln — *to plane*
Valentin sang vom Tod, der alle gleichhobelt. *Valentin sang of death, which levels everyone.*
Wo gehobelt wird, da fallen Späne. *You can't make an omelette without breaking eggs.*

hoch, höher, höchst — *high, higher, highest*
hoch hinaus wollen — *to have big ideas/ambitions.*
Ich liebte sie, aber sie wollte hoch hinaus und heiratete den Millionär.
I loved her, but she had great ambitions and married the millionaire.

die höchste Zeit sein — *to be high time.*
Es ist die höchste Zeit, dass wir uns auf den Weg machen. *It's high time we got started.*

hoch und heilig versprechen — *to promise faithfully, solemnly.*
Hoch und heilig versprach er ihr, keinen mehr zu heben. *He solemnly promised her not to drink anymore.*

zu hoch sein — *to be beyond.*
Die Relativitätstheorie ist uns zu hoch. *The theory of relativity is beyond us.*

hohes Alter — *advanced age.*
Trotz ihres hohen Alters hat unsere Hündin noch Freude am Essen.
Despite her advanced age, our dog still enjoys eating.

das Hochhaus — *high-rise.*
In diesem Viertel gibt es viele Hochhäuser. *There are many high rises in this section.*

hochnäsig — *stuck-up.*
Das Personal in dem Nobelhotel ist sehr hochnäsig. *The staff in that ritzy hotel is very stuck-up.*

die Hochrechnungen — *electoral projections.*
Den ersten Hochrechnungen zufolge, wird die Senatorin wieder gewählt werden. *According to early projections the senator will be re-elected.*

der Hocker — *stool*

locker vom Hocker — *free and easy.*

Es gibt keinen Zwang; du kannst locker vom Hocker mit mir darüber reden. *There's no constraint; you can talk about it freely with me.*

vom Hocker hauen — *to astound s.o.*

Das hat uns glatt vom Hocker gehauen, dass sie sich scheiden lassen. *We were flabbergasted to hear they're getting a divorce.*

vom Hocker locken — *to arouse interest.*

Mit solch alten Kamellen lockt man keinen heutzutage vom Hocker. *Nobody goes for old chestnuts like that nowadays.*

der Hof — *court; courtyard*

den Hof machen — *to court.*

Jahrelang machte er ihr den Hof, aber sie heiratete einen anderen. *He courted her for years, but she married someone else.*

die Höhe — *height*

auf der Höhe sein — *to feel great, fit; to be in fine form.*

Trotz ihres hohen Alters ist Oma geistig und körperlich noch auf der Höhe. *Despite her advanced age, grandma is still in great shape mentally and physically.*

in die Höhe gehen — *to blow one's top.*

Der Chef geht gleich in die Höhe, wenn man das Thema berührt. *The boss blows his top when the subject is mentioned.*

nicht ganz auf der Höhe sein — *to be a bit under the weather.*

Onkel Otto hat wieder zu viel gefeiert und ist heute nicht ganz auf der Höhe. *Uncle Otto did a little too much celebrating again and is a bit under the weather today.*

das Holz — *wood*

Holz in den Wald tragen — *to carry coals to Newcastle.*

nicht aus Holz sein — *not to be made of stone; to have feelings.*

Glaubst du, dass ich aus Holz bin? *Don't you think I have feelings too?*

die Holzhammermethode — *hard-sell methods.*

In ihrer eleganten Boutique ist die Holzhammermethode fehl am Platz. *In her elegant boutique hard sell methods are out of place.*

auf dem Holzweg sein — *to be on the wrong track.*
Die Polizei war wieder auf dem Holzweg. *The police were on the wrong track again.*

der Honig — *honey*
Honig um den Bart (Mund) schmieren — *to flatter, to butter up.*
Alle versuchten, dem Chef Honig um den Bart zu schmieren. *They all tried to butter up the boss (m).*
Alle versuchten, der Chefin Honig um den Mund zu schmieren. *They all tried to butter up the boss (f).*

kein Honig(sch)lecken sein — *to be no picnic, no bed of roses.*
Eine so lange Reise mit ihm war kein Honiglecken. *A long trip like that with him was no picnic.*

strahlen wie ein Honigkuchenpferd — *to grin like a Cheshire cat.*
Da strahlt er wieder wie ein Honigkuchenpferd. *There he is grinning like a Cheshire cat again.*

der Hopfen — *hops*
Bei (an) ihm ist Hopfen und Malz verloren. *He's worthless, a hopeless case.*

das Horn — *horn*
ins gleiche Horn stoßen — *to take the same line, sing the same tune.*
Sie gehören nicht derselben Partei an, doch stoßen sie oft ins gleiche Horn. *They don't belong to the same party, but they often take the same line.*

sich die Hörner ablaufen — *to sow one's wild oats.*
Er hat sich jetzt genug die Hörner abgelaufen! *He's sown enough wild oats now!*

das Huhn — *chicken*
das Huhn, das goldene Eier legt, schlachten — *to kill the goose that lays the golden eggs.*
Nimm dich in acht, das Huhn, das goldene Eier legt, nicht zu schlachten. *Be careful not to kill the goose that lays the golden eggs.*

ein Hühnchen zu rupfen haben — *to have a bone to pick.*
Ich habe noch ein Hühnchen mit dir zu rupfen. *I have another bone to pick with you.*

---

das Hühnerauge — *corn (foot)*
    jemandem auf die Hühneraugen treten — *to step on someone's toes.*
Pass auf, ihm nicht auf die Hühneraugen zu treten. *Be careful not to step on his toes.*

---

der Hund — *dog*
    auf den Hund kommen — *to go to the dogs.*
Er ist auf den Hund gekommen. *He's gone to the dogs.*

    bekannt wie ein bunter Hund — *to be a well-known figure.*
Aber einst war er bekannt wie ein bunter Hund. *But once he was a well-known figure.*

    Da wird der Hund in der Pfanne verrückt! *That's mindboggling!*

    ein dicker Hund — *an incredible, shocking bit of news.*
Das ist ein dicker Hund, dass sie so durchgebrannt ist! *That's incredible, her running off like that!*

    mit allen Hunden gehetzt sein — *to know all the tricks.*
Ihre Anwältin ist mit allen Hunden gehetzt. *Her lawyer knows all the tricks.*

    vor die Hunde gehen — *to go to the dogs; be ruined.*
Er und sein Geschäft sind vor die Hunde gegangen. *He and his business have gone to the dogs.*

    wissen, wo der Hund begraben liegt — *to know the reason behind s.t., to know what's at the bottom/root of a matter.*
Ich weiß, wo der Hund begraben liegt. Seine Tante lässt ihm heimlich Geld zukommen. *I know what's behind that. His aunt's having money sent to him secretly.*

    Ach, da liegt der Hund begraben! *So that's the real reason!*

---

hundert — *hundred*
    vom Hundertsten ins Tausendste kommen — *to go from one subject to another.*

Nicht alle Studenten schätzen Professoren, die vom Hundertsten ins Tausendste kommen. *Not all students appreciate professors who go from one subject to another.*

der Hunger — *hunger*
Hunger ist der beste Koch. *Hunger is the best sauce.*

Hunger haben — *to be hungry.*
Habt ihr noch Hunger? *Are you still hungry?*

eine Hungerkur machen — *to go on a fasting diet.*
Er musste abspecken und eine Hungerkur machen. *He had to slim down and go on a fasting diet.*

hüpfen — *to hop*
gehüpft wie gesprungen sein — *to not matter either way.*
Jetzt oder später — das ist gehüpft wie gesprungen. *Now or later, it doesn't matter either way.*

der Hut — *hat*
aus dem Hut machen — *to pull out of a hat; to come up with right away.*
Sie sagte, sie könne die Sache nicht so gleich aus dem Hut machen, und müsse darüber nachdenken. *She said she couldn't come up with something right away and would have to think about the matter.*

Das kannst du dir an den Hut stecken! Ich will's nicht. *You can have that! I don't want it.*

den Hut nehmen müssen — *to have to resign.*
Wegen der Korruptionsskandale mussten einige Senatoren den Hut nehmen. *Because of corruption scandals some senators had to resign.*

eins auf den Hut kriegen — *to be rebuked; to get a chewing out.*
Er kam spät nach Hause und kriegte eins auf den Hut. *He came home late and got a chewing out.*

Hut ab! — *Hats off!*
Hut ab vor ihrer Leistung! *Hats off to her accomplishment.*

nichts am Hut haben — *to have nothing to do with.*
Mit Fanatikern jeder Art haben wir nichts am Hut. *We have nothing to do with fanatics of any kind.*

unter einen Hut bringen — *to reconcile.*
Es gelang der Präsidentin, verschiedene Interessen unter einen Hut zu
bringen. *The president succeeded in reconciling diverse interests.*

die Hut — *keeping, care*
auf der Hut sein — *to be on guard; be cautious, wary.*
Die Witwe war auf der Hut vor Schwindlern. *The widow was wary of
swindlers.*

in guter Hut sein — *to be in good hands.*
In der Pension meiner Tante wärst du in guter Hut. *You'd be in good
hands in my aunt's rooming house.*

die Idee — *idea*
Das Kleid ist eine Idee zu eng. *The dress is just a little too tight.*

das Inland — *one's own country*
Im In- und Ausland verkauft sich die Maschine gut. *The machine is
selling well at home and abroad.*

der I-Punkt; das I-Tüpfelchen — *the dot over the i*
bis auf den I-Punkt — *down to the last detail.*
Ich bestehe darauf, dass die Rechnung bis auf den I-Punkt stimmt. *I insist
that the bill be correct down to the last detail.*

bis auf das letzte I-Tüpfelchen — *down to the smallest detail.*
Nicht alle Beamten sind bis auf das I-Tüpfelchen genau. *Not all officials
are precise down to the smallest detail.*

der I-Tüpfel-Reiter — *stickler for detail, nitpicker.*
Ja, aber der Beamte, mit dem wir zu tun hatten,war ein I-Tüpfel-Reiter.
Yes, but the official we had to do with was a stickler for detail.

inwendig — *inside*
  in- und auswendig kennen — *to know inside out.*
  Ich glaubte, ihn in- und auswendig zu kennen, aber ich irrte mich.
  I thought I knew him inside out, but I was mistaken.

Ja - *yes*
  sich das Jawort/das Jawort fürs Leben geben — *to get married.*
  Sie haben sich endlich das Jawort gegeben. *They finally got married.*

die Jacke — *jacket*
  sich die Jacke anziehen — *to take something personally.*
  Du hast dir die Jacke gleich angezogen; ich sprach aber ganz im
    Allgemeinen. *You took it personally, but I was only speaking in general
    terms.*

  Wem die Jacke passt, der zieht sie an. *If the shoe fits, wear it.*

  Jacke wie Hose sein — *to make no difference.*
  Ob Sie mit Dollars oder Euros bezahlen, das ist Jacke wie Hose. *Whether
    you pay with dollars or euros, it makes no difference.*

  eine alte Jacke — *old hat.*
  Das wissen wir schon; deine Geschichte ist eine alte Jacke. *We know that
    already; your story is old hat.*

jagen — *to hunt*
  eins jagt das andere — *following in close succession.*
  Zuerst jagte ein Erfolg den anderen. Später aber jagte eine
    Pleite/Katastrophe die andere. Jetzt jagt ein Unglück das andere.
    *At first, it was one success after another. But later one bankruptcy/
    catastrophe followed hard on the heels of the other. It's one misfortune
    after another now.*

  ins Bockshorn jagen — *to intimidate.*
  Lassen Sie sich von ihm nicht ins Bockshorn jagen! *Don't let him
    intimidate you.*

mit etwas jagen — *to detest.*

Mit Rock-Pop Musik kann man ihn jagen. *He detests Rock-Pop music.*

das Jahr — year

in die Jahre kommen — *to get older; to get to an age.*

Wir kommen jetzt in die Jahre, wo wir lieber zu Hause bleiben. *We're now getting to an age when we prefer to stay at home.*

in jungen Jahren — *at an early age.*

Das haben wir schon in jungen Jahren gelernt. *We already learned that at an early age.*

Jahr und Tag — *many years; a year and a day.*

Wir sind seit Jahr und Tag nicht da gewesen. *We haven't been there for many years.*

Jakob — *Jacob*

der billige Jakob — *thrift shop; the junkman.*

Sie ist millionenschwer, aber ihre Kleider sehen aus, als ob sie vom billigen Jakob kämen. *She's worth millions, but her clothes look like they come from a thrift shop.*

der wahre Jakob — *the right and proper thing; the real McCoy, genuine article.*

Den ganzen Tag nur herumlungern, du musst doch einsehen, das ist nicht der wahre Jakob. *You must realize that loafing around all day isn't the right thing to do.*

Die vermeintliche Rolexuhr, die du vom Straßenhändler gekauft hast, ist nicht der wahre Jakob. *That supposed Rolex you bought from the street peddler isn't the genuine article.*

jobben — *to work at a job*

Die meisten Studenten auf dieser Uni müssen jobben. *Most students at this university have to get jobs.*

jung — young

Jung getan, alt gewohnt. *Do something early on and it'll be easier to do later.*

junge Hunde regnen — *to rain cats and dogs.*
Als wir ankamen, regnete es junge Hunde. *When we arrived it was raining cats and dogs.*

zum Junge-Hunde-Kriegen — *enough to make you flip out, give you kittens.*
In Las Vegas haben wir nur verloren. Es war zum Junge-Hunde-Kriegen! *All we did was lose in Las Vegas. It was enough to give you kittens!*

der Jux — *joke, lark*
sich einen Jux machen — *to do as a lark, spree.*
Die Jungen wollten in die Großstadt, um sich einen Jux zu machen. *The boys wanted to go to the big city to go on a spree.*

der Kaffee — *coffee*
kalter Kaffee — *stale, flat; old hat.*
Alles, was der Vorsitzende sagte, war nur kalter Kaffee. *Everything the chairman said was old hat.*
Kalter Kaffee macht schön. *Drink coffee cold and never look old.*

der Kaiser — *emperor*
das Kaiserwetter — *splendid weather.*
Alle Werktätigen erfreuten sich des Kaiserwetters bei der Gewerkschaftsfeier. *All the workers enjoyed the splendid weather at the union festivity.*

der Kakao — *cocoa*
durch den Kakao ziehen — *to ridicule.*
Der Senator versuchte, seinen Gegner durch den Kakao zu ziehen. *The senator tried to ridicule his opponent.*

kalt — *cold*
auf die kalte Tour; auf kaltem Wege — *with no fuss; without violence.*

Es gelang ihr, alles auf die kalte Tour zu erledigen. *She succeeded in settling everything without any fuss.*

kalt erwischen — *to catch off guard, unprepared.*
Die Hochwasserkatastrophe hat Tausende kalt erwischt. *The flood disaster caught thousands unprepared.*

kaltmachen — *to do in.*
Der Detektiv war nicht der erste, den der Gangster kaltgemacht hatte. *The detective wasn't the first one the gangster had done in.*

---

der Kamm — *comb*
über einen Kamm scheren — *to lump together.*
Alle Bündnispartner sind nicht über einen Kamm zu scheren. *All the partners in the alliance shouldn't be lumped together.*

---

der Kanal — *canal, channel*
den Kanal voll haben — *to be plastered; to have had as much as one can take.*
Er hat den Kanal schon voll, aber er will noch mehr. *He's already plastered, but he wants more.*
Die Wähler hatten den Kanal voll von den Versprechungen des Senators. *The voters had as much as they could take of the senator's promises.*

---

die Kandare — *curb (horses)*
an die Kandare nehmen — *to take a strong line with.*
Der Diktator beschloss, die streikenden Arbeiter an die Kandare zu nehmen. *The dictator decided to take a strong line with the striking workers.*

---

die Kanone — *cannon*
mit Kanonen auf Spatzen schießen — *to shoot at sparrows with cannons; to overkill.*
Das tun, hieße mit Kanonen auf Spatzen schießen. *To do that would be overkill.*

unter aller Kanone — *very bad(ly).*
Wieder hat die Mannschaft unter aller Kanone gespielt. *The team played very badly again.*

---

die Kante — *edge*
auf die hohe Kante legen — *to put money by.*
Du solltest jede Woche etwas auf die hohe Kante legen. *Every week you should put a little money by.*

kapern — *to seize a ship; to hook*
Sie hat endlich den Milliardär gekapert. *She finally hooked the multimillionaire.*

kapern — *to rope into.*
Sie versuchten, den Geistlichen für ihren Plan zu kapern. *They tried to rope the clergyman into their scheme.*

das Kapitel — *chapter*
Das ist ein anderes Kapitel. *That's another story.*
Das is ein Kapitel für sich. *That's quite another story.*

kaputt — *broken*
kaputtmachen — *to break; to ruin, wreck.*
Das Kind hat ihre Puppe wieder kaputtgemacht. *The child has broken its doll again.*
Die Zwangsarbeit in Sibirien machte ihn kaputt. *Forced labor in Siberia left him a wreck.*

kaputtreden — *to talk to death.*
Das Thema wurde kaputtgeredet. *The subject was talked to death.*

die Karte — *card*
alles auf eine Karte setzen — *to stake everything on one chance; to go for broke.*
Der Chef musste alles auf eine Karte setzen. *The boss had to stake everything on one chance.*

auf die falsche Karte setzen — *to back the wrong horse; to choose the wrong means.*
Er hat leider auf die falsche Karte gesetzt. *Unfortunately he backed the wrong horse.*

kartenlegen — *to read cards (tarot, etc.).*
Carmen und die anderen Kartenlegerinnen legten Karten. *Carmen and the other fortune tellers read the cards.*

die Kartoffel — *potato*
Rein (rin) in die Kartoffeln, raus aus den Kartoffeln. *First it's "do this," then it's "do that."*

die Kasse — *cash box, cash register*
getrennte Kasse machen — *to go Dutch.*
Sie sagte ihm, dass sie nicht mehr getrennte Kasse machen wollte. *She told him she didn't want to go Dutch anymore.*

Kasse machen — *to tally up receipts.*
Die Abteilungsleiterin machte Kasse. *The department head tallied up the receipts.*

Kasse machen — *to make a lot of money.*
Einige wenige deutsche Filme konnten international Kasse machen. *Very few German movies have made a lot of money internationally.*

der Kassenschlager — *box office hit.*
Ihr letzter Film ist ein Kassenschlager. *Her latest movie is a box office hit.*

knapp bei Kasse sein — *to be short of funds.*
Wir sind wieder knapp bei Kasse und können uns das leider nicht leisten. *Unfortunately, we're short of funds again and can't afford that.*

zur Kasse bitten — *to ask to pay for.*
Nach der Katastrophe wurden die Umweltverschmutzer zur Kasse gebeten. *After the catastrophe, the environmental polluters were asked to pay for it.*

kassieren — *to collect; to receive money for services*
ganz schön kassieren — *to make a bundle.*
Bei dem Geschäft hat er ganz schön kassiert. *He made a bundle on the deal.*

der Kater — *tomcat*

einen Kater haben — *to have a hangover.*
Onkel Otto hat oft einen furchtbaren Kater. *Uncle Otto often has a terrible hangover.*

die Katerstimmung — *gloomy/morning after mood.*
Nach der Wahlschlappe herrscht Katerstimmung bei uns. *After losing the election we're in a gloomy mood here.*

der Muskelkater — *sore muscles.*
Nach den Anstrengungen von gestern hab ich heute ein bisschen Muskelkater. *After yesterday's efforts my muscles are a bit sore today.*

die Katze — *cat*

die Katze aus dem Sack lassen — *to let the cat out of the bag.*
Du hast wieder die Katze aus dem Sack gelassen. *You let the cat out of the bag again.*

die Katze im Sack kaufen — *to buy a pig in a poke.*
Wir wollen keine Katze im Sack kaufen. *We don't want to buy a pig in a poke.*

Die Katze lässt das Mausen nicht. *A leopard can't change its spots.*

für die Katz sein — *to be wasted, for nothing.*
Sie kamen nicht, und unsere ganze Arbeit war für die Katz. *They didn't come, and all our work was for nothing.*

Wenn die Katze aus dem Haus ist, tanzen die Mäuse auf dem Tisch. *When the cat's away, the mice will play.*

ein Katzensprung sein — *to be a stone's throw away.*
Zu Fuß ist es ziemlich weit, aber mit dem Wagen ist es nur ein Katzensprung. *On foot it's rather far, but with the car it's just a stone's throw away.*

Katzenwäsche machen — *to wash quickly, superficially, cat lick.*
Statt sich zu duschen, machte er nur Katzenwäsche. *Instead of taking a shower, he just washed superficially.*

der Kauf — *purchase*

in Kauf nehmen — *to put up with as part of a deal.*

Die Pauschalreise war schön, doch mussten wir einige Unannehmlichkeiten in Kauf nehmen. *The package tour was nice, but we had to put up with some things we didn't like.*

der Kavalier — *gentleman; nobleman*
das Kavaliersdelikt — *trivial offense, peccadillo.*
Trunkenheit am Steuer ist kein Kavaliersdelikt. *Drunk driving is no trivial offense.*

der Keks — *cookie*
auf den Keks gehen — *to get on someone's nerves, to grate.*
Die Fotografen gingen der Schauspielerin auf den Keks. *The photographers got on the actress's nerves.*

einen weichen Keks haben — *to be soft in the head.*
Sie glauben, du hast einen weichen Keks. *They think you're soft in the head.*

Kauf dir 'nen Keks! *Go take a walk/hike./Go jump in the lake.*

der Keller — *cellar*
im Keller sein — *to be at rock bottom/at the bottom of the barrel.*
Die Witschaft ist im Keller und der Beliebtheitsgrad des Präsidenten ist auch im Keller. *The economy's at rock-bottom and the president's approval ratings are at rock-bottom too.*

in den Keller fallen/gehen — *to drop drastically.*
Computerpreise sind in den Keller gegangen. *Computer prices have dropped dramatically.*

das Kind — *child*
das Kind beim rechten Namen nennen — *to call a spade a spade.*
Es war immer ihre Art, das Kind beim rechten Namen zu nennen. *It was always her style to call a spade a spade.*

das Kind mit dem Bad ausschütten — *to throw out the baby with the bathwater.*
Er hat voreilig gehandelt und das Kind mit dem Bad ausgeschüttet. *He acted rashly and threw out the baby with the bathwater.*

das Kind schon schaukeln — *to get things sorted out.*
Trotz aller Schwierigkeiten werden wir das Kind schon schaukeln.
Despite all difficulties, we'll get things sorted out.

mit Kind und Kegel — *with bag and baggage.*
Sie sind mit Kind und Kegel angekommen. *They have arrived with bag
and baggage.*

sich lieb Kind machen — *to ingratiate oneself.*
Sie versuchten sofort, sich lieb Kind bei den Siegern zu machen. *They
immediately tried to ingratiate themselves with the conquerors.*

der Kinderschuh — *child's shoe*
den Kinderschuhen entwachsen sein — *not to be a child any more.*
Du bist doch den Kinderschuhen entwachsen. *You're really not a child
anymore.*

die Kinderschuhe ausziehen — *to grow up.*
Ich glaube, sie hat jetzt endlich die Kinderschuhe ausgezogen. *I think
she's really grown up now.*

in den Kinderschuhen stecken — *to be still in its infancy.*
Die Mikrotechnik steckt noch in den Kinderschuhen. *Microtechnology is
still in its infancy.*

von Kindesbeinen an — *from earliest childhood*
Schon von Kindesbeinen an musste Zsupan arbeiten. *From earliest
childhood Zsupan had to work.*

die Kippe — *slag heap*
auf der Kippe stehen — *to be touch and go.*
Mit diesem Patienten steht es auf der Kippe. *It's touch and go with this
patient.*

die Kirche — *church*
Die Kirche hat einen guten Magen. *The church has a great appetite for
riches, whatever their source.*

die Kirche im Dorf lassen — *to keep a sense of proportion; not to go
overboard.*

Ja, er hätte es nicht tun sollen; aber lassen wir doch die Kirche im Dorf.
Yes, he shouldn't have done it; but let's not go overboard.

kein großes Kirchenlicht sein — *to be rather dim-witted.*
Er ist kein großes Kirchenlicht, trotzdem hat er den Posten bekommen.
He's not very bright; nevertheless he got the position.

die Kirchturmpolitik — *narrow, sectarian, local outlook.*
Uns fehlt Weitsicht; mit unserer Kirchturmpolitik erreichen wir wenig. *We
lack vision; we won't get very far with our sectarian behavior.*

die Kirsche — *cherry*
Mit dem/der/denen ist nicht gut Kirschen essen. *You'd better not
tangle/mess with him/her/them.*

sich wie reife Kirschen verkaufen — *to sell like hotcakes.*
Die neue Puppe verkauft sich wie reife Kirschen. *The new doll is selling
like hotcakes.*

der Klacks — *dollop, blob*
nur ein Klacks sein — *to be easy, a cinch.*
Für die Sportlerin war es nur ein Klacks, da hinaufzuklettern. *For the
athlete, climbing up there was a cinch.*

klappen — *to succeed; to go off; to work out*
Es hat alles gut geklappt. *Everything went off smoothly.*

mit etwas klappen — *to work out.*
Auch mit der dritten Ehe hat's nicht geklappt. *The third marriage didn't
work out either.*

der Klaps — *smack, slap*
einen Klaps haben — *to be off one's rocker.*
Ich glaube, dein Bruder hat einen Klaps. *I think your brother's off his rocker.*

klar — *clear*
bei klarem Verstand sein — *to be in full possession of one's faculties.*
Die Neffen wollten nicht glauben, dass ihr verstorbener Onkel bei klarem
Verstand war. *The nephews wouldn't believe that their deceased uncle
was in full possession of his faculties.*

klar wie Klärchen sein — *to be as plain as the nose on one's face.*
Es ist klar wie Klärchen, dass er in sie verliebt ist. *It's as plain as the nose on your face that he's in love with her.*

klarkommen — *to come to terms with.*
Mit seiner neuen Lage ist er noch nicht klargekommen. *He hasn't yet come to terms with his new situation.*

Klartext reden — *to talk in plain language; to be frank.*
Ich will mit Ihnen Klartext reden. *I'll be frank with you.*

klipp und klar sagen — *to say quite plainly.*
Der Senator hat es nicht klipp und klar, sondern durch die Blume gesagt. *The senator didn't come right out and say so, but he did say it in a roundabout way.*

---

die Klasse — *class*
In ihrem Garten zählt Klasse nicht Masse. *It's quality not quantity that counts in her garden.*

klasse sein — *to be first rate, classy.*
Die Vorstellung war wirklich klasse. *The performance was really first rate.*

---

klatschen — *to gossip; to slap*
Gestern war Kaffeeklatsch bei meiner Tante; dabei gestattet sie das Klatschen nur in Grenzen. *Yesterday my aunt had people over for coffee and a chat (a coffeeklatsch); but she permits gossiping only within limits.*

Beifall klatschen — *to applaud.*
Begeistert haben wir alle der Sopranistin Beifall geklatscht. *We all applauded the soprano enthusiastically.*

---

kleckern — *to make a mess; to mess with trifles*
nicht kleckern, sondern klotzen — *to forget halfway measures and go all out.*
Jetzt heißt es, nicht kleckern, sondern klotzen. *Now it's necessary to go all out and forget halfway measures.*

---

der Klee — *clover*
  über den grünen Klee loben — *to praise to the skies.*
  Er lobte die Aufführung über den grünen Klee. *He praised the*
  performance to the skies.

die Kleider — *dresses; clothes*
  Kleider machen Leute. *Clothes make the man (persons).*

klein — *small*
  es kleiner haben — *to have a smaller bill.*
  Fünfhundert Euro! Haben Sie es nicht kleiner? *A five hundred euro note!*
  Don't you have a smaller bill?

  klein, aber fein — *small but very nice.*
  Der Computer ist klein, aber fein. *The computer is small but very nice.*

  klein, aber mein — *small but mine.*
  Die Wohnung ist klein, aber mein. *The apartment is small, but it's mine.*

  klein beigeben — *to make concessions.*
  In einigen Punkten war die Chefin bereit, klein beizugeben. *The boss was*
  prepared to make concessions on some points.

  von klein auf — *from childhood on.*
  Von klein auf hat sie nur Traurigkeit gekannt. *From childhood on she has*
  known only sadness.

  Die Kleinen hängt man; die Großen lässt man laufen. *The small fish*
  get fried; the big ones get off scot free.

  Wer das Kleine nicht ehrt, ist des Großen nicht wert. *Those who slight*
  small things are not worthy of great ones.

Kleinkleckersdorf — *any out-of-the-way hamlet*
  Kleinkleckersdorf find ich nicht auf dieser Karte. *I can't find godforsaken*
  on this map.

kleinkriegen — *to intimidate*
  Opa ist nicht kleinzukriegen. *You can't keep grandpa down.*

  sich kleinkriegen lassen — *to let oneself be intimidated.*
  Er lässt sich von niemand kleinkriegen. *He won't let anyone intimidate him.*

kleinschreiben — *to write in small letters; to minimize*
Bei uns wird sein Reichtum kleingeschrieben. *His wealth counts for little with us.*

die Klemme — *clip (paper, hair)*
in der Klemme sitzen — *to be in a fix, bind.*
Sie haben alles auf eine Karte gesetzt, und sitzen jetzt in der Klemme. *They put all their eggs in one basket and are now in a fix.*

die Klinge — *blade*
die Klingen kreuzen mit — *to cross swords with.*
Der Senator und die Reporterin kreuzten wieder die Klingen. *The senator and the reporter crossed swords again.*

eine scharfe Klinge führen — *to be a formidable opponent in a discussion.*
Die Reporterin führt eine der schärfsten Klingen in der Hauptstadt. *The reporter is one of the most formidable opponents in the capital.*

über die Klinge springen lassen — *to kill; to ruin someone deliberately; to throw out of work.*
Rücksichtslos ließ der Senator seine früheren Kollegen über die Klinge springen. *Ruthlessly the senator ruined his former colleagues.*
Der neue Inhaber ließ die Hälfte der Angestellten über die Klinge springen. *The new owner threw half the employees out of work.*

die Klinke — *door handle*
sich die Klinke in die Hand geben — *to come and go without interruption.*
Seitdem er das Grosse Los gezogen hat, geben sich seine Verwandten die Klinke in die Hand. *Ever since he won the lottery his relatives are waiting in line to visit him.*

der Klinkenputzer — *door-to-door salesman; beggar.*
Dagwald Bumstedt kaufte dieses Gerät von einem Klinkenputzer. *Dagwood Bumpstead bought this appliance from a door-to-door salesman.*

der Kloss — *dumpling*
einen Kloss im Hals haben — *to have a lump in one's throat.*
Sie sah ihn an und hatte einen Kloss im Hals, als er aus dem Krieg
zurückkam. *She looked at him and had a lump in her throat when he
came back from the war.*

der Klotz — *block of wood, log*
auf einen groben Klotz gehört ein grober Keil — *to reply to rudeness
with (more) rudeness; to fight fire with fire.*
Auf seine unverschämte Mitteilung werde ich bald gehörig antworten —
auf einen groben Klotz gehört ein grober Keil. *I'll soon reply
appropriately to his impertinent communication — you've got to fight
fire with fire.*

ein Klotz am Bein sein — *to be a millstone around someone's neck.*
Sie meinte, sie wäre Filmstar geworden, wenn ihr die Kinder nicht ein
Klotz am Bein gewesen wären. *She thinks she would have become a
movie star if her children hadn't been a millstone around her neck.*

klug — *clever*
aus etwas nicht klug werden können — *be unable to make head or tail
of.*
Ich hab's mehrmals gelesen, aber daraus kann ich nicht klug werden. *I've
read it over several times, but I can't make head or tail of it.*

Der Klügere gibt nach. *Discretion is the better part of valor.*

die Kneifzange — *pincers*
mit der Kneifzange anfassen — *to touch with a ten-foot pole.*
So etwas möchte ich nicht mit der Kneifzange anfassen. *I don't want to
touch that with a ten-foot pole.*

das Knie — *knee*
etwas übers Knie brechen — *to push/rush through.*
Die Präsidentin sah ein, dass sie die Reformen nicht übers Knie brechen
konnte. *The president realized that she couldn't push through the
reforms.*

121

in die Knie gehen — *to cave/give in to.*

Die Regierung weigerte sich, vor den Terroristen in die Knie zu gehen. *The government refused to give in to the terrorists.*

---

der Knochen — *bone*

auf die Knochen gehen — *to be backbreakingly difficult.*

Diese Arbeit geht auf die Knochen. Warum muss ich immer die Knochenarbeit machen? *This work is backbreakingly difficult. Why do I always have to do the menial jobs?*

bis auf die Knochen — *through and through.*

Es regnete und wir wurden bis auf die Knochen nass. *It rained and we got wet through and through.*

in den Knochen sitzen/stecken — *to be deeply felt.*

Nach dem Terroranschlag sitzen die Angst und der Schock noch tief in den Knochen. *After the terrorist attack people are still afraid and in a profound state of shock.*

die Knochenarbeit — *backbreaking job.*

Für diese Knochenarbeit hab ich nur einen Hungerlohn bekommen. *All I got for that backbreaking job was a miserable pittance.*

---

der Koch, die Köchin — *cook*

Viele Köche verderben den Brei. *Too many cooks spoil the broth.*

War die Köchin verliebt? *Was the cook in love? (i.e., Did she have her mind on other things and neglect the food?)*

---

kochen — *to cook*

auch nur mit Wasser kochen — *to be basically the same, to put one's pants on the same way as everyone else.*

Wir Rockstars kochen auch nur mit Wasser. *We rock stars are really just like everybody else.*

---

der Komfort — *comfort*

mit allem Komfort und zurück — *with every imaginable luxury.*

Einer der Preise ist ein Aufenthalt in einem Hotel mit allem Komfort und zurück. *One of the prizes is a stay in a hotel with every imaginable luxury.*

kommen — *to come*
Wie's kommt, so kommt's. *What will be will be.*

abhanden kommen — *to misplace, lose.*
Mir ist wieder ein Handschuh abhanden gekommen. *I've lost a glove again.*

Erstens kommt es anders, und zweitens als man denkt. *First, expect the unexpected, then expect it to be different from what you thought it might be.*
Mit 30 wollte ich schon Millionär sein, aber im hohen Alter muss ich noch schuften—erstens kommt es anders, und zweitens als man denkt. *I wanted to be a millionaire at 30, but even at my advanced age I still have to slave away—things never turn out as you think.*

im Kommen sein — *to be the latest thing; be on the way up.*
Roboter sind ganz groß im Kommen. *Robots are very much on the way up.*
Der Weinhändler behauptete, australische Weine wären im Kommen. *The wine merchant declared that Australian wines were the latest thing.*

kommen zu — *occur.*
Nur selten kam es zu Aufführungen seiner Musik. *His music was performed only rarely.*

zu Geld kommen — *to get rich.*
Niemand weiß, wie er zu Geld gekommen ist. *No one knows how he got rich.*

können — *to be able; to know a language*
Sie kann einige Fremdsprachen. *She knows a few foreign languages.*

nichts dafür können — *not to be able to help it.*
"Ich kann ja nichts dafür, dass ich so schön und stark bin," behauptete unbescheiden der Fußballer. *"I can't help being so handsome and strong," declared the football player immodestly.*

das Konto — *account*
  auf jemands Konto gehen — *to be someone's fault.*
  Die Niederlage der Partei geht vor allem aufs Konto des Senators. *The electoral defeat is primarily the senator's fault.*

das Kontor — *office; branch office*
  ein Schlag ins Kontor — *an unpleasant surprise.*
  Der Schatzmeister verschwand mit dem Geld—war das aber ein Schlag ins Kontor! *The treasurer disappeared with the money—was that ever a shock!*

der Kopf — *head*
  Was man nicht im Kopf hat, muss man in den Füßen haben. *What your head forgets means extra fetching for your feet.*

  einen dicken Kopf haben — *to have a hangover.*
  Onkel Otto hat wieder einen dicken Kopf. *Uncle Otto has a hangover again.*

  Kopf an Kopf — *neck and neck.*
  Der Favorit erreichte das Ziel Kopf an Kopf mit unserem Pferd. *The favorite finished neck and neck with our horse.*

  Kopf stehen — *to be in a hubub, go wild.*
  Nach unserem Fußballsieg stand die ganze Stadt Kopf. *After our soccer win the whole town went wild.*

  vor den Kopf stoßen — *to offend.*
  Der Senator will keine Sozialgruppe vor den Kopf stoßen. *The senator doesn't want to offend any social group.*

der Korb — *basket*
  einen Korb geben — *to turn down.*
  Grete gab Kai einen Korb und verlobte sich mit Uwe. *Grete turned down Kai and got engaged to Uwe.*

das Korn — *seed, grain*
  etwas aufs Korn nehmen — *to take aim at.*

Gemeinsam nahmen Goethe und Schiller die Schwächen der Zeit aufs Korn. *Together, Goethe and Schiller took aim at the weaknesses of their time.*

kosten — *to cost*

sich etwas kosten lassen — *to be prepared to pay good money for.*
Einige sind bereit, sich Qualitätsarbeit etwas kosten zu lassen. *Some are prepared to pay good money for quality work.*

auf seine Kosten kommen — *to get one's money's worth; to be satisfied*
In Bills Ballhaus kam jeder auf seine Kosten. *In Bill's ballroom everyone was satisfied.*

koste es, was es wolle — *at any cost.*
Der Milliardär wollte das Gemälde, koste es, was es wolle. *The billionaire wanted the painting, no matter what the cost.*

die Kraft — *strength*

bei Kräften sein — *to feel fit.*
Onkel Otto war lange im Krankenhaus; aber jetzt ist er wieder bei Kräften. *Uncle Otto was in the hospital for a long time, but he's feeling fit again.*

wieder zu Kräften kommen — *to regain one's strength.*
Die Krankenschwestern waren froh, dass Onkel Otto wieder zu Kräften gekommen war. *The nurses were glad that uncle Otto had regained his strength.*

der Kragen — *collar*

an den Kragen gehen — *to be threatened, endangered.*
Nicht nur im Regenwald geht es vielen Tier- und Pflanzenarten an den Kragen. *Not only in the rain forest are there many endangered species of plants and animals.*

der Kragen platzen — *to be the last straw.*
Mir (ihm, ihr, uns, ihnen) platzte der Kragen! *That was the last straw (for me, him, her, us, them)!*

jemands Kragenweite sein — *to be someone's cup of tea.*
Die kleine Brünette war genau seine Kragenweite. *The little brunette was just his cup of tea.*

die Krähe — *crow*

Eine Krähe hackt der anderen kein Auge aus. *One dog does not eat another. (Colleagues stick up for each other).*

die Kreide — *chalk*

in der Kreide stehen — *to be in debt.*
Seine Firma steht tief in der Kreide. *His firm is deep in debt.*

der Kreis — *circle*

jemandem dreht sich alles im Kreis — *someone is dizzy/tipsy.*
Schon nach dem ersten Schnaps drehte sich ihm alles im Kreis. *He felt dizzy after just one whisky.*

den Kreis (schon) eckig kriegen — *to iron out a difficult problem, square the circle.*
Sie glauben sie werden den Kreis schon eckig kriegen, aber sie sind wohl etwas blauäugig. *They think they're going to be able to solve their throny problem, but they're probably a bit naïve.*

Kreise ziehen — *to have repercussions, make waves.*
Die Schmiergeldaffäre zieht immer weitere Kreise. *That bribery scandal is having ever wider repercussions.*

das Kreuz — *cross*

ein Kreuz mit etwas haben — *to have a burden to bear.*
Mit seinem Geschäft hat er ein Kreuz. *His business is a heavy burden to him.*

mit jmdm. über Kreuz sein/stehen — *to be at cross purposes/on bad terms with.*
Seit langem steht er mit uns über Kreuz. *He's been on the outs with us for some time.*

zu Kreuze kriechen — *to eat humble pie.*
Bismarck weigerte sich, zu Kreuze zu kriechen. *Bismarck refused to eat humble pie.*

das Kriegsbeil — *hatchet*

Wir hatten das Kriegsbeil begraben, aber Lisa grub es wieder aus. *We had buried the hatchet but Lisa dug it up again.*

der Krimi — *whodunit; crime novel*

Agathe hat zahlreiche Krimis geschrieben. *Agatha has written numerous whodunits.*

die Krippe — *crib; feeding trough* (**Futterkrippe**)

an der Krippe sitzen — *to have a cushy job, feed at the trough.*

Alle glauben, ich sitze an der Krippe, aber schuften muss ich. *Everyone thinks I've got a cushy job, but I have to slave away.*

sich an die Krippe drängen — *to jockey for position.*

Die Chefin weiß, dass die Abteilungsleiter sich an die Krippe drängen und amüsiert sich darüber. *The boss knows the department chiefs are jockeying for position and she's amused.*

die Krone — *crown*

allem die Krone aufsetzen — *to take the cake.*

Das setzt allem die Krone auf! *That takes the cake! (That beats all!)*

in die Krone steigen — *to go to one's head.*

Der Champagner, nicht der Erfolg, stieg ihr in die Krone. *The champagne, not her success, went to her head.*

der Kuckuck — *cuckoo*

zum Kuckuck schicken — *to send away.*

Schick sie alle zum Kuckuck, wir haben keine Zeit. *Send them all away; we have no time.*

sich als Kuckucksei erweisen — *to turn out to be a liability.*

Die Erbschaft erwies sich als Kuckucksei. *The inheritance turned out to be a liability.*

die Kuh — *cow*

die Kuh fliegen lassen — *to have a blast.*

Beim Tanz haben wir alle die Kuh fliegen lassen. *We all had a blast at the dance.*

die Kuh vom Eis bringen — *to solve a difficult problem.*

Glauben Sie, dass wir je die Kuh vom Eis bringen werden? *Do you think we'll ever solve this difficult problem?*

der Kuhhandel — *shady horse trading; dirty deal.*
Der Senator verneinte, dass es sich um einen Kuhhandel handelte. *The senator denied that it was a dirty deal.*

auf keine Kuhhaut gehen — *to be beyond belief.*
Die Gräueltaten der Kriegsteilnehmer gehen auf keine Kuhhaut. *The atrocities of the belligerents are beyond belief.*

der Kulturbeutel — *shaving/grooming kit*
Sein einziges Gepäck war ein Kulturbeutel und ein Flachmann. *His only baggage was a shaving kit and a hip flask.*

die Kunst — *art*
Das ist keine Kunst! *There's nothing to it.*

Was macht die Kunst? *How are things?*

der Kurs — *course, rate*
hoch im Kurs stehen — *to be selling at a high price; to have a high opnion of.*
Deutsche Aktien stehen jetzt hoch im Kurs. *German stocks are selling at a high price now.*
Er steht bei ihr hoch im Kurs. *She has a high opinion of him.*

kurz — *short*
binnen Kurzem — *in a short time; shortly.*
Binnen Kurzem ist sie wieder da. *She'll be back shortly.*

den Kürzeren ziehen — *to lose; to get the worst of.*
Er machte erneut einen Prozess und zog wieder den Kürzeren. *He sued again and lost again.*

kurz und gut — *in short.*
Ich kann Ihnen keinen Kuchen backen, weil mir Butter, Eier, Mehl fehlen—kurz und gut alles, was zum Backen nötig ist. *I can't bake a cake for you because I haven't got butter, eggs, flour—in short, everything necessary for baking.*

seit Kurzem — *a short time ago.*
Erst seit Kurzem sind wir angekommen. *We arrived just a short time ago.*

Über Kurz oder lang — *sooner or later.*

über Kurz oder lang werden wir's schaffen. *We'll manage it sooner or later.*

vor Kurzem — *a short time ago.*

Bis vor Kurzem hat er bei Siemens gearbeitet. *Until a short time ago he worked for Siemens.*

zu kurz kommen — *not to get one's share.*

Du hast immer Angst, dass du zu kurz kommst. *You're always afraid you won't get your share.*

lachen — *to laugh*

Das ich nicht lache! *Don't make me laugh!*

sich einen Ast lachen — *to double over with laughter.*

Bei seinen Geschichten lachten wir uns einen Ast. *We doubled over with laughter listening to his stories.*

Wer zuletzt lacht, lacht am besten. *Who laughs last, laughs best.*

der Lack — *varnish*

Der Lack ist ab. *The bloom is off the rose.*

Die Sache hat nicht mehr ihren alten Reiz — der Lack ist ab. *The matter no longer has its old charm. The bloom is off the rose.*

laden — *to load*

schief geladen haben — *to be drunk, loaded.*

Gestern Abend hat er wieder schief geladen. *He was loaded again last night.*

der Laden — *store*

Der Laden läuft. *Business is good.*

den Laden schmeißen — *to run a very efficient business; to keep things moving smoothly.*

Ich weiß nicht, ob ich weiterhin den Laden ganz allein schmeißen kann. *I don't know if I can continue to run the business efficiently all alone.*

Tante-Emma-Laden — *Mom and Pop store.*
Wir würden gern auf dem Land wohnen, und einen Tante-Emma-Laden aufmachen. *We'd like to live in the country and open a Mom and Pop store.*

der Ladenhüter — *slow seller*

In unserem Winterschlussverkauf versuchen wir, die Ladenhüter loszuwerden. *In our winter clearance sale we try to get rid of the slow sellers.*

die Lage — *position*
in der Lage sein — *to be able to, be in a position to.*
Tante Erna ist nicht in der Lage, alles im Haus allein zu tun. *Aunt Erna isn't able to do everything in the house alone.*

die Lampe — *lamp*
einen auf die Lampe gießen — *to wet one's whistle.*
Während der Predigt hatte er große Lust, sich einen auf die Lampe zu gießen. *During the sermon he really felt like wetting his whistle.*

lang — *long*
lang und breit — *at great length; in great detail.*
Sie erklärte uns ihren Computer lang und breit; trotzdem verstanden wir nichts. *She explained her computer to us in great detail, but we still didn't understand anything.*

die Länge — *length*
sich in die Länge ziehen — *to go on and on.*
Der Film über den Hundertjährigen Krieg zog sich in die Länge. *The movie about the Hundred Years' War went on and on.*

die Lanze — *lance*
eine Lanze brechen für — *to go to bat for.*
Er brach eine Lanze für die Ideen seiner Freundin. *He went to bat for his friend's ideas.*

der Lappen — *cloth, rag*
   durch die Lappen gehen — *to slip through one's fingers.*
   Die Terroristen gingen den Soldaten durch die Lappen. *The terrorists
      slipped through the soldiers' fingers.*

   sich auf die Lappen machen — *to get underway.*
   Du musst dich jetzt auf die Lappen machen. *You've got to get underway
      now.*

der Lärm — *noise*
   Viel Lärm um nichts. *Much ado about nothing.*

lassen — *to let, allow*
   etwas lassen — *to stop,*
   Lass doch das Rauchen; es schadet nur deiner Gesundheit. *Stop smoking;
      it's harmful to your health.*

   gut sein lassen — *to let pass.*
   Es stimmt nicht genau, aber wir können's schon gut sein lassen. *It's not
      exact, but we can let it pass.*

   lassen müssen — *to have to give/grant.*
   Eines muss man ihm lassen—tanzen kann er gut. *You've got to give him
      that—he dances well.*

   in Ruhe lassen — *to leave alone.*
   Lass mich in Ruhe mit deinen ewigen Schimpfereien. *Leave me alone
      with your endless complaining.*

   lassen + infinitive — *to have something done.*
   Sie ließ sich ein neues Kleid machen. *She had a new dress made for
      herself.*

   sich lassen + infinitive — *to be able to be done.*
   Lässt sich das jetzt machen? *Can that be done now?*
   Lassen Sie sich's gut gehen! *Take it easy. Take care of yourself.*
   Das lässt sich leicht sagen. *That's easy to say.*
   Hier lässt es sich leben! *Life is good here.*
   Es lässt sich nicht leugnen, dass er Geld unterschlagen hat. *There's no
      hiding the fact that he embezzled money.*

die Last — *load, burden*

zu Lasten gehen — *to charge.*

Die Versandkosten gehen zu Lasten der Kunden. *Customers must pay the shipping charges.*

zur Last fallen — *to be troublesome; to inconvenience.*

Hoffentlich fällt euch unser Besuch nicht zu sehr zur Last. *We hope our visit isn't too much of an inconvenience for you.*

Ihr fallt uns gar nicht zur Last; wir freuen uns euch zu sehen. *You're not inconveniencing us at all; we're glad to see you.*

das Latein — *Latin*

mit seinem Latein am Ende sein — *not know what more to do.*

Die Ärzte waren mit ihrem Latein am Ende. *The doctors didn't know what to do any more.*

laufen — *to run*

auf dem Laufenden halten — *to keep informed.*

Unser Spion hielt uns über die Rüstungspläne auf dem Laufenden. *Our spy kept us informed about armament plans.*

wie am Schnürchen laufen — *to run like clockwork.*

Als sie Abteilungsleiterin war, lief alles wie am Schnürchen. *When she was department head, everything ran like clockwork.*

wie geschmiert laufen — *to run smoothly.*

Alles lief, wie geschmiert. *Everything ran smoothly.*

die Laune — *mood*

gute/schlechte Laune haben — *to be in a good/bad mood.*

Er hat heute wieder schlechte Laune. *He's in a bad mood again today.*

(nicht) bei Laune sein —*(not) to be in a good mood.*

Wenn sie bei Laune ist, wird's vielleicht klappen. *If she's in a good mood, it may work out.*

das Leben — *life*

am Leben sein — *to be alive.*

Ihre Großeltern sind noch am Leben. *Her grandparents are still alive.*

auf Leben und Tod kämpfen — *to be engaged in a life-and-death struggle; to fight to the finish.*

In allen seinen Filmen muss er auf Leben und Tod kämpfen. *In all his movies he has to fight to the finish.*

aus dem Leben gegriffen — *realistic, true to life.*

Aus dem Leben gegriffene Filme gefallen Blanche nicht. *Blanche doesn't like realistic movies.*

ins Leben rufen — *to bring into being; to found.*

Sie hat eine neue Zeitschrift ins Leben gerufen. *She founded a new periodical.*

Leben in die Bude bringen — *to liven the place up.*

Wenn Fritz nur hier wäre, würde er ein bisschen Leben in die Bude bringen. *If Fritz were only here, he'd liven up the place a bit.*

---

leben — *to live*

Leben und leben lassen ist sein Motto. *Live and let live is his motto.*

wie die Made im Speck leben — *to live off the fat of the land.*

Sie sind reich geworden und leben jetzt wie die Made im Speck. *They got rich and are now living off the fat of the land.*

---

die Leber — *liver*

frei von der Leber weg reden — *to speak freely, frankly.*

Frei von der Leber weg hab ich ihm meine Meinung gesagt. *I frankly told him my opinion.*

---

die Leberwurst — *liver sausage*

die beleidigte Leberwurst spielen — *to pout, to have a chip on one's shoulder.*

Meine Kritik war wohlwollend, aber jetzt spielt er die beleidigte Leberwurst. *My criticism was well meaning, but now he's pouting.*

---

leer — *empty*

ins Leere gehen — *to fall on deaf ears; come to nothing.*

Meine Vorschläge gingen ins Leere. *My suggestions fell on deaf ears.*

---

der Leib — *body*

   am eigenen Leib — *personally.*

Hunger und Vertreibung haben sie am eigenen Leib erfahren. *They've experienced hunger and expulsion personally.*

   bei lebendigem Leibe verbrennen — *to burn alive.*

Die Inquisition verbrannte angebliche Ketzer bei lebendigem Leib. *The inquisition burned alleged heretics alive.*

   mit Leib und Seele — *dedicated.*

Sie is mit Leib und Seele Lehrerin. *She is a dedicated teacher.*

   zu Leib gehen/rücken — *to tackle.*

Die Präsidentin wollte vielen schweren Sozialproblemen zu Leibe rücken. *The president wanted to tackle many severe social problems.*

   die Leib- und Magenspeise — *favorite dish.*

Der Professor behauptete, Berliner Buletten wären Zilles Leib- und Magenspeise gewesen. *The professor declared that rissole was Zille's favorite dish.*

   das Leibgericht — *favorite dish.*

Er behauptete auch, Wiener Schnitzel wäre Artur Schnitzlers Leibgericht gewesen. *He also claimed that breaded veal cutlet was Artur Schnitzler's favorite dish.*

leiblich — *physical*

Die leibliche und die Adoptivmutter stritten sich um das Kind. *The biological and the adoptive mother quarreled over the child.*

   das leibliche Wohl — *food; creature comforts.*

In der Pension unserer Tante wird bestens für das leibliche Wohl gesorgt. *In our aunt's rooming house creature comforts are well provided for.*

die Leiche — *corpse*

   eine Leiche im Keller haben — *to have a skeleton in the closet.*

Die Reporterin war sicher, dass der Senator mehr als eine Leiche im Keller hatte. *The reporter was sure the senator had more than one skeleton in the closet.*

   Nur über meine Leiche! *Over my dead body!*

über Leichen gehen — *to be utterly ruthless.*

Um ihre Karriere zu fördern, war die Reporterin bereit, über Leichen zu gehen. *To further her career, the reporter was prepared to be utterly ruthless.*

der Leichenschmaus — *funeral banquet, wake.*

Sein Geschäft geht schlecht, aber noch ist es nicht Zeit für einen Leichenschmaus. *His business is doing badly but it's too early to bury it.*

leid — *sorry*

es leid sein — *to be tired of.*

Sie war es leid, immer dieselben Vorwürfe zu hören. *She was tired of listening to the same reproaches.*

leidtun — *to be sorry.*

Bei der Prüfung tat es ihr leid, *Die Leiden des Jungen* Werther nicht gelesen zu haben. *At the exam she was sorry she hadn't read* The Sufferings of Young Werther.

leiden — *to suffer*

nicht leiden können — *to be unable to stand.*

Deinen Onkel kann ich nicht leiden. *I can't stand your uncle.*

gern/gut leiden können/mögen — *to like.*

Aber deine ganze Verwandschaft kann ich gut leiden. *But I like all your relatives.*

der Leim — *glue*

auf den Leim gehen — *to be taken in.*

Fast alle gingen dem Quecksalber auf den Leim. *Almost everyone was taken in by the quack.*

aus dem Leim gehen — *to come unglued.*

Der Stuhl ist wieder aus dem Leim gegangen. *The chair has come unglued again.*

aus dem Leim gehen — *to put on a lot of weight.*

Nach dem Militärdienst ging er aus dem Leim. *After military service he put on a lot of weight.*

die Leine — *rope, leash*

an der Leine halten — *to keep a tight rein on.*

Der Parteichef versuchte, die Mitglieder an der Leine zu halten. *The leader of the party tried to keep a tight rein on the members.*

Leine ziehen — *to clear off, beat it.*

Kurz darauf zog er Leine. *Shortly after that, he cleared off.*

leise — *quiet*

Bei leiser Musik und leisem Regen kochte leise sein Abendessen. *His dinner simmered gently as soft music played and gentle rain fell.*

leiser stellen — *to turn down.*

Trotzdem bat ihn sein Nachbar, die Musik leiser zu stellen. *Still, his neighbor asked him to turn down the music.*

der Leisten — *shoemaker's last*

alles über einen Leisten schlagen — *to lump together.*

Man kann alle ihre Anhänger nicht über einen Leisten schlagen. *You can't lump together all her devotees.*

bei seinem Leisten bleiben — *to stick to one's trade and not venture into other areas.*

Hans Sachs dachte an das Sprichwort: "Schuster bleib bei deinem Leisten!" *Hans Sachs thought of the proverb, "Cobbler stick to your last."*

Dichter, bleib bei deinem Geistesleisten und lass die Politik! *Poet, stay with your spiritual trade and leave politics alone.*

leisten — *to work; to accomplish*

einen Beitrag leisten — *to make a contribution.*

Unser Verein wollte einen Beitrag zur Völkerverständigung leisten. *Our club wanted to make a contribution to better understanding among peoples.*

einen Eid leisten — *to swear an oath.*

Siegfried vergaß, daß er einen Eid geleistet hatte. *Siegfried forgot that he had sworn an oath.*

sich leisten — *to treat/permit oneself.*

Herr Weintraub leistet sich jeden Luxus. *Mr. Weintraub permits himself every luxury.*

sich etwas leisten können — *to be able to afford.*
Das alles können wir uns nicht leisten. *We can't afford all that.*

die Leitung — *telephone line, connection*
eine lange Leitung haben — *to be slow on the uptake.*
Dein Bruder hat eine lange Leitung. *Your brother is slow on the uptake.*

letzt — *last*
    bis aufs Letzte; bis zum Letzten — *totally, to the utmost.*
    Die Einbrecher hatten die Wohnung bis aufs Letzte ausgeraubt. *The burglars cleaned out the apartment totally.*
    Sie verteidigte ihn bis zum Letzten. *She defended him to the utmost.*

    bis ins Letzte — *in every detail.*
    Wir wollen die Rechnung bis ins Letzte überprüfen. *We want to check the bill in every detail.*

    die Letzten Dinge — *death and eternity.*
    Die Mystikerin sprach von den Letzten Dingen und möglichen Reinkarnationen. *The mystic spoke of death, eternity, and possible reincarnations.*

    in der letzten Zeit — *recently.*
    In der letzten Zeit gibt es erneuertes Interesse dafür. *There has been renewed interest in it recently.*

    letzten Endes — *in the last analysis.*
    Letzten Endes musst du die Verantwortung dafür tragen. *In the last analysis you'll have to take responsibility for it.*

das Licht — *light*
Beim Unterrichten ist ihr manches Licht über das Fach aufgegangen. *When teaching, she gained many insights into the subject.*

    das Licht der Welt erblicken — *to be born.*
    Die jetzige Schlossherrin erblickte das Licht der Welt in einem Berliner Hinterhof. *The present owner of the castle was born in a Berlin tenement.*

    hinters Licht führen — *to fool.*
    Es gelang dem Verbrecher, die Polizei hinters Licht zu führen. *The criminal succeeded in fooling the police.*

ein Licht aufstecken — *to put wise.*
Ich versuchte, ihm ein Licht aufzustecken. *I tried to put him wise.*

kein großes Licht sein — *not to be very bright.*
Das Kind ist kein großes Licht, aber ich wollte es der Mutter nicht sagen.
The child isn't very bright, but I didn't want to say that to his mother.

lichten — *to become lighter.*
Das Geheimnis um die gestohlenen Kunstwerke hat sich gelichtet. *The mystery concerning the stolen works of art has been cleared up.*

---

die Liebe — *love*
aus Liebe — *for love.*
Das erste Mal hat sie aus Liebe geheiratet. *The first time, she married for love.*

bei aller Liebe — *despite all sympathy.*
Bei aller Liebe kann ich ihm nicht mehr helfen. *However much I sympathize, I can't help him anymore.*

Die Liebe geht durch den Magen. *The way to a man's heart is through his stomach.*

---

das Lied — *song*
das gleiche Lied singen — *to repeat the same story; to complain constantly*
Er wird nie müde, das gleiche Lied zu singen. *He never tires of telling the same story.*

ein Lied/Liedchen singen können — *to be able to tell a thing or two about.*
Von solchen Problemen könnte auch ich ein Lied singen. *I, too, could tell you a thing or two about such problems.*

---

liefern — *to deliver*
einen Beweis liefern — *to prove.*
Können Sie den Beweis dafür liefern? *Can you prove that?*

geliefert sein — *to be sunk; to have had it.*
Wenn es diesmal seine Schulden nicht zahlen kann, dann ist sein Geschäft ̈ ̇ ̃rt. *If he can't pay his debts this time, his business has had it.*

sich Kämpfe liefern — *to engage in armed conflict.*
Sie liefern sich noch erbitterte Kämpfe. *They're still waging fierce battles.*

liegen — *to lie, be situated; to be*
Das alles liegt noch vor uns. *All that is still before us.*

an etwas /jemandem liegen — *to be due to; to be the responsibility of.*
Dass man die Sänger oft kaum hören konnte, liegt vielleicht an der
Straußschen Musik. *The fact that we often could barely hear the
singers, was perhaps due to Strauss's music.*
Es liegt an Ihnen, ob wir hingehen oder nicht. *It's up to you whether we
go or not.*

liegen — *to appeal.*
"Treu sein, das liegt mir nicht," sang der Tenor. *"Staying faithful doesn't
appeal to me," sang the tenor.*

liegen bleiben — *to stay down; remain unsold, be a non-starter*
Fallen ist menschlich. Liegen bleiben ist teuflisch. *To fall is human. To
stay down is devlish.*
Wir hofften auf Publikumsrenner, aber die meisten Waren sind uns liegen
geblieben. *We hoped for runaway sales, but most of these goods are still
on our hands.*

Lieschen Müller — *the average person*
Das Werk ist zugleich hohe Kunst und für Lieschen Müller zugänglich.
The work is great art and also accessible to the average person.

die Linie — *line*
auf der ganzen Linie — *all along the line; in every respect.*
Sie haben auf der ganzen Linie Fortschritte gemacht. *You've made
progress in every respect.*

in erster/zweiter Linie — *of primary/secondary importance; primarily/
secondarily.*
"In erster Linie interessiert uns seine Gesundheit: sein Geld spielt nur in
zweiter Linie eine Rolle," erklärten die Verwandten. *"We're primarily
interested in his health; his money is only of secondary importance,"
declared the relatives.*

links — *on the left*

Das Geschäft befindet sich in der nächsten Straße, links. *The store is on the next street, on the left.*

etwas links liegenlassen — *to ignore.*

Die Demonstranten schrieen, dass die Gesellschaft sie links liegengelassen hätte. *The demonstrators screamed that society had ignored them.*

mit links — *with the left hand; with no difficulty.*

Das ist nicht schwer; ich könnte es mit links machen. *That isn't hard; I could do it easily.*

die Lippe — *lip*

an den Lippen hängen — *to hang on every word.*

Entzückt hingen ihre Anhänger an den Lippen der Prophetin. *Enraptured, her disciples listened to every word the prophetess uttered.*

nicht über die Lippen bringen können — *to be unable to bring oneself to say.*

Sie brachte es nicht über die Lippen, dass sie ihn nicht mehr liebte. *She couldn't bring herself to say that she didn't love him anymore.*

über die Lippen kommen — *to pass one's lips.*

Kein Wort davon soll mir über die Lippen kommen. *Not a word about it will pass my lips.*

das Lob — *praise*

Ein Lob dem Küchenchef. *My/our compliments to the chef.*

über alles Lob erhaben — *beyond all praise.*

Die *Lohengrin* Aufführung war über alles Lob erhaben. *The performance of* Lohengrin *was beyond all praise.*

loben — *to praise*

Das lob ich mir! *That's really to my liking!*

Als Goethe dort studierte, sagte er: "Mein Leipzig lob ich mir." *When Goethe studied there he said, "Leipzig is a place really to my liking."*

ein Loblied anstimmen — *to sing the praises of; to praise extravagantly.*

Alle Gäste sangen ein Loblied auf ihre Kochkunst. *All the guests sang the praises of her cooking.*

das Loch — *hole*

auf dem letzten Loch pfeifen — *to be on one's last legs.*
Geschäftlich pfeifen wir auf dem letzten Loch. *Our business is on its last legs.*

ein Loch in den Bauch fragen — *to ply/pester with questions.*
Ihre Kinder fragen sie ein Loch in den Bauch, aber das stört sie nicht. *Her children ply her with questions, but that doesn't bother her.*

ein Loch in den Bauch reden — *to talk one's head off.*
Wir vermeiden ihn, weil er uns immer ein Loch in den Bauch redet. *We avoid him because he always talks his head off at us.*

ein Loch in den Tag schlafen — *to sleep the day away.*
Statt zu arbeiten, schläft er wieder ein Loch in den Tag. *Instead of working, he's sleeping the day away again.*

Löcher in die Luft gucken — *to gaze at space.*
Ich weiß nicht, ob er ein Genie, ein Idiot oder beides ist, aber er guckt oft Löcher in die Luft. *I don't know whether he's a genius, an idiot, or both, but he often gazes into space.*

der Lohn — *wages; reward*

in Lohn und Brot sein — *to be gainfully employed.*
In den neuen Fabriken stehen jetzt wieder Tausende in Lohn und Brot. *Thousands are now again gainfully employed in the new factories.*

sich lohnen — *to be worthwhile*
Der Film lohnt sich sehr. *The movie is well worth seeing.*

das Los — *lot*

das große Los ziehen — *to win big, hit the jackpot,*
Millionen sind mit ihrem Los unzufrieden und hoffen das große Los im Lotto zu ziehen. *Millions are dissatisfied with their lot and hope to win big in the lottery.*

das Lot — *perpendicular, plumb line*

im Lot sein — *to be in order.*
In ihrem Leben ist jetzt alles wieder im Lot. *Everything is now in order in their lives.*

ins Lot bringen — *to put in order, to straighten out.*
Dem Eheberater gelang es, die Familie ins Lot zu bringen. *The marriage counselor succeeded in straightening out the family.*

die Luft — *air*
Wenn die Luft rein ist, komm zu uns. *When the coast is clear, come to us.*

die Luft anhalten — *to hold one's breath.*
Halt doch die Luft an! *Keep quiet!*

in die Luft sprengen — *to blow up.*
Der Terrorist versuchte, die Botschaft in die Luft zu sprengen. *The terrorist tried to blow up the embassy.*

wie Luft behandeln — *to snub; to ignore.*
Warum hast du uns wie Luft behandelt? *Why did you snub us?*

die Lüge — *lie*
Lügen haben kurze Beine. *Lies come back to haunt the liar.*

Lügen strafen — *to give the lie to; to prove wrong.*
Durch ihr Benehmen hat sie das üble Gerede Lügen gestraft. *Through her behavior she gave the lie to the vicious gossip.*

lügen — *to lie*
wie gedruckt lügen — *to lie like mad; to be an out-and-out liar.*
Sie behauptete, der Senator lüge wie gedruckt. *She declared the senator was an out-and-out liar.*

(sich nicht) lumpen lassen — *(not) to be outdone*
Als Gastgeber ließen sich die Indianer des Nordwestens nicht lumpen. *As hosts, the Northwest Indians would not allow themselves to be outdone.*

die Lupe — *magnifying glass*
mit der Lupe suchen müssen — *to be rare.*
Restaurants, die noch Innereiengerichte bieten, muss man mit der Lupe suchen. *Restaurants that still serve giblets are rare.*

unter die Lupe nehmen — *to take a close look at.*
Sherlock Holmes beschloss, das Treiben des Professors unter die Lupe zu nehmen. *Sherlock Holmes decided to take a close look at the professor's doings.*

die Lust — *joy*
Lust haben — *to feel like.*
Ich hätte jetzt keine große Lust dazu. *I don't particularly feel like it now.*

lustig — *merry*
sich lustig machen — *to make fun of.*
Alle machten sich über sein Kostüm lustig. *They all made fun of his costume.*

machen — *to make*
Das macht nichts. *That doesn't matter.*

Mach, dass du fortkommst. *See that you get started.*

Was macht die Arbeit? *How are things at work?*

mächtig — *mighty*
einen mächtigen Hunger haben — *to be very hungry.*
Die Arbeiter hatten alle einen mächtigen Hunger auf unsere Currywürste. *The workers were all very hungry for our curry sausages.*

einer Sprache mächtig sein — *to have a command of a language.*
Elfriede ist vieler Fremdsprachen mächtig. *Elfriede has a command of many foreign languages.*

seiner selbst nicht mächtig sein — *to lose control.*
Als er von dem Betrug erfuhr, war er seiner selbst nicht mächtig. *When he learned of the betrayal, he lost control of himself.*

das Machtwort — *word of command*
    ein Machtwort sprechen — *to lay down the law; to put one's foot down.*
    Warum sprechen die Eltern kein Machtwort? *Why don't the parents put their foot down?*

das Mädchen — *girl*
    Mädchen für alles — *maid of all work; girl (man) Friday.*
    Wir haben ein neues Mädchen für alles im Büro. *We have a new girl (man) Friday in the office.*

madig — *maggot-ridden*
    etwas madig machen — *to ruin.*
    Du hast uns die Party madig gemacht. *You ruined the party for us.*

der Magen — *stomach*
    im Magen haben — *to detest.*
    Sprich nicht von meinem Anwalt, den hab ich im Magen. *Don't talk about my lawyer; I detest him.*

die Makulatur — *spoiled / waste paper*
    Makulatur reden — *to talk nonsense.*
    Die Opposition behauptete, der Präsident rede nur Makulatur. *The opposition alleged that the president was talking nonsense.*

das Mal — *time*
    ein für alle Mal — *once and for all.*
    Ein für alle Mal sag ich dir, ich will nichts damit zu tun haben. *I'm telling you once and for all, I don't want anything to do with it.*

    mit einem Mal — *all of a sudden.*
    Mit einem Mal war sie nicht mehr da. *All of a sudden she wasn't there any more.*

    zum ersten Mal — *for the first time.*
    Heute tritt sie zum ersten Mal vor die Öffentlichkeit. *She's appearing before the public for the first time today.*

der Mann — *man*

an den Mann bringen — *to know how to market.*
Haydn wusste Bescheid, seine Musik an den Mann zu bringen. *Haydn
knew how to market his music.*

auf den Mann dressiert — *trained to attack people.*
Seine Dobermänner sind auf den Mann dressiert. *His dobermans are
trained to attack people.*

Ein Mann, ein Wort. *An honest man is as good as his word.*

mit Mann und Maus untergehen — *to go down with all on board.*
Das Schiff ist mit Mann und Maus untergegangen. *The ship went down
with all on board.*

seinen Mann stehen — *to demonstrate one's ability; to show one's worth.*
Auch auf diesem technischen Gebiet können Frauen ihren Mann stehen.
In this technical area too, women can demonstrate their ability.

---

die Manschette — *cuff*

Manschetten haben — *to be afraid.*
Alle glaubten, Zorro hätte vor dem Fechten Manschetten. *Everyone
thought Zorro was afraid of fencing.*

---

das Mark — *marrow*

bis ins Mark — *to the quick, core.*
Die erschütternde Nachricht traf uns bis ins Mark. *The shattering news cut
us to the quick.*

das Mark aus den Knochen saugen — *to bleed white.*
Uriah gefiel es, seinen Mandanten das Mark auszusaugen. *Uriah enjoyed
bleeding his clients white.*

---

das Maß — *measure*

Das Maß ist voll. *Enough is enough.*

ein gerüttelt (und geschüttelt) Maß — *a good measure.*
Wie viele ehemalige Romantiker hat er ein gerüttelt Maß von Zynismus in
sich. *Like many former romantics, he has a good measure of cynicism in him.*

in/mit Maßen — *in moderation, moderately.*
Er macht jetzt den Versuch, in Maßen zu leben. *He's making an effort to live moderately now.*

mit zweierlei Maß messen — *to apply different sets of standards.*
Sie warfen dem Richter vor, mit zweierlei Maß zu messen. *They accused the judge of applying two sets of standards.*

über die (alle) Maßen — *extremely.*
Wir waren über die Maßen glücklich, von ihr einen Brief zu bekommen. *We were extremely happy to get a letter from her.*

weder Maß noch Ziel kennen — *to be immoderate, undisciplined.*
Er isst und trinkt zu viel, weil er weder Maß noch Ziel kennt. *He eats and drinks too much because he's undisciplined.*

maßhalten — *to exercise moderation.*
Er hat nie maßhalten gelernt. *He never learned to exercise moderation.*

das Maul — *mouth (animals)*
das Maul aufreißen — *to shoot one's mouth off.*
Er hat wieder das Maul weit aufgerissen. *He shot his mouth off again.*

das Maul halten — *to shut one's trap.*
Halt's Maul! *Shut your trap!*

ein schiefes Maul ziehen — *to pull a long face.*
Zieh mir kein schiefes Maul! *Don't pull a long face on me!*

sich das Maul zerreißen — *to gossip viciously.*
Hinter ihrem Rücken haben sie sich das Maul über sie zerrissen. *Behind her back they gossiped viciously about her.*

die Maulsperre kriegen — *to be flabbergasted, speechless.*
Sag's ihr nicht gleich, sonst kriegt sie die Maulsperre. *Don't tell her right away or she'll be flabbergasted.*

die Maus — *mouse*
weiße Mäuse sehen — *to see pink elephants.*
Er betrank sich und sah weiße Mäuse. *He got drunk and saw pink elephants.*

mein — *my*

Meine Damen und Herren! *Ladies and gentlemen!*

mein und dein verwechseln — *to steal.*

Einige Deutsche behaupten, sie verwechselten manchmal "mir" und "mich" aber niemals "mein" und "dein." *Some Germans allege they sometimes confused "me" and "mine," but never "mine" and "thine" (yours).*

---

die Meise — *titmouse*

eine Meise unterm Pony haben — *to have bats in the belfry.*

Manchmal glaub ich, du hast eine Meise unterm Pony. *Sometimes I think you've got bats in your belfry.*

---

der Meister — *master*

Es ist noch kein Meister vom Himmel gefallen. *Practice makes perfect.*

In der Beschränkung zeigt sich erst der Meister. *True champions respond successfully to challenges/limitations.*

---

die Menge — *quantity*

in rauhen Mengen — *in huge amounts.*

Vor Jahren aß er alles — und in rauhen Mengen. *Years ago he ate everything, and in huge amounts.*

jede Menge — *loads of.*

Das Kind hat schon jede Menge Spielzeug. *The child already has loads of toys.*

---

merken — *to notice*

die Absicht merken und verstimmt werden — *to see what someone is getting at and be displeased.*

In allen seinen Filmen merkt man die propagandistische Absicht und wird verstimmt. *In all his movies you can tell he's grinding a propaganda axe, and it's annoying.*

---

das Messer — *knife*

ans Messer liefern — *to betray, hand over.*

Der Spitzel hat sie alle ans Messer geliefert. *The spy betrayed them all.*

auf des Messers Schneide stehen — *to be touch and go.*
Ob sie vom Senatsausschuss bestätigt wird, steht auf des Messers
Schneide. *It's touch and go whether the senate committee will confirm
her.*

bis aufs Messer — *to the bitter end; with no holds barred.*
Die Rivalen kämpften bis aufs Messer. *The rivals fought to the bitter end.*

ins offene Messer laufen — *to play right into someone's hands.*
Mit seinen unbedachten Äußerungen lief er der Opposition ins Messer.
*With his ill-considered statements he played right into the opposition's
hands.*

die Miene — *face; facial expression*
gute Miene zum bösen Spiel machen — *to put a good face on it.*
Wir sind mit dem Abkommen sehr unzufrieden, aber wir versuchen, gute
Miene zum bösen Spiel zu machen. *We're very dissatisfied with the
agreement, but we're trying to put a good face on it.*

keine Miene verziehen — *not to turn a hair.*
Der Reporter beobachtete die Hinrichtung und verzog keine Miene. *The
reporter observed the execution and didn't turn a hair.*

Miene machen — *to show signs of starting.*
Mehrmals machte er Miene, fortzugehen. *Several times he showed signs
of starting to leave.*

die Miete — *rent*
die halbe Miete sein — *to be halfway to success; half the battle.*
Du hast diese Prüfung gut bestanden; das ist schon die halbe Miete.
You've done well on this exam; that's half the way there (to your goal).

die Mine — *explosive mine*
alle Minen springen lassen — *to go all out.*
Wir lassen alle Minen springen, um den Auftrag zu bekommen. *We're
going all out to get the contract.*

eine Mine legen — *to plot, cook up a surprise.*
Was hast du wieder für eine kleine Mine gelegt? *What little surprise have
you cooked up now?*

mir — *to me*

mir nichts, dir nichts — *just like that.*

Mir nichts, dir nichts ist sie ausgezogen. *She moved out just like that.*

wie du mir, so ich dir — *to repay in kind.*

Du willst dich für einen Heiligen ausgeben, trotzdem sagst du: "Wie du
mir, so ich dir." *You want to pass yourself off as a saint, yet you say,
"as you do unto me, I do unto you."*

---

mithalten — *to keep up with; to be up to*

Der Tristan versuchte mit der Isolde mitzuhalten, aber seine Stimme
versagte ihm. *The Tristan tried to keep up with the Isolde, but his voice
gave out.*

Ich würde gerne das Matterhorn ersteigen, aber meine Beine halten nicht
mehr mit. *I'd love to climb the Matterhorn, but my legs aren't up to it
anymore.*

---

mitmachen — *to take part in*

Er wollte den Krieg nicht mehr mitmachen und wurde fahnenflüchtig. *He
didn't want to take part in the war anymore and deserted.*

---

der Mittag — *noon*

Mittag machen — *to take a break for lunch.*

Genug gearbeitet! Jetzt machen wir Mittag. *That's enough work. We'll
take a break for lunch now.*

zu Mittag essen — *to eat lunch.*

Nach dem Sektfrühstück hatten wir keine Lust zu Mittag zu essen. *After
the champagne breakfast we didn't feel like eating lunch.*

---

mogeln — *to cheat*

die Mogelpackung — *deceptive packaging; sham*

Die Senatorin hielt die Versprechungen der Regierung, keine Steuern zu
erhöhen, für Mogelpackung. *The senator thought the government's
promises not to raise taxes were a sham.*

---

das Moment — *factor*
das auslösende Moment sein — *to trigger.*
Die Scheidung war das auslösende Moment seines Wahnsinns. *The divorce triggered his madness.*

der Moment — *moment*
einen lichten Moment (lichte Momente) — *lucid interval(s).*
Dann und wann hat er einen lichten Moment. *Now and then he has a lucid interval.*

jeden Moment — *(at) any moment.*
Jeden Moment kann sie zurückkommen. *She can come back any moment.*

die Morgenluft — *morning air*
Morgenluft wittern — *to see one's chance.*
Die Opposition witterte Morgenluft. *The opposition saw its chance.*

die Morgenstunde — *early morning hour(s)*
Morgenstund hat Gold im Mund. Wer verschläft sich geht zugrund. *The morning hours are wonderful for getting things done. Oversleepers come to grief.*

das Moos — *moss*
Moos ansetzen — *to get old.*
Ohne Selbstironie, stellte er fest, dass seine Schulfreunde Moos angesetzt hatten. *Without irony, he determined that his school friends had gotten old.*

die Mücke — *gnat*
aus einer Mücke einen Elefanten machen — *to make a mountain out of a molehill.*
Wie gewöhnlich, machst du aus einer Mücke einen Elefanten. *As usual, you're making a mountain out of a molehill.*

die Mücke machen — *to clear out, scram.*
Mach schnell die Mücke, dass der Chef dich nicht erwischt. *Clear out fast so the boss doesn't catch you.*

der Muckefuck — *watery coffee; coffee substitute*

Ohne zu mucken, trank der Patient den Muckefuck. *Without grumbling, the patient drank his watery coffee.*

die Mucken — *whims*

seine Mucken haben — *to have one's moods, be temperamental; not to run right (machines).*

Mein Bruder hat seine Mucken. *My brother has his moods.*

Besonders im Winter hat der Wagen seine Mucken. *The car is a bit temperamental, especially in the winter.*

der Mund — *mouth*

aus dem Mund riechen — *to have bad breath.*

Gib auch mir etwas Knoblauch, damit wir beide aus dem Mund riechen. *Give me some garlic too, so that we can both have bad breath.*

den Mund voll nehmen — *to talk big.*

Er taugt wenig, aber er nimmt gern den Mund voll. *He's not good for much, but he likes to talk big.*

in aller Munde sein — *to be widely talked about.*

Nach ihrem Olympiasieg war sie in aller Munde. *After her Olympic victory, she was talked about everywhere.*

nach dem Mund reden — *to be a yes person; to tell someone what they want to hear.*

Alle redeten dem verrückten Diktator nach dem Munde. *They all told the crazy dictator what he wanted to hear.*

nicht auf den Mund gefallen sein — *not to be at a loss for words*

Normalerweise bist du nicht auf den Mund gefallen. *Usually you're not at a loss for words.*

wie aus einem Munde — *as if with one voice.*

Die Abgeordneten riefen wie aus einem Munde: "Verrat!" *The congresspersons cried as if with one voice, "Treason!"*

mundtot machen — *to silence.*

Die Dissidenten wurden mundtot gemacht. *The dissidents were silenced.*

das Mündel — *ward (person under a guardian's care)*
mündelsicher — *gilt-edged, blue chip.*
Selbst ihre mündelsicher geglaubten Wertpapiere sind jetzt wertlos. *Even their supposedly gilt-edged securities are now worthless.*

die Münze — *coin*
für bare Münze nehmen — *to take at face value.*
Seine Schwärmereien sind nicht für bare Münze zu nehmen. *His effusions aren't to be taken at face value.*

in/mit gleicher Münze heimzahlen — *to pay back in kind.*
Diese Frechheit werde ich dir in gleicher Münze heimzahlen. *I'll pay you back in kind (in your own coin) for that impudence.*

klingende Münze — *hard cash.*
Hier musst du mit klingender Münze bezahlen, mein Freund. *You've got to pay with hard cash here, my friend.*

die Muse — *muse*
die leichte Muse — *light entertainment; operettas; musical comedies.*
In unserem Opernhaus wird die leichte Muse nicht venachlässigt. *In our opera house operettas are not neglected.*

von der Muse geküsst werden — *to be inspired.*
Seit langem ist er nicht von der Muse geküsst worden. *He hasn't been inspired for some time.*

musisch veranlagt — *to be artistic.*
Sie ist ein musisch veranlagter Mensch. *She's a very artistic person.*

der Nabel — *navel*
der Nabel der Welt — *the hub of the universe.*
Viele Orte halten sich noch für den Nabel der Welt. *Many places still think they're the hub of the universe.*

die Nabelschau — *navel contemplation; ego trip.*

Der Film ist mehr als eine selbstgefällige Nabelschau. *The movie is more than a self-satisfied ego trip.*

nach — *after*

nach und nach — *gradually, little by little.*

Nach und nach wurde uns alles klar. *Gradually everything became clear to us.*

nach wie vor — *still, as always.*

Nach wie vor ist er ein Publikumsliebling. *He's still popular with the public.*

nach — *according to, by.*

Ich kenne ihn nur dem Namen nach. *I know him only by name.*

nach Adam Riese — *correctly calculated; according to my arithmetic.*

Nach Adam Riese macht das 50 nicht 60 Euro. *According to my arithmetic, that makes 50, not 60 euros.*

im Nachhinein — *after the event; with hindsight.*

Im Nachhinein ist man natürlich immer klüger. *Of course one is always wiser after the event.*

nachsehen — *to go (look and) see*

das Nachsehen bleiben — *to be duped/disadvantaged.*

Der Direktor verschwand mit dem Geld und den Aktionären blieb das Nachsehen. *The director disappeared with the money, and the shareholders were left holding the bag.*

nächst — *next*

Jeder ist sich selbst der Nächste. *Everyone looks out for number one. (Charity begins at home.)*

die Nächstenliebe — *love of one's fellow (hu)man; philanthropy.*

Im Alter entdeckte der Milliardär die Nächstenliebe. *In old age the billionaire discovered philanthropy.*

nachstehen — *to lag behind*

in nichts nachstehen — *to be in no way inferior.*

Dieses Modell steht den anderen in nichts nach. *This model is in no way inferior to the others.*

die Nacht — *night*
bei Nacht und Nebel — *under cover of darkness.*
Bei Nacht und Nebel schlich er in das Schloss. *Under cover of darkness he sneaked into the castle.*

die Nacht um die Ohren schlagen — *to stay up all night.*
Er hat sich wieder die Nacht um die Ohren geschlagen. *He stayed up all night again.*

das Nachthemd — *nightshirt*
ein aufgeblasenes Nachthemd sein — *to be a pretentious fool/a stuffed shirt.*
Onkel Otto ist doch alles andere als ein aufgeblasenes Nachthemd. *Onkel Otto is really anything but a pretentious fool.*

die Nachtigall — *nightingale*
Nachtigall, ich hör dir trapsen! *I know what you're after!*

der Nacken — *neck*
jemandem im Nacken sitzen — *to be breathing down one's neck; to threaten.*
Ich half ihm, sein Geschäft auf die Beine zu bringen, und jetzt sitzt mir seine Konkurrenz im Nacken. *I helped him to start up his business, and now competition from him is threatening me.*

den Nacken steifhalten — *to keep one's chin up.*
Im Moment geht das Geschäft schlecht, aber ich halte noch den Nacken steif. *At the moment business is bad, but I'm still keeping my chin up.*

den Nacken steifen/stärken — *to give moral support; to comfort*
Nach dem Tod seiner Frau versuchten wir, ihm den Nacken zu stärken. *After his wife's death, we tried to comfort him.*

die Nadel — *needle*
Man konnte eine Nadel fallen hören. *One could hear a pin drop.*

die/eine Nadel im Heuschober/Heuhaufen suchen — *to look for a needle in a haystack.*
Du suchst ein geräumiges, trotzdem billiges Hotelzimmer in Wien? Das ist wie eine Nadel im Heuschober suchen. *You're looking for a spacious*

yet inexpensive hotel room in Vienna? That's like looking for a needle in a haystack.

mit der heißen Nadel genäht — *done hurriedly/carelessly.*
In der letzten Zeit ist nicht nur ihre Näharbeit mit der heißen Nadel genäht. *Recently, it's not just her sewing that's been done carelessly.*

---

der Nagel — *nail*
an den Nagel hängen — *to give up.*
Wegen der Knieverletzung musste er den Sport an den Nagel hängen. *Because of a knee injury, he had to give up sports.*

auf den Nägeln brennen — *to be urgent.*
Das Problem brennt uns allen auf den Nägeln. *We all consider the problem urgent.*

auf den Nägeln brennend liegen — *to be of great concern/urgency.*
Dieses Thema liegt uns brennend auf den Nägeln. *This subject is of great concern to us.*

den Nagel auf den Kopf treffen — *to hit the nail on the head.*
Diesmal hast du den Nagel auf den Kopf getroffen. *This time you've hit the nail on the head.*

Nägel mit Köpfen machen — *to make a good job of.*
Wir wollen Nägel mit Köpfen machen. *We want to make a good job of it.*

sich etwas unter den Nagel reißen — *to make off with.*
Lass die Sachen nicht so herumliegen, sonst reißt er sie sich unter den Nagel. *Don't let things lie around like that, or he'll make off with them.*

---

nagen — *to gnaw*
am Hungertuch nagen — *to be starving; be destitute.*
"Man hält mich für reich, aber ich nage am Hungertuch!" klagte der Geizhals. *"People think I'm rich, but I'm destitute!" complained the miser.*

---

nah — *near*
aus nah und fern — *from far and wide.*
Unsere Gäste kommen aus nah und fern. *Our guests come from far and wide.*

nahe treten — *to give offense.*

Ohne Ihnen nahe treten zu wollen, muss ich Ihnen doch die Wahrheit sagen. *Without wishing to give offense, I must nevertheless tell you the truth.*

die Nahrung — *food*
Nahrung geben — *to fan the flames.*

Die Presseberichte gaben dem Skandal neue Nahrung. *The reports in the press fanned the flames of the scandal.*

das Nähkästchen — *sewing kit*
aus dem Nähkästchen plaudern — *to spill the beans.*

Der Senator betrank sich und plauderte aus dem Nähkästchen. *The senator got drunk and spilled the beans.*

der Name — *name*
Name ist Schall und Rauch. *What's in a name?*

der Narr, die Närrin — *fool*
einen Narren gefressen haben — *to be smitten with.*

Meine Tochter hat an dem Filmstar einen Narren gefressen. *My daughter is smitten with the movie star.*

zum Narren halten — *to fool.*

Mit der erfundenen Geschichte hat der Reporter alle zum Narren gehalten. *With that made-up story the reporter fooled everybody.*

die Nase — *nose*
an der Nase herumführen — *to lead by the nose.*

Er hat uns lange genug an der Nase herumgeführt. *He's led us by the nose long enough.*

die Nase in die Bücher stecken — *to buckle down and study.*

Wann steckst du endlich die Nase in die Bücher? *When will you finally buckle down and study?*

die Nase rümpfen — *to turn up one's nose.*

Sie hat eigentlich kein Recht, die Nase über diesen armen Menschen zu rümpfen. *She really has no right to turn up her nose at this unfortunate individual.*

die Nase voll haben — *to be fed up with.*

Von Krieg und Zerstörung hatten sie die Nase voll. *They were fed up with war and destruction.*

die Nase vorn haben — *to be leading.*

Auf dem internationalem Markt haben wir die Nase vorn. *We're leading on the international market.*

die Nase zu tief ins Glas stecken — *to get roaring drunk.*

Er hat die Nase zu tief ins Glas gesteckt. *He got roaring drunk.*

auf der Nase herumtanzen — *to walk all over.*

Er lässt sich von allen auf der Nase herumtanzen. *He lets everybody walk all over him.*

sich die Nase begießen — *to have a few drinks.*

Nach der Arbeit begießt er sich gern die Nase. *After work he likes to have a few drinks.*

sich eine goldene Nase verdienen — *to make a lot of money.*

Mit seinem Elixir hat sich der Scharlatan eine goldene Nase verdient. *With his elixir the charlatan made a lot of money.*

---

nehmen — *to take*

Woher nehmen und nicht stehlen? *Just where am I supposed to get a hold of that?*

nicht für voll nehmen — *not to take seriously.*

Nur weil ich jung und schön bin, nimmt man mich nicht für voll. *Just because I'm young and beautiful, they don't take me seriously.*

---

die Neige — *dregs; lees*

bis zur Neige auskosten — *to enjoy to the fullest.*

Sie hat ihren Tennistriumph bis zur Neige ausgekostet. *She enjoyed her tennis triumph to the fullest.*

bis zur Neige leeren — *to drink to the dregs.*

Wir haben das Glas voll Muscadet Wein zur Neige geleert. *We drank our glass of Muscadet to the dregs.*

zur Neige gehen — *to run low.*

Der Honig geht zur Neige. *The honey is running low.*

zur Neige gehen — *to draw to a close.*
Der Tag ging zur Neige und er war noch nicht gekommen. *The day was drawing to a close, and he hadn't come yet.*

neppen — *to rook; to rip off*
sich neppen lassen — *to get ripped off.*
Wir wollen uns von niemand neppen lassen. *We don't want to get ripped off by anyone.*

das Nepplokal — *clip joint.*
Leider sind wir in einem Nepplokal gelandet. *Unfortunately, we wound up in a clip joint.*

der Nerv — *nerve*
an den Nerv der Sache rühren — *to get to the heart of the matter.*
Sie hat an den Nerv der Sache gerührt. *She got to the heart of the matter.*

einen sonnigen Nerv haben — *to be naive and foolish.*
Wenn du weiterhin daran glauben willst, hast du einen ganz sonnigen Nerv. *If you choose to continue to believe that, then you're quite naive and foolish.*

den letzten Nerv rauben — *to drive up the wall.*
Mit seiner Trunksucht raubt er mir den letzten Nerv. *He's driving me up the wall with his drinking.*

nerven — *to get on one's nerves.*
Sein Benehmen nervt mich. *His behavior gets on my nerves.*

die Nessel — *nettle*
sich in die Nesseln setzen — *to get into hot water.*
Tu's nicht; du wirst dich nur in die Nesseln setzen. *Don't do it; you'll just get into hot water.*

neu — *new*
aufs Neue — *(once) again.*
Leider muss ich Sie aufs Neue darauf aufmerksam machen. *Unfortunately, I must once again bring it to your attention.*

von Neuem — *(all over) again.*
Wir sollten eigentlich alles von Neuem beginnen. *We really ought to make a fresh start.*

neun(e) — *nine*
Ach, du grüne Neune! — *Oh, for heaven's sake!/Well I'll be darned!*
Ach, du grüne Neune, der Hund ist wieder fortgelaufen! *Oh, for heaven's sake, the dog's run off again!*

Verrückt und fünf ist neune! — *The world is full of madness!/The crazies are out there!*
Opa will snowboarden gehen—verrückt und fünf ist neune! *Gramps wants to go snowboarding—he's gone off the deep end!*

das Nichts — *nothingness*
aus dem Nichts — *from nothing.*
Das einst blühende Unternehmen hat er aus dem Nichts aufgebaut. *He built up his once flourishing enterprise from nothing.*

vor dem Nichts stehen — *to be facing ruin.*
Jetzt steht er vor dem Nichts. *Now he is facing ruin.*

nichts — *nothing*
für nichts und wieder nichts — *for nothing at all; in vain.*
Für nichts und wieder nichts hat er gearbeitet. *He's worked in vain.*

die Niere — *kidney*
an die Nieren gehen — *to stir deeply.*
Die Fernsehbilder von den Kriegsopfern gingen uns an die Nieren. *The TV pictures of the war victims stirred us deeply.*

die Niete — *rivet*
alles, was nicht niet- und nagelfest ist — *everything that isn't nailed or screwed down.*
Die abziehenden Soldaten nahmen alles mit, was nicht niet- und nagelfest war. *The departing soldiers took with them everything that wasn't nailed or screwed down.*

nicht alle Nieten an der Hose haben — *not to have all one's marbles.*

Sein Benehmen ist mir unerklärlich; der hat wohl nicht alle Nieten an der Hose. *I can't understand his behavior; he probably hasn't got all his marbles.*

das Niveau — *level*

an Niveau einbüßen — *to decline in quality.*

Das Restaurant hat an Niveau eingebüßt, doch sind die Preise gestiegen. *The restaurant has declined in quality but the prices have gone up.*

Niveau haben — *to be of quality.*

Die Sendung über Händel in Halle und Hannover hatte hohes Niveau. *The program about Händel in Halle and Hanover was of high quality.*

das Nickerchen — *nap*

ein Nickerchen halten/machen — *to take a nap.*

Jeden Nachmittag macht er sein Nickerchen. *Every afternoon he takes his nap.*

auf Nimmerwiedersehen verschwinden — *to disappear forever*

Der Betrüger nahm das Geld und verschwand auf Nimmerwiedersehen. *The con-man took the money and disappeared forever.*

die Not — *need; emergency*

Not bricht Eisen. *Necessity is the mother of invention.*

Spare in der Zeit, dann hast du in der Not. *Save beforehand; then you'll be provided for when you need it.*

nottun — *to need, be needed.*

In diesem Betrieb tut eine Reform not. *This company needs reform.*

der Notnagel — *last resort, fill in, stopgap*

Leider halten die meisten Jugendlichen ein Job in der Landwirtschaft für eine Notnagel für Schlusslichter. *Unfortunately, most young people think a job on the farm is a last resort for those at the bottom of the class.*

die Null — *zero*

  in Null Komma nichts — *in no time at all.*

  In Null Komma nichts kam sie zurück. *In no time at all she returned.*

  Null Komma nichts erreichen — *to get nowhere at all.*

  Bei den Beamten hat er Null Komma nichts erreicht. *He got nowhere at all with the officials.*

  nullachtfünfzehn — *run-of-the-mill, humdrum.*

  Meiner Ansicht nach war die Vorstellung alles andere als nullachtfünfzehn. *In my opinion the performance was anything but humdrum.*

  die Null-Bock-Generation — *turned-off generation.*

  Sie sagten, sie gehörten der Null-Bock-Generation an. *They said they belonged to the dropout generation.*

  die Nulldiät — *starvation diet.*

  Er ging auf Nulldiät. *He went on a starvation diet.*

  zum Nulltarif — *free of charge.*

  Er hält sich berechtigt, zum Nulltarif zu fahren. *He thinks he's entitled to ride free of charge.*

die Nummer — *number*

  auf Nummer Sicher gehen — *to play it safe.*

  Die meisten Wähler wollten auf Nummer Sicher gehen. *Most voters wanted to play it safe.*

  eine dicke Nummer haben — *to be well thought of.*

  Bei allen Nachbarn hat er eine dicke Nummer. *He's well thought of by all the neighbors.*

oben — *above*

  oben nicht ganz richtig sein — *to be not quite right in the head (upstairs).*

  Ich glaube er ist oben nicht ganz richtig. *I don't think he's quite right in the head.*

von oben herab — *condescendingly.*

Ehe sie ihn heiratete, behandelte sie ihren Chauffeur von oben herab. *Before she married him she treated her chauffeur condescendingly.*

obenhinaus wollen — *to be a social climber.*

Einst wollte sie obenhinaus, jetzt aber lebt sie nur der Liebe. *Once she was a social climber, now she lives only for love.*

---

ober — *upper*

die oberen Zehntausend — *the upper crust.*

Suzannes Galerie ist für die oberen Zehntausend. *Suzanne's gallery is for the upper crust.*

---

offen — *open*

offen gesagt — *frankly speaking.*

Offen gesagt, glaub ich das nicht. *Frankly speaking, I don't believe that.*

offene Türen einrennen — *to fight battles already won.*

Wir sind ganz deiner Meinung; du rennst nur offene Türen ein. *We agree with you completely; you're fighting a battle already won.*

---

das Ohr — *ear*

bis über beide Ohren in Schulden stecken — *to be up to one's neck in debt.*

Bis über beide Ohren steckt er in Schulden. *He's up to his neck in debt.*

bis über beide Ohren verliebt sein — *to be very much in love.*

Einst waren sie bis über beide Ohren in einander verliebt. *Once they were very much in love with each other.*

bis über die Ohren rot werden — *to blush all over.*

Er wurde bis über die Ohren rot. *He blushed all over.*

die Ohren steif halten — *to maintain morale.*

Halt die Ohren steif! *Keep smiling!/Keep a stiff upper lip!*

etwas hinter den Ohren haben — *to be smart.*

Sie hat was hinter den Ohren. *She's got something upstairs.*

etwas hinter die Ohren schreiben — *to be sure to remember; to take due note of.*

Vor Mitternacht musst du zu Hause sein — schreib dir das hinter die
Ohren. *You must be home before midnight. Be sure to remember that.*

ganz Ohr sein — *to be all ears.*

Wenn geklatscht wird, ist er immer ganz Ohr. *Whenever anyone gossips,
he's always all ears.*

jemandem die Ohren langziehen — *to give s.o. a good talking-to/an
earful.*

Dem Lausbuben hat Mutti ganz schön die Ohren langgezogen. *Mom gave
that rotten kid a good talking-to.*

**jemandem in den Ohren liegen/jemandem mit etwas auf den Ohren
liegen** — *to nag; importune someone.*

Ach, wenn er nur aufhören würde, mir mit seinen Theorien endlos in den
Ohren zu liegen. *Oh, if he'd only quit going on and on about his theories.*

sich aufs Ohr legen/hauen — *to turn in, hit the hay.*

Ich leg mich jetzt ein bisschen aufs Ohr. *I'm going to have a little lie
down now.*

übers Ohr hauen — *to cheat.*

Prüfen Sie die Echtheit genau, damit Sie nicht übers Ohr gehauen werden.
Check the authenticity carefully, so that you aren't cheated.

viel um die Ohren haben — *to have a lot to do.*

Diese Woche hatte ich viel um die Ohren. *I had a lot to do this week.*

---

das Öl — *oil*

Öl auf die Wogen gießen — *to pour oil on troubled waters.*

Sie goß Öl auf die Wogen und setzte dem Streit ein Ende. *She poured oil
on troubled waters and put an end to the quarrel.*

Öl ins Feuer gießen — *to add fuel to the flames.*

Die Reporterin wusste, dass der Artikel Öl ins Feuer gießen würde. *The
reporter knew that the article would add fuel to the flames.*

ölen — *to lubricate*

wie geölt — *like clockwork.*

Alles lief wie geölt. *Everything went like clockwork.*

---

die Olympiade — *Olympic Games*
Auf der Olympiade gewann sie Gold. *She won a gold medal at the Olympics.*

olympiaverdächtig — *Olympics material; outstanding in sports.*
Unsere Kleine ist immer auf der Piste; sie ist wohl olympiaverdächtig. *Our little daughter is always on the ski lanes; she's Olympics material.*

der Olympionike, die Olympionikin — *Olympics victor/participant.*
Er treibt gern Sport, aber Olympionike wird er wohl nie. *He loves sports, but it's doubtful he'll ever make the Olympics.*

die Oper — *opera*
ein Opernnarr sein — *to be avidly fond of the opera.*
Er ist zugleich Opernnarr und Leseratte. *He's both a bookworm and an opera nut.*

Opern quatschen — *to talk too much.*
Quatsch keine Opern! *Don't talk so much.*

Otto Normalverbraucher — *the average person; John Q. Public.*
Würde so etwas Otto Normalverbraucher ansprechen? *Would something like that appeal to the average person?*

pachten — *to lease*
Glauben Sie, die Straße für sich gepachtet zu haben? *Do you think you own the street?*

das Päckchen — *small parcel*
sein Päckchen (zu tragen) haben — *to have one's cross (to bear); to have one's troubles.*
Jeder hat sein Päckchen (zu tragen). *Everyone has his troubles.*

die Palme — *palm tree*
auf die Palme bringen — *to drive up the wall.*

Sein moralinsaueres Benehmen bringt mich auf die Palme. *His holier-than-thou behavior drives me up the wall.*

der Pantoffel — *slipper*
unter dem Pantoffel stehen — *to be henpecked.*
Lange Jahre stand er unter dem Pantoffel. *He was henpecked for many years.*

der Pantoffelheld — *henpecked husband.*
Man nannte ihnen einen Pantoffelhelden, aber er war glücklich. *They called him henpecked, but he was happy.*

der Pappenstiel — *trifle*
für einen Pappenstiel — *for a song.*
Sie hat den Wagen für einen Pappenstiel gekauft. *She bought the car for a song.*

die Parade — *parade*
in die Parade fahren — *to oppose vigorously.*
Sie fuhr dem Senator oft in die Parade. *She often opposed the senator.*

die Partei — *political party*
es mit beiden Parteien halten — *to keep a foot in both camps.*
Er versucht es, mit beiden Parteien zu halten. *He's trying to keep a foot in both camps.*

Partei ergreifen — *to take sides; to take a stand.*
Sehr früh ergriff sie für den Umweltschutz Partei. *Very early on she took a stand for environmental protection.*

die Partie — *part; game*
eine gute Partie sein — *to be a good match.*
Ihre Mutter nannte ihn eine gute Partie, aber sie wollte nichts von ihm wissen. *Her mother called him a good match, but she didn't want anything to do with him.*

mit von der Partie sein — *to join in.*
Wenn wir aufs Land gingen, war sie oft mit von der Partie. *When we went to the country, she often joined us.*

die Pauke — *kettle drum*

  auf die Pauke hauen — *to have a blast.*

  Gestern abend haben wir auf die Pauke gehauen. *Last night we had a blast.*

  auf die Pauke hauen — *to blow one's own trumpet.*

  Seitdem er das Vermögen geerbt hat, haut er auf die Pauke. *Ever since he inherited the fortune he's been blowing his own trumpet.*

das Pech — *pitch; bad luck*

  Pech im Spiel, Glück in der Liebe. *Unlucky at cards, lucky in love.*

der Pechvogel — *unlucky person*

  Dein Bruder hat wieder einen Unfall gehabt? Er ist ein richtiger Pechvogel. *Your brother had another accident? He's a walking disaster area.*

die Pelle — *skin; peel*

  auf die Pelle rücken — *to harrass, be after.*

  Er rückt mir dauernde auf die Pelle, damit ich Geld bei ihm anlege. *He's always after me to invest money with him.*

  von der Pelle gehen — *to leave in peace.*

  Er will mir nicht von der Pelle gehen. *He won't leave me in peace.*

der Pelz — *fur; pelt*

  eins auf den Pelz geben — *to tan someone's hide.*

  Sie drohen oft, den Kindern eins auf den Pelz zu geben, aber es bleibt bei der Drohung. *They often threaten to tan their kids' hides, but threatening is all they do.*

perfekt — *perfect; a done deal*

  Das Abkommen ist perfekt. *The agreement is a done deal.*

die Pfanne — *frying pan*

  in die Pfanne hauen — *to pan.*

  Das Stück wurde von den meisten Kritikern in die Pfanne gehauen. *The play was panned by most of the critics.*

der Pfeffer — *pepper*
hingehen, wo der Pfeffer wächst — *to go to hell; get lost.*
Deine besoffenen Kumpane sollen hingehen, wo der Pfeffer wächst. *Your drunken buddies can go to hell.*

pfeffern — *to season with pepper*
eine pfeffern — *to whack.*
Lass mich in Ruh, oder ich pfeffre dir eine. *Leave me alone or I'll whack you.*

gepfeffert — *steep.*
Die gepfefferten Preise for Spitzenweine können wir nicht zahlen. *We can't pay the steep prices for top-quality wines.*

gepfeffert — *racy; spicy.*
Beim Gewürztraminertrinken erzählen sie sich gepfefferte Geschichten. *While drinking Gewürztraminer they tell spicy stories.*

pfeifen — *to whistle*
auf etwas pfeifen — *not to care a damn about.*
Wir pfeifen auf seine Befehle. *We don't care a damn about his orders.*

der Pfeil — *arrow*
alle seine Pfeile verschossen haben — *to have used up all one's arguments.*
Alle glaubten, die Anwältin hätte ihre Pfeile verschossen. *Everyone thought the lawyer had used up all her arguments.*

der Pfennig — *penny, cent*
Wer den Pfennig nicht ehrt, ist des Talers nicht wert. *Whoever doesn't respect the penny doesn't deserve the dollar.*

auf den Pfennig genau — *correct to the last cent.*
Die Rechnung stimmte auf den Pfennig genau. *The bill was correct to the last cent.*

auf Heller und Pfennig — *down to the last cent/detail.*
Er hatte alles auf Heller und Pfennig gerechnet. *He had figured everything out down to the last detail.*

bis auf den letzten Pfennig — *down to the last cent.*
Er hat alles verloren, bis auf den letzten Pfennig. *He lost everything, down
to the last cent.*

---

das Pferd — *horse*
das Pferd am Schwanz aufzäumen — *to make a false start.*
Vielleicht wäre das Projekt besser gelungen, wenn er das Pferd nicht am
Schwanz aufgezäumt hätte. *Perhaps the project would have worked out
better if he hadn't made a false start of it.*

die Pferde durchgehen — *to lose control, composure.*
Wenn man dieses Thema berührt, gehen ihm die Pferde durch. *When that
subject comes up, he loses control.*

einen vom Pferd erzählen — *to tell a fish story, a fib.*
Er hat dir wohl wieder einen vom Pferd erzählt. *He probably told you a
fib again.*

keine zehn Pferde — *wild horses.*
Keine zehn Pferde bringen mich wieder in sein Restaurant. *Wild horses
couldn't get me to go back to his restaurant.*

mit jemandem Pferde stehlen können — *to be game for anything.*
Die beiden sind alte Schulkameraden, mit denen man Pferde stehlen kann.
Both are old school chums who are game for anything.

---

der Pferdefuß — *horse's foot*
einen Pferdefuß haben — *to have a (hidden) disadvantage/drawback.*
Erst nach Unterzeichnung des Kaufvertrags, sah er ein, dass das Haus
einen Pferdefuß hatte. *Only after signing the sales contract did he
realize that the house had a drawback.*

---

der Pfifferling — *chanterelle mushroom*
keinen Pfifferling wert sein — *to be worthless.*
Sie behauptete, die Versprechungen des Senators wären keinen Pfifferling
wert. *She alleged the senator's promises were worthless.*

---

das Pflaster — *sticking plaster; pavement*
ein heißes Pflaster — *a dangerous spot.*

ein teures Pflaster — *an expensive district.*

Dieser Gangster wohnt in Hamburg-Blankenese, ein teures und jetzt auch ein heißes Pflaster. *That gangster lives in Hamburg-Blankenese, an expensive area, and now a dangerous one, too.*

piepen — *to peep, chirp*

Bei dir piept's wohl! Du hast einen Vogel! *You must be off your rocker. You're bonkers!*

Der Film war zum Piepen! *The movie was a scream/hoot!*

die Pike — *pike*

von der Pike auf dienen/lernen — *to start at the bottom and work one's way up.*

Er sollte im Geschäft seines Vaters von der Pike auf dienen. *He was supposed to work his way up in his father's business.*

die Piksieben — *seven of spades*

dastehen wie Piksieben — *to stand there looking stupid.*

Keiner bewegte sich; alle standen da wie Piksieben. *No one moved; they all stood there looking stupid.*

die Pistole — *pistol*

die Pistole auf die Brust setzen — *to hold a gun to someone's head.*

Niemand setzte ihm eine Pistole auf die Brust; er tat es aus freien Stücken. *No one put a gun to his head; he did it of his own accord.*

wie aus der Pistole geschossen — *unhesitatingly.*

Wie aus der Pistole geschossen antwortete sie auf alle Fragen. *She answered all questions unhesitatingly.*

die Platte — *record*

die alte Platte laufen lassen — *to put on the same broken record.*

Er lässt immer die alte Platte laufen. *He always puts on the same broken record.*

die Platte kennen — *to have heard it before.*

Die Platte kennen wir schon. *We've heard that tune before.*

die Platte putzen — *to make oneself scarce.*

Ohne dass es die anderen merkten, putzte er die Platte. *Without the others' noticing, he made himself scarce.*

eine andere Platte auflegen — *to put another record on; to change the subject.*

Leg doch 'ne andere Platte auf — das alles kennen wir schon. *Put on another record. We know all that.*

---

der Platz — *place*

am Platz sein — *to be fitting.*

An diesem Feiertag ist es am Platz, dass wir an unsere verstorbenen Kameraden denken. *On this holiday it is fitting that we think of our dead comrades.*

der Platzhirsch — *the dominant stag; the boss, the big cheese.*

Er hält sich für den Platzhirsch hier. *He thinks he's the boss around here.*

---

das Porzellan — *porcelain*

das Porzellan zerschlagen — *to cause a lot of trouble.*

Mit seinen Beschuldigungen hat er viel Porzellan zerschlagen. *His accusations caused a lot of trouble.*

---

die Post — *mail; post office; mail coach* (**Postkutsche**)

Jetzt geht die Post ab! *It's time to get going now!*

In dem Film geht richtig die Post ab. *There's plenty of action in that movie.*

Wir hätten gerne größere Marktanteile in China—dort wird die Post abgehen! *We'd like a larger share of the market in China—that's where the action will be!*

---

der Posten — *post, position*

auf verlorenem Posten stehen — *to be fighting for a lost cause.*

Nicht alle Anhänger des Kreationismus wissen, dass sie auf verlorenem Posten stehen. *Not all devotees of creationism know that they're fighting for a lost cause.*

---

der Pott — *pot*

  zu Pott(e) kommen — *to get to the point; to make up one's mind.*

  Nixon bat Eisenhower zu Potte zu kommen. *Nixon asked Eisenhower to make up his mind.*

der Pranger — *pillory*

  an den Pranger stellen — *to pillory.*

  Die Presse stellte den Senator an den Pranger. *The press pilloried the senator.*

die Probe — *test*

  auf die Probe stellen — *to put to the test.*

  Ihre Liebe wurde auf die Probe gestellt. *Their love was put to the test.*

  auf Probe — *on a trial basis.*

  Könnten Sie mich vielleicht auf Probe einstellen? *Could you maybe hire me on a trial basis?*

  die Probe aufs Exempel machen — *to decide by trying.*

  Ob meiner der beste Apfelstrudel ist? Machen Sie die Probe aufs Exempel! *As to whether mine is the best apple strudel, try some and decide!*

  Probieren geht über Studieren. *The proof of the pudding is in the eating.*

das Profil — *profile*

  Profil haben — *to have a distinctive image.*

  Unter den Wählern hat er Profil. *He has a distinctive image among the voters.*

  sich profilieren — *to make one's name/mark.*

  Auf der Schule profilierte er sich mehr als Athlet denn als Schüler. *In school he made more of a name for himself as an athlete than as a student.*

das Protokoll — *written record*

  das Protokoll führen — *to take the minutes.*

  Bei der CIA Sitzung führte ein Doppelagent das Protokoll. *A double agent took the minutes at the CIA meeting.*

  etwas zu Protokoll geben — *to make a statement (for the record).*

  Er gab zu Protokoll, dass er die Ermordete seit zwei Jahren nicht gesehen hätte. *He stated that he hadn't seen the murdered woman for two years.*

der Prozess — *trial; lawsuit*
den Prozess machen — *to sue.*
Er drohte, ihnen den Prozess zu machen. *He threatened to sue them.*

kurzen Prozeß machen — *to make short work of.*
Die Tennis Weltmeisterin machte mit der Konkurrenz kurzen Prozess. *The world champion tennis player made short work of the competition.*

der Pudel — *poodle*
Das war also des Pudels Kern! *So that's what was behind the matter!*

wie ein begossener Pudel — *crestfallen.*
Wie ein begossener Pudel zog er ab. *He went off crestfallen.*

sich pudelwohl fühlen — *to feel on top of the world.*
In der neuen Wohnung im Hochhaus fühlte Sie sich pudelwohl. *In the new apartment in the high rise she felt on top of the world.*

das Pulver — *powder; gunpowder*
das Pulver nicht erfunden haben — *not to be very bright.*
Er hat das Pulver nicht erfunden, aber sein Vater ist reich. *He's not particularly bright, but his father's rich.*

sein Pulver verschossen haben — *to have used up one's ammunition.*
Er konnte wenig mehr sagen, denn er hatte schon sein Pulver verschossen. *He couldn't say much more, for he'd already used up his ammunition.*

der Punkt — *point; period*
auf den Punkt bringen — *to sum up; to put in a nutshell.*
Um es auf den Punkt zu bringen, wenn wir keine Lohnerhöhung bekommen, streiken wir. *To put it in a nutshell, if we don't get a wage raise, we'll go on strike.*

der springende Punkt — *the essential factor; the main thing.*
Ja, schön ist es, aber zu teuer — das ist der springende Punkt. *Yes, it's nice, but too expensive; that's the main thing.*

den toten Punkt überwinden — *to get one's second wind.*
Ein Schluck Schnaps half ihm, den toten Punkt zu überwinden. *A swig of schnapps helped him get his second wind.*

ohne Punkt und Komma reden — *to talk nonstop.*

Da verstummte er, obwohl er gewöhnlich ohne Punkt und Komma redet. *He fell silent then, although he usually talks nonstop.*

die Puppe — *doll*

bis in die Puppen — *for a long time; till all hours.*

Sie tanzten bis in die Puppen. *They danced till all hours.*

die Puppen tanzen lassen — *to let it all hang out.*

Gestern abend vergaß er seine Hemmungen und ließ alle Puppen tanzen. *Last night he forgot his inhibitions and let it all hang out.*

die Puppen tanzen lassen — *to kick up a fuss.*

Wenn wir seinen Befehlen nicht genau gehorchen, wird er die Puppen tanzen lassen. *If we don't obey his orders exactly, he will kick up a fuss.*

putzen — *to clean*

jmdn. herunterputzen — *to put s.o. down.*

Ihm macht's Spaß, alle herunterzuputzen. *He enjoys putting everybody down.*

die Qual — *torment*

Wer die Wahl hat, hat die Qual. *It's terrible making up your mind when there's so much to choose from.*

der Quark — *sour curd cheese*

Getretener Quark wird breit, nicht stark. *Under pressure jellyfish (weaklings) get wider, not stronger.*

seine Nase in jeden Quark stecken — *to stick one's nose in everywhere.*

Er fühlt sich bemüßigt, seine Nase in jeden Quark zu stecken. *He feels obliged to stick his nose in everywhere.*

quasseln — *to babble; chatter*
Quasselwasser getrunken haben — *to chatter on and on.*
Er schien Quasselwasser getrunken zu haben und ließ keinen zu Wort
kommen. *He chattered on and on and didn't let anyone get a word in
edgewise.*

das Quecksilber — *mercury, quicksilver*
Quecksilber im Leib haben — *to have ants in one's pants.*
Jungen in seinem Alter haben Quecksilber im Leib. *Boys his age have
ants in their pants.*

quer — *sideways*
Die Kunstziele des Bauhaus standen dem breiten Publikum quer. *The
artistic goals of the Bauhaus were at odds with the public at large.*

quer durch — *straight through.*
Die Karnevalstimmung geht quer durch die Stände. *The carnival
atmosphere cuts across class lines.*

der Querdenker — *independant thinker; maverick.*
Von Dogmen will er nichts wissen; er ist Querdenker. *He wants nothing to
do with dogmas; he's an independant thinker.*

in die Quere kommen — *to get in someone's way.*
Keiner soll mir jetzt in die Quere kommen. *Just don't let anybody get in
my way now.*

quer schießen — *to make trouble, raise objections.*
Wir glaubten alle, eine Lösung gefunden zu haben, aber natürlich musste
Gero wieder quer schießen. *We all thought we'd found a solution, but of
course Gero had to raise objections again.*

der Quertreiber — *troublemaker.*
Der wirkliche Quertreiber ist Fritz, der seine Querflöte zu ungelegener
Zeit spielt. *The real troublemaker is Fritz, who plays his transverse
flute at inopportune times.*

der Quirl — *kitchen blender*
ein Quirl sein — *to be a real live wire.*
Kai ist ein richtiger Quirl. *Kai is a real live wire.*

der Rabe — *raven*

ein weißer Rabe — *a great rarity; very unusual.*
Er sieht niemals fern, und gilt bei seinen Schulkameraden als ein weißer Rabe. *He never watches television, and his schoolmates think he's very unusual.*

klauen wie ein Rabe — *to pinch everything one can lay one's hands on.*
Überall wo Hedi hingeht, klaut sie wie ein Rabe. *Everywhere Hedi goes she pinches everything she can lay her hands on.*

schwarz wie ein Rabe — *black as pitch.*
Draußen war es schwarz wie ein Rabe. *Outside it was black as pitch.*

die Rabenmutter — *cruel and uncaring mother*
Die Milliardärin sagte, ihre Mutter wäre eine Rabenmutter. *The billionairess said her mother was cruel and uncaring.*

die Rache — *revenge*
Rache ist süß/Blutwurst. *Revenge is sweet.*

das Rad — *wheel*

das fünfte Rad am Wagen sein — *to be a fifth wheel.*
Ich hatte keine Lust das fünfte Rad am Wagen zu sein und blieb zu Hause. *I had no wish to be a fifth wheel and stayed home.*

unter die Räder kommen — *to get run over.*
Die Kinder kamen fast unter die Räder des Lkws. *The children almost got run over by the truck.*

unter die Räder kommen — *to go to rack and ruin; go to the dogs.*
Trotz, oder vielleicht wegen seiner Begabungen, kam er unter die Räder. *Despite, or perhaps because of his talents, he went to the dogs.*

das Rädchen — *small wheel, cog*

ein Rädchen zuviel haben — *to be cuckoo, weird.*
Einige glauben, er hat ein Rädchen zuviel. *Some think he's weird.*

nur ein Rädchen im Getriebe sein — *to be a mere cog in the machinery.*
Der Beamte behauptete, er wäre nur ein Rädchen im Getriebe gewesen.
The official declared he was a mere cog in the machinery.

das Radieschen — *radish*
die Radieschen von unten betrachten — *to push up daisies.*
Es störte die pantheistische Botanikerin nicht im geringsten, dass sie eines
Tages die Radieschen von unten betrachten würde. *It didn't in the least
disturb the pantheistic botanist that one day she'd be pushing up daisies.*

das Rampenlicht — *the footlights*
im Rampenlicht stehen — *to be in the limelight.*
Sie träumt davon, im Rampenlicht zu stehen. *She dreams of being in the
limelight.*

der Rang — *rank*
alles, was Rang und Namen hat — *anybody who is anybody.*
Alles, was in der Stadt Rang und Namen hatte, erschien für die
Erstaufführung. *Anyone who was anyone in the city appeared for the
first performance.*

den Rang ablaufen — *to surpass.*
Der Werbung nach läuft dieses neue Waschmittel allen anderen den Rang
ab. *According to the commercials, this new detergent surpasses all the
others.*

ersten Ranges — *of the greatest importance.*
Für uns ist das eine Entscheidung ersten Ranges. *For us that is a decision
of the greatest importance.*

rasten — *to rest*
Wer rastet, der rostet. *Use it or lose it.*

der Rat — *advice*
Da ist guter Rat teuer. *This is a difficult situation to find a solution for.*

keinen Rat wissen — *to know no way out of a situation; to be at one's
wit's end.*
Er wusste keinen Rat mehr, und sah sich gezwungen, das Geschäft zu
verkaufen. *He knew no other way out and sold the business.*

mit Rat und Tat — *with moral and practical support.*

Unsere Freunde standen uns mit Rat und Tat zur Seite. *Our friends stood by us offering moral and practical support.*

mit sich zu Rate gehen — *to think over carefully.*

Wir müssen erst mit uns zu Rate gehen, bevor wir Ihr Angebot annehmen können. *We'll have to think it over carefully before we can accept your offer.*

zu Rate ziehen — *to consult.*

Sie haben eine Fachärztin zu Rate gezogen. *They consulted a specialist.*

---

der Raubbau — *ruthless exploitation*

Raubbau mit seiner Gesundheit treiben — *to undermine one's health.*

Um sein Geschäft aufzubauen, trieb er mit seiner Gesundheit Raubbau. *In building up his business he undermined his health.*

---

die Raupe — *caterpillar*

Raupen im Kopf haben — *to have odd ideas.*

Mit 80 Jahren will er wieder zur See fahren. Na, er hat ja immer Raupen im Kopf gehabt. *At 80 he wants to go to sea again. Well, he's always had odd ideas.*

---

rechnen — *to reckon; calculate*

gut/schlecht rechnen können — *to be good/bad at figures.*

Käthi kann gut rechnen, besser als ihr Bruder. *Käthi is good at figures, better than her brother.*

sich rechnen — *to show a profit; pay off.*

Das Projekt ist teuer, aber in wenigen Jahren wird es sich rechnen. *The project is expensive, but in a few years it will show a profit.*

---

die Rechnung — *calculation*

auf eigene Rechnung — *at one's own risk.*

Er hat es auf eigene Rechnung getan. *He did it at his own risk.*

auf seine Rechnung kommen — *to get one's money's worth.*

In dem Restaurant kommt jeder auf seine Rechnung. *All get their money's worth in that restaurant.*

einen Strich durch die Rechnung machen — *to ruin plans.*
Wir wollten aufs Land, aber der Wettergott hat uns einen Strich durch die Rechnung gemacht. *We wanted to go to the country, but the weather ruined our plans.*

recht — *right*

jemandem recht geben — *to admit that someone is right.*
Ich musste ihr recht geben. *I had to admit that she was right.*

recht behalten — *to be proved right.*
Also hat sie doch recht behalten. *So she was proved right anyway.*

recht haben — *to be right.*
Die Partei hatte nicht immer recht. *The party wasn't always right.*

Was dem einen recht ist, ist dem anderen billig. *What is justice for one person is justice for another, too.*

reden — *to speak*

reden wie einem der Schnabel gewachsen ist — *to talk freely and easily.*
In der Kiezkneipe kann der Chef reden, wie ihm der Schnabel gewachsen ist. *In that neighborhood bar the boss can talk freely and easily.*

der Regen — *rain*

ein warmer Regen — *a windfall.*
Er hofft auf einen warmen Regen. *He's hoping for a windfall.*

im Regen stehen lassen — *to leave in the lurch.*
Er ließ seine Familie im Regen stehen. *He left his family in the lurch.*

vom Regen in die Traufe kommen — *to go from the frying pan into the fire.*
Wir zogen um und kamen vom Regen in die Traufe. *We moved and went from the frying pan into the fire.*

der Regenbogen — *rainbow*

die Regenbogenpresse — *gossip/scandal/romance print media.*
In der Regenbogenpresse steht viel über Filmstars, Politiker und Adlige. *In scandal sheets there's a lot about movie stars, politicians, and royals.*

das Register — *register, index; organ stop*
  alle Register ziehen/alle Register spielen lassen — *to pull out all the stops.*
  Um den Vertrag zu bekommen, mussten wir alle Register ziehen. *We had to pull out all the stops to get the contract.*

  andere Register ziehen — *to take a different approach.*
  Sie werden immer unverschämter; wir müssen jetzt andere Register ziehen. *They're growing more and more brazen; we'll have to take a different tack.*

reichen — *to reach; to be/have enough*
  Die Demonstranten schrien: "Uns reicht's!" *The demonstrators shouted, "We've had enough!"*

die Reihe — *row*
  an der Reihe sein — *to be someone's turn.*
  Jetzt bist du an der Reihe. *It's your turn now.*

  an die Reihe kommen — *to get one's turn.*
  Wann komme ich an die Reihe? *When do I get my turn?*

  aus der Reihe tanzen — *to be different.*
  In der Militärschule durfte niemand aus der Reihe tanzen. *In military school no one was allowed to be different.*

  nicht alle in der Reihe haben — *not to be all there.*
  Ich glaube, er hat nicht alle in der Reihe. *I don't think he's all there.*

  wieder in die Reihe kommen — *to get back on one's feet again.*
  Ich hoffe, bald wieder in die Reihe zu kommen. *I hope to get back on my feet again soon.*

rein — *pure, clear*
  ins Reine kommen — *to sort/straighten out.*
  Sie versucht, mit ihren inneren Konflikten ins Reine zu kommen. *She's trying to sort out her inner conflicts.*

  reinen Wein einschenken — *to be honest, forthcoming.*
  Die Politiker müssen uns reinen Wein einschenken. *The politicians must be more honest with us.*

reinsten Wassers — *through and through.*
Sie ist eine Dichterin reinsten Wassers. *She's a poet through and through.*

die Reise — *trip*
eine Reise machen — *to take a trip.*
Jedes Jahr machen wir eine Reise in die Berge. *Every year we take a trip to the mountains.*

sich auf die Reise machen — *to start (out) on a trip.*
Bald machen wir uns auf die Reise. *We'll be starting out soon.*

viel auf Reisen sein — *to be away; to travel.*
Geschäftlich ist er viel auf Reisen. *He travels a lot on business.*

der Reiter — *horseman, rider; cavalryman*
der Paragraphenreiter — *stickler for the rules, pedant.*
Der Chef ist kein Paragraphenreiter; manchmal lässt er auch fünf gerade sein. *The boss is no petty bureaucrat; sometimes he bends the rules a little.*

der Spitzenreiter — *front-runner, top seller; number-one hit.*
Das altbekannte Waschmittel ist nicht mehr Spitzenreiter. *The well-known old detergent isn't the market leader anymore.*

der Vorreiter — *avant-gardist, pioneer.*
Sein Unternehmen war Vorreiter bei der Unterstützung junger Künstler. *Our company was a trailblazer in the support of young artists.*

das Rennen — *race*
Das Rennen ist gelaufen. *The race is over (the matter is settled).*

das Rennen machen — *to win the race.*
Jede der drei Parteien sagte, sie würde das Wahlrennen machen. *Each of the three parties said they'd win the electoral race.*

die Rente — *pension*
in Rente gehen — *to retire*
Seit Jahren denkt er daran, in Rente zu gehen. *For years he's been thinking of retiring.*

sich rentieren — *to be profitable*
Sie glauben, dass die Magnetschwebebahn sich rentieren wird. *They believe the magnetic levitation train will be profitable.*

der Rest — *rest, remainder*
den Rest geben — *to wipe out, finish off.*
Die Gier nach Kaviar hat dem europäischen Stör fast den Rest gegeben. *Greed for caviar has almost wiped out the European sturgeon.*

riechen — *to smell*
etwas nicht riechen können — *not be able to know.*
Ich konnte nicht riechen, dass er ein Spion war. *How was I supoosed to know that he was a spy?*

nicht riechen können — *not to be able to stand.*
Sie kann ihn nicht riechen. *She can't stand him.*

der Riecher — *smeller; nose*
den richtigen Riecher (einen guten Riecher) haben — *to have a sense/instinct for.*
Ich hatte den richtigen Riecher und wusste, dass es Schwindel war. *I had the right instinct and knew that it was a swindle.*

der Riemen — *belt*
den Riemen enger schnallen — *to tighten one's belt.*
Im Krieg mussten wir uns den Riemen enger schnallen und dabei wurden wir gesünder. *In the war we had to tighten our belts and were healthier for it.*

sich am Riemen reißen — *to pull oneself together.*
Wenn du dich am Riemen reißt, besteht noch Hoffnung für dich. *If you pull yourself together there's still hope for you.*

sich kräftig in die Riemen legen — *to put one's nose to the grindstone.*
Wenn ihr euch kräftig in die Riemen legt, werden wir noch vor Abend fertig. *If you put your nose to the grindstone, we'll be done before evening.*

der Ritt — *ride*

auf einen Ritt — *all at once.*

Du brauchst den Kuchen nicht auf einen Ritt aufzuessen. *You don't have to eat up the cake all at once.*

der Rock — *skirt; jacket*

Der letzte Rock hat keine Taschen. *You can't take it with you.*

die Rolle — *roll*

aus der Rolle fallen — *to behave inappropriately.*

Bei seinem Empfang betrank sich der Botschafter und fiel aus der Rolle. *At his reception the ambassador got drunk and behaved inappropriately.*

eine Rolle spielen — *to be of importance.*

Ihre Unterstützung hat eine entscheidende Rolle gespielt. *Her support was of crucial importance.*

röntgen — *to take X-rays*

Man hat geröngt, aber nichts gefunden. *They took X-rays but found nothing.*

das Ross — *horse; steed*

auf dem hohen Ross sitzen — *to lord it over others.*

Sie sind reich und sitzen gern auf dem hohen Ross. *They're rich and like to lord it over others.*

Ross und Reiter nennen — *to name names.*

Warum nennt die Zeitung Ross und Reiter nicht? *Why doesn't the newspaper name names?*

die Rosskur — *drastic measure/remedy.*

Er will den Betrieb einer Rosskur unterziehen. *He wants to apply drastic measures to save the company.*

rot — *red*

auf der roten Liste stehen — *to be endangered.*

Viele Tierarten stehen auf der roten Liste. *Many species are endangered.*

die rote Laterne tragen — *to be last.*
Wirtschaftlich trägt unser Bundesland noch die rote Laterne.
Economically, our state still brings up the rear.

Heute rot, morgen tot. *Here today, gone tomorrow. (Today in the pink,
tomorrow in the drink.)*

der Rubel — *Russian ruble*
Der Rubel rollt. *Business is booming.*

das Ruder — *rudder; oar.*
  am Ruder sein — *to be in power.*
  Trotz Unruhen ist der Diktator noch am Ruder. *Despite disturbances, the
  dictator is still in power.*

  das Ruder (he)rumreißen — *to right a course, reverse a trend.*
  Die Präsidentin will alles versuchen, vor der Wahl das Ruder noch
  herumzureißen. *The president wants to do all she can to reverse the
  trend before the elections.*

  das Ruder in der Hand haben — *to be in control.*
  Sie hat noch das Ruder in der Hand—aber wie lange noch? *She's still in
  control—but for how long?*

der Ruf — *call; reputation*
  Ist der Ruf erst ruiniert, lebt man völlig ungeniert. *Once your reputation's
  ruined, you can do as you please/If you've got the name, you might as
  well have the game.*

rufen — *to call*
  wie gerufen kommen — *to come at just the right moment.*
  Du kommst wie gerufen! *You've come just at the right moment.*

der Rufmord — *character assassination*
  Der Filmstar drohte, den Journalisten wegen Rufmord zu verklagen.
  *The movie star threatened to sue the journalist for character
  assassination.*

die Ruhe — *calm*

Immer mit der Ruhe! *Just take it easy.* Don't panic.

in aller Ruhe — *quite calmly.*
In aller Ruhe erörterten wir die Lage. *We discussed the situation quite calmly.*

aus der Ruhe bringen — *to make nervous*
Jetzt hast du mich wieder aus der Ruhe gebracht. *Now you've made me nervous again.*

sich zur Ruhe setzen — *to retire.*
Sie will sich noch nicht zur Ruhe setzen. *She doesn't want to retire yet.*

der Ruhestand — *retirement*
in den Ruhestand treten — *to retire.*
Mit 48 Jahren ist er schon in den Ruhestand getreten. *He retired at 48.*

rund — *round*
rund um die Uhr — *round-the-clock.*
Diese Patienten brauchen Pflege rund um die Uhr. *These patients require round-the-clock care.*

die Runde — *round*
die Runde machen — *to make the rounds.*
Üble Gerüchte machten die Runde durch die Stadt. *Nasty rumors made the rounds in the city.*

eine runde Kugel schieben — *to have a cushy job.*
Jahrelang schob Lars eine runde Kugel im Auswärtigen Amt. *For years Lars had a cushy job in the State Dept./Foreign Office.*

eine Runde schmeißen — *to buy a round of drinks.*
Gestern hat er allen eine Runde Bier geschmissen. *Yesterday he bought a round of beer for everybody.*

über die Runden kommen — *to make ends meet.*
Mit seinem so niedrigen Gehalt kommt seine Familie kaum über die Runden. *His family scarcely makes ends meet on his low salary.*

die Sache — *thing; matter*

nicht bei der Sache sein — *not to be committed; not to be with it.*

Er ist sehr begabt, scheint aber nicht ganz bei der Sache zu sein. *He's very talented but doesn't seem to be entirely with it.*

zur Sache kommen — *to get to the point.*

Wann kommen Sie endlich zur Sache? *When will you finally get to the point?*

---

der Sack — *bag*

im Sack haben — *to have in the bag.*

Die Firma glaubte, den Auftrag im Sack zu haben. *The firm thought it had the contract in the bag.*

mit Sack und Pack — *with bag and baggage.*

Sie wollen mit Sack und Pack kommen. *They want to come with bag and baggage.*

---

säen — *to sow*

dünn gesät — *few and far between.*

Solche Gelegenheiten sind dünn gesät. *Such opportunities are few and far between.*

wie gesät — *spread out in quantity.*

Die Pflaumen lagen auf dem Gras wie gesät. *Quantites of plums were all spread out on the grass.*

---

der Saft — *juice*

im eigenen Saft schmoren lassen — *to let someone stew in his/her own juices.*

Sie sagte nichts, und ließ ihn im eigenen Saft schmoren. *She said nothing and let him stew in his own juices.*

ohne Saft und Kraft — *insipid; limp.*

Seine Argumente waren ohne Saft und Kraft. *His arguments were limp.*

---

sagen — *to say*

das Sagen haben — *to say what goes.*

Niemand weiß, ob der Präsident oder der General das Sagen im Land hat. *No one knows whether it's the president or the general who says what goes in that country.*

nichts zu sagen haben — *not to mean anything.*

Sein "Nein" hat nichts zu sagen. *His "No" doesn't mean anything.*

sage und schreibe — *really; no kidding.*

Sie hat sage und schreibe 200 Millionen Dollar geerbt. *She inherited 200 million dollars, no kidding.*

unter uns gesagt — *between you and me.*

Unter uns gesagt, ich suche eine andere Stelle. *Between you and me, I'm looking for another job.*

der Salat — *salad*

den Salat haben — *to be in a (fine) fix.*

Jetzt haben wir den Salat; der Wagen springt nicht an. *Now we're in a fix; the car won't start.*

der Salon — *parlor, living-room*

salonfähig — *socially acceptable, presentable.*

Seine radikale Partei ist jetzt salonfähig geworden. *His radical party's now socially acceptable.*

der Salonkommunist/Salonanarchist — *parlor pink/armchair revolutionary.*

Dieser Salonkommunist ist millionenschwer. *That parlor pink's got millions.*

der Salontiroler — *armchair yodeler* (Northerner/city slicker enthusiastic about the Alps).

Dieser Salontiroler will Unterricht im Jodeln und Skifahren von mir. *That armchair yodller wants skiing and yodeling lessons from me.*

das Salz — *salt*

nicht das Salz in der Suppe gönnen — *to begrudge everything; not to want to give someone the time of day.*

Sie gönnen uns nicht das Salz in der Suppe. *They begrudge us everything.*

Salz auf die Wunde streuen — *to rub salt into the wound.*
Musst du noch Salz auf meine Wunde streuen? *Do you have to rub salt into the wound?*

weder Salz noch Schmalz haben — *to have neither wit nor intensity.*
Das Stück hatte weder Salz noch Schmalz. *The play had neither wit nor intensity.*

Sankt-Nimmerleins-Tag — *"Saint Neverly's Day"; Doomsday; never*
bis zum Sankt-Nimmerleins-Tag warten — *to wait forever.*
Bevor ich mich bei ihm entschuldige, kann er bis zum Sankt-Nimmerleins-Tag warten. *He can wait forever before I apologize to him.*

die Sau — *sow*
die Sau rauslassen — *to let it all hang out.*
Wir wollten uns amüsieren und die Sau richtig rauslassen. *We wanted to have a good time and let it all hang out.*

Perlen vor die Säue werfen — *to cast pearls before swine.*
Er bildete sich ein, seine Perlen vor die Säue zu werfen. *In his conceit he thought he was casting his pearls before swine.*

unter aller Sau — *beneath contempt, really rotten.*
Sein Vortrag war unter aller Sau. *His presentation was pathetic.*

sauer — *sour; ticked off*
Die Mannschaft war auf den Schiedsrichter sauer. *The team was ticked off at the umpire.*

saufen — *to drink (animals); to guzzle*
saufen wie ein Loch/Schlauch — *to drink like a fish.*
Onkel Otto säuft wie ein Loch. *Uncle Otto drinks like a fish.*

saugen — *to suck*
sich etwas aus den Fingern saugen — *to make s.t. up; figure out.*
Das wär's also? Nichts mehr? Das hätte ich mir selber aus den Fingern saugen können. *So that's it? Nothing more? I could have come up with that myself.*

in Saus und Braus leben — *to live the life of Riley*
Mit dem gestohlenen Geld lebten sie eine Zeitlang in Saus und Braus. *For a while they lived the life of Riley with the money they stole.*

die Sause — *pub crawl*
eine Sause machen — *go barhopping.*
Er machte eine Sause, trank zu viel vom Sauser, und wurde krank. *He went barhopping, drank too much new wine, and got sick.*

sausen — *to roar (wind)*
durchs Examen sausen — *to fail an exam.*
Er sauste wieder durchs Examen. *He failed the exam again.*

sausenlassen — *not to bother about; to drop.*
Er bot mir eine Stelle an, aber ich ließ sie sausen. *He offered me a job, but I didn't bother about it.*

der Schaden — *damage*
Durch Schaden wird man klug. *One learns by negative experiences.* *(Experience is the best teacher.)*

Wer den Schaden hat, braucht nicht für Spott zu sorgen. *The laugh is always on the loser.*

zu Schaden kommen — *to be harmed.*
Durch seine Trunksucht ist seine Karriere zu Schaden gekommen. *His career was harmed by his alcoholism.*

die Schadenfreude — *malicious pleasure*
Schadenfreude heißt, sich über das Unglück anderer freuen.
"Schadenfreude" means taking malicious pleasure in others' misfortunes.

schadenfroh — *with malicious pleasure.*
Schadenfroh beobachtete Iago den eifersüchtigen Othello. *With malicious pleasure Iago observed jealous Othello.*

das Schäfchen — *little lamb*
sein Schäfchen ins Trockene bringen — *to look out for one's own interests.*

Der Börsenmakler brachte sein Schäfchen ins Trockene, ohne sich um seine Auftraggeber zu kümmern. *The stockbroker looked out for his own interests with no concern for his clients.*

der Schalk — *imp, jokester*
jemandem sitzt der Schalk im Naken — *s.o. is impish.*
Diesem Satiriker sitzt der Schalk im Nacken. *That satirist is quite a Merry Devil.*

der Schall — *sound*
Schall und Rauch — *meaningless.*
Seine Versprechungen waren nur Schall und Rauch. *His promises were meaningless.*

scharf — *sharp*
scharf auf — *keen on; fond of.*
Sie ist scharf auf Gesundheit. *She's keen on (maintaining) health.*
Ich esse gern scharf. *I'm fond of spicy foods.*

scharf schießen — *to use live amunition; to aim to hit.*
Es wurde scharf geschossen. *They used live ammunition.*

der Schatten — *shade; shadow*
über seinen eigenen Schatten springen — *to transcend one's nature/feelings by making a great effort.*
Sie sprang über ihren eigenen Schatten und vergab ihm. *She mastered her feelings and forgave him.*

Über seinen eigenen Schatten kann man nicht springen. *A leopard can't change its spots.*

das Schattendasein — *shadowy existence*
ein Schattendasein fristen — *to be insignificant.*
Einst fristete die Umweltschutzpolitik ein Schattendasein; heute steht sie im Mittelpunkt. *Once the political aspects of environmental protection were insignificant; today they're central.*

die Schau — *show*
zur Schau stellen — *to exhibit.*
Ihre Gemälde werden jetzt in mehreren Galerien zur Schau gestellt. *Her paintings are now on exhibition in several galleries.*

zur Schau tragen — *to make a show of.*
Der Heuchler trug seine Frömmigkeit zur Schau.
The hypocrite made a show of his piety.

der Schaum — *foam*
Schaum schlagen — *to boast, talk big.*
Wird er's wirklich tun, oder hat er nur Schaum geschlagen? *Will he really do it, or was he just talking big?*

die Scheibe — *slice*
eine Scheibe abschneiden — *to learn a thing or two.*
Von ihr könntest du dir eine Scheibe abschneiden. *You could learn a thing or two from her.*

der Schein — *appearance*
Der Schein trügt. *Appearances are deceptive.*

den Schein wahren — *to keep up appearances.*
Die Geschäftspartner vertragen sich nicht, aber sie versuchen noch, den Schein zu wahren. *The business partners don't get along, but they're still trying to keep up appearances.*

zum Schein — *as a pretense; to pretend to do.*
Der Polizeibeamte sollte die Drogen nur zum Schein kaufen. *The policeman was supposed only to pretend to buy the drugs.*

der Schickimicki — *trendy; glitzy, fancy-shmantzy*
Die Nordseeinsel Sylt gilt als Schickimicki. *The North Sea island Sylt is considered trendy.*

schießen — *to shoot*
ausgehen wie das Hornberger Schießen — *to fizzle out.*
Monatelang gab es viel Rummel, aber schließlich ging alles wie das Hornberger Schießen aus. *For months there was a lot of fuss, but at the end everything fizzled out.*

zum Schießen sein — *to be very funny.*
Diese Komikerin ist wirklich zum Schießen. *This comic is really very funny.*

der Schild — *shield*
auf den Schilde heben — *to make one's leader.*
Die Gruppe suchte einen Helden, den sie auf den Schilde erheben konnte. *The group was looking for a hero they could make their leader.*

etwas im Schilde führen — *to be plotting; to be up to no good.*
Ich glaube, er führt gegen uns etwas im Schilde. *I think he's plotting against us.*

der Schildbürger — *Gothamite, big fool*
Es stellte sich heraus, dass die vermeintlichen Schildbürger alles andere als Bauernopfer waren. *It turned out that the supposedly foolish villagers were anything but dumb country bumpkins.*

der Schimmer — *gleam; shimmer*
keinen (blassen) Schimmer haben — *to have no (not the faintest) idea.*
Wir hatten keinen Schimmer davon, dass sie heute kommen sollten. *We had no idea they were coming today.*

der Schlag — *blow; stroke*
auf einen Schlag — *all at once; simultaneously.*
Die Gefangenen begannen alle, auf einen Schlag zu schreien. *The prisoners all began shouting simultaneously.*

ein Schlag ins Wasser — *a washout.*
Sein Versuch, den Betrieb zu retten, war ein Schlag ins Wasser. *His attempt to save the company was a washout.*

mit einem Schlag — *suddenly.*
Nach ihrem ersten Film wurde sie mit einem Schlag berühmt. *After her first movie she was suddenly famous.*

Schlag auf Schlag — *in rapid succession.*
Nach dem missglückten Staatsstreich kamen die Nachrichten Schlag auf Schlag. *After the unsuccessful coup, the news came in rapid succession.*

schlagen — *to beat*
    Brücken schlagen — *to build bridges; create bonds.*
    Wir wollen alle mithelfen, Brücken zwischen den Menschen zu schlagen.
    We all want to help in building bridges between people.

    Vorteil schlagen — *to turn to one's advantage.*
    Aus allen Lagen weiß er, Vorteil zu schlagen. *He knows how to turn every
    situation to his own advantage.*

    Wurzeln schlagen — *to put down roots.*
    Sie haben schon in der neuen Heimat Wurzeln geschlagen. *They've
    already put down roots in their new homeland.*

die Schlange — *snake*
    Die Schlange beißt sich in den Schwanz. *This business just keeps going
    round in circles.*

    Schlange stehen — *to wait in line.*
    Wir mussten fast eine Stunde Schlange stehen. *We had to wait in line for
    almost an hour.*

    der Schlangenmensch — *contortionist.*
    Ich kann's nicht, bin doch kein Schlangenmensch. *I can't do it, I'm no
    contortionist.*

schlecht — *bad*
    mehr schlecht als recht — *after a fashion.*
    Das Buch langweilte sie und sie las es mehr schlecht als recht. *The book
    bored her and she read it only after a fashion.*

schlechthin — *quintessential(ly); the very embodiment of*
    Nietzsche war der individuelle Denker schlechthin. *Nietzsche was the very
    embodiment of the individualistic thinker.*

der Schliff — *cut; polish*
    der letzte Schliff — *the finishing touch.*
    Es schien ihr, dass der Maler vergessen hatte, dem Gemälde den letzten
    Schliff zu geben. *It seemed to her that the painter had forgotten to give
    the painting the finishing touch.*

Schliff backen — *to do a poor job.*

Sie haben mit dem Projekt Schliff gebacken. *They did a poor job on the project.*

schlucken — *to swallow*

eine Kuh/Kröte schlucken müssen — *to have to accept something, make difficult/unpleasant compromises.*

Die Senatoren mussten manche Kröte schlucken, aber sie stimmten doch fur den Plan. *The senators had to accept many things they didn't like but nevertheless they voted for the plan.*

der Schlüssel — *key*

schlüsselfertig — *ready to move into.*

Der Makler sagte, das Haus wäre schlüsselfertig. *The real estate agent said the house was ready to move into.*

das Schloss — *lock*

hinter Schloss und Riegel — *behind bars; under lock and key.*

Die Betrogenen freuten sich, dass der Betrüger hinter Schloss und Riegel saß. *The people he cheated were glad the conman was behind bars.*

der Schlot — *chimney*

wie ein Schlot qualmen — *to smoke like a chimney.*

Er weiß, daß es seiner Gesundheit schadet, trotzdem qualmt er wie ein Schlot. *He knows it's harmful to his health, still he smokes like a chimney.*

der Schlotbaron — *industrial tycoon.*

Er gibt sich gern für einen Schlotbaron aus. *He likes to pass himself off as a tycoon.*

der Schluss — *conclusion*

Schluss machen — *to stop; to break off a relationship.*

Erst gegen Mitternacht machten sie Schluss mit dem Lärm. *They stopped making noise only around midnight.*

Sie überlegte sich, wie sie mit ihm Schluss machen könnte. *She pondered how she could break off with him.*

schlüssig — *convincing; logical*
sich schlüssig werden — *to make up one's mind.*
Sie konnten sich über ihre Reisepläne nicht schlüssig werden. *They couldn't make up their minds about their travel plans.*

das Schlusslicht — *taillight*
Schlusslicht sein — *to be in last position, bring up the rear.*
Dieses Jahr ist unsere Mannschaft wieder Schlusslicht. *Our team's in last position again this year.*

schmecken — *to taste*
"Hat es Ihnen geschmeckt?" fragte die Kellnerin. *"Did you enjoy your meal?" asked the waitress.*
Wie schmeckte Ihnen die Linsensuppe? *How did you like the lentil soup?*

nach gar nichts schmecken; nicht nach ihm und nicht nach ihr schmecken — *to be flat-tasting.*
Das Gemüse schmeckte nach gar nichts. *The vegetables were flat-tasting.*

nach mehr schmecken — *to taste like more.*
Der Nachtisch schmeckt nach mehr. *The dessert tastes like more.*

der Schmied — *blacksmith*
Jeder ist seines Glückes Schmied. *Life is what you make it.*

der Schmock — *hack writer*
Weil sie eifersüchtig waren, nannten sie ihn einen Schmock. *Because they were jealous, they called him a hack writer.*

der Schmöker — *light reading (adventure, romance).*
Sie liest gern dicke Schmöker. *She likes to read fat, fast-moving books.*

schmökern — *to bury oneself in a book.*
Sie wollte schmökern, nicht fernsehen. *She wanted to bury herself in a book instead of watching television.*

schmettern — *to hurl; bellow*
einen schmettern — *to belt down alcohol.*
Er hatte Lust, einen zu schmettern. *He felt like belting one down.*

das Schnäppchen — *bargain*
  ein Schnäppchen machen — *to get a bargain.*
  Er glaubte, ein Schnäppchen gemacht zu haben, aber das Gemälde war
  nicht echt. *He thought he'd gotten a bargain, but the painting wasn't*
  genuine.

die Schnapsfahne — *boozy breath*
  Bleib mir weg mit deiner Schnapsfahne. *Stay away from me with your*
  boozy breath.

die Schnapsidee — *hare-brained scheme*
  Dieser Vorschlag ist nicht als Schnapsidee abzutun. *This proposal*
  shouldn't be dismissed as a hare-brained scheme.

die Schnapszahl — *multidigit number with all digits identical,*
numerical palindrome, fanciful number
  Sie heirateten am 8.8 2008, weil sie an die Numerologie glauben, und ihr
  Leben nach Schnapszahlen richten. *They got married on August 8, 2008*
  because they believe in numerology and live their lives according to
  fanciful numbers.

der Schneider — *tailor*
  aus dem Schneider/vom Schneider sein — *to be in the clear/off the*
  hook/out of the woods.
  Gegen den Senator wird noch ermittelt; er ist noch nicht vom Schneider.
  The senator's still being investigated; he's not off the hook yet.

schneien — *to snow*
  ins Haus schneien — *to snow into the house; to descend unannounced on*
  someone.
  Wir müssen es ihm abgewöhnen, uns ins Haus zu schneien. *We'll have to*
  get him to break the habit of descending unannounced on us.

der Schock — *shock*
  unter Schock stehen — *to be in shock.*
  Die Passagiere stehen noch unter Schock. *The passengers are still in a*
  state of shock.

der Schönheitsfehler — *blemish; (minor) drawback*
Es gibt mehr als einen Schönheitsfehler in seinem Plan. *There's more than one drawback in his plan.*

der Schrei — *cry; scream*
der letzte Schrei — *the latest fashion.*
In den sechziger Jahren war der Minirock der letzte Schrei. *In the sixties the mini skirt was the latest fashion.*

der Schrecken — *horror*
mit dem Schrecken davonkommen — *to have had a close call but be safe.*
Beim Zugunfall gab es zwei leicht Verletzte, aber die meisten Passagiere kamen mit dem Schrecken davon. *Two were slightly injured in the train accident, but most passengers were scared but safe.*

der Schritt — *step*
Schritt halten — *to keep up with.*
Seiner Firma fällt es schwer, auf dem internationalen Markt Schritt zu halten. *It's difficult for his firm to keep pace with the international market.*

die Schuld — *guilt; debt*
Schulden machen — *to go into debt.*
Wir wollen keine Schulden machen. *We don't want to go into debt.*

die Schule — *school*
Schule machen — *to find imitators; be taken up.*
Diese Idee macht jetzt überall Schule. *This idea is being taken up everywhere now.*

schulmeistern — *to lecture in a prescriptive way.*
Ich will mich nicht weiter von ihm schulmeistern lassen. *I won't be lectured to anymore by him.*

die Schulter — *shoulder*
auf die Schulter klopfen — *to give a pat on the back.*

Der Chef klopfte mir auf die Schulter, gab mir aber keine
Gehaltserhöhung. *The boss gave me a pat on the back but no salary
raise.*

auf die leichte Schulter nehmen — *to underestimate.*
Nehmen Sie seine Drohungen nicht auf die leichte Schulter! *Don't
underestimate his threats.*

der Schulterschluss — *act of solidarity.*
Das Abkommen wurde als Schulterschluss bezeichnet. *The agreement was
called an act of solidarity.*

der Schuss — *shot*
   ein Schuss in den Ofen — *a total waste of effort.*
   Der Oppositionschef behauptete, das Regierungsprogramm sei ein Schuss
   in den Ofen. *The head of the opposition said the government's program
   was a total waste of effort.*

   in Schuss — *in working order.*
   Die Straßenbeleuchtung ist nicht immer in Schuss. *The street lights aren't
   always in working order.*

der Schwamm — *sponge*
   Schwamm drüber! Ich will nichts mehr davon hören. *Drop it! I don't want
   to hear anymore about it.*

schwarz — *black*
   schwarzarbeiten — *to do work not reported for taxes.*
   Er bezieht Arbeitslosengeld und arbeitet auch ein bisschen schwarz.
   *He collects unemployment and also does a little unreported work on
   the side.*

   schwarzbrennen — *to distill illegally; make moonshine.*
   Sie las Burns' Gedichte über das Schwarzbrennen von Scotch vor. *She
   recited Burns' poems about the illegal distilling of scotch.*

   schwarzfahren — *to ride without having paid.*
   Man hat uns erwischt, als wir in Wien mit der Straßenbahn
   schwarzgefahren sind. *They caught us in Vienna when we rode the
   streetcar without paying.*

schwarzsehen — *to be pessimistic.*

Was die Wirtschaft betrifft, sehen die meisten Experten noch schwarz.
Most experts are still pessimistic about the economy.

die Schwebe — *state of suspension*
in der Schwebe liegen — *to be uncertain, open.*
Die Entscheidung liegt noch in der Schwebe. *The decision is still open.*

das Schwein — *pig*
Schwein haben — *to be (very) lucky.*
Das ist das erste Mal, das wir beim Lotto Schwein haben. *That's the first
time we've been lucky in the lottery.*

schwer — *heavy*
schwer fallen — *to find difficult.*
Am Golf von Biskaya fiel es der hübschen Brünette schwer, sich von
ihrem blonden Matrosen zu trennen. *The pretty brunette found it hard to
part from her blond sailor by the Bay of Biscay.*

schweres Geld kosten — *to cost a lot of money, a bundle.*
So ein Wagen muss schweres Geld gekostet haben. *A car like that must
have cost a lot of money.*

der Schwerpunkt — *center of gravity; focus.*
Der Schwerpunkt unserer heutigen Berichterstattung ist der
Regierungswechsel. *The focus of our reporting today is the change in
government.*

sich schwertun mit — *to have trouble with.*
Viele Wähler in einigen Ländern tun sich schwer mit der Idee einer
Europäischen Union. *Many voters in some countries have trouble with
the idea of a European union.*

der Schwerverbrecher — *serious offender.*
Die Polizei verfolgte die Schwerverbrecher. *The police pursued the
serious offenders.*

schwimmen — *to swim*
ins Schwimmen kommen — *to be all at sea.*

Er verhaspelte sich und kam bald ins Schwimmen. *He stumbled on his words and was soon all at sea.*

die See — *sea, ocean*
  zur See fahren — *to go to sea, be a sailor.*
  Ich bin mehrere Jahre zur See gefahren. *I was a sailor for many years.*

die Seele — soul
  die Seele baumeln lassen — *to relax, drift and dream.*
  Am Strand haben wir die Seele baumeln lassen. *We relaxed on the beach.*

das Seil — *rope*
  in den Seilen hängen — *to be on the ropes (boxing); be exhausted.*
  Tag und Nacht hab ich geastet; kein Wunder, dass ich jetzt in den Seilen hänge. *I slaved away night and day; no wonder I'm knocked out now.*

  die Seilschaft — *mountain climbers joined by ropes; coterie, clique.*
  Gegen den alten Parteichef und seine Seilschaft kommst du nicht an. *You can't buck the old party boss and his coterie.*

sehen — *to see*
  sich sehen lassen — *to be impressive.*
  Trotz des Rückgangs lässt sich die Handelsbilanz noch sehen. *Despite the decline, the balance of trade is still impressive.*

seinesgleichen — *similar to oneself*
  wie seinesgleichen behandeln — *to treat as an equal.*
  Die Königin hat mich wie ihresgleichen behandelt. *The queen treated me as an equal.*

  seinesgleichen suchen — *to be unequaled.*
  Ihre Skulpturen suchen auf der Welt ihresgleichen. *Her sculptures are unequaled anywhere.*

selig — *blessed*
  nach seiner Fasson selig werden — *to pursue happiness in one's own way.*

"Jeder soll nach seiner Fasson selig werden," sagte Friedrich der Große. *"Let everyone turn on to religion in his/her/their own way," said Frederick the Great.*

der Senkel — *shoelace; plumbline*
jmdm. auf den Senkel gehen — *to get on s.o.'s nerves.*
Du gehst mir echt auf den Senkel mit deiner Nörgelei. *Your nagging is really getting on my nerves.*

jmdn. in den Senkel stellen — *to put s.o. in his/her place; lay down the law to s.o.*
Diesen Aufmüpfigen werden wir bald in den Senkel stellen. *We'll soon put that uppity guy in his place.*

senkrecht — *vertical*
Immer schön senkrecht bleiben! *Keep your spirits up/don't let things get you down.*

das einzig Senkrechte — *the only good choice, only thing that stands up to comparison.*
In der ganzen Stadt ist dieses Restaurant das einzig Senkrechte. *This restaurant's the only good choice in the whole town.*

die Serie — *series*
serienreif — *ready for mass production.*
Dieses Modell ist noch nicht serienreif. *This model isn't ready for mass production yet.*

serienweise — *in series; in great quantities.*
Serienweise schrieb Dumas Romane. *Dumas cranked out quantities of novels.*

setzen — *to put; to set*
auf etwas setzen — *to bet on, count on.*
Wir setzen auf einen Konjunkturaufschwung. *We're counting on an economic upturn.*

eins/einen drauf setzen — *to go one better/one step further; add insult to injury.*

Seiner bisherigen Leistung will er noch eins draufsetzen. *He wants to go beyond his previous record.*

Signale/Zeichen setzen — *to send a message; indicate a trend.*
Mit dieser Äußerung wollte der Kanzler Zeichen setzen. *With that statement the chancellor wanted to indicate a trend.*

sieben — *seven*
die Siebensachen — *belongings.*
Vor Einbruch der Soldaten packten die Einwohner ihre Siebensachen zusammen und flohen. *Before the soldiers broke through, the inhabitants packed up their belongings and fled.*

sitzen — *to sit*
auf sich sitzen lassen — *to take lying down.*
Diesen Vorwurf will der Senator nicht auf sich sitzen lassen. *The senator won't take that accusation lying down.*

sitzenbleiben — *to lag behind; be left back in school.*
Auf technischem Bereich läuft unsere Firma Gefahr, sitzenzubleiben. *In technical areas our firm is in danger of lagging behind.*
In der Schule ist er oft sitzengeblieben; später ließ ihn seine Verlobte sitzen. *He often got left back in school; later his fiancée jilted him.*

sitzenlassen — *to jilt.*
Er hatte Angst, dass sie ihn sitzenlassen würde. *He was afraid that she would jilt him.*

die Socke — *sock*
sich auf die Socken machen — *to get a move on; get going.*
Mach dich auf die Socken! *Get a move on!*

spanisch — *Spanish*
Das kommt mir spanisch vor. *That seems odd to me (that's Greek to me).*
spanische Reiter — *barbed-wire barricades.*
Wir konnten nicht durch, weil die Polizei spanische Reiter aufgestellt hatte. *We couldn't get through because the police had set up barbed-wire barricades.*

der Sparren — *rafter*
  einen Sparren (zu viel/zu wenig) haben — *to be off the beam.*
  Ja, sie hat einen Sparren, aber lustig und nett ist sie doch. *Yes, she's got bats in the belfry but still, she's jolly and kind.*

der Spaß — *fun*
  an etwas Spaß haben — *to enjoy.*
  Sie hat viel Spaß an ihrem Beruf. *She enjoys her profession very much.*

  nur zum Spaß machen — *to do just for fun.*
  Er behauptet, er hätte es nur zum Spaß getan. *He alleges that he did it just for fun.*

  keinen Spaß verstehen — *to have no sense of humor.*
  Der versteht keinen Spaß. *He has no sense of humor.*

  Spaß machen — *to kid.*
  Ach, ich hab nur Spaß gemacht. *Oh, I was only kidding.*

  der Spaßverderber — *killjoy; spoilsport.*
  Sei doch kein Spaßverderber! *Don't be a spoilsport.*

der Speck — *bacon*
  abspecken — *to lose weight.*
  Ihr seid zu dick und musst abspecken. Ran an den Speck! *You're overweight and have to get the lard off. Tackle that fat!*

  leben wie die Made im Speck — *to live off the fat of the land.*
  Er wurde reich und lebt jetzt wie die Made im Speck. *He got rich and lives off the fat of the land.*

  Mit Speck fängt man Mäuse. *You need a sprat to catch a mackerel.*

  Ran an den Speck! — *Let's get going/let's tackle the goal/job. It's time for action!*

spendieren — *to treat, make a present of*
  die Spendierhosen anhaben — *to be in a generous mood.*
  Damals hatte ich oft die Spendierhosen an, aber ich wurde arbeitslos und musste sie ausziehen. *In those days I often gave treats to everybody, but I lost my job and I've had to tighten my belt.*

die Spesen — *expenses*

's war wieder 'n Flop. Außer Spesen nichts gewesen; die Firma hat zu viele Spesenrittter. *Another flop. Money spent with nothing to show for it; the firm's got too many expense account jockeys.*

auf Spesen — *on an expense account.*

Weil er auf Spesen ist, sucht er sich die besten Restaurants aus. *Because he's on an expense account, he seeks out the best restaurants.*

das Spiel — *game*

auf dem Spiel stehen — *to be at stake.*

Seine Glaubwürdigkeit steht auf dem Spiel. *His credibility is at stake.*

ein abgekartetes Spiel — *a rigged, put-up job.*

Das Ganze war nur ein abgekartetes Spiel. *The whole thing was just a put-up job.*

spielen — *to play*

die Muskeln spielen lassen — *to make a show of force.*

Die neue Regierung will in der Außenpolitik die Muskeln spielen lassen. *The new government wants to make a show of force in its foreign policy.*

spinnen — *to spin; to be daft; to plot an intrigue*

Es ist nichts so fein gesponnen, es kommt doch ans Licht der Sonnen. *Truth will out, however elaborate the intrigues that conceal it.*

etwas spinnen — *to make up, spin out of whole cloth.*

Das hast du wohl gesponnen. *You probably made that up.*

Ich hätt's getan? Ach, du spinnst, du Spinner! *I did it? You're making that up, you screwball!*

die Spitze — *point*

auf die Spitze treiben — *to carry things too far.*

Immer muss er alles auf die Spitze treiben. *He always has to carry things too far.*

die Sprechstunde — *office hours*
Außerhalb ihrer Sprechstunden kann sie Sie nicht sprechen. *She can't see you outside of her office hours.*

der Sprung — *leap; crack in crockery*
auf die Sprünge helfen — *to help get started; give hints.*
Nachdem sie ihm auf die Sprünge geholfen hatte, konnte er das Rätsel lösen. *After she helped him get started, he solved the riddle.*

den Sprung schaffen — *to succeed in making a transition.*
Er hat den Sprung zum Tonfilm nicht geschafft. *He didn't succeed in making the transition to talking pictures.*

einen Sprung in der Schüssel haben — *to be cracked; to be off one's rocker.*
Der hat einen Sprung in der Schüssel. *He's cracked.*

keine großen Sprünge machen können — *to be unable to spend much money.*
Im Augenblick können wir keine großen Sprünge machen. *At the moment we can't afford to spend much money.*

die Spucke — *spit*
die Spucke bleibt weg — *left speechless/breathless/flabbergasted.*
Mir blieb die Spucke weg, als ich sie nach 20 Jahren wieder sah. *I was flabbergasted when I saw her again after 20 years.*

stampfen — *to stamp (feet); mash (potatoes, etc.)*
etwas aus dem Boden stampfen — *to create from nothing; to put up a building, etc. rapidly.*
Die Fabrik wurde in kürzester Zeit aus dem Boden gestampft. *The factory was put up in the shortest possible time.*

die Stange — *pole*
bei der Stange bleiben — *to keep at it.*
Bleibt noch bei der Stange; wir sind bald am Ziel. *Keep at it; we'll soon reach the goal.*

die Stange halten — *to stick up for.*
Die Kollegen hielten mir die Stange. *My colleagues stuck up for me.*

der Staub — *dust*

sich aus dem Staub machen — *to clear off (out).*

Statt Rede und Antwort zu stehen, machte er sich aus dem Staub. *Instead of explaining his actions he cleared off.*

staubsaugen — *to vacuum.*

Ich habe aber gestern gestaubsaugt. *But I vacuumed yesterday.*

der Stegreif — *stirrup*

aus dem Stegreif — *extemporaneously; without a prepared text.*

Wenn der Professor aus dem Stegreif spricht, ist er interessanter. *When the professor talks without a prepared text, he's more interesting.*

stehen — *to stand; to be*

gut/schlecht um etwas stehen — *to do/go well/badly.*

In einigen Ländern steht es nicht gut um die Pressefreiheit. *In some countries freedom of the press is not doing well.*

stehen auf — *to point to.*

Die Zeichen stehen auf Streik. *The indicators point to a strike.*

stehen — *to suit.*

Kleider und Röcke stehen mir besser als Hosen. *Dresses and skirts suit me (look better on me) than pants.*

das Stehaufmännchen — *tumbler, acrobat*

Hans ist ein richtiges Stehaufmännchen. *Nothing can keep Hans down.*

steil — *steep*

eine steile Karriere machen — *to have a meteoric career.*

Trotz aller Hindernisse hat sie eine steile Karriere gemacht. *Despite all obstacles, she's had a meteoric career.*

der Stein — *stone*

bei jemandem einen Stein im Brett haben — *to be in someone's good graces.*

Es gelang ihm, beim Chef einen Stein im Brett zu haben. *He succeeded in getting into the boss's good graces.*

den Stein ins Rollen bringen — *to set things in motion.*

Ein Brief seiner Exehefrau brachte den Stein ins Rollen; jetzt wird gegen ihn ermittelt. *A letter from his ex-wife got things started; now he's being investigated.*

Stein des Anstoßes — *bone of contention.*

Seit Jahrhunderten ist diese Provinz ein Stein des Anstoßes zwischen beiden Ländern. *For centuries this province has been a bone of contention between the two countries.*

der Stern — *star*

in den Sternen stehen — *to be in the lap of the gods.*

Das Ergebnis steht noch in den Sternen. *The outcome is still in the lap of the gods.*

nach den Sternen greifen — *to reach for the moon.*

Auch mit zunehmendem Alter griff sie noch nach immer höheren Sternen. *Even in advancing years she still reached for the moon and beyond.*

die Sternstunde — *great moment, memorable experience.*

Mit diesem sehr alten Wein können Sie eine Sternstunde erleben, oder sehr enttäuscht werden. *With this very old wine you might have a memorable experience or be very disappointed.*

still — *quiet, silent*

im Stillen — *privately, secretly.*

Sie hatte sich im Stillen etwas Schöneres gehofft. *Secretly she'd hoped for something nicer.*

die Stimme — *voice*

seine Stimme abgeben — *to vote.*

Ich habe meine Stimme für die Senatorin abgegeben. *I voted for the senator.*

stimmen — *to tune an instrument; to be correct.*

Alles, was sie berichtet hat, stimmt. *Everything she reported is correct.*

die Stirn — *forehead*

die Stirn bieten — *to defy.*

Mutig bot sie dem Diktator die Stirn. *She courageously defied the dictator.*

jmdm. hinter die Stirn sehen — *to read s.o.'s mind.*

Wieso hätte ich's wissen sollen? Ich konnte ihm nicht hinter die Stirn sehen. *How am I supposed to have known? I couldn't read his mind.*

stoßen — *to push, shove*
vor den Kopf stoßen — *to insult, offend.*

Hüte dich, diesen Milliardär vor den Kopf zu stoßen. *Be careful not to offend that billionaire.*

der Strich — *line*
auf den Strich gehen — *to be a streetwalker, practice prostitution.*

Die Armut zwang sie, auf den Strich zu gehen. *Poverty compelled her to be a streetwalker.*

einen Strich unter etwas machen/ziehen — *to make a clean break.*

Jetzt versucht sie, einen Strich unter die Vergangenheit zu ziehen. *Now she's trying to make a clean break with the past.*

unterm Strich — *all things considered.*

Unterm Strich ist ihr Leben interessant und positiv zu bewerten. *All things considered, her life must be rated as interesting and positive.*

unterm Strich sein — *to be feeling under the weather, not to be up to snuff/scratch.*

Onkel Otto ist heute wieder unterm Strich. *Uncle Otto's feeling a bit under the weather again today.*

das Stück — *piece*
aus freien Stücken — *of one's own free will.*

Sie behaupteten, sie hätten ihr Grundstück in der DDR nicht aus freien Stücken verkauft. *They claimed they didn't sell their property in the GDR of their own free will.*

ein ganzes/gutes Stück — *quite a bit.*

Das Kind ist wieder ein ganzes Stück gewachsen. *The child has grown quite a bit.*

große Stücke halten auf — *to have a high opinion of.*
Ihre Lehrer halten große Stücke auf sie. *Her teachers have a high opinion of her.*

die Stunde — *hour*
zur vollen Stunde — *on the hour.*
Mehr berichten wir darüber in den Nachrichten zur vollen Stunde. *We'll have more to say about that in the news on the hour.*

der Sturm — *storm*
ein Sturm im Wasserglas — *a tempest in a teapot.*
Weil es dich nicht betrifft, tust du's als Sturm im Wasserglas ab. *Because it doesn't affect you, you dismiss it as a tempest in a teapot.*

Sturm laufen — *to be up in arms.*
Umweltschützer laufen Sturm gegen die geplante Talsperre.
Environmentalists are up in arms about the planned dam.

stürzen — *to plunge*
sich in Unkosten stürzen — *to go to great expense.*
Ja, das Haus ist schön, aber jetzt will ich mich nicht in Unkosten stürzen.
Yes, the house is beautiful, but I don't want to incur great expense now.

die Suche — *search*
sich auf die Suche machen — *to start looking for.*
Hänsel und Gretels Eltern machten sich auf die Suche nach den Kindern.
Hänsel and Gretel's parents started to look for the children.

suchen — *to look for*
zu suchen haben — *to have business; be pertinent.*
Sie haben hier nichts zu suchen. *You have no business here.*
Was haben solche komplizierten Bücher in unserem Lehrplan zu suchen?
What place is there for complicated books like that in our curriculum?

die Suppe — *soup*
jemandem die Suppe versalzen — *to put a spoke in someone's wheel, rain on someone's parade, spoil someone's plans.*

Du versuchst wieder, mir die Suppe zu versalzen. *You're trying to rain on my parade again.*

seine eigene Suppe/sein eigenes Süppchen kochen — *to pursue a private agenda.*

Bei den Verhandlungen wollte jeder nur sein eigenes Süppchen kochen. *During the negotiations everyone just wanted to pursue a private agenda.*

die Szene — *scene*

sich in Szene setzen — *to get noticed.*

Der Senator weiß, sich in Szene zu setzen und benutzt die Medien zu seinen Zwecken. *The senator knows how to get media attention and exploits it.*

Tacheles reden — *to do some straight talking*

Wann wird er endlich mit uns Tacheles reden? *When will he finally talk straight to us?*

der Tag — day

alle Tage — *every day.*

Alle Tage sieht man dergleichen nicht. *One doesn't see things like that every day.*

an den Tag legen — *to display.*

Er hat eine neue Hilfsbereitschaft an den Tag gelegt. *He displayed a new readiness to help.*

den Tag vor dem Abend loben — *to count one's chickens before they're hatched.*

Man soll den Tag nicht vor dem Abend loben. *One shouldn't count one's chickens before they're hatched.*

dieser Tage — *recently.*

Dieser Tage stand etwas darüber in der Zeitung. *There was something about it recently in the newspaper.*

in den Tag hineinleben/von Tag zu Tag leben — *to live day by day with no thought for the future*
Sie sind verliebt und wollen von Luft und Liebe in den Tag hineinleben. *They're in love and want to live day by day on love and air.*

über Tage — *above ground (mining);* **unter Tage** — *below ground.*
Jahrelang arbeitete er unter Tage aber er wurde krank und kann jetzt nur über Tage arbeiten. *For years he worked in an underground mine, but he got sick and now can only work above ground.*

unter Tags — *during the day.*
Schon unter Tags sitzt er in der Kneipe. *Even during the day he's in the bar.*

---

die Talfahrt — *descent into the valley; decline*
Durch Kostensenkungen versuchte sie, die Talfahrt der Firma aufzuhalten. *By reducing costs she tried to stop the firm's decline.*

sich auf Talfahrt befinden — *to be on a downhill course.*
Er behauptete, die Wirtschaft befinde sich auf stetiger Talfahrt. *He alleged that the economy was on a steady downhill course.*

---

das Tamtam — *tomtom; noise; ballyhoo*
Die neue Entfettungspille wird mit viel Tamtam vermarktet. *The new weight-reducing pill is being marketed with much ballyhoo.*

---

die Tapete — *wallpaper*
die Tapeten wechseln — *to have a change of scenery.*
Der Hausmann (die Hausfrau) sehnte sich danach, die Tapeten zu wechseln. *The houseman/housewife longed for a change of scenery.*

---

die Taufe — *baptism*
aus der Taufe heben — *to launch, start.*
Die Salzburger Festspiele wurden 1920 aus der Taufe gehoben. *The Salzburg Festival was started in 1920.*

---

tausend — *thousand*
Tausende und Abertausende — *thousands upon thousands.*

Tausende und Abertausende besuchen jetzt die einst abgelegene Insel.
Thousands upon thousands now visit that once remote island.

---

das Techtelmechtel — *amorous dalliance; hanky-panky*
Die so fromm geglaubte Helene wurde beim Techtelmechtel erwischt.
Helene, thought so pious, was caught in amorous dalliance.

---

der Teich — *pond*
  der große Teich — *the Atlantic Ocean.*
Oma will wieder über den großen Teich, um unsere Verwandten in
  Amerika zu besuchen. *Grandma wants to cross the Atlantic again to
  visit our relatives in America.*

---

der Teufel — *devil*
  auf Teufel komm raus — *to beat the band; like all get-out*
Er und seine ganze Familie lügen auf Teufel komm raus. *He and his
  whole family lie like all get-out.*

  den Teufel an die Wand malen — *to imagine the worst; tempt fate.*
Brauchst nicht gleich den Teufel an die Wand zu malen. *You don't have to
  imagine the worst-case scenario right away.*

  in Teufels Küche kommen — *to get into deep trouble.*
Seine beiden Söhne waren Fixer und kamen in Teufels Küche. *His two
  sons were drug addicts and got into deep trouble.*

  der Teufelskreis — *vicious circle.*
Die Ärztin will ihnen helfen, den Teufelskreis von Sucht und Kriminalität
  zu sprengen. *The doctor wants to help them to break the vicious cycle of
  addiction and criminality.*

---

ticken — *to tick*
  Bei dem tickt's nicht richtig. *That guy's off his rocker.*

  anders ticken — *to be of a different mentality.*
In Bayern ticken die Uhren anders. *Bavaria's in its own (political) time-
  zone/Bavaria marches to a different drummer.*

---

das Tier — *animal*

ein hohes/großes Tier — *a big shot.*
Sie will sich mit den großen Tieren des Betriebs zusammentreffen. *She wants to meet with the big shots in the company.*

Jedem Tierchen sein Pläsierchen. *To each his/her own/Whatever turns you on.*

tierischer Ernst — *deadly seriousness.*
Er betreibt alles mit tierischem Ernst. *He does everything with deadly seriousness.*

das Tierkreiszeichen — *sign of the zodiac.*
Welches Tierkreiszeichen bist du? *Under what sign were you born?*

---

die Tinte — *ink*

in der Tinte sitzen — *to be in a mess.*
Das ganze Land saß in der Tinte. *The whole country was in a mess.*

Tinte gesoffen haben — *to be out of one's mind.*
Du musst wohl Tinte gesoffen haben, wenn du das wieder versuchen willst. *You must be out of your mind if you want to try that again.*

---

der Tisch — *table*

am grünen Tisch (vom grünen Tisch aus) — *entirely theoretical.*
Das, was sie am grünen Tisch geplant und beschlossen haben, ist völlig wirklichkeitsfremd. *What they planned and decided is entirely theoretical and totally unrealistic.*

über den Tisch ziehen — *to outmaneuver, cheat.*
Lassen Sie sich von ihm und seinem unehrlichen Anwalt nicht über den Tisch ziehen. *Don't let him and his unethical lawyer outmaneuver you.*

vom Tisch sein — *to be settled; to no longer be an issue.*
Die meisten Streitfragen sind jetzt vom Tisch. *Most of the issues have now been settled.*

Toi, toi, toi — *good luck*
Toi, toi, toi für dein Examen! *Good luck in your exam!*

unberufen, toi, toi, toi — *knock on wood.*

Viele meiner Kumpel in der Fabrik sind entlassen; mich haben sie noch nicht gefeuert — unberufen, toi, toi, toi. *Many of my buddies in the factory were let go; they haven't fired me yet, knock on wood.*

der Ton — *tone*

Der Ton macht die Musik. *It's not what you say, but how you say it.*

den Ton angeben — *say what goes.*

Warum soll immer nur der den Ton angeben? *Why should it always be just he who says what goes?*

Jede Bohn' hat ihren Ton. *Each bean has its own tone.*

Der Kellner riet uns davon ab, Bohnen zu essen, denn jede Bohn' hat ihren Ton. *The waiter recommended we not eat beans, for each bean has its own tone.*

große/dicke Töne reden/spucken — *to talk big.*

Du spuckst wieder große Töne, aber wann folgen Taten den Tönen? *You're talking big again, but will you when we see action?*

der Topf — *pot*

alles in einen Topf werfen — *to lump everything together.*

So etwas Kompliziertes kannst du doch nicht in einen Topf werfen. *You really can't lump together such complicated things.*

Leere Töpfe klappern und leere Köpfe plappern am meisten. *Empty pots and empty heads make the most noise/Among walnuts only the empty one speaks.*

Hurrapatrioten schreien am lautesten—ohne zu wissen warum, meinte Mark Twain. Ja, leere Töpfe klappern und leere Köpfe plappern am meisten. *Super-patriots yell the loudest—without knowing why, declared Mark Twain. Yes, empty pots and empty heads make the most noise.*

der Topfgucker — *a busybody*

Unser Nachbar ist nett, aber leider ein alter Topfgucker. *Our neighbor is nice but, unfortunately, a busybody.*

Jeder Topf findet seinen Deckel. *No matter how ugly you are there's somebody for you/Every Jack has his Jill/There's a cover to fit every pot.*

das Tor — *gate*

die Torschlusspanik — *last minute panic; fear of being left out.*
Ihn erwischte Torschlusspanik, sonst hätte er mich nicht geheiratet. *He wouldn't have married me if he hadn't been afraid of being left on the shelf.*

kurz vor Torschluss — *at the last minute, 11th hour.*
Kurz vor Torschluss besann er sich anders. *He had a change of heart at the last minute.*

tot — *dead*

sich totlachen — *to die laughing.*
Wir haben uns über ihre Witze fast totgelacht. *We almost died laughing at her jokes.*

totschlagen — *to beat to death.*
Du kannst mich totschlagen, aber ich kann mich nicht mehr daran erinnern. *For the life of me I can't remember it any more.*

die Tour — *tour*

auf vollen Touren laufen — *to operate at full capacity/speed/volume.*
Die Klimaanlage läuft schon auf vollen Touren. *The air conditioner is already operating at full capacity.*

in einer Tour — *all the time.*
Er hatte große Lust, ihr in einer Tour noch mehr Schmuckstücke und Pelzmäntel zu schenken. *He longed to give her even more jewels and fur coats all the time.*

der Trab — *trot*

auf Trab — *on the go.*
Oma ist immer auf Trab. *Granny's always on the go.*

treiben — *to drive*

Kurzweil treiben — *to have fun.*
Er will immer nur Kurzweil treiben, statt an den Ernst des Lebens zu denken. Vielleicht hat er recht. *All he wants is to have fun, instead of thinking of the serious side of life. Maybe he's right.*

trinken — *to drink*

Brüderschaft trinken — *to pledge close friendship (by intertwining arms, drinking, and using the* du *form).*

Sie betranken sich und tranken Brüderschaft. *They got drunk and pledged close friendship.*

einen trinken gehen — *to go for a drink (or two).*

Nach der Arbeit gingen sie einen trinken. *After work they went for a drink.*

trinkfest — *able to hold one's liquor.*

Sie will nur trinkfeste Männer um sich. *She wants only men who are able to hold their liquor around her.*

---

trocken — *dry*

auf dem Trockenen sein/sitzen — *to be bankrupt, economically stranded/high and dry; to be without anything to drink.*

Der Vorstand hat das Unternehmen heruntergewirtschaftet und es ist jetzt auf dem Trockenen. *The executive board ran the company into the ground and now it's in a tight spot.*

Hier sitzen wir, arbeitslos und auf dem Trockenen; schenk uns doch endlich ein! *We're sitting here unemployed and without a drink; set us up, will you!*

sein Schäfchen ins Trockene bringen — *to look out for one's own interests.*

Mit seiner großzügigen Abfindung wusste der alte Firmenchef sein Schäfchen ins Trockene zu bringen; die neue Chefin versucht das Unternehmen wieder flottzubekommen. *With his golden parachute the old CEO looked out for number one; the new boss is trying to get the company on its feet again*

---

der Tropf — *intravenous feeding apparatus, drip feeder*

am Tropf hängen — *to be extremely weak.*

Die Wirtschaft der ehemaligen Kolonie hängt noch am Tropf. *The former colony's economy is still entirely dependent on outside aid.*

---

der Tropfen — *drop*

    ein Tropfen auf den heißen Stein — *a drop in the bucket.*

    Danke fürs Geld; es ist aber nur ein Tropfen auf den heißen Stein. Ich brauche noch viel mehr. *Thanks for the money, but it's just a drop in the bucket. I need lots more.*

    Steter Tropfen höhlt den Stein. *Constant dripping erodes the stone (sustained effort will eventually pay off).*

der Trost — *consolation, comfort*

    nicht bei Trost sein — *not to be all there.*

    Im Krieg hat er viel Schweres erlitten und ist nicht mehr ganz bei Trost. *He suffered much in the war and isn't quite all there any more.*

    Trost spenden — *to comfort.*

    Sie hat den Armen Trost gespendet. *She comforted the poor.*

das Trostpflaster — *consolation prize*

    Als Trostpflaster bekam sie einen Plüschbären. *As a consolation prize she got a teddy bear.*

trüb — *dreary*

    im Trüben fischen — *to fish in troubled waters.*

    Das liegt mir nicht, im Trüben zu fischen, um Profit zu schlagen. *Fishing in troubled waters to make a profit doesn't appeal to me.*

das Tuch — *cloth; towel*

    das Handtuch werfen — *to throw in the towel.*

    Endlich musste sie das Handtuch werfen. *She finally had to throw in the towel.*

    in trockene Tücher bringen — *to accomplish, wrap up.*

    Sie will ihre Doktorarbeit in trockene Tücher bringen, bevor sie an ihrem Roman weiterschreibt. *She wants to complete her doctoral dissertation before continuing her novel.*

die Tür — *door*

    mit der Tür ins Haus fallen — *to come right out and say what one wants.*

Ich muss leider gleich mit der Tür ins Haus fallen, denn ich brauche das Geld sofort. *Unfortunately, I've got to come right out and say so, for I need the money right away.*

Tür und Tor öffnen — *to open wide the door.*

In den zwanziger Jahren öffnete die Prohibition der Kriminalität Tür und Tor. *In the twenties Prohibition opened the door wide for criminal behavior.*

vor die Tür setzen — *to throw out.*

Der Wirt musste den Betrunkenen vor die Tür setzen. *The tavern owner had to throw the drunk out.*

vor seiner eigenen Tür kehren — *to set one's own house in order.*

Er sollte zuerst vor seiner eigenen Tür kehren, statt andere zu beschuldigen. *He should set his own house in order before accusing others.*

übel — *bad*

einem übel werden — *to feel sick.*

Es wurde mir übel. *I felt sick.*

zu allem Übel — *on top of everything else.*

Zu allem Übel sprang der Wagen nicht an. *On top of everything else, the car didn't start.*

über — *over*

über sein — *to be superior.*

Liesl ist mir in Mathe über. *Liesl is superior to me in math.*

über und über — *completely.*

Der U-Bahnhof war über und über mit Graffiti besprüht. *The subway station was completely sprayed with graffiti.*

zu allem Überfluss — *on top of it all.*

Zu allem Überfluss fing es zu schneien an. *On top of it all, it began to snow.*

übertrumpfen — *to trump; to surpass, best*
In allem übertrumpfte ihn seine Schwester. *His sister bested him in everything.*

übrig — *remaining*
   ein Übriges tun — *to contribute.*
   Das unsympatische Personal tat noch ein Übriges, uns den Aufenthalt zu verleiden. *The unpleasant staff contributed to spoiling our stay.*

   nichts übrig haben für — *not to care for.*
   Für moderne Malerei hat er nichts übrig. *He doesn't care for modern painting.*

   übrigbleiben — *to be left (over),*
   Es blieb uns nichts anderes übrig als auszuziehen. *We had no other choice but to move out.*

   übrigens — *by the way, incidentally.*
   Übrigens, gestern hab ich deine Freundin gesehen. *By the way, I saw your friend yesterday.*

das Ufer — *shore*
   ins Uferlose gehen — *to have no end; to know no boundaries*
   Sie schreibt noch an ihrem Roman, der ins Uferlose geht. *She's still working on her novel that never ends.*

umbringen — *to kill*
   nicht umzubringen sein — *to be indestructible.*
   Columbos alter Regenmantel ist nicht umzubringen. *Columbo's old raincoat is indestructible.*

der Umgang — *contact; dealings*
   die Umgangssprache — *colloquial speech.*
   Die Lehrerin erklärte den Unterschied zwischen der gehobenen und der Umgangssprache. *The teacher explained the distinction between elevated and colloquial speech.*

umgehen — *to go round; to deal/work with*
Sie versteht es, mit Computern umzugehen. *She knows how to work with computers.*

mit etwas nicht umgehen können — *to be unable to handle something.*
Ihr Vater kann nicht mit Geld umgehen. *Her father doesn't know how to handle money.*

ummünzen — *to convert into something else*
eine Niederlage in einen Sieg ummünzen — *to turn defeat into victory.*
Sie wusste, ihre Niederlagen in Siege umzumünzen. *She knew how to turn her defeats into victories.*

umsonst — *free, gratis*
Umsonst ist nur der Tod, und der kostet das Leben. *Everything comes with a price; there's no free lunch.*

nicht umsonst — *not for nothing, for good reason.*
Nicht umsonst hab ich euch vor ihm gewarnt. *I had good reason to warn you about him.*

der Umstand — *circumstance*
den Umständen entsprechend — *as can be expected in the circumstances.*
Es geht dem Patienten den Umständen entsprechend gut. *The patient is doing as well as can be expected in the circumstances.*

keine Umstände machen — *not to make a fuss.*
Valentin wusste, dass er sterben musste, und machte keine Umstände. *Valentin knew he had to die and didn't make a fuss.*

unter Umständen — *perhaps; possibly.*
Unter Umständen wird sich das machen lassen. *Perhaps that can be done.*

ungefähr — *approximate*
nicht von ungefähr sein — *not be unjustified.*
Sein schlechter Ruf ist nicht von ungefähr. *His bad reputation is not unjustified.*

ungefähr können — *to know more or less how to do.*
Wenn man's kann ungefähr, ist's nicht schwer. *If you more or less know how to do it, it isn't difficult.*

wie von ungefähr — *as if by chance,*
Er kam ihr wie von ungefähr entgegen. *He came toward her as if by chance.*

der Unrat — *garbage*
Unrat wittern — *to smell a rat.*
Der Polizist witterte sofort Unrat. *The policeman smelled a rat right away.*

die Urne — *urn*
zur Urne gehen — *to vote.*
Nicht alle Wahlberechtigten gingen zur Urne. *Not all those eligible to vote did so.*

der Urnengang — *way to the polls; election.*
Nächstes Jahre finden viele Urnengänge statt. *Next year many elections will take place.*

der Urknall — *the big bang*
Die Wissenschaftler sprachen vom Urknall. *The scientists talked of the big bang.*

die Urzeit — *primeval times*
seit Urzeiten — *since time immemorial.*
Der Bauer behauptete, die Wiese hätte seit Urzeiten seiner Familie angehört. *The farmer maintained that the meadow had belonged to his family since time immemorial.*

die Verachtung — *contempt*
mit Verachtung strafen — *to treat with contempt.*
Die Malerin konnte seine Meinung nur mit Verachtung strafen. *The painter could treat his opinion only with contempt.*

verboten — *forbidden*
verboten aussehen — *to look weird.*
Als Fledermaus verkleidet, sah er verboten aus. *He looked weird dressed as a bat.*

der Verdacht — *suspicion*
auf Verdacht — *just in case.*
Auf Verdacht hab ich große Mengen gekauft. *Just in case, I bought large amounts.*

verhexen — *to bewitch*
wie verhext — *jinxed.*
Alles, was mit der Feier in Hornberg zu tun hatte, war wie verhext. *Everything that had to do with the celebration in Hornberg seemed jinxed.*

die Verlegenheit — *embarrassment*
in Verlegenheit bringen — *to embarrass.*
Im Restaurant brachte das Kind die Eltern in Verlegenheit. *In the restaurant the child embarrassed his parents.*

die Vernunft — *reason*
Vernunft annehmen — *to be reasonable; come to one's senses.*
Du kannst unmöglich diesen Kerl heiraten — nimm doch Vernunft an! *It's impossible for you to marry that fellow. Come to your senses!*

zur Vernunft bringen — *to make someone listen to reason.*
Sie versuchten vergebens, die Fanatiker zur Vernunft zu bringen. *They tried in vain to make the fanatics listen to reason.*

zur Vernunft kommen — *to see reason; to come to one's senses.*
Es wird Generationen dauern, bevor sie zur Vernunft kommen. *It will take generations before they see reason.*

das Vertrauen — *trust, confidence*
ins Vertrauen ziehen — *to take into one's confidence.*
Erst als es zu spät war, zogen sie uns ins Vertrauen. *Only when it was too late did they take us into their confidence.*

verwechseln — *to confuse*
  zum Verwechseln ähnlich sehen — *to be the spitting image of.*
  Er sieht seinem Vater zum Verwechseln ähnlich. *He is the spitting image of his father.*

das Vitamin — *vitamin*
  durch Vitamin B (Beziehungen) kriegen — *to get through connections.*
  Ohne Vitamin B hätte er es nicht gekriegt. *Without connections he never would have gotten it.*

der Vogel —*bird*
  einen Vogel haben — *to have bats in one's belfry, be nuts.*
  Er hat einen Vogel, ist aber sehr liebenswürdig. *He's nuts but very nice.*

  das Vögelchen — *little bird.*
  Woher ich's weiß? Das hat mir ein Vögelchen gesungen. *How do I know? A little bird told me.*

voll — *full*
  voll und ganz — *totally, 100 percent.*
  Wir stehen voll und ganz auf deiner Seite. *We're 100 percent behind you.*

  voll — *plastered.*
  Gib ihm nichts mehr; er ist schon voll. *Don't give him any more (to drink); he's already plastered.*

von — *of; from*
  ein von und zu sein — *to be an aristocrat, have a very aristocratic name.*
  Er ist ein richtiger von und zu, ist aber bettelarm. *He's a genuine aristocrat, but poor as a church mouse.*

  mit einer/einem von verheiratet sein — *to be married to an aristocrat.*
  Sie glaubte, mit einem von verheiratet zu sein, aber alles an ihm war Schwindel. *She thought she was married to an aristocrat, but everything about him was fraudulent.*

  von vornherein — *from the (very) beginning.*
  Von vornherein hat er unehrlich gehandelt. *His behavior was unethical from the very beginning.*

von wegen — *By no means/Not at all/You must be joking/No way!*
Die Böttcherei ein veraltetes Handwerk? Von wegen! Holzfässer werden
noch stark gefragt. *A cooper's trade old-fashioned? Not at all! Wooden
barrels are still in great demand.*

vor — *in front of*
vor allem — *above all.*
Du musst vor allem danach streben, ein guter Mensch zu sein. *Above all,
you must strive to be a good human being.*

im Voraus — *in advance.*
Wir hatten leider alles im Voraus bezahlt. *Unfortunately, we had paid for
everything in advance.*

vorbei — *past, gone.*
Dicht vorbei ist auch daneben. *Close, but no cigar. (A miss is as good as
a mile.)*

vorbestraft — *to have previous convictions, be an ex-con.*
Obwohl er vorbestraft ist, wird man ihn einstellen. *Although he's an ex-
con, they're going to hire him.*

der Vordermann — *person in front*
auf Vordermann bringen — *to get/keep in good order.*
Sie weiß, Garten und Haushalt auf Vordermann zu bringen. *She knows
how to keep the garden and the house in good order.*

der Vorsatz — *intention; resolution*
Der Weg zur Hölle ist mit guten Vorsätzen gepflastert. *The road to hell
is paved with good intentions.*

Vorsätze fassen — *to make resolutions.*
Am Silvesterabend fasste er wieder große Vorsätze. *On New Year's Eve he
made many ambitious resolutions again.*

die Vorsicht — *caution*
mit Vorsicht zu genießen sein — *to take with caution; to be wary of.*
Alles, was er behauptet, ist mit Vorsicht zu genießen. *You must be wary
of everything he says.*

die Vorsorge — *precaution*
Vorsorge treffen — *to take precautions.*
Die Behörden behaupteten, Vorsorge gegen Terroristen getroffen zu
haben. *The authorities claimed to have taken precautions against
terrorists.*

der Vorwurf — *reproach*
zum Vorwurf machen — *to reproach; to hold against.*
Man soll ihm sein bisheriges Verhalten nicht zum Vorwurf machen. *One
shouldn't hold his former behavior against him.*

die Waage — *scale*
das Zünglein an der Waage sein — *to tip the scales; to hold the balance
of power.*
Im neuen Parlament könnte diese kleine Splitterpartei das Zünglein an der
Waage sein. *In the new parliament this little splinter party could hold
the balance of power.*

sich die Waage halten — *to be equally divided.*
In dem Wahlreformstreit halten sich Befürworter und Gegner die Waage.
*In the electoral reform dispute, supporters and opponents are equally
divided.*

wachsen — *to grow*
etwas gewachsen sein — *to be able to handle.*
Diese Straße ist dem immer stärkeren Verkehr nicht gewachsen. *This road
can't handle the ever increasing traffic.*

über den Kopf wachsen — *to become too much for.*
Die Arbeit wuchs ihm über den Kopf. *The job became too much
for him.*

die Waffel — *waffle*

einen an der Waffel haben — *to be a bit crazy/cracked.*

Die ganze Mannschaft hat einen an der Waffel. *The whole team is a bit cracked.*

---

wagen — *to dare*

Wer nicht wagt, der nicht gewinnt. (Frisch gewagt ist halb gewonnen.) *Nothing ventured, nothing gained.*

---

wahr — *true*

nicht wahr — *isn't that so.*

Ihr seid müde, nicht wahr? *You're tired, aren't you?*

Du hast es für mich getan, nicht wahr? *You did it for me, didn't you?*

Er hat es gründlich überprüft, nicht wahr? *He's checked it thoroughly, hasn't he?*

---

der Wald — *forest*

Wie man in den Wald hineinruft, so schallt es heraus. *As you sow, so shall you reap. (Others will treat you as you treat them.)*

den Wald vor lauter Bäumen nicht sehen — *to not see the forest for the trees.*

Er warf mir vor, den Wald vor lauter Bäumen nicht zu sehen. *He accused me of not seeing the forest for the trees.*

einen vom Wald erzählen — *to tell a fib.*

Erzähl mir nicht wieder einen vom Wald. *Don't tell me another fib.*

---

die Wand — *wall*

dass die Wände wackeln — *so as to raise the roof.*

Die Mannschaft feierte, dass die Wände wackelten. *The team was celebrating so as to raise the roof.*

gegen eine Wand reden — *to talk to a wall.*

Weitere Gespräche sind zwecklos — mit ihm reden heißt gegen eine Wand reden. *Further conversations serve no purpose. Talking to him is like talking to a wall.*

---

warm — *warm*
warm ums Herz werden — *to be touched.*
Mir wurde warm ums Herz, als ich ihre tröstenden Worte las. *I was touched when I read her comforting words.*

die Warte — *watchtower; observatory*
von höherer Warte aus — *from a loftier perspective.*
Seit seiner Reise nach Tibet glaubt er, alles von höherer Warte aus zu sehen. *Ever since his trip to Tibet, he thinks he sees everything from a loftier perspective.*

warten — *to wait; to service*
warten auf — *to wait for.*
Ich habe lange auf dich gewartet. *I waited for you for a long time.*

warten bis man schwarz wird — *to wait till one is blue in the face.*
Ihr könnt warten, bis ihr schwarz werdet — das tu ich nie. *You can wait till you're blue in the face. I'll never do that.*

die Wartung — *service.*

wartungsfreundlich — *easy to service; requiring little service.*
Dies ist ein wartungsfreundliches Gerät. *This is an easy-to-service appliance.*

was — *what*
Was Sie nicht sagen! *You don't say!*
Was man nicht weiß, macht man nicht heiß. *Ignorance is bliss. No news is good news.*

die Wäsche — *laundry*
schmutzige Wäsche waschen — *to wash one's dirty linen.*
Einige Kinder von Filmstars schrieben Bücher, in denen schmutzige Wäsche gewaschen wird. *Some children of movie stars wrote books in which dirty linen is washed in public.*

dumm aus der Wäsche gucken — *to look dumbfounded.*
Nachdem sie das hörte, guckte sie dumm aus der Wäsche. *After she heard that, she looked dumbfounded.*

waschecht — *dyed-in-the-wool.*
Der Verkäufer war ein waschechter Lügner. *The salesperson was a dyed-in-the-wool liar.*

waschen — *to wash*
wasch mir den Pelz, aber mach mich nicht nass. — *to want benefits without any drawbacks/expense/work.*
Oma meint, heute handeln zu viele nach dem Spruch: wasch mir den Pelz, aber mach mich nicht nass. *Grandma thinks that too many behave according to the saying, "I'd like the job done, but I don't want to get my hands dirty."*

das Wasser — *water*
einem das Wasser reichen — *to hold a candle to.*
Trotz Fusionen kann keine andere Börse Wall Street das Wasser reichen. *Despite mergers, no other stock exchange can hold a candle to Wall Street.*

ins Wasser fallen — *to fall through.*
Unsere Urlaubspläne sind ins Wasser gefallen. *Our vacation plans have fallen through.*

jemandem das Wasser abgraben — *to cut the ground from someone's feet.*
Durch die neue Technik wurde uns das Wasser abgegraben. *We were left high and dry/cut off at the pass because of the new technology.*

mit allen Wassern gewaschen sein — *to know all the tricks.*
Ihre Anwältin ist mit allen Wassern gewaschen. *Her lawyer knows all the tricks.*

Wasser auf die Mühle — *grist for the mill.*
Der letzte Skandal ist Wasser auf die Mühle der Opposition. *The latest scandal is grist for the mill of the opposition.*

der Wecker — *alarm clock*
auf den Wecker fallen/gehen — *to get on someone's nerves.*
Ich vermeide ihn, weil er mir auf den Wecker geht. *I avoid him because he gets on my nerves.*

weg — *away; gone*

in einem weg — *constantly.*

Beim Essen klingelte das Telefon in einem weg. *The telephone rang constantly while we were eating.*

über etwas weg sein — *to have gotten over something.*

Ihr Kind starb letztes Jahr und sie sind noch nicht darüber weg. *Their child died last year, and they haven't gotten over it yet.*

weg sein — *to be carried away.*

Lola tanzte, und alle Männer waren weg. *Lola danced, and all the men were carried away.*

---

der Weg — *way, path*

Hier trennen sich unsere Wege. *This is where we part company.*

an etwas geht kein Weg vorbei — *to be unavoidable.*

An den Haushaltskürzungen geht kein Weg vorbei. *There's no getting around having to make budget cuts.*

auf den Weg bringen — *to get started, initiate.*

Ein neues Drogenbekämpfungsgesetz wurde auf den Weg gebracht. *New anti-drug legislation was introduced.*

aus dem Weg räumen — *to get out of the way.*

Jetzt sind alle Hindernisse aus dem Weg geräumt. *All obstacles are now out of the way.*

den Weg des geringsten Widerstandes gehen — *to take the line of least resistance.*

Er ging den Weg es geringsten Widerstandes, und behauptete, er sei oft der beste Weg. *He took the line of least resistance and said it was often the best line to take.*

etwas in die Wege leiten — *to start s.t. on its way through channels.*

Ihren Antrag werden wir in die Wege leiten. *We'll start processing your request.*

sich auf den Weg machen — *to set out.*

Erst spät in der Nacht machten wir uns auf den Weg. *It wasn't till late at night that we set out.*

sich selbst im Weg stehen — *to be one's own worst enemy.*
Wenn sie sich selbst nicht im Weg stünde, könnte sie mehr erreichen.
If she weren't her own worst enemy, she could achieve more.

wegdenken — *to imagine as not there*
nicht wegzudenken sein — *to be inconceivable without.*
Sie ist aus der jüngsten Geschichte ihres Landes nicht wegzudenken.
The recent history of her country is inconceivable without her.

wegsehen — *to look away*
vom Wegsehen kennen — *to want nothing to do with.*
Seit er mich betrogen und belogen hat, kenn ich ihn nur vom Wegsehen.
Ever since he cheated and lied to me, I want nothing to do with him.

das Weh — *woe*
das Fernweh — *longing for far-off places, wanderlust.*

das Heimweh — *nostalgia for one's home(land), homesickness.*
In der Heimat hab ich Fernweh; in der Ferne hab ich Heimweh. *At home
I yearn for far-off places; when abroad I'm homesick.*

wehtun — *to hurt*
Wo tut's denn weh? *What's the problem?*

die Weiche — *switch*
die Weichen stellen — *to set a course.*
Durch Namenwechsel und ein neues Programm will die Partei die
Weichen für die Zukunft stellen. *By changing its name and with a new
program the party wants to set a course for the future.*

der Weihnachtsmann — *Santa Claus, Father Christmas*
noch an den Weihnachtsmann glauben — *to still believe in Santa
Claus; be very naïve.*
Virginia glaubt noch an den Weihnachtsmann, und den Märchenprinzen
auch. *Virginia still believes in Santa Claus, and in Prince Charming
too.*

weinen — *to cry*

zum Weinen bringen — *to make cry.*
Der bloße Anblick der Trümmer brachte mich zum Weinen. *The mere sight of the ruins made me weep.*

weit — *far*

weit entfernt sein — *to be a long way from.*
Von einem Abkommen sind wir noch weit entfernt. *We're still a long way from an agreement.*

bis auf weiteres — *for the present; until further notice.*
Bis auf weiteres können Sie hier bleiben. *For the present you can stay here.*

die Welle — *wave*

die weiche Welle — *the soft approach/line.*
Zuerst versuchte er's mit der weichen Welle. *At first he took a soft line.*

hohe Wellen schlagen — *to cause a commotion, make waves.*
Die Enthüllungen der Journalistin schlugen hohe Wellen. *The journalist's revelations made waves.*

die Welt — *world*

Davon geht die Welt nicht unter. *That's not the end of the world.*

alle Welt — *everyone.*
Das weiß schon alle Welt. *Everybody knows that already.*

aus der Welt schaffen — *to get rid of, put an end to.*
Der Senator verlangte eine Ermittlung, um die Gerüchte aus der Welt zu schaffen. *The senator demanded an investigation to put an end to the rumors.*

bis ans Ende der Welt — *to the ends of the earth.*
Er reist oft bis ans Ende der Welt, um seinen Gral zu suchen. *He often travels to the ends of the earth looking for his Grail.*

die große Welt — *high society.*
Er verließ die große Welt und wohnt jetzt im Himalaja. *He left high society and lives in the Himalayas now.*
Die Welt ist ein Dorf. *It's a small world.*

Dich hier im Himalaja zu sehen — *ach die Welt ist wahrhaftig ein Dorf!*
To see you here in the Himalayas — it sure is a small world!

heile Welt — *ideal, picture-pefect, Norman Rockwell world.*
Wir schauten uns Omas Photoalbum an—das war noch eine heile Welt!
We looked at grandma's photo album—that was a saner age!

die Weltanschauung — *world view; philosophy of life.*
Nietzsches Weltanschauung ist noch viel umstritten. *Nietzsche's*
philosophy of life is still very controversial.

---

der Wermut — *wormwood; vermouth*
   der Wermutstropfen (im Becher der Freude) — *the drop of bitterness*
   (in the cup of joy).
   Bei der Olympiade gewann sie Gold; einziger Wermutstropfen, sie hat
   sich dabei das Fußgelenk leicht verstaucht. *She won gold at the*
   Olympics; the only little problem was a sprained ankle.

---

der Wert — *value*
   Wert auf etwas legen — *to be a great believer in.*
   Mutter legte großen Wert auf eine gesunde Ernährung. *Mother was a*
   great believer in a healthy diet.

---

die Westentasche — *vest pocket*
   wie seine Westentasche kennen — *to know inside out.*
   Er kennt Wien wie seine Westentasche. *He knows Vienna inside out.*

   im Westentaschenformat — *pocket-sized; tin-pot.*
   Sie kaufte einen Rechner im Westentaschenformat. *She bought a pocket-*
   sized calculator.
   Der General, der über die kleine Insel herrscht, ist ein Diktator im
   Westentaschenformat. *The general who rules the little island is a tin-pot*
   dictator.

---

die Wette — *bet, wager*
   etwas um die Wette tun — *to compete; try to outdo.*
   In Mozarts *Der Schauspieldirektor* singen die Sopranistinnen um die Wette.
   In Mozart's "The Impresario" the sopranos try to outsing each other.

---

der Wettergott — *god of the Weather; the weather*
Wir hoffen, dass der Wettergott uns gnädig sein wird. *We hope the weather will be kind to us (cooperate).*

wichtig — *important*
  sich wichtig machen/tun — *to behave pompously.*
Er machte sich wichtig und gab seinen Senf dazu. *He behaved pompously and put an oar in.*

wie — *how; as*
  Wie du mir, so ich dir. *Tit for tat. I'll pay you back in kind.*

die Wiege — *cradle*
  in die Wiege legen — *to bestow at birth.*
Die Muse hat ihm keine dichterischen Gaben in die Wiege gelegt, trotzdem hält er sich für einen großen Dichter. *The Muse didn't bestow any poetic gifts on him at birth, nevertheless he thinks he's a great poet.*

der Wind — *wind*
  Wer Wind sät, wird Sturm ernten. *Sow the wind, and reap the whirlwind.*

  im Ab-/Aufwind sein — *to be (on the way) down/up.*
Im gestrigen Kurs stand der Dollar im Auf- die Euro im Abwind. *At yesterday's rates the dollar was up, the euro down.*

  in den Wind schlagen — *to disregard.*
Unsere Warnungen hat er in den Wind geschlagen. *He disregarded our warnings.*

  in den Wind schreiben — *to give up as lost.*
Er denkt daran, seine Karriere als Rechtsanwalt in den Wind zu schreiben, weil er dreimal beim Examen durchgefallen ist. *He's thinking of giving up a career as a lawyer, because he failed the (bar) exam three times.*

  Wind machen — *to brag.*
Das stimmt nicht; er hat nur Wind gemacht. *That's not true; he was just bragging.*

  der Gegenwind — *headwind; opposition.*

der Rückenwind — *tail wind; support.*
Rückenwind haben wir von der Regierung nicht erwartet, aber mit Gegenwind haben wir nicht gerechnet. *We didn't expect the government's support, but we didn't count on their opposition.*

das Windei — *dud, non-starter, wind egg.*
Der vermeintlich geniale Plan stellte sich als Windei heraus. *The supposedly brilliant plan turned out to be a dud.*

der Wink — *sign; hint*
ein Wink mit dem Zaunpfahl — *a broad hint.*
Alle verstanden sofort den Wink mit dem Zaunpfahl. *Everyone immediately understood the broad hint.*

der Winterschlaf — *hibernation*
Winterschlaf halten — *to hibernate.*
Diese Tiere halten jetzt ihren Winterschlaf. *These animals are now hibernating.*

wissen — *to know*
Von ihm will ich nichts mehr wissen. *I don't want anything more to do with him.*

weder ein noch aus wissen — *not to thave the remotest idea of what to do.*
In seiner Verzweiflung wußte er weder ein noch aus. *In his despair he didn't have the remotest idea of what to do.*

die Woge — *wave; surge*
die Wogen glätten — *to calm things down.*
Wenn sich die Wogen wieder geglättet haben, fangen wir wieder an. *When things have calmed down, we'll start again.*

der Wolf — *wolf; meat grinder*
wie durch den Wolf gedreht — *thoroughly exhausted.*
Während der Weinlese war ich jede Nacht wie durch den Wolf gedreht. *During the grapepicking season (vintage), I was thoroughly exhausted every night.*

die Wolke — *cloud*
aus allen Wolken fallen — *to be dumbfounded.*
Sie fiel aus allen Wolken, als sie erfuhr, dass er in Honolulu eine Frau
hatte. *She was dumbfounded when she found out that he already had a
wife in Honolulu.*

die Wolkenfelder — *cloud banks*
Wolkenfelder schieben — *to drift and dream, deal in abstractions.*
Statt Wolkenfelder zu schieben, hilf mir den Schnee schaufeln. *Instead of
drifting and dreaming, help me shovel the snow.*

das Wolkenkuckucksheim — *cloud-cuckoo-land, dream world.*
Mein verträumter Bruder wohnt in einem Wolkenkratzer und lebt im
Wolkenkukucksheim. *My absent-minded brother resides in a skyscraper
and lives in cloud-cuckoo-land.*

die Wolle — *wool*
sich in die Wolle geraten — *to get into a squabble.*
Die Verbündeten gerieten sich in die Wolle. *The allies got into a squabble.*

wollen — *to want; claim*
Sie will das Loch Ness-Ungeheur oft gesehen haben. *She claims to have
seen the Loch Ness monster often.*

das Wort — *word*
zu Wort kommen lassen — *to allow to speak.*
Die Parteiführer ließen die neue Abgeordnete selten zu Wort kommen.
The party leaders rarely allowed the new congresswoman to speak.

wund — *sore*
sich die Hände wund arbeiten — *to work one's fingers to the bone.*
Die Chefin ist ein richtiges Arbeitstier und arbeitet sich die Hände wund.
The boss is a real workaholic and works her fingers to the bone.

sich wund laufen — *to walk until one's feet are sore; walk one's feet off.*
Auf der Suche nach Arbeit lief sie sich einst wund. *Once she walked her
feet off looking for work.*

der Wurf — *throw*
  einen großen/glücklichen Wurf tun — *to score a great success.*
Mit der Rolle tat sie einen glücklichen Wurf. *She scored a great success with that role.*

der Würfel — *cube; dice; die*
  die Würfel sind gefallen — *the die is cast.*
Jetzt hast du dich anders besonnen aber es ist zu spät; die Würfel sind gefallen. *You've changed your mind now but it's too late—the die is cast.*

der Wurm — *worm*
  die Würmer aus der Nase ziehen — *to worm out; to get to spill the beans.*
Durch List gelang es der Polizei, ihm die Würmer aus der Nase zu ziehen. *Through cunning the police succeeded in getting him to spill the beans.*

die Wurst — *sausage*
Alles hat ein Ende, nur die Wurst hat zwei. *Everything must come to an end.*

um die Wurst gehen — *to be down to the nitty-gritty.*
Das ist deine letzte Chance — es geht jetzt um die Wurst. *This is your last chance. Things are down to the nitty-gritty now.*

Wurst sein — *to be all the same.*
Er kann machen, was er will — es ist mir Wurst. *He can do what he wants. It's all the same to me.*

wursteln — *to putter about; muddle through.*
Ja, es geht alles schlecht, aber wir wollen doch weiter wursteln. *Yes, everything is going badly, but we'll continue to muddle through.*

X
  ein X für ein U vormachen — *to pull a fast one.*
Die Rechnung ist unverschämt; man will uns ein X für ein U vormachen. *The bill is outrageous; they're trying to pull a fast one on us.*

X-Beine — *knock-knees*

Seine Frau findet seine X-Beine schön. *His wife thinks his knock-knees are nice.*

X-Beine haben — *to be knock-kneed.*

Hat er X- oder O-Beine? *Is he knock-kneed or bowlegged?*

---

x-beliebig — *just any old (thing)*

In der Galerie werden nicht x-beliebige, sondern wohlbekannte Maler ausgestellt. *In that gallery they don't exhibit just any old painters, only well-known ones.*

---

das x-temal — *the umpteenth time*

zum x-tenmal — *for the umpteenth time.*

Zum x-tenmal, wir wollen es nicht kaufen. *For the umpteenth time, we don't want to buy it.*

---

die Zahl — *number*

rote/schwarze Zahlen schreiben — *to be in the red/black.*

Unser Theater schreibt noch rote Zahlen, aber nächstes Jahr hoffen wir schwarze Zahlen schreiben zu können. *Our theater is still in the red this year, but next year we hope to be in the black.*

---

zahlen — *to pay*

Herr Ober! Wir möchten bitte zahlen. *Waiter! We'd like the check please.*

---

der Zahn — *tooth*

Ihm tut kein Zahn mehr weh. *He has no toothache anymore. (He's dead, out of it.)*

auf den Zahn fühlen — *to sound out/check out.*

Bevor wir ihn akzeptieren, müssen wir ihm auf den Zahn fühlen. *We'll have to check him out before accepting him.*

die Zähne zusammenbeißen — *to grit one's teeth.*

Sie musste die Zähne zusammenbeißen, um nicht zu heulen. *She had to grit her teeth to keep from screaming.*

dritte Zähne — *false teeth.*
Opa trägt nur ungern seine dritten Zähne. *Grandpa doesn't like to wear his false teeth.*

einen Zahn zulegen — *to hurry it up, get a move on.*
Legt doch einen Zahn zu, sonst werden wir nicht fertig. *Hurry it up, or we won't get done.*

zappeln — *to wriggle; fidget*
zappeln lassen — *to let dangle; to keep guessing.*
Sie ließ ihn zappeln. *She kept him guessing.*

zart — *tender*
zartbesaitet — *high-strung, oversensitive.*
Der Film ist nichts für zartbesaitete Naturen. *The movie isn't for oversensitive sorts.*

der Zauber — *magic*
einen großen Zauber ausüben — *to fascinate.*
Mozarts Werke üben großen Zauber auf viele aus. *Mozart's works fascinate many.*

fauler Zauber — *fraud.*
Mach uns keinen faulen Zauber vor! *Don't try to defraud us!*

der Zaum — *bridle*
im Zaum halten — *to keep under control, in check.*
Der Tiger konnte seinen Instinkt nicht im Zaume halten und fraß seine Dompteuse auf. *The tiger couldn't keep his instinct under control and devoured his trainer.*

der Zaun — *fence*
einen Streit vom Zaun brechen — *to start a quarrel suddenly.*
Ohne Grund brach er einen Streit vom Zaun. *For no reason he suddenly picked a fight.*

das Zeichen — *sign*

im Zeichen eines Tierkreises geboren sein — *to be born under an astrological sign.*

Sie ist im Zeichen des Wassermans geboren. *She was born under the sign of Aquarius.*

im Zeichen von etwas stehen — *to be influenced/determined/characterized by.*

Ihr letztes Schuljahr stand ganz im Zeichen der bevorstehenden Abschlussprüfung. *Her last year in school was entirely influenced by the finals she had to take.*

die Zeit — *time*

Kommt Zeit, kommt Rat. *If you give it time, the solution will come.*

auf Zeit — *temporarily.*

Ihm wurde der Führerschein auf Zeit entzogen. *His driver's license was temporarily suspended.*

Das waren noch Zeiten! *Those were the days!*

Einst waren wir jung, reich und verliebt — das waren noch Zeiten! *Once we were young, rich, and in love. Those were the days!*

es wird (höchste/allerhöchste) Zeit — *it's about time (it's high time).*

Einige im Publikum meinten, es wird Zeit, dass sie nicht mehr Rollen wie Julia spielt. *Some in the audience thought it was about time that she stopped playing roles like Juliet.*

das Zeug — *stuff*

sich ins Zeug legen — *to work very hard.*

Sie hat sich ins Zeug gelegt und den ersten Preis gewonnen. *She knuckled down and won the first prize.*

was das Zeug hält — *like all get out, to beat the band.*

Man muss den Werbetrommel rühren, was das Zeug hält. *We'll have to go all out on an advertising campaign.*

die Zicke — *she goat*

Zicken machen — *to act up.*

Der alte Wagen macht wieder Zicken und muss repariert werden. *The old car is acting up again and needs repair.*

ziehen — *to pull*

Es zieht wie Hechtsuppe hier! *There's a terrible draft here.*

die Augen aller auf sich ziehen — *to attract everyone's attention.*
In ihrem roten Ballkleid zog sie die Augen aller auf sich. *In her red ball gown she attracted everyone's attention.*

zittern — *to tremble; to shiver*

mit Zittern und Zagen — *with fear and trembling.*
Mit Zittern und Zagen erinnerte er sich an die Vergangenheit. *With fear and trembling he remembered the past.*

wie Espenlaub zittern — *to shake like a leaf.*
Als er das Gespenst erblickte, zitterte er wie Espenlaub. *When he saw the ghost, he shook like a leaf.*

die Zitterpartie — *cliff-hanger; nail-biter*
Bis zum Ende war die Wahl eine Zitterpartie. *Till the very end the election was a cliff-hanger.*

der Zoll — *inch*

jeder Zoll; Zoll für Zoll — *every inch.*
Auch im Elend war sie noch jeder Zoll eine Dame. *Even in wretched circumstances she was still every inch a lady.*

das Zubrot — *supplementary income.*
Mit ihrem Singen in Kirchen und Kneipen verdient sie sich ein schönes Zubrot. *Singing in churches and bars brings her in a nice bit of extra cash.*

der Zucker — *sugar*

Zuckerbrot und Peitsche — *carrot and stick.*
Die Politik von Zuckerbrot und Peitsche ging nicht auf. *The politics of carrot and stick didn't work out.*

der Zug — *train; draught*

In einem Zug leern — *to empty in one go.*
Er leerte den Maßkrug in einem Zug. *He emptied his beermug in one go.*

Im Zug von etwas sein — *in the course/process of.*
Im Zuge der Sparmaßnahmen hat die Stadt die Subventionen an unser Theater gestrichen. *In the course of economy measures, the city cut subsidies to our theater.*

zugrunde gehen — *to die; to be destroyed, ruined*
In Mozarts Lied hofft Luise, dass ihr untreuer Liebhaber zugrunde gehen wird. *In Mozart's song, Luise hopes that her unfaithful lover will drop dead.*

zum einen . . . zum ander(e)n — *for one thing . . . for another*
Zum einen haben wir das dafür nötige Geld nicht, zum andern, wenn wir's hätten, würden wir's für etwas anderes ausgeben. *For one thing, we haven't got the money needed for it, for another, if we had it, we'd spend it on something else.*

zumute sein — *to feel*
Ihr war traurig zumute. *She felt sad.*

zumuten — *to ask/expect something unreasonable.*
Willst du mir noch zumuten, dass ich nach der Arbeit noch die Hausarbeit mache? *Do you expect me to do the housework after getting home from work?*

zuschieben — *to push shut*
den schwarzen Peter zuschieben — *to pass the buck; to blame someone else.*
Der Senator versuchte, seinem Sekretär den schwarzen Peter zuzuschieben. *The senator tried to pass the buck to his secretary.*

der Zweig — *branch*
auf (k)einen grünen Zweig kommen — *(not) to amount to something.*
Trotz seiner reichen Familie kam er auf keinen grünen Zweig. *Despite his wealthy family, he never amounted to anything.*

zwicken — *to pinch*
zwicken und zwacken — *to suffer aches and pains.*

Ihn zwickt's und zwackt's öfters, aber trotz seines hohen Alters ist seine
Gesundheit verhältnismäßig gut. *He's often plagued by aches and pains,
but despite his age his health is relatively gut.*

das Zwielicht — *twilight*
ins Zwielicht geraten — *to come under suspicion.*
Der Vorsitzende ist ins Zwielicht geraten. *The chairman has come under
suspicion.*

zwielichtig — *shady*
Seine Frau hat nichts von seinen zwielichtigen Geschäften gewusst. *His
wife knew nothing of his shady dealings.*

zwischen — *between*
zwischen Tod und Teufel/zwischen Baum und Borke sein — *to be
between the devil and the deep blue sea/between a rock and a hard
place.*
Beide Lösungen gingen mir gegen den Strich; ich war zwischen Tod und
Teufel. *Both solutions went against my grain; I was between the devil
and the deep blue sea.*

zwischen Tür und Angel — *hurriedly; haphazardly.*
Mittags esse ich nur zwischen Tür und Angel. *I always have lunch on
the run.*

zwitschern — *to chirp*
einen zwitschern — *to tipple.*
Nach dem Essen wollten sie noch einen zwitschern. *After eating they
wanted to tipple some more.*

Deutsches Register (German Index)

D
E
U
T
S
C
H
E
S

R
E
G
I
S
T
E
R

Deutsches Register

D E U T S C H E S   R E G I S T E R

aus den Angeln gehen, 12
aus den Angeln heben, 12
aus den Angeln sein, 12
Aus den Augen aus dem Sinn., 21
aus der Haut fahren, 61
aus der Reihe tanzen, 179
aus der Rolle fallen, 182
aus der Ruhe bringen, 184
aus der Taufe heben, 210
aus der Welt schaffen, 230
aus Dummsdorf sein, 48
aus eigenem Antrieb, 15
aus einer Hand, 91
aus einer Mücke einen Elefanten machen, 150
aus etwas nicht klug werden können, 121
aus freien Stücken, 207
ausgedient haben, 44
ausgehen, 21
ausgehen wie das Hornberger Schießen, 190
auskommen, 21–22
Ausland, 22
auslasten, 22
auslernen, 22
aus Liebe, 138
auslöffeln, 22
das auslösende Moment sein, 150
aus nah und fern, 155
ausrutschen, 22
ausschildern, 22
aus seinem Dornröschenschlaf erwachen, 46

B

Bach, 22
Bahn, 23
Bahn frei!, 23
Bahnhof, 23
Bahnhof verstehen, 23
Balken, 23
Ball, 23
Bandage, 24
Bank, 24
Bär, 24
bärbeißg, 24
Bart, 25
Bauch, 25
bauen, 25
bauen auf, 25
Bauklotz, 25
Bauklötze staunen, 25
Baum, 25
Bäume ausreißen können, 25
baumeln, 26
Bäume wachsen nicht in den Hemmel—in der Beschränkung zeigt sich der Meister., 26
bedienen, 26
Begriff, 26
bei, 27
bei aller Liebe, 138
Bei (an) ihm ist Hopfen und Malz verloren., 104
Beichte abnehmen, 3
Bei dem tickt's nicht richtig., 211
bei den Frauen Glück haben, 82
bei der Stange bleiben, 204

C

D

D
E
U
T
S
C
H
E
S
R
E
G
I
S
T
E
R

D E U T S C H E S R E G I S T E R

D
E
U
T
S
C
H
E
S

R
E
G
I
S
T
E
R

ins Blaue hineinreden, 33
ins Blaue schießen, 33
ins Bockshorn jagen, 108
in Schuss, 197
ins Fettnäpfchen treten, 65
ins Garn gehen, 74
ins Gebet nehmen, 75
ins Geld gehen, 78
ins Gerede kommen, 79
ins Gericht gehen, 80
ins gleiche Horn stoßen, 104
ins Gras beißen, 84
ins Handwerk pfuschen, 93
ins Haus schneien, 195
ins Haus stehen, 95
ins Leben rufen, 133
ins Leere gehen, 133
ins Lot bringen, 142
ins offene Messer laufen, 148
ins Reine kommen, 179
ins Schwimmen kommen, 198
ins Stocken geraten, 79
in Strömen gießen, 81
ins Uferlose gehen, 218
ins Vertrauen ziehen, 221
ins Wasser fallen, 227
ins Zwielicht geraten, 241
in Teufels Küche kommen, 211
in trockene Tücher bringen, 216
in- und auswendig kennen, 108
in Verlegenheit bringen, 221
inwendig, 108
in wilder Ehe leben, 51
I-Punkt, 107
Das ist ein Hammer!, 90

Das ist keine Kunst!, 128
I-Tüpfelchen, 107
I-Tüpfel-Reiter, 107

J

Ja, 108
Jacke, 108
Jacke wie Hose sein, 108
jagen, 108
Jahr, 109
Jahr und Tag, 109
Jakob, 109
Jede Bohn' hat ihren Ton, 36
Jede Bohn' hat ihren Ton., 213
jede Menge, 147
Jedem Tierchen sein Pläsierchen., 212
jeden Moment, 150
Jeder ist seines Glückes Schmied, 194
Jeder ist sich selbst der Nächste., 153
Jeder Topf findet seinen Deckel., 213
jeder Zoll, 239
Jedes Böhnchen gibt sein Tönchen, 36
Jedes Böhnchen hat sein Tönchen, 36
jemandem auf die Hühneraugen treten, 105
jemandem das Wasser abgraben, 227
jemandem den Marsch blasen, 32
jemandem die Ohren langziehen, 163

K

L

Deutsches Register

Wer Wind sät, wird Sturm
ernten, 232
Wer zuletzt lacht, lacht am
besten., 129
Westentasche, 231
Wette, 231
Wettergott, 232
wichtig, 232
wie, 232
wie am Schnürchen laufen,
132
wie angewurzelt stehenbleiben,
16
wie aus dem Ei gepellt, 52
wie aus der Pistole geschossen,
169
wie aus einem Munde, 151
wieder auf dem Damm sein,
41
wieder auf den Beinen sein, 28
wieder auf die Beine kommen,
28
wieder in die Reihe kommen,
179
wieder zu Kräften kommen,
125
wie die Made im Speck leben,
133
Wie du mir, so ich dir, 232
wie du mir, so ich dir, 149
wie durch den Wolf gedreht,
233
wie ein begossener Pudel, 172
wie ein Schlot qualmen, 193
wie Espenlaub zittern, 239
Wiege, 232
wie gedruckt lügen, 142
wie gehabt, 88

wie geölt, 163
wie gerufen kommen, 183
wie gesät, 185
wie geschmiert laufen, 132
wie Gott in Frankreich leben,
84
wie Luft behandeln, 142
Wie man in den Wald
hineinruft, so schallt es
heraus., 225
wie seinesgleichen behandeln,
199
wie seine Westentasche
kennen, 231
wie verhext, 221
wie von/durch Geisterhand, 77
wie von ungefähr, 220
Wind, 232
Windei, 233
Wind machen, 232
Wink, 233
Winterschlaf, 233
Winterschlaf halten, 233
wissen, 233
wissen, was die Glocke
geschlagen hat, 82
wissen, wie der Hase läuft, 94
wissen, wo der Hund begraben
liegt, 105
Woge, 233
Woge glätten, 233
Wo gehobelt wird, da fallen
Späne., 102
Woher nehmen und nicht
stehlen?, 157
wohnen, wo sich die Füchse
gute Nacht sagen, 71
Wolf, 233

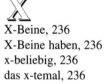

PART II:
ENGLISH-GERMAN
TEIL II:
ENGLISCH-DEUTSCH

PREFACE

"Idiom" derives from the Greek for "to make one's own." Even if you have mastered the basic structure of a language, you cannot be said to have made it your own until you understand its idioms. "Idiom" is also related to a word meaning "private." A knowledge of idioms affords an entry into private areas of the language, usually reserved only for natives, for initiates. Dictionaries of idioms, such as those Barron's has already published in other languages, are invaluable providers of inside, essential information. In convenient form they offer students, travelers, and business persons definitions not usually obtainable in pocket dictionaries and frequently difficult to ferret out and comprehend in comprehensive, multivolume dictionaries.

This volume, like the others in the series, offers a mix of fanciful expressions (which all, including native speakers, would consider idioms), along with more basic expressions, which students of the language will take as idioms because word-forword translations are not possible. Thus, many simple idioms such as *Hunger/ Durst/Angst/ recht haben* (to be hungry, thirsty, afraid, right) are included, as well as more elaborate ones. An attempt has been made to balance old sayings with idioms that pertain to contemporary social and political situations. Whether it was old sayings, picturesque phrases, or grammatical constructions that might seem "peculiar," even "idiotic" to a student of the language, the chief criterion for selecting them was their being different, unique, "idiomatic." Obviously therefore, sentences like *Er ist hier. Wir trinken Bier. Das Gras ist grün.* did not qualify for inclusion.

Sometimes, attempting to translate idioms with a conventional dictionary produces disastrous results. Basic meanings can lead you astray. For instance, if you saw the German *über den Berg* you might be tempted to translate it as "over the hill." It really means "out of the woods." Smaller dictionaries give few idioms, and users often flounder trying to find them in large ones. Using a conventional dictionary, you might conclude that the expression *auf den Busch klopfen* meant "to beat about the bush." In this book you'll learn easily that it means "to sound out." You will also quickly find the German for "to beat about the bush"—*um den heißen Brei herumreden*. With this book you will be able to access idioms easily and avoid making errors.

Perhaps to an even greater extent than in English, contemporary German writing still abounds in proverbs and picturesque phrases, i.e. idioms. Very often idioms appear in variations—put downs, take offs, and puns on them. To appreciate all that, you must first be familiar with the basic phrase, the idiomatic starting point.

This volume contains over 2,000 English and German idioms. The idioms are listed in alphabetical order according to their key words. Each entry consists of four parts: an idiom (in boldface), its meaning or translation in the other language (in italics), a sentence that exemplifies the use of the idiom in context (in roman type), and a translation of that sentence into the other language (in italics). Although the key words are translated literally, you may note that their meaning can change considerably when they are used in an idiomatic expression.

The reference works most frequently consulted were *Duden: Redewendungen und sprichwörtliche Redensarten*, volume 11 of the 12 volume Duden standard reference work on the German language, as well as the standard multivolume Duden and Langenscheidt German-English/English-German dictionaries.

Merely translating word-for-word from one language to another has enabled humorists from Mark Twain to Art Buchwald to get laughs. To master a language and avoid getting laughed at, a knowledge of idioms is indispensable. You can have plenty of fun—and also be more correct—in comparing and distinguishing the numerous idiomatic connections and divergencies between English and German. On rare occasions idioms in the two languages correspond in all particulars. Usually, however, there are variations on a basic idea. Thus, a "bull in a china shop" is, in German an *Elefant im Porzellanladen*. German drunks see *weiße Mäuse* (white mice) instead of pink elephants. If they get rowdy, the police might take them away in a *Grüne Minna* (a "Black Maria" in English). In English it's a "goose that lays the golden eggs," whereas in German the largesse-dispensing fowl is a *Huhn* (chicken). Whether one "puts the fox in charge of the henhouse," as in English, or one "makes the goat the gardener," as in German, the idea is the same, though the animals, colors, names, and images are different. To expand the language menagerie, to broaden the spectrum with a greater variety of picturesque phrases in the language gallery, you must learn idioms. The judicious use of them will make your speech more colorful. Studying them is also an interesting, colorful way to appreciate essential human unity as manifested in linguistic diversity.

ENGLISH IDIOMS (Englische Redewendungen)

about — *ungefähr*

   to be about — *handeln von.*
   What is this novel about? *Wovon handelt dieser Roman?*

   to be about to — *im Begriff sein.*
   We were just about to eat when the telephone rang. *Wir waren gerade im Begriff zu essen, als das Telefon klingelte.*
   How (what) about . . . ? *Wie wär's mit . . . ?*
   How about a glass of wine now? *Wie wär's mit einem Glas Wein jetzt?*

   not to be about to — *nicht daran denken.*
   We're not about to lend him money again. *Wir denken nicht daran, ihm wieder Geld zu leihen.*

---

ace — *das As*
   an ace in the hole (up one's sleeve) — *ein Trumpf in der Hand.*
   They thought he was beaten, but he still had an ace in the hole. *Man hielt ihn für geschlagen, aber er hatte noch einen Trumpf in der Hand.*

---

acid — *die Säure*
   acid test — *die Feuerprobe.*
   The new car didn't pass the acid test of the long trip. *Der neue Wagen bestand die Feuerprobe der langen Fahrt nicht.*

---

act — *die Tat; der Akt* (theater)
   to be caught in the act — *auf frischer Tat ertappt werden.*
   The thief was caught in the act. *Der Dieb wurde auf frischer Tat ertappt.*

   to get one's act together — *sich zusammenreißen, ins richtige Gleis kommen.*
   Get your act together, man! *Reiß dich doch mal zusammen, Mensch!*

to get in on the act — *sich einmischen.*

He always tries to get in on the act. *Der versucht immer sich einzumischen.*

to put on an act — *Theater spielen.*

Don't believe him; he's just putting on an act. *Glauben Sie ihm nicht; er spielt nur Theater.*

to add — *hinzufügen*

to add insult to injury — *noch einen drauf setzen.*

The swindler added insult to injury and made fun of his victims. *Der Schwindler setzte noch einen drauf und machte sich über seine Opfer lustig.*

to add up to something — *einen Sinn ergeben.*

His arguments don't add up to anything. *Aus seinen Argumenten ergibt sich keinen Sinn.*

advance — *der Fortschritt*

in advance — *im Voraus.*

We thank you for it in advance. *Wir danken Ihnen im Voraus dafür.*

to be in advance of one's time — *seiner Zeit voraus sein.*

Some painters were in advance of their time. *Einige Maler waren ihrer Zeit voraus.*

to get an advance — *einen Vorschuß bekommen.*

She got a large advance for her novel. *Sie bekam einen großen Vorschuss für ihren Roman.*

to make advances — *Annäherungsversuche machen.*

He wanted to make advances to them, but he was too shy. *Er wollte ihnen Annäherungsversuche machen, war aber zu schüchtern.*

to be advanced in years — *in fortgeschrittenem Alter sein.*

She is now advanced in years. *Sie ist jetzt in fortgeschrittenem Alter.*

age — *das Alter*

to come of age — *volljährig werden.*

The rich heiress will come of age this year. *Die reiche Erbin wird dieses Jahr volljährig.*

age-old — *uralt*

The little old granny told us age-old stories. *Das alte Mütterchen erzählte uns uralte Märchen.*

air — *die Luft*

to be made of thin air — *aus der Luft gegriffen.*

Such assertions are made entirely of thin air. *Solche Behauptungen sind völlig aus der Luft gegriffen.*

to be up in the air — *in der Schwebe sein.*

Everything is still up in the air. *Alles ist noch in der Schwebe.*

open air theater — *das Freilichttheater.*

It rained, but we enjoyed the concerts in the open air theater anyway. *Es regnete, aber trotzdem erfreuten uns die Konzerte im Freilichttheater.*

to put on airs — *vornehm tun.*

Since he married the rich heiress, he puts on airs. *Seitdem er die reiche Erbin geheiratet hat, tut er vornehm.*

alive — *lebendig*

to be alive — *am Leben sein.*

Her great-grandparents are still alive. *Ihre Urgroßeltern sind noch am Leben.*

to be alive and kicking — *gesund und munter sein.*

Her whole family is alive and kicking. *Ihre ganze Familie ist gesund und munter.*

to be alive with — *wimmeln von.*

His room is alive with cockroaches. *In seiner Bude wimmelt es von Kakerlaken.*

all — *all, ganz*

all along — *die ganze Zeit.*

She knew all along that he was lying. *Sie wusste die ganze Zeit, dass er log.*

all day long — *den ganzen Tag.*

all night long — *die ganze Nacht.*

They travelled all day long and couldn't sleep all night long. *Sie reisten den ganzen Tag und konnten die ganze Nacht nicht schlafen.*

all the better — *um so besser.*

All the better if they don't come. *Um so besser, wenn sie nicht kommen.*

all but — *fast.*

The dress is all but finished. *Das Kleid ist fast fertig.*

to be all the same to — *einem gleich/egal/piepegal/wurstegal/schnuppe sein.*

Whether we go or not, it's all the same to them. *Ob wir hingehen oder nicht, es ist ihnen gleich.*

to be all ears — *ganz Ohr sein.*

When she told the horrible story, everyone was all ears. *Als sie die grausame Geschichte erzählte, waren alle ganz Ohr.*

to be all in — *völlig erledigt sein.*

After the trip we were all in. *Nach der Reise waren wir völlig erledigt.*

to be all over — *aus sein.*

"It's all over between us," said Carmen. *"Zwischen uns ist alles aus," sagte Carmen.*

That's you (him, her) all over! *Das sieht dir (ihm, ihr) ähnlich!*

to be all right — *in Ordnung sein.*

They had problems, but everything is all right again now. *Sie hatten Probleme, aber jetzt ist alles wieder in Ordnung.*

to be all right with — *einverstanden sein mit.*

That's all right with me. *Ich bin damit einverstanden.*

when all is said and done — *letzten Endes.*

When all is said and done, you must make the decision. *Letzten Endes müssen Sie die Entscheidung treffen.*

not to be all there — *nicht bei Trost sein.*

After his experiences in the war, he's no longer quite all there. *Nach seinen Kriegserlebnissen ist er nicht mehr ganz bei Trost.*

also — *auch*

also-ran — *ferner liefen.*

He was fed up with always being only an also-ran. *Er hatte es satt, immer nur unter "ferner liefen" zu rangieren.*

to amount to — *sich belaufen auf*

to amount to the same thing — *auf dasselbe hinauslaufen.*

All these proposals amount to the same thing. *All diese Vorschläge laufen auf dasselbe hinaus.*

not to amount to anything — *auf keinen grünen Zweig kommen.*

He'll never amount to anything. *Der kommt auf keinen grünen Zweig.*

to animate — *beleben*

animated cartoon — *der Zeichentrickfilm.*

That animated cartoon was made in Japan. *Dieser Zeichentrickfilm wurde in Japan gedreht.*

to appeal — *Berufung einlegen gegen*

to appeal to — *ansprechen.*

Her works appeal more to the senses than the intellect. *Ihre Werke sprechen eher das Gefühl als den Verstand an.*

appearance — *das Erscheinen*

Appearances are often deceptive. *Der Schein trügt oft.*

to put in an appearance — *sich sehen lassen.*

He hasn't put in an appearance for a long time. *Seit langem hat er sich nicht sehen lassen.*

by all appearances — *allem Anschein nach.*

By all appearances, no one lived in it. *Allem Anschein nach wohnte niemand darin.*

apple — *der Apfel*

the apple of one's eye — *der Augenstern.*

The little boy was the apple of their eye. *Das Bübchen war ihr Augenstern.*

to apple-polish — *sich lieb Kind machen; sich anbiedern.*

He tried to do some apple polishing with the new masters. *Er versuchte, sich bei den neuen Herren lieb Kind zu machen.*

to upset the applecart — *einen Strich durch die Rechnung machen.*

We wanted to travel around the world, but unforeseen difficulties upset our applecart. *Wir wollten um die Welt reisen, aber unvorhergesehene Schwierigkeiten machten uns einen Strich durch die Rechnung.*

---

apple pie — *das Apfelgebäck, der Apfelkuchen*
easy as apple pie — *kinderleicht; mit links tun können.*
Answering those quiz questions was easy as apple pie. *Es war kinderleicht die Quizfragen zu beantworten.*

in apple-pie order — *picobello/in bester Ordnung/in Butter.*
At Craig's wife's house everything is always in apple-pie order. *Bei Craigs Frau ist alles immer picobello.*

Mom's apple-pie — *etwas Hausbackenes; vom echten Schrot und Korn.*
At first we didn't notice anything sinister in their house; it all seemed like Mom's apple pie. *Zuerst merkten wir nichts Unheimliches bei ihnen, alles schien uns eher hausbacken.*

---

apron — *der Schurz*
to be tied to s.o.'s apron strings — *am Gängelband sein.*
He's still a moma's boy and likes being tied to her apron strings. *Er ist noch Muttersöhnchen und lässt sich gern von ihr am Gängelband führen.*

---

arm — *der Arm*
to be up in arms — *Sturm laufen.*
The environmentalists were up in arms about the planned expansion of the airport. *Die Umweltschützer liefen Sturm gegen die geplante Flughafenerweiterung.*

---

at — *an, in, bei, zu*
at last — *endlich.*
At last the check came. *Endlich kam der Scheck.*

at least — *wenigstens.*
At least you tried. *Wenigstens haben Sie den Versuch gemacht.*

at (the) present (time) — *zur Zeit/derzeit.*
At the present time she's playing in a dance band. *Zur Zeit spielt sie in einer Tanzkapelle.*

At present this little group of anarchists is no great danger. *Derzeit bildet diese kleine Gruppe von Anarchisten keine große Gefahr.*

average — *der Duchschnitt*

on average — *im Schnitt; durchschnittlich.*

How fast did you travel on average in the Himalayas? *Wie schnell sind Sie im Schnitt im Himalaja gefahren?*

the average consumer — *Otto Normalverbraucher.*

This appliance is too complicated for the average consumer. *Dieses Gerät ist für Otto Normalverbraucher zu kompliziert.*

the average woman/person — *Lieschen Müller.*

They're trying to make movies for the average person. *Sie versuchen, Filme für Lieschen Müller zu drehen.*

back — *der Rücken*

to put one's back into it — *sich ins Zeug legen.*

Let's put our back into it, so that the job gets done sooner. *Legen wir uns ins Zeug, damit die Arbeit schneller fertig wird.*

back and forth — *hin und her.*

He walked back and forth impatiently. *Ungeduldig lief er hin und her.*

to back the wrong horse — *auf das falsche Pferd setzen.*

You backed the wrong horse. *Sie haben auf das falsche Pferd gesetzt.*

to back down — *nachgeben.*

They had to back down after all. *Sie mussten doch nachgeben.*

to back off — *auf Distanz gehen.*

They agreed to it, but now they're backing off. *Sie waren damit einverstanden aber jetzt gehen Sie auf Distanz.*

to back into a corner — *in die Enge treiben.*

Are you trying to back me into a corner? *Versuchst du mich in die Enge zu treiben?*

to back out of — *abspringen.*
They're trying to back out of the agreement now. *Sie versuchen jetzt, vom Abkommen abzuspringen.*

to be back — *wieder da sein.*
I'll be back in two weeks. *In zwei Wochen bin ich wieder da.*

backbiting — *die Verleumdung.*
There was much backbiting in the last electoral campaign. *Bei der letzten Wahlkampagne gab es viel Verleumdung.*

backseat — *der Rücksitz*
to take a backseat — *die zweite Geige spielen.*
Ecological problems take a backseat with that compay. *Bei dem Unternehmen spielen Umweltfragen nur eine zweite Geige.*

bad — *schlecht; böse*
too bad — *(wie) schade.*
It's too bad they couldn't come along. *Wie schade, dass sie nicht mitkommen konnten.*

bag — *der Sack*
bag and baggage — *Sack und Pack.*
They left with bag and baggage. *Sie sind mit Sack und Pack abgereist.*

bag of tricks — *die Trickkiste.*

to exhaust one's bag of tricks — *sein Pulver verschießen.*
He's long since exhausted his bag of tricks. *Der hat längst schon sein Pulver verschossen.*

to be in the bag — *so gut wie sicher sein.*
Her appointment to this post is in the bag. *Ihre Ernennung zu diesem Posten ist so gut wie sicher.*

to be a bag of bones — *Haut und Knochen sein.*
After the war he was just a bag of bones. *Nach dem Krieg war er nur noch Haut und Knochen.*

to leave holding the bag — *die Schuld aufhalsen.*
Although he had relatively little to do with the matter, his accomplices left him holding the bag. *Obwohl er mit der Sache verhältnismäßig wenig zu tun hatte, halsten ihm seine Komplizen die Schuld auf.*

old bag — *alte Schachtel.*
How could Fritz fall for that old bag? *Wie hat sich Fritz in diese alte Schachtel verknallen können?*

ugly old bag — *die Schreckschraube.*
She's very motherly and certainly no ugly old bag. *Sie ist sehr mütterlich und gewiss keine Schreckschraube.*

---

ball — *der Ball*
   to be on the ball — *auf Draht sein.*
   During the first few weeks in the business he was really on the ball. *In den ersten paar Wochen im Geschäft war er wirklich auf Draht.*

   to have a ball/blast — *auf die Pauke hauen; einen draufmachen.*
   He doesn't study, because every night he just wants to have a ball. *Er lernt nichts, weil er jede Nacht nur auf die Pauke hauen will.*

   to get the ball rolling — *den Stein ins Rollen bringen.*
   We must try to get the ball rolling. *Wir müssen versuchen, den Stein ins Rollen zu bringen.*

---

bargain — *das Schnäppchen*
   to get a bargain — *ein Schnäppchen machen.*
   She hoped to get a bargain at the clearance sale. *Sie hoffte beim Schlussverkauf ein Schnäppchen zu machen.*

   A bargain is a bargain. *Was einmal abgemacht ist, gilt.*

---

to bark — *bellen*
   to bark up the wrong tree — *auf dem Holzweg sein.*
   If you expect anything like that from us, then you're barking up the wrong tree. *Wenn Sie so 'was von uns erwarten, dann sind Sie auf dem Holzweg.*

   His bark is worse than his bite. *Hunde, die bellen, beißen nicht.*
   "Barking dogs don't bite" is another proverb that isn't always true.
   "Bellende Hunde beißen nicht" ist noch ein Sprichwort, das nicht immer stimmt.

   to bark orders at — *Befehle zubrüllen.*
   The general still barked orders at the soldiers after they had already deserted. *Der General brüllte den Soldaten noch Befehle zu, nachdem sie schon fahnenflüchtig waren.*

basket — *der Korb*
   to be a basket case (economically) — *am Tropf hängen, hoffnungslos sein.*
   After the war the whole country's a basket case. *Nach dem Krieg hängt das ganze Land am Tropf.*

   to be a basket case (mentally) — *reif für die Klapse/Irrenanstalt.*
   His family, business partner, they all betrayed him. He's a basket case. *Familie, Geschäftspartner, alle haben ihn betrogen. Er ist reif für die Klapse.*

bat — *die Fledermaus; das Schlagholz*
   to have bats in the belfry — *einen Vogel haben.*
   Many say he's got bats in the belfry, but others think he's a genius. *Viele sagen, er habe einen Vogel, aber andere meinen, er sei ein Genie.*

   to be blind as a bat — *blind wie ein Maulwurf sein.*
   Although he's blind as a bat, he still drives. *Obwohl er blind wie ein Maulwurf ist, fährt er noch.*

   like a bat out of hell — *als ob der Teufel hinterher wäre.*
   He drove off like a bat out of hell. *Er ist abgefahren, als ob der Teufel hinter ihm her wäre.*

   right off the bat — *gleich auf Anhieb.*
   We hope it'll be successful right off the bat. *Wir hoffen, es klappt gleich auf Anhieb.*

   to go to bat for — *eine Lanze brechen für; sich ins Zeug legen für.*
   With her songs and poems she wanted to go to bat for her home town. *Mit ihren Liedern und Gedichten wollte sie eine Lanze für ihre Heimatstadt brechen.*
   If the mayor hadn't gone to bat for her, grandma would never have gotten her pension. *Wenn die Bürgermeisterin sich für sie nicht ins Zeug gelegt hätte, hätte Oma ihre Rente nicht bekommen.*

   to bat an eyelash — *mit der Wimper zucken.*
   Without batting an eyelash, she told him that she loved someone else. *Ohne mit der Wimper zu zucken, sagte sie ihm, dass sie einen anderen liebte.*

bathroom — *das Badezimmer*

to go to the bathroom — *aufs Klo gehen.*

Unfortunately, during the flight the children had to go to the bathroom often. *Während des Flugs mussten die Kinder leider oft aufs Klo.*

battle — *die Schlacht*

half the battle — *die halbe Miete.*

A good start is half the battle. *Ein guter Start ist die halbe Miete.*

to be — *sein; sich befinden*

We were in the cathedral when the bombs fell. *Wir befanden uns im Dom, als die Bomben fielen.*

to be in a bad way — *aufgeschmissen sein.*

He's unemployed and really in a bad way. *Er ist arbeitslos und voll aufgeschmissen.*

to be in cahoots with — *unter einer Decke stecken mit.*

The reporter asserted that the mayor was in cahoots with the gangsters. *Die Reporterin behauptete, der Bürgermeister stecke unter einer Decke mit der Verbrecherbande.*

beam — *der Balken*

to be off the beam/mark — *danebenliegen.*

With ideas like that, you're off the beam. *Mit solchen Ideen liegst du daneben.*

to be on the beam/mark — *richtigliegen.*

You're more on the beam with that theory. *Du liegst richtiger mit dieser Theorie.*

bean — *die Bohne*

to be full of beans — *springlebendig sein.*

Grandpa is still full of beans. *Opa ist noch springlebendig.*

not to know beans about — *keinen blassen Schimmer haben.*

He got the job, although he doesn't know beans about the subject. *Er bekam den Posten, obwohl er keinen blassen Schimmer vom Fach hat.*

to spill the beans — *alles ausquatschen.*
One of the crooks spilled the beans. *Einer der Gauner quatschte alles aus.*

The whole shebang doesn't add up to a hill of beans. *Der ganze Kram ist keinen Pfifferling wert.*

to bear — *ertragen*
to bear a grudge against — *böse sein.*
She is so charming one can't hold a grudge against her. *Sie ist so charmant, man kann ihr nicht böse sein.*

to beat — *schlagen*
That beats me! — *Das ist mir zu hoch!*

to beat about the bush — *um den heißen Brei herumreden.*
Stop beating about the bush and tell me everything straight out. *Hör doch auf, um den heißen Brei herumzureden, und sag mir alles gerade heraus.*

to beat (be superior to) — *gehen über.*
You can't beat Lulu's Apfelstrudel. *Es geht nichts über Lulus Apfelstrudel.*

to beat out the competition — *die Konkurrenz aus dem Feld schlagen.*
Through a big advertising campaign, her firm succeeded in beating out the competition. *Durch einen großen Werbefeldzug gelang es ihrer Firma, die Konkurrenz aus dem Felde zu schlagen.*

to beat the band — *dass sich die Balken biegen/auf Teufel komm raus/was das Zeug hält.*
He lies to beat the band. *Er lügt, dass sich die Balken biegen.*

to beat the drum for — *die (Werbe)Trommel rühren für.*
That film star is so famous there's no need to beat the drum for her. *Die Filmdiva ist so berühmt, dass man die Werbetrommel für sie nicht zu rühren braucht.*

bee — *die Biene*
busy as a bee — *bienenfleißig.*
Debbie is always busy as a bee. *Debbie ist immer bienenfleißig.*

to have a bee in one's bonnet — *einen Fimmel/Tick haben.*
She has a bee in her bonnet about higher education and insists that her son is to go to college. *Sie hat einen Bildungsfimmel und besteht darauf, dass ihr Sohn auf die Universität gehen soll.*

to make a beeline for — *auf etwas schnurstracks zugehen.*
The children made a beeline for the birthday presents. *Die Kinder gingen schnurstracks auf die Geburtstagsgeschenke zu.*

before — *bevor; vorher; zuvor*
before you could say Jack Robinson — *in Null Komma nichts, im Nu, ehe man sich's versieht.*
Before you could say Jack Robinson he disappeared. *In Null Komma nichts verschwand er.*

beggar — *der Bettler*
Beggars can't be choosers. *In der Not frisst der Teufel Fliegen/In der Not schmeckt jedes Brot.*

bell — *die Glocke*
to be sound as a bell — *kerngesund sein.*
Uncle Otto was always sound as a bell until he suddenly took sick. *Onkel Otto war immer kerngesund, bis er plötzlich erkrankte.*

belly — *der Bauch*
to have had a bellyful — *die Nase voll haben.*
I've had a bellyful of your constant bellyaching. *Ich hab die Nase voll von deinem ewigen Gemurre.*

belt — *der Gürtel*
to tighten one's belt — *den Gürtel enger schnallen.*
Because of poor economic conditions we had to tighten our belt. *Wegen der schlechten Konjunktur mussten wir den Gürtel enger schnallen.*

below the belt — *unter der Gürtellinie.*
That was a blow below the belt. *Das war ein Schlag unter der Gürtellinie.*

to bend — *sich beugen*
to bend over backwards — *sich ein Bein ausreißen.*
He said he'd bend over backwards to help us. *Er sagte, er würde sich ein Bein ausreißen, um uns zu helfen.*

to bet — *wetten*

to bet on a sure thing — *auf Nummer Sicher gehen/setzen.*
He only bets on a sure thing. *Er geht nur auf Nummer Sicher.*

to bet one's bottom dollar on — *auf etwas Gift nehmen.*
You can bet your bottom dollar that that scoundrel won't be back. *Du kannst Gift darauf nehmen, der Schuft kommt nicht wieder.*

better — *besser*

to get the better of — *ausstechen.*
He tried to get the better of his rival. *Er versuchte, seinen Rivalen auszustechen.*

for better or for worse — *in Freud und Leid.*
Ännchen von Tharau and her husband stood by each other for better or worse. *Ännchen von Tharau und ihr Mann hielten zu einander in Freud und Leid.*

between — *zwischen*

to be between the devil and the deep blue sea — *zwischen Baum und Borke sein.*
Because of poor planning, he's between the devil and the deep blue sea again. *Wegen schlechter Planung ist er wieder zwischen Baum und Borke.*

bird — *der Vogel*

A bird in the hand is worth two in the bush. *Ein Spatz in der Hand ist besser als eine Taube auf dem Dach.*

Birds of a feather flock together. *Gleich und gleich gesellt sich gern.*

to bite — *beißen*

to bite the bullet — *in den sauren Apfel beißen.*
Unfortunately, we had to bite the bullet and pay a lot of money for the property. *Leider mussten wir in den sauren Apfel beißen und viel Geld für das Grundstück bezahlen.*

to bite the dust — *ins Gras beißen.*
That actor has bitten the dust in many westerns. *In vielen Westerns hat dieser Schauspieler ins Gras gebissen.*

Once bitten twice shy. *Gebranntes Kind scheut das Feuer.*

black — *schwarz*

Black Maria — *die grüne Minna.*

The police arrested so many that there wasn't enough room in the Black Maria. *Die Polizei verhaftete so viele, dass es in der grünen Minna nicht genug Platz gab.*

in black and white — *schwarz auf weiß.*

I'll have to see that in black and white. *Das muss ich schwarz auf weiß sehen.*

to be in the black — *schwarze Zahlen schreiben.*

For years this firm has been in the black. *Jahrelang schreibt diese Firma schwarze Zahlen.*

---

blanket — *die Decke*

wet blanket — *Spielverderber.*

When one gets to know him better one realizes that he's not really a wet blanket. *Wenn man ihn besser kennt, sieht man ein, dass er wirklich kein Spielverderber ist.*

---

blarney — *die Schmeichelei, Flunkerei; der Schmus*

to have kissed the Blarney Stone — *Beredsamkeit haben (nach Küssen des Blarney Steines (irische Burg); beschwatzen können; nicht auf den Mund gefallen sein.*

He's kissed the Blarney Stone and can talk his way out of anything. *Er ist nicht auf den Mund gefallen und kann sich aus allem herausreden.*

---

blow — *der Schlag*

to come to blows — *zu Handgreiflichkeiten kommen.*

At first the congresspersons yelled at each other; then they came to blows. *Zuerst schrieen sich die Abgeordneten an; dann kam es zu Handgreiflichkeiten.*

---

to blow — *blasen*

to blow a fuse — *die Sicherung durchbrennen.*

When he found out about it, he blew a fuse. *Als er das erfuhr, brannte ihm die Sicherung durch.*

to blow hot and cold — *rin in die Kartoffeln, raus aus den Kartoffeln.*
First it was yes, then no—they blow hot and cold. *Zuerst hieß es ja, dann nein—rin in die Kartoffeln, raus aus den Kartoffeln.*

to blow someone's cover — *jemandes Tarnung auffliegen lassen.*
His lover blew his cover. *Seine Geliebte hat seine Tarnung auffliegen lassen.*

to wait until something blows over — *warten bis Gras über etwas wächst.*
Better wait until it blows over. *Besser wär's, du wartest bis Gras darüber wächst.*

blue — *blau*

out of the blue/like a bolt from the blue — *aus heiterem Himmel.*
Everything was peaceful until out of the blue he started screaming. *Es war alles ruhig, bis er aus heiterem Himmel zu schreien anfing.*

to have the blues — *in gedrückter Stimmung sein.*
He's unemployed and has the blues. *Er ist arbeitslos und in gedrückter Stimmung.*

to sing the blues — *Trübsal blasen.*
People are avoiding you because you're always singing the blues. *Man vermeidet dich, weil du immer Trübsal bläst.*

boat — *das Boot*

to be in the same boat — *im selben Boot sitzen, in einem Boot sitzen.*
"We came over on different ships, but we're all in the same boat now," said the governor. *"Wir sind auf verschiedenen Schiffen rübergekommen, aber jetzt sitzen wir alle im selben Boot," sagte der Gouverneur.*

to boil — *sieden*

to make one's blood boil — *einem die Galle hochbringen.*
His behavior made my blood boil. *Sein Benehmen brachte mir die Galle hoch.*

bone — *der Knochen*

I feel it in my bones that you're not telling me the whole truth. *Mein kleiner Finger sagt mir, dass du mir nicht die ganze Wahrheit sagst.*

bone of contention — *der Zankapfel.*

That province was for a long time a bone of contention between the two countries. *Diese Provinz war lange ein Zankapfel zwischen beiden Ländern.*

to have a bone to pick — *ein Hühnchen zu rupfen haben.*

Unfortunately, I have a bone to pick with you again. *Leider hab ich wieder ein Hühnchen mit dir zu rupfen.*

bone tired — *völlig erschöpft.*

After work they were bone tired. *Nach der Arbeit waren sie völlig erschöpft.*

to make no bones about — *keinen Hehl aus etwas machen.*

Goethe made no bones about his religious views. *Goethe machte keinen Hehl aus seinen religiösen Ansichten.*

---

book — *das Buch*

to do everything by the book — *alles genau nach den Vorschriften machen; ein Paragraphenreiter sein.*

Unfortunately we met with someone who wanted to do everything by the book. *Leider sind wir auf einen Paragraphenreiter gestossen.*

---

bookworm — *die Leseratte*

My husband never reads and just watches TV; but I'm a bookworm. *Mein Mann ist Lesemuffel und guckt nur fern; ich aber bin Leseratte.*

(the) boondocks/boonies — *wo sich Hase und Fuchs gute Nacht sagen*

We live in the boonies now. *Wir wohnen jetzt in einer Gegend, in der sich Hase und Fuchs gute Nacht sagen.*

---

boot — *der Stiefel*

to give someone the Order of the Boot — *jemanden laufen lassen/den Passierschein geben.*

After years of faithful service they're giving me the Order of the Boot. *Jahrelang hab ich treu gedient, jetzt gibt man mir den Passierschein.*

---

to bow — *sich beugen*
   to bow and scrape — *katzbuckeln.*
   Now he's got the upper hand, but for a long time he bowed and scraped to his masters. *Jetzt hat er die Oberhand, aber lange katzbuckelte er vor seinen Herren.*

to break — *brechen*
   to (take a) break — *Pause machen.*
   We'll break for ten minutes. *Wir machen 10 Minuten Pause.*

   Break a leg! *Hals- und Beinbruch!*

   to break a habit — *sich etwas abgewöhnen.*
   Only with the greatest effort did he break his smoking habit. *Nur mit größter Mühe hat er sich das Rauchen abgewöhnt.*

   to break in (a vehicle) — *einfahren.*
   The new trucks aren't yet broken in. *Die neuen Lkws sind noch nicht eingefahren.*

   to break off a relationship — *Schluss machen.*
   Udo became a soldier because his girl friend broke off with him. *Udo wurde Soldat, weil seine Freundin mit ihm Schluss gemacht hatte.*

   breakneck — *halsbrecherisch.*
   The soccer player approached the goal at breakneck speed. *Der Fußballspieler kam mit halsbrecherischer Geschwindigkeit auf das Tor zu.*

   to be broke — *pleite/blank sein.*
   Because of his passion for gambling, he's always broke. *Seiner Spielleidenschaft wegen ist er immer pleite.*

bridge — *die Brücke*
   Don't cross your bridges before you come to them. *Kümmere dich nicht um ungelegte Eier.*

   That's all water under the bridge. *Das alles ist Schnee von gestern.*

   to bridge the gap between people — *die Kluft zwischen den Menschen überbrücken.*

As a diplomat I'm trying to build bridges, to bridge the gap between people. *Als Diplomat versuche ich Brücken zu schlagen, die Kluft zwischen den Menschen zu überbrücken.*

to bring — *bringen*
to bring down — *zu Fall bringen.*
The revolutionaries tried to bring down the president. *Die Putschisten versuchten, den Präsidenten zu Fall zu bringen.*

to bring down the house — *einen Bombenerfolg haben.*
Last night the soprano brought down the house. *Gestern Abend hatte die Sopranistin einen Bombenerfolg.*

to bring to bear — *Beziehungen spielen lassen.*
His uncle brought influence to bear to get the job for his nephew. *Der Onkel hat seine Beziehungen spielen lassen, um seinem Neffen den Posten zu besorgen.*

to bring up — *großziehen.*
They want to bring up their children in the country. *Sie möchten ihre Kinder auf dem Lande großziehen.*

to bring up the rear — *Schlusslicht sein.*
We were the frontrunners last year, but now we're bringing up the rear. *Letztes Jahr waren wir Spitzenreiter; jetzt sind wir Schlusslicht.*

to bring up the past — *die Vergangenheit aufrühren.*
Stop bringing up the past constantly. *Hör doch auf, immer wieder die Vergangenheit aufzurühren.*

broad — *breit*
in broad daylight — *am helllichten Tag.*
A vampire in broad daylight? Impossible! *Ein Vampir am helllichten Tag? Unmöglich!*

broom — *der Besen*
A new broom sweeps clean. *Neue Besen kehren gut.*

bucket — *der Kübel*
It's coming down in buckets. *Es gießt wie aus Kübeln.*

to kick the bucket — *abkratzen/ins Gras beißen/den Löffel abgeben.*
Jenny kicked the bucket at 76. *Mit 76 Jahren kratzte Jenny ab.*

bud — *die Knospe*
to nip in the bud — *im Keim ersticken.*
The tyrant tried to nip the revolt in the bud. *Der Gewaltherrscher versuchte, den Aufstand im Keim zu ersticken.*

budding — *angehend.*
The number of priestesses of Gaia is rising steadily. *Die Zahl der angehenden Priesterinnen Gaias steigt ständig.*

bull — *der Bulle*
like a bull in a china shop — *wie ein Elefant im Porzellanladen.*
Don't behave like a bull in a china shop again. *Benimm dich nicht wieder wie ein Elefant im Porzelanladen!*

hit the bull's-eye — *ins Schwarze treffen.*
Her well-aimed arguments hit the bull's-eye. *Ihre treffsicheren Argumente trafen ins Schwarze.*

to burn — *brennen*
to burn the midnight oil — *sich die Nacht um die Ohren schlagen.*
He had to cram and burn the midnight oil. *Er musste büffeln und schlug sich die Nacht um die Ohren.*

business — *das Geschäft*
Business is good. *Der Laden läuft.*

to be someone's business — *jemanden etwas angehen.*
Her private life is no business of yours. *Ihr Privatleben geht dich gar nichts an.*

to do a big business — *Hochkonjunktur haben.*
Her art works are doing a big business. *Ihre Kunstwerke haben jetzt Hochkonjunktur.*

to do business — *Geschäfte machen; ins Geschäft kommen.*
We're still hoping to do business with them. *Wir hoffen noch, mit ihnen ins Geschäft kommen zu können.*

to get down to business — *zur Sache kommen, Tacheles reden.*
Come on now, let's get down to business. *Kommen wir doch endlich zur Sache!*

---

to bust — *kaputtmachen*

to be/get busted — *verhaftet werden.*
When'd you get busted? *Wann hat man dich verhaftet?*

to bust a gut — *sich kaputtmachen, sich einen abbrechen.*
Here I am busting a gut and you just lounge around. *Da mach ich mich kaputt und du lungerst nur herum.*

to go bust — *Pleite gehen/machen.*
If you keep on like that, you'll soon go bust. *Wenn du so weiter machst, gehst du bald Pleite.*

---

butter — *die Butter*
to melt butter — *Butter zerlassen.*
He looks as if butter wouldn't melt in his mouth. *Er hat den Anschein, als ob er kein Wässerchen trüben könnte.*

to butter up — *Honig um den Mund schmieren.*
He really buttered up the boss, but she saw through him. *Er schmierte der Chefin viel Honig um den Mund, aber sie durchschaute ihn.*

---

butterfly — *der Schmetterling*
to break a butterfly on the wheel — *mit Kanonen nach Spatzen schießen.*
Yes, you're right, but you're breaking a butterfly on the wheel. *Ja, du hast recht, aber du schießt mit Kanonen nach Spatzen.*

to do the butterfly — *im Delphinstil schwimmen; delphinschwimmen.*
She likes to do the butterfly. *Sie schwimmt gern im Delphinstil.*

to have butterflies in one's stomach — *einen Bammel haben.*
Before the concert the singer had butterflies in her stomach. *Vor dem Konzert hatte die Sängerin einen Bammel.*

---

button — *der Knopf*
  to bust one's buttons — *es platzt einem der Kragen.*
  "Humor is the button that keeps us from busting our buttons," said
  Ringelnatz. You've got to be able to laugh at yourself and the world.
  "Humor ist der Knopf, der verhindert, dass uns der Kragen platzt,"
  sagte Ringelnatz. Man muss über die Welt und sich selbst lachen
  können.

by — *von*
  by and large — *im Großen und Ganzen.*
  By and large, we're satisfied with it. *Im Großen und Ganzen sind wir*
  damit zufrieden.

bygones — *das Vergangene*
  to let bygones be bygones — *die Vergangenheit ruhen lassen.*
  We've been at odds for some time, but let's let bygones be bygones. *Wir*
  waren lange zerstritten, aber lassen wir jetzt die Vergangenheit ruhen.

cake — *der Kuchen*
  a piece of cake — *ein Kinderspiel sein.*
  The exam was a piece of cake for her. *Die Prüfung war für sie nur ein*
  Kinderspiel.

  to have one's cake and eat it too — *auf allen Hochzeiten tanzen wollen.*
  He tried to have his cake and eat it too. *Er versuchte, auf allen Hochzeiten*
  zu tanzen.

  to sell like hotcakes — *wie warme Semmeln weggehen.*
  All her novels are selling like hotcakes. *Alle ihre Romane gehen wie*
  warme Semmeln weg.

  to take the cake — *dreizehn schlagen.*
  He's done many dumb things, but that takes the cake! *Er hat schon viel*
  Dummes angerichtet, aber jetzt schlägt's dreizehn!

to call — *rufen*

to call the shots — *das große Wort führen*

Although grandpa has retired from the family business, he still wants to call the shots. *Obwohl Opa sich aus dem Familiengeschäft zurückgezogen hat, will er noch das große Wort führen.*

to call it a day — *Feierabend machen.*

We're tired and want to call it a day. *Wir sind müde und wollen Feierabend machen.*

to call it quits — *einpacken/aufhören/Schluss machen.*

If things keep on this way we can soon call it quits. *Wenn's so weitergeht, können wir bald einpacken.*

to call names — *beschimpfen.*

He called all his opponents names. *Er beschimpfte alle seine Gegner.*

to call for — *verlangen.*

The king called for his pipe. *Der König verlangte nach seiner Pfeife.*

to call for — *bestellen.*

We called for a taxi. *Wir bestellten ein Taxi.*

to call for — *abholen.*

When will you call for your luggage? *Wann holen Sie Ihr Gepäck ab?*

to call for a celebration — *etwas feiern müssen.*

Her triumph calls for a celebration. *Ihr Triumph muss gefeiert werden.*

to call in — *zu Rate ziehen.*

A specialist was called in. *Eine Fachärztin wurde zu Rate gezogen.*

to call on — *besuchen.*

Call on us anytime. *Besuchen Sie uns jederzeit!*

to call off — *abblasen.*

Many hoped that the president would call off the invasion. *Viele hofften, dass der Präsident die Invasion abblasen würde.*

to call off a wedding engagement — *eine Verlobung lösen.*

In tears, she called off the engagement. *Weinend löste sie die Verlobung.*

to call (up) — *anrufen.*

She called us from Tahiti last night. *Sie rief uns gestern Abend aus Tahiti an.*

to be uncalled for — *unangebracht sein.*
Such remarks are uncalled for. *Solche Bemerkungen sind unangebracht.*

candle — *die Kerze*
  (not) to be worth the candle — *der Mühe (nicht) wert.*
  The game is (not) worth the candle. *Die Sache ist (nicht) der Mühe wert.*

  to burn the candle at both ends — *mit seiner Gesundheit aasen.*
  Edna burned the candle at both ends. *Edna aaste mit ihrer Gesundheit.*

  to hold a candle to — *einem das Wasser reichen.*
  No other heroic tenor can hold a candle to him. *Kein anderer Heldentenor kann ihm das Wasser reichen.*

card — *die Karte*
  to put one's cards on the table — *mit offenen Karten spielen.*
  Let's put our cards on the table! *Spielen wir mit offenen Karten!*

  to play one's cards right — *seine Karten geschickt ausspielen.*
  She played her cards right and became a member of the board of directors. *Sie spielte ihre Karten geschickt aus und wurde zum Vorstandsmitglied.*

  to throw in the cards — *die Flinte ins Korn werfen.*
  Now is not the time to throw in the cards. *Jetzt ist nicht die Zeit, die Flinte ins Korn zu werfen.*

care — *die Sorge*
  in care of — *per Adresse; bei.*
  You can write him in care of his aunt. *Sie können ihn per Adresse seiner Tante schriftlich erreichen.*

  to care about (something) — *ausmachen.*
  Do you care much if we're late? *Macht es Ihnen viel aus, wenn wir spät kommen?*

  not to care about (something) — *einem einerlei/gleichgültig sein.*
  They didn't care if people saw them kiss. *Es war ihnen einerlei, ob man sah, dass sie sich küssten.*

to carry — *tragen*

to carry coals to Newcastle — *Eulen nach Athen tragen.*

Don't give him a bottle of wine; that would be carrying coals to
Newcastle, since he owns a liquor store. *Schenk ihm keine Flasche
Wein; das hieße Eulen nach Athen tragen, denn er ist Inhaber eines
Spirituosengeschäfts.*

to carry on — *sich wild benehmen.*

The parents weren't home, and the kids carried on. *Die Eltern waren nicht
zu Hause, und die Kinder benahmen sich wild.*

carry-on luggage — *das Handgepäck.*

How much carryon luggage do you have? *Wieviel Handgepäck haben
Sie?*

to carry things too far — *es zu weit treiben.*

In Ibsen's and O'Neill's works some characters carry things too far with
the love of truth. *Bei Ibsen und O'Neill treiben es einige Personen mit
der Wahrheitsliebe zu weit.*

to carry oneself well — *eine gute Haltung haben.*

He's a bit corpulent but he carries himself well. *Er ist etwas beleibt aber
er hat eine gute Haltung.*

to carry (goods) — *führen.*

Do you carry luxury articles? *Führen Sie Luxuswaren?*

to get carried away — *sich hinreißen lassen.*

The mob got carried away by the demagogue. *Der Pöbel ließ sich vom
Demagogen hinreißen.*

---

cart — *der Karren*

to put the cart before the horse — *das Pferd am Schwanz aufzäumen.*

The professor claimed that Descartes put the cart before the horse. *Der
Professor behauptete, Descartes hätte das Pferd am Schwanz
aufgezäumt.*

---

cash — *das Bargeld*

cash-and-carry — *gegen Bargeld und Selbstabholung.*

We're selling these items on a cash-and-carry basis only. *Wir verkaufen
diese Stücke nur gegen Bargeld und Selbstabholung.*

cash in hand — *bar auf die Hand.*

I want 500 euros cash in hand for it. *Dafür will ich 500 Euro bar auf die Hand.*

to be short of cash — *knapp bei Kasse sein.*

Gamblers are often short of cash. *Spieler sind oft knapp bei Kasse.*

to cash in on — *Kapital schlagen.*

He knew how to cash in on the stock market crisis. *Aus der Börsenkrise wusste er Kapital zu schlagen.*

---

to cast — *werfen*

to cast doubt on — *in Zweifel stellen.*

She cast doubt on their intentions. *Sie hat ihre Absichten in Zweifel gestellt.*

to cast light on — *Licht in etwas bringen.*

Let us try to cast light on this dark affair. *Versuchen wir Licht in diese dunkle Geschichte zu bringen.*

to cast a role — *besetzen.*

The leading roles aren't cast yet. *Die Hauptrollen sind noch nicht besetzt.*

to cast a spell — *bezaubern, behexen.*

Merlin knew that Viviane was trying to cast a spell on him. *Merlin wusste, dass Viviane versuchte, ihn zu bezaubern.*

to cast about — *sich umsehen nach.*

She is casting about for a new secretary. *Sie sieht sich nach einem neuen Sekretär um.*

to cast off — *losmachen.*

Mutinous sailors refused to cast off. *Meuternde Matrosen weigerten sich, das Boot loszumachen.*

The die is cast. *Die Würfel sind gefallen.*

---

castle — *das Schloss*

to build castles in the air/in Spain — *Luftschlösser bauen.*

Pierette indulged in naïve fantasies and built castles in Spain for herself. *Pierette machte sich Milchmädchenrechnungen und baute sich Luftschlösser.*

---

cast-iron — *(guß)eisern*

Once he had a cast-iron stomach. but now he has ulcers. *Einst hatte er einen eisernen Magen aber jetzt hat er Magengeschwüre.*

a cast-iron alibi — *ein hieb- und stichfestes Alibi.*

The district attorney doesn't believe his cast-iron alibi. *Die Staatsanwältin glaubt nicht an sein hieb- und stichfestes Alibi.*

cat — *die Katze*

the cat's pyjamas/whiskers — *das Gelbe vom Ei.*

He thinks he's the cat's pyjamas. *Er hält sich für das Gelbe vom Ei.*

When the cat's away, the mice will play. *Wenn die Katze aus dem Haus ist, tanzen die Mäuse auf dem Tisch.*

to be a different breed of cat — *zwei Paar Schuhe/Stiefel sein.*

That's a totally different breed of cat. *Das sind zwei verschiedene Paar Stiefel.*

to be like a cat on a hot tin roof — *wie auf glühenden Kohlen sitzen.*

Maggie was like a cat on a hot tin roof. *Maggie saß wie auf glühenden Kohlen.*

to grin like a Cheshire cat — *wie ein Honigkuchenpferd grinsen.*

Why are you grinning like a Cheshire cat? *Warum grinst du wie ein Honigkuchenpferd?*

to let the cat out of the bag — *die Katze aus dem Sack lassen.*

We kept quiet, but you let the cat out of the bag. *Wir haben geschwiegen, aber du hast die Katze aus dem Sack gelassen.*

to see how the cat jumps — *abwarten, wie der Hase läuft.*

Before he decides, he wants to see how the cat jumps. *Bevor er sich entscheidet, will er abwarten, wie der Hase läuft.*

catch — *der Fang*

to be a good catch — *eine gute Partie sein.*

Not all the girls thought the young millionaire was a good catch. *Nicht alle Mädchen hielten den jungen Millionär für eine gute Partie.*

Where's the catch? *Wo ist der Haken?*

to catch — *fangen*

  to catch a cold — *sich erkälten.*

  Linus rarely caught a cold. *Linus erkältete sich nur selten.*

  to be in a catch-22 situation — *in der Zwickmühle sitzen.*

  He tried to set up a super-subtle deal and now he's in a catch-22 situation.
    Er versuchte, ein äußerst spitzfindiges Geschäft einzufädeln und jetzt
    sitzt er in der Zwickmühle.

  to catch on — *ankommen bei.*

  This model never really caught on with the public. *Dieses Modell ist beim*
    Publikum nie so richtig angekommen.

  to catch on — *kapieren.*

  Despite many broad hints, they didn't catch on. *Trotz vieler Winke mit*
    dem Zaunpfahl kapierten sie nichts.

  to catch someone's meaning — *mitbekommen.*

  I caught little of the meaning of everything he said. *Von allem, was er*
    sagte, hab ich nur wenig mitbekommen.

  to catch out (in errors, lies) — *etwas am Zeug flicken.*

  The district attorney couldn't catch her out in anything. *Der Staatsanwalt*
    konnte ihr nichts am Zeug flicken.

  to catch it — *es kriegen.*

  If you don't mend your ways, you'll catch it from me. *Wenn du dich nicht*
    besserst, kriegst du's von mir.

  to catch someone's eye — *ins Auge fallen.*

  Her new dress caught the eye of all the other women. *Ihr neues Kleid fiel*
    all den anderen Frauen ins Auge.

  to catch a likeness — *treffen.*

  The painter caught his likeness very well. *Die Malerin hat ihn gut getroffen.*

  to catch up — *aufholen.*

  He played hooky a lot, but now he wants to catch up. *Er hat viel*
    geschwänzt, aber jetzt will er aufholen.

ceiling — *die Decke*

  to hit the ceiling — *an die Decke gehen.*

When he found out about that, he hit the ceiling. *Als er das erfuhr, ging er an die Decke.*

cent — *der Cent*
to put in one's two cents worth — *seinen Senf dazu geben.*
He felt obliged to put in his two cents' worth again. *Er fühlte sich wieder bemüssigt, seinen Senf dazu zu geben.*

ceremony — *die Feier; Feierlichkeit; Förmlichkeit*
Please don't stand on ceremony. *Bitte keine Förmlichkeiten!/Sei doch nicht so förmlich.*

character — *der Charakter*
to be a character — *ein Original sein.*
Uncle Otto is a real character. *Onkel Otto ist ein richtiges Original.*

character actor — *der Chargenspieler.*
The director is looking for character actors. *Der Regisseur sucht Chargenspieler.*

character assassination — *der Rufmord.*
Character assassination is that journalist's specialty. *Der Rufmord ist die Spezialität dieses Journalisten.*

to be out of character/place — *aus dem Rahmen fallen.*
His remarks were entirely out of character. *Seine Bemerkungen fielen ganz aus dem Rahmen.*

charity — *die Wohltätigkeit*
Charity begins at home. *Das Hemd ist näher als der Rock/Jeder ist sich selbst der Nächste.*

chatterbox — *die Plaudertasche/Schwatzbase*
Your uncle is a real chatterbox. *Dein Onkel ist echt eine Plaudertasche.*

to cheat — *betrügen, schummeln, mogeln*
to cheat death — *dem Tod von der Schippe (Schaufel) springen (hopfen).*
Grandpa's left the hospital and is going to celebrate his 107th birthday at home. He's often cheated death. *Opa hat das Krankenhaus verlassen*

und wird zu Hause seine 107 Jahre feiern. Dem Tod ist er oft von der Schaufel gesprungen.

card cheat — *der, die Falschspieler-in, Mogler-in.*

Minnie, the card-cheat, shuffled and cut the cards often. Nevertheless she won, of course. *Minnie die Moglerin mischte die Karten und hob sie mehrmals ab. Trotzdem gewann sie, natürlich.*

cheese — *der Käse*

the big cheese — *der Gröfaz, Platzhirsch.*

He thinks he's the big cheese here, but we know different. *Er hält sich für den Platzhirsch hier; wir aber wissen's anders.*

chest — *die Brust*

to get something off one's chest — *sich Luft machen/seinem Herzen Luft machen.*

He writes letters to the editor to get all that anger off his chest. *Er schreibt Briefe an die Zeitungsredaktion um seinem Ärger Luft zu machen.*

chestnut — *die Kastanie/Marone*

to pull s.o.'s chestnuts out of the fire — *jemandem. die Kohle/ Kartoffeln/Kastanien aus dem Feuer holen.*

This is the last time I'll pull your chestnuts out of the fire. *Dies ist das letzte Mal, das ich dir die Kohle aus dem Feuer hole.*

to chew — *kauen*

to chew the fat — *schwatzen.*

They chewed the fat all day. *Sie schwatzten den ganzen Tag.*

to chew out — *zusammenstauchen.*

Dagwood Bumsted and all the employees were chewed out by the boss again. *Dagwood Bumsted und alle Angestellten wurden wieder vom Chef zusammengestaucht.*

chicken — *das Huhn*

to count one's chickens before they're hatched — *das Fell verkaufen, ehe man den Bären erlegt hat.*

You shouldn't count your chickens before they are hatched. *Verkauf nicht das Fell, ehe du den Bären erlegt hast. Man soll den Tag nicht vor Abend loben.*

to call chicken — *einen Angsthasen nennen.*

He's not chicken at all and is, in fact, more courageous than you. *In der Tat ist er mutiger als euch und gar kein Angsthase.*

no spring chicken — *nicht mehr der/die Jüngste sein.*

I'm no spring chicken, but many still find me attractive. *Ich bin nicht mehr die Jünste aber viele finden mich noch attraktiv.*

childhood — *die Kindheit*

from earliest childhood — *von Kindesbeinen an.*

From earliest childhood she's been active in many types of sports. *Schon von Kindesbeinen an treibt sie viele Sportarten.*

chip — *die Scheibe*

to be a chip off the old block — *ganz der Vater sein.*

His mother doesn't want to admit it, but the boy is a chip off the old block. *Seine Mutter will's nicht zugeben, aber der Junge ist ganz der Vater.*

to have a chip on one's shoulder — *die beleidigte Leberwurst spielen.*

They didn't give him the job, and now he's got a chip on his shoulder. *Man gab ihm den Posten nicht, und jetzt spielt er die beleidigte Leberwurst.*

to chip in — *beisteuern.*

Some chipped in more money than others for the gift. *Einige steuerten mehr Geld als andere für das Geschenk bei.*

city — *(Groß)Stadt*

city slicker — *der Großstadtmensch/die Großstadtpflanze.*

What does that city-slicker know about our problems here in the country? *Was versteht diese Großstadtpflanze von unseren Problemen hier auf dem Lande?*

clam — *die Venusmuschel; Schwertmuschel; Mördermuschel*
  as happy as a clam (at high water) — *quietschvergnügt sein, sich
  pudelwohl fühlen.*
At the clambake we ate clams and sang happy songs. We were happy as
clams. *Beim Strandpicknick aßen wir Muscheln und sangen frohe
Lieder. Wir waren quietschvergnügt.*

  to clam up — *plötzlich wortkarg werden, verstummen.*
When I asked about his uncle and the CIA, he clammed up. *Als ich nach
seinem Onkel und der CIA fragte, verstummte er.*

clean — *sauber/rein*

  to come clean/make a clean breast of — *alles gestehen/reinen Tisch
  machen.*
After years of silence the accused came clean. *Nach jahrelangem
Schweigen machte der Angeklagte reinen Tisch.*

  to make a clean sweep of — *aufräumen.*
Her film made a clean sweep of the Oscars. *Bei der Oscarverleihung
räumte ihr Film auf.*

cleaners (dry cleaning) — *die (chemische) Reinigung*
  to take to the cleaners — *ausnehmen/ausziehen.*
In that clip joint they really take you to the cleaners. *In dem Nepplokal
wird man wirklich ausgezogen.*

cliff — *der Felsen, das Kliff, die Klippe*
  cliff-hanger — *die Hängepartie/ Zitterpartie.*
The last election was a real cliff-hanger. *Die letzte Wahl war eine echte
Zitterpartie.*

clock — *die Uhr*
  clockwise — *im Uhrzeigersinn.*
Should I turn it clockwise or counterclockwise? *Soll ich das im
Uhrzeigersinn oder gegen den Uhrzeigersinn drehen?*

clockwork — *das Uhrhaus*
>**to work/go like clockwork** — *wie am Schnürchen laufen/klappen.*
>For a while at least, everything went like clockwork. *Wenigstens eine Zeitlang lief alles wie am Schnürchen.*

close — *nahe*
>**to be a close call** — *beinahe ins Auge gehen.*
>That was a close call. *Das ging beinahe ins Auge.*

cloth — *das Tuch*
>**made up of whole cloth** — *aus der Luft gegriffen.*
>The story is made up of whole cloth. *Die Geschichte ist völlig aus der Luft gegriffen.*

cloud — *die Wolke*
>**under a cloud** — *unter zweifelhaften Umständen.*
>He resigned under a cloud. *Er trat unter zweifelhaften Umständen vom Amt zurück.*
>
>**to cloud the issue** — *die Sache verunklaren.*
>Now he's trying to cloud the issue. *Jetzt versucht er die Sache zu verunklaren.*
>
>**to have one's head in the clouds** — *in den Wolken schweben.*
>The best poets have their head in the clouds and their feet firmly on the ground. *Die besten Dichter schweben in den Wolken und stehen auch mit festen Füßen auf der Erde.*

clover — *der Klee*
>**to be in clover** — *an der Krippe sitzen.*
>After years of poverty, he's finally in clover. *Nach Jahren der Armut sitzt er endlich an der Krippe.*

coast — *die Küste*
>**the coast is clear** — *die Luft ist rein.*
>We'll have to stay hidden until the coast is clear. *Wir müssen uns noch versteckt halten, bis die Luft rein ist.*

cock — *der Hahn*
  cock of the walk — *der Hahn im Korb.*
  He dominated the scene in the role of the sultan and felt like the cock of
    the walk. *In der Rolle des Sultans beherrschte er die Szene und fühlte
    sich wie der Hahn im Korb.*

  cock-and-bull story — *die Lügengeschichte/das Lügenmärchen/die
    Räuberpistole.*
  Münchhausen told his cock-and-bull stories at the inn. *Im Wirtshaus
    erzählte Münchhausen seine Lügenmärchen.*

cold — *kalt*
  cold comfort — *ein schwacher Trost.*
  That's only cold comfort. *Das ist nur ein schwacher Trost.*

  cold facts — *nackte Tatsachen.*
  Cold facts leave Blanche cold. *Nackte Tatsachen lassen Blanche kalt.*

  to give the cold shoulder — *die kalte Schulter zeigen.*
  At first she gave him the cold shoulder. *Zuerst zeigte sie ihm die kalte
    Schulter.*

  to leave out in the cold — *links liegen lassen.*
  His superiors left the agent out in the cold. *Seine Vorgesetzten ließen den
    Agenten links liegen.*

color — *die Farbe*
  to come through with flying colors — *sich glänzend bewähren.*
  The world champion in figure skating has come through with flying
    colors again. *Die Weltmeisterin im Eiskunstlaufen hat sich wieder
    glänzend bewährt.*

to come — *kommen*
  to come clean — *alles eingestehen.*
  "When are you going to come clean with us?" asked the policemen.
    "Wann gestehst du uns alles ein?," fragten die Polizeibeamten.

  to come off it — *mal einen Punkt machen.*
  Come off it now! They didn't say ask for that at all. *Nun mach aber mal
    einen Punkt. Das haben sie gar nicht verlangt.*

to come to blows — *tätlich/handgemein werden.*

The soccer fans quarrelled and soon came to blows. *Die Fußballfans stritten sich und wurden bald tätlich.*

to come to nothing — *ins Wasser fallen; ausgehen wie das Hornberger Schießen.*

Our travel plans came to nothing. *Unsere Reisepläne sind ins Wasser gefallen.*

His big plans for restructuring the business all came to nothing. *Seine großen Pläne, das Geschäft neu zu gestalten, gingen aus wie das Hornberger Schießen.*

to come true — *sich erfüllen.*

She thought her most beautiful dream had come true. *Sie glaubte, ihr schönster Traum hätte sich erfüllt.*

to come up with — *aufbringen.*

They couldn't come up with the money right away. *Sie konnten das Geld nicht sofort aufbringen.*

to get what's coming to one — *sein Fett kriegen.*

You'll soon be getting what's coming to you. *Du wirst schon dein Fett kriegen.*

---

to commit — *begehen*

totally committed — *mit Leib und Seele dabei.*

The biologist is totally committed to her work. *Die Biologin ist mit Leib und Seele bei ihrer Arbeit.*

---

confidence — *das Vertrauen*

con(fidence) man — *der Trickbetrüger; der Hochstapler; der Bauernfänger.*

The old swindler wanted to start a school for con men. *Der alte Hochstapler wollte eine Schule für Trickbetrüger gründen.*

---

control — *die Kontrolle*

to control oneself — *sich im Zaum halten.*

She wanted to throw a plate at him, but she controlled herself. *Sie wollte einen Teller nach ihm werfen, aber sie hielt sich im Zaum.*

to get under control — *in den Griff bekommen.*
The government tried to get inflation under control. *Die Regierung versuchte, die Inflation in den Griff zu bekommen.*

cook — *der Koch*
Too many cooks spoil the broth. *Zu viele Köche verderben den Brei.*

to cook up a story — *eine Geschichte aushecken.*
Nobody believed the story they cooked up. *Niemand glaubte an die von ihnen ausgeheckte Geschichte.*

What's cooking? *Was gibt's?*

cookie — *der Keks*
That's the way the cookie crumbles. *So ist nun mal das Leben/So läuft der Hase.*

copy — *die Kopie/Abschrift; das Exemplar*
copycat — *der Nachahmer, Nachmacher.*
That doesn't count, you copycat! *Nachmachen gilt nicht!*

copycat criminal — *der Nachahmungstäter; Trittbrettfahrer.*
After the first anthrax cases, copycat criminals sent salt, powder, sugar, and flour through the mail. *Nach den ersten Milzbrandfällen schickten die Trittbrettfahrer Salz, Puder, Zucker und Mehl durch die Post.*

cork — *der Korken*
to be a real corker — *echt Spitze sein.*
That was a real corker of a joke. *Der Witz war echt Spitze.*

corner — *die Ecke*
to be just around the corner — *vor der Tür stehen.*
The leaves are falling, and winter is just around the corner. *Die Blätter fallen, und der Winter steht vor der Tür.*

to drive into a corner — *in die Enge treiben.*
The journalist drove the senator into a corner. *Die Journalistin trieb den Senator in die Enge.*

from the four corners of the earth — *aus aller Herren Länder.*
"Our guests come from the four corners of the earth," said the hotel owner proudly. *"Unsere Gäste kommen aus aller Herren Länder," sagte stolz die Hotelbesitzerin.*

to corner the market — *den Markt aufkaufen.*
Mr. Dorn once cornered the grain market. *Herr Dorn kaufte einmal den Getreidemarkt auf.*

to cost — *kosten*
to cost an arm and a leg — *ein Vermögen kosten.*
I like the car but it costs an arm and a leg. *Der Wagen gefällt mir, aber es kostet ein Vermögen.*

couch — *das Sofa*
couch potato — *der Stubenhocker/Dauerglotzer.*
That old couch potato doesn't go walking anymore. *Der alte Stubenhocker geht nicht mehr spazieren.*

to cough — *husten*
to cough up (money) — *berappen.*
For admission tickets you have to cough up 100 euros or more. *Für Eintrittskarten muss man hundert Euro oder noch mehr berappen.*

to count — *zählen*
to count on — *sich verlassen auf.*
There's no counting on him. *Auf den ist kein Verlass.*

to count out (exclude) — *nicht mitmachen.*
You can count me out. *Ich mache nicht mit.*

counter — *der Tresen*
over the counter — *freiverkäuflich, nicht rezeptpflichtig.*
Over the counter medications can be dangerous too. *Auch freiverkäufliche Medikamente können gefährlich sein.*

to court — *freien*
   to go courting — *auf Freiersfüßen gehen.*
   Is it true that grandpa is going courting now? *Stimmt es, dass Opa jetzt
   auf Freiersfüßen geht?*

to cover — *decken*
   to cover ground/distance — *zurücklegen.*
   Many migratory birds cover huge distances. *Viele Zugvögel legen
   ungeheure Wege zurück.*

cover — *die Deckung/Tarnung*
   to blow s.o.'s cover — *jmds. Tarnung auffliegen lassen, enttarnen.*
   See to it that you don't blow your cover. *Sieh zu, dass du nicht enttarnt
   wirst.*

crack — *der Riss*
   at the crack of dawn — *in aller Herrgottsfrühe.*
   He likes to get up at the crack of dawn. *Er steht gern in aller
   Herrgottsfrühe auf.*

   to have a crack at — *es einmal versuchen.*
   Even though the chances for success are slight, you could have a crack at
   it. *Obwohl die Erfolgsaussichten gering sind, könntest du's doch einmal
   damit versuchen.*

to crack — *knacken*
   to crack down on — *hart durchgreifen.*
   The candidate promised to crack down on the growing crime rate. *Die
   Kandidatin versprach, gegen die wachsende Kriminalität hart
   durchzugreifen.*

   to crack jokes. *Witze reißen.*
   He's always cracking jokes. *Er reißt immer Witze.*

   to crack open a bottle — *einer Flasche den Hals brechen.*
   Shall we crack open another bottle? *Sollen wir noch einer Flasche den
   Hals brechen?*

to get cracking — *sich ins Zeug legen.*
No more waiting. Let's get cracking. Time for action!
Genug gewartet! Legen wir uns ins Zeug. Ran an den Speck!

creek — *der Bach*
up the creek — *aufgeschmissen, in der Tinte sitzen.*
Without the foreign workers agriculture would be up the creek. *Ohne die ausländischen Arbeiter wäre die Landwirtschaft aufgeschmissen.*

to creep — *kriechen*
to creep in — *sich einschleichen.*
Many errors crept into the report. *Viele Irrtümer haben sich in den Bericht eingeschlichen.*

to give the creeps — *eine Gänsehaut über den Rücken jagen.*
The idiotic horror film was full of monsters who were supposed to give us the creeps. *Der idiotische Horrorfilm strotzte vor Fieslingen, die uns eine Gänsehaut über den Rücken jagen sollten.*

criticism — *die Kritik*
to engage in sharp criticism — *etwas aufs Korn nehmen.*
In that cabaret church and state come in for sharp criticism. *In dem Kabarett werden Kirche und Staat aufs Korn genommen.*

to cross — *kreuzen*
to cross one's mind — *in den Sinn kommen.*
That never would have crossed my mind. *Das wäre mir nie in den Sinn gekommen.*

to cross someone's path — *jemandem über den Weg laufen.*
Guess who crossed my path yesterday. *Rate mal, wer mir gestern über den Weg gelaufen ist.*

to keep one's fingers crossed (for) — *den/die Daumen drücken für.*
Keep your figers crossed so that I do well on the exam. *Drück mir die Daumen, dass ich ein gutes Examen mache.*

crow — *die Krähe*
   as the crow flies —*in der Luftlinie.*
   It's not far as the crow flies. *In der Luftlinie ist es nicht weit.*

   to eat crow — *zu Kreuze kriechen.*
   The proud industrialist had to eat crow. *Der stolze Industrielle musste zu Kreuze kriechen.*

cuff — *die Manschette*
   off the cuff — *aus dem Handgelenk, aus dem Stegreif.*
   I don't care to comment on that off the cuff; I'll have to think about it.
   Dazu möchte ich mich aus dem Handgelenk nicht äußern; darüber muss ich nachdenken.

   on the cuff — *auf Kredit/Pump/Stottern.*
   They bought everything on the cuff and can't meet the payments now. *Sie haben alles auf Stottern gekauft und können jetzt die Zahlungen nicht mehr leisten.*

cup — *die Tasse*
   to be one's cup of tea — *jemands Fall sein.*
   Horror movies are not her cup of tea. *Horrorfilme sind nicht ihr Fall.*

curiosity — *die Neugier*
   curiosity killed the cat — *Neugier ist der Katze Tod/Neugierige Katzen verbrennen sich die Tatzen.*
   "Curiosity didn't kill just the cat," said Bluebeard to his new wife.
   "Neugier ist nicht nur der Katze Tod," sagte Blaubart seiner neuen Frau.

to cut — *schneiden*
   to cut dead — *wie Luft behandeln.*
   She cut her former boyfriend dead. *Sie behandelte ihren ehemaligen Freund wie Luft.*

   to cut down on — *einschränken.*
   He's trying to cut down on his alcohol intake again. *Er versucht wieder, seinen Alkoholverbrauch einzuschränken.*

to cut loose — *die Sau rauslassen.*

The professor is usually quiet and modest, but sometimes he really cuts loose. *Meistens ist der Professor ruhig und bescheiden, aber manchmal lässt er die Sau so richtig raus.*

to cut off — *abschneiden; über den Mund fahren.*

During the press conference the chancellor cut off reporters frequently. *Während der Pressekonferenz fuhr der Kanzler den Reportern wiederholt über den Mund.*

to cut short — *vorzeitig beenden.*

A grave illness cut short her career. *Eine schwere Krankheit hat ihre Karriere vorzeitig beendet.*

to cut the cards/deck — *abheben.*

Cut the cards, please. *Abheben, bitte.*

dagger — der Dolch

   to be at daggers (drawn) — *auf Kriegsfuß stehen.*

   The former friends are now at daggers (drawn) with each other. *Die ehemaligen Freunde stehen jetzt mit einander auf Kriegsfuß.*

   to look daggers at — *hasserfüllt ansehen; mit Blicken zerfleischen.*

   She looked daggers at her rival. *Hasserfüllt sah sie ihre Rivalin an.*

daisy — *das Gänseblümchen*

   fresh as a daisy — *wie aus dem Ei gepellt.*

   Despite the heat you look fresh as a daisy. *Trotz der Hitze siehst du aus wie aus dem Ei gepellt.*

day — *der Tag*

   day off — *Ruhetag, Feiertag.*

   to get a day off — *einen Tag frei bekommen.*

   Can you get a few days off next week? *Kannst du nächste Woche einige Tage frei bekommen?*

the other day — *dieser Tage.*

We saw them the other day. *Wir haben sie dieser Tage gesehen.*

to call it a day — *Feierabend machen.*

Let's call it a day now. *Machen wir jetzt Feierabend.*

to have had its day — *ausgedient haben.*

This model has had its day. *Dieses Modell hat ausgedient.*

day-care center — *die (Kinder) krippe.*

The parents are at work and the child is at the day-care center. *Die Eltern arbeiten und das Kind ist in der Krippe.*

---

daylight — *das Tageslicht*

to beat the (living) daylights out of — *windelweich schlagen, zu Brei schlagen.*

In broad daylight the hoodlums beat the daylights out of him. *Am hell-lichten Tage haben ihn die Hooligans zu Brei geschlagen.*

daylight saving time — *die Sommerzeit.*

Daylight saving time began yesterday and I forgot to set the clock ahead one hour. *Gestern begann die Sommerzeit und ich vergaß, die Uhr um eine Stunde vorzustellen.*

---

dead — *tot*

dead as a doornail — *mausetot.*

The police found him dead as a doornail in front of the TV set. *Die Polizei fand ihn mausetot vor dem Fernseher.*

to be dead wrong — *sich in den Finger schneiden.*

If you think that's enough money, then you're dead wrong. *Wenn Sie meinen das sei genug Geld, dann schneiden Sie sich in den Finger.*

---

deadbeat — *tote Hose*

She called him a deadbeat and also found life in the village deadly dull. *Sie nannte ihn 'ne tote Hose; fand auch das Dorfleben total tote Hose.*

---

deadly — *tödlich*

deadly dull — *todlangweilig; tote Hose.*

Some students thought his lectures were deadly dull. *Einige Studenten hielten seine Vorlesungen für todlangweilig.*

deadly serious(ly) — *bierernst.*

The situation is serious, but let's try not to take it so deadly seriously. *Die Lage ist ernst, aber versuchen wir sie nicht so bierernst zu nehmen.*

to deal with — *sich befassen mit.*

She's now dealing with the problem. *Sie befasst sich jetzt mit dem Problem.*

to get a good/bad deal — *ein gutes/schlechtes Geschäft machen.*

You got a good deal there. *Da hast du ein gutes Geschäft gemacht.*

---

deaf — *taub*

to turn a deaf ear — *einen Rat in den Wind schlagen.*

He's drinking, smoking, and on the way to Las Vegas again. He turned a deaf ear to my advice. *Er trinkt, raucht und ist wieder nach Las Vegas unterwegs. Meinen Rat hat er in den Wind geschlagen.*

---

debut — *das Debüt*

to make one's debut — *sein Debüt geben.*

Tomorrow I make my debut as a tap dancer. *Morgen geb ich mein Debüt als Stepptänzerin.*

---

deck — *das Deck; das Kartenspiel*

not to be playing with a full deck — *nicht (ganz) bei Groschen sein, nicht alle Tassen im Schrank haben.*

I can't explain his behavior; he's not playing with a full deck. *Ich kann mir sein Benehmen nicht erklären; er ist nicht bei Groschen.*

---

devil — *der Teufel*

The devil is in the details. *Der Teufel steckt im Detail.*

The devil take (me)— *Hol (mich) der Teufel.*

The devil take me if that isn't our teacher. *Hol mich der Teufel, wenn das nicht unser Lehrer ist.*

to be a lucky devil — *ein Glückspilz sein/bleiben.*

In all his adventures he was always a lucky devil. *Bei allen seinen Abenteuern blieb er ein Glückspilz.*

devil-may-care — *sorglos, leichtsinnig; nach mir die Sintflut.*

Louis XV is supposed to have said "After me, the deluge," but he wasn't as devil-may-care as people think. *"Nach mir die Sintflut" soll Ludwig XV. gesagt haben, aber er war nicht so leichtsinnig, wie man meint.*

to have the devil in one — *den Teufel im Leib haben.*

His youngest son has the devil in him. *Sein jüngster Sohn hat den Teufel im Leib.*

to have the devil's own luck — *verteufeltes Glück haben.*

In Monte Carlo, Las Vegas, and Baden-Baden she had the devil's own luck. *In Monte Carlo, Las Vegas und Baden-Baden hatte sie verteufeltes Glück.*

---

diamond — *der Diamant*

a rough diamond — *ein Rauhbein.*

He's quite a rough diamond, but the princess loves him. *Er ist ein richtiges Rauhbein; die Prinzessin liebt ihn aber trotzdem.*

---

to die — *sterben*

to be dying for — *nach etwas lechzen.*

On the job he was dying for a glass of beer. *Bei der Arbeit lechzte er nach einem Glas Bier.*

to be dying to do something — *darauf brennen, etwas zu tun.*

We're dying to know how the story turns out. *Wir brennen darauf zu wissen, wie die Geschichte ausgeht.*

to die in the war — *im Krieg bleiben/fallen.*

Her two sons died in the war. *Ihre beiden Söhne sind im Krieg geblieben.*

---

different — *anders*

He's different from the others. *Er ist anders als die andern.*

a different ballgame/ballpark/breed of cat/kettle of fish — *zwei Paar Schuhe, ein anderes Paar Schuhe, ein anderes Kapitel.*

Theory and practice, they're different ballgames. *Theorie und Praxis, das sind zwei Paar Schuhe.*

---

difficult — *schwer*

to be difficult for — *es schwer haben.*

Because of supermarkets, things are difficult for most Mom and Pop stores. *Wegen der Supermärkte haben es die meisten Tante-Emma-Läden schwer.*

to be difficult for — *es schwer fallen.*

It was difficult for the sailor's girl to have to be separated from him so often. *Es fiel der Seemannsbraut schwer, sich so oft von ihm trennen zu müssen.*

---

to dig — *graben*

to dig in — *zugreifen.*

Dig in right now if you're hungry. *Greif schon jetzt zu, wenn du Hunger hast.*

to dig in one's heels — *sich auf die Hinterbeine stellen.*

If you don't dig in your heels, they'll push you aside. *Wenn du dich nicht auf die Hinterbeine stellst, wird man dich beiseite schieben.*

to dig up — *aufgabeln.*

The reporter dug up many unpleasant things about the senator. *Die Reporterin gabelte viel Unangenehmes über den Senator auf.*

---

dirt — *der Dreck*

dirt cheap — *spottbillig.*

He bought a sports car dirt cheap. *Er hat einen Sportwagen spottbillig gekauft.*

dirt-poor — *bettelarm.*

We were dirt-poor then. *Damals waren wir bettelarm.*

to do dirt to — *eins auswischen.*

The senator tried to do her dirt. *Der Senator versuchte, ihr eins auszuwischen.*

dirty — *dreckig.*

to be dirty (in politics) — *Dreck am Stecken haben.*

The reporter claimed the senator was dirty. *Die Reporterin behauptete, der Senator habe Dreck am Stecken.*

to give s.o. a dirty look — *jmdm. einen bösen/finsteren Blick zuwerfen.*
I don't know why he gave me such a dirty look. *Ich weiß nicht, warum er mir einen so bösen Blick zuwarf.*

to disappear — *verschwinden*
    to disappear into thin air — *von der Bildfläche verschwinden.*
    The sorceress disappeared into thin air. *Die Zauberin verschwand von der Bildfläche.*

discretion — *die Diskretion*
    Discretion is the better part of valor. *Vorsicht ist besser als Nachsicht.*

    to use one's own discretion — *nach eigenem Ermessen handeln.*
    But you told me to use my own discretion at the auction! *Aber du hast mir gesagt, ich sollte bei der Versteigerung nach meinem eigenen Ermessen handeln!*

to do — *tun*
    Do unto others as you would they do unto you. *Was du nicht willst, dass man dir tu, das tu keinem anderen zu.*

    to do — *abschneiden.*
    He hopes to do better in the run-off election. *Bei der Stichwahl hofft er besser abzuschneiden.*

    to do — *besichtigen.*
    To do Vienna properly, you need at least a week. *Um Wien richtig zu besichtigen, braucht man wenigstens eine Woche.*

    to do — *gehen.*
    How are you doing? *Wie geht es Ihnen (dir, euch)?*

    to do — *reichen.*
    That will do. *Das reicht.*

    to do in — *umbringen; den Garaus machen.*
    The gardener tried to do in the bugs by natural means. *Der Gärtner versuchte, dem Ungeziefer durch natürliche Mittel den Garaus zu machen.*

    to do without (something) — *entbehren; sich etwas nehmen lassen.*

Although we're short of funds, we don't want to do without our vacation trip. *Trotz knapper Kasse wollen wir uns die Urlaubsreise nicht nehmen lassen.*

done — *getan*

What's done is done. *Getan ist getan! (Geschehen ist geschehen!)*

to be all done in — *erschöpft sein, fix und fertig sein.*
After that bone-breaking job I was all done in. *Nach der Knochenarbeit war ich fix und fertig.*

---

dog — *der Hund*

Let sleeping dogs lie. *Schlafende Hunde soll man nicht wecken.*

every dog has its day — *für jeden kommt eine Chance.*
Every dog has its day, but you slept through it and missed out on the 15 minutes of fame you might have had. *Für jeden kommt eine Chance, aber du hast sie verschlafen und deine 15 Minuten Berühmtheit verpasst.*

to dog s.o's tracks. *Jmdm. auf Schritt und Tritt folgen.*
The reporters dogged the princess' track. *Die Reporter folgten der Prinzessin auf Schritt und Tritt.*

to go to the dogs — *vor die Hunde gehen.*
He lost so much money at the dog races that he's gone to the dogs. *Bei den Windhundrennen hat er so viel Geld verloren, dass er vor die Hunde gegangen ist.*

to put on the dog — *einen großen Aufwand treiben, protzen, auf fein machen.*
You don't have to put on the dog for us. *Für uns musst ihr keinen großen Aufwand treiben.*

to work like a dog — *ackern, malochen.*
I worked like a dog all day and I'm dog-tired now. *Den ganzen Tag hab ich geackert und jetzt bin ich hundemüde.*

---

doll — *die Puppe*

to get all dolled up — *sich auftakeln.*
Cinderella's sisters got all dolled up for the ball. *Aschenputtels Schwestern takelten sich für den Ball auf.*

---

double — *doppelt*

On the double! *Im Laufschritt!*

"On the double!" ordered the sergeant. *"Im Laufschritt!" befahl der Feldwebel.*

to apply a double standard — *mit zweierlei Maß messen.*

Thanks to the womens' movement, society applies the double standard less. *Dank der Frauenbewegung misst die Gesellschaft weniger mit zweierlei Maß.*

to double-cross — *ein falsches Spiel treiben.*

The double agent double-crossed his government for many years. *Viele Jahre trieb der Doppelagent ein falsches Spiel mit seiner Regierung.*

to double up — *sich ein Zimmer teilen.*

We had to double up in the hotel. *Im Hotel mussten wir uns das Zimmer teilen.*

---

down — *herunter*

down to the present day — *bis in unsere Tage.*

In that region many traditions have been preserved down to the present day. *In der Gegend haben sich bis in unsere Tage viele Traditionen erhalten.*

to be down and out — *elend dran sein.*

He is homeless, down and out, but he's learning to play the violin. Er ist obdachlos, ganz elend dran, lernt aber Geige spielen.

to be down at the heels — *heruntergekommen sein.*

He is down at the heels. *Er ist ganz heruntergekommen.*

to be down in the dumps — *ganz niedergeschlagen sein.*

She left him, and he's down in the dumps. *Sie hat ihn verlassen, und er ist ganz niedergeschlagen.*

to be down on one's luck — *vom Pech verfolgt sein.*

Ever since the divorce he's been down on his luck. *Seit der Scheidung wird er vom Pech verfolgt.*

to get down (depress) — *kirre machen.*

The reports about the many harmful substances in the environment have really gotten us down. *Die Berichte von den vielen Schadstoffen in der Umwelt haben uns kirre gemacht.*

dozen — *das Dutzend*
  baker's dozen — *dreizehn Stück.*
  She's very nice and always gives us a baker's dozen for the price of a
  dozen. *Sie ist sehr nett und gibt uns immer dreizehn Stück zum
  Dutzendpreis.*

  six of one, half dozen of the other — *Jacke wie Hose.*
  I see no difference there; it's six of one, half dozen of the other. *Da seh
  ich keinen Unterschied; das ist Jacke wie Hose.*

---

drain — *das Abflussrohr*
  to go down the drain — *ins Wasser fallen.*
  Our vacation plans have gone down the drain. *Unsere Urlaubspläne sind
  ins Wasser gefallen.*

---

drawer — *die Schublade*
  top-drawer — *von höchster Qualität, der Extraklasse.*
  If it isn't top-drawer, you can keep it. *Wenn's nicht von höchster Qualität
  ist, können Sie's behalten.*

---

to dress — *sich anziehen*
  dressed to kill — *aufgedonnert sein.*
  Dressed to kill, the lady in red entered the movie house. *Ganz
  aufgedonnert, trat die Dame in Rot ins Kino ein.*

  to give a dressing down — *die Leviten lesen/eine Standpauke halten.*
  The boss gave him quite a dressing down/really chewed him out. *Die
  Chefin hat ihm eine gehörige Standpauke gehalten.*

---

drink — *das Getränk*
  That calls for a drink! *Das müssen wir begießen!*

  a soft drink — *ein alkoholfreies Getränk.*
  Unfortunately it has to be a soft drink. *Leider muss es ein alkoholfreies
  Getränk sein.*

  to be dying/gagging for a drink — *verdursten.*
  Open that bottle fast; I'm really dying for a drink. *Mach schnell die
  Flasche auf; ich verdurste gleich.*

to buy someone a drink — *jemandem einen ausgeben.*
Are you going to buy me a drink? *Gibst du mir einen aus?*

to have a drink — *einen trinken.*
Let's have a drink! *Trinken wir einen!*

to drink like a fish — *wie ein Loch/Schlauch saufen.*
God, you drink like a fish. *Mensch, du säufst ja wie ein Loch.*

to drink up — *austrinken, aussaufen.*
Drink up and I'll pour you some more. *Trink aus und ich schenk dir wieder ein.*

to drive — *treiben; fahren*
   to drive at — *auf etwas hinauswollen.*
What are you driving at with that? *Wo wollen Sie damit hinaus?*

   to drive up the wall — *auf die Palme bringen.*
The undermining of the language drives many French scholars up the wall. *Die Unterwanderung der Sprache bringt viele französische Gelehrte auf die Palme.*

drop — *der Tropfen*
   a drop in the bucket — *ein Tropfen auf den heißen Stein.*
These donations are just a drop in the bucket. *Diese Spenden sind nur ein Tropfen auf den heißen Stein.*

to drop — *fallen lassen*
   to drop a line — *ein paar Zeilen schreiben.*
Drop us a line now and then. *Schreib uns dann und wann ein paar Zeilen.*

   to drop the subject — *das Thema wechseln.*
We'd better drop the subject. *Wechseln wir lieber das Thema!*

   to drop in — *hereinschauen.*
Drop in on us some time. *Schauen Sie mal bei uns 'rein!*

   to drop off — *absetzen.*
Can you drop me off at the station? *Können Sie mich am Bahnhof absetzen?*

   to drop out — *aussteigen.*
After a brilliant career, he dropped out of society. *Nach einer glänzenden Karriere stieg er aus der Gesellschaft aus.*

to drop out — *zusammenbrechen.*

On that Friday the bottom dropped out of the stock market. *An dem Freitag brach der Börsenmarkt zusammen.*

drummer — *der Trommler*

to walk/march to the beat of a different drummer — *aus der Reihe tanzen, aus dem Schritt/Tritt/Takt kommen.*

Yes, we know he likes to walk to the beat of a different drummer, but now he has to get into step with us. *Ja, wir wissen, er tanzt gern aus der Reihe, aber jetzt muss er im Gleichschritt mit uns mitmarschieren.*

drunk — *betrunken; besoffen*

to be dead drunk — *sternhagelblau/voll sein.*

All saw that he was dead drunk. *Alle sahen, dass er sternhagelblau war.*

duck — *die Ente*

to be like water off a duck's back — *glatt ablaufen.*

All threats were like water off a duck's back to her. *Alle Drohungen liefen an ihr glatt ab.*

to take to like a duck to water — *bei etwas gleich in einem Element sein.*

The children took to the new electronic game like ducks to water. *Bei dem neuen elektronischen Spiel waren die Kinder gleich in ihrem Element.*

dust — *der Staub*

dry as dust — *todlangweilig, knochentrocken.*

The subject's dry as dust; but she knows how to bring it to life. *Das Thema ist knochentrocken, aber sie weiß, es zu beleben.*

dust jacket — *der Schutzumschlag.*

That's a first edition, but the dust jacket is missing. *Das ist eine Erstausgabe, aber der Schutzumschlag fehlt.*

dust-jacket blurb — *der Klappentext.*

The dust-jacket blurb has an interesting but inaccurate description of the book. *Im Klappentext steht eine interessante aber irreführende Beschreibung des Buches.*

to let the dust settle — *das Gras über etwas wachsen lassen.*
It would be advisable to let the dust settle on the matter. *Es wäre ratsam, das Gras darüber wachsen zu lassen.*

Dutch — *holländisch*
Dutch courage — *angetrunkener Mut.*
Thanks to Dutch courage, he told the boss off. *Dank angetrunkenem Mut schimpfte er den Chef aus.*

to go Dutch — *getrennte Kasse machen.*
We went Dutch. *Wir haben getrennte Kasse gemacht.*

to dye — *färben*
dyed-in-the-wool — *eingefleischt.*
Victoria Augusta is a dyed-in-the-wool monarchist/democrat/republican. *Viktoria Augusta ist eine eingefleischte Monarchistin/ Demokratin/Republikanerin.*

eager — *eifrig*
to be an eager beaver — *ein Streber sein; übereifrig sein.*
Even at school he was an eager beaver and he's still too eager. *Schon in der Schule war er ein Streber und übereifrig ist er geblieben.*

ear — *das Ohr*
to be all ears — *ganz Ohr sein.*
Whenever anyone's gossiping, he's always all ears. *Wenn geklatscht wird, ist er immer ganz Ohr.*

to be out on one's ear — *fliegen.*
Do it again and you'll be out on your ear. *Tu's wieder und du fliegst.*

to be up to one's ears in work — *viel um die Ohren haben.*
If I weren't so up to my ears in work today, I'd come along. *Wenn ich heute nicht so viel um die Ohren hätte, würde ich schon mitkommen.*

to bend s.o.'s ear — *jemanden voll quatschen.*

I was in a hurry but he wanted to keep on bending my ear. *Ich hatte es eilig, aber er wollte mich noch voll quatschen.*

to have a good ear — *ein gutes Gehör haben.*

She has a good ear for music. *Sie hat ein gutes Gehör für Musik.*

---

easy — *leicht*

easy as pie/ABC — *kinderleicht.*

"With this gadget, cooking is as easy as pie," said the salesman. *"Mit diesem Gerät ist das Kochen kinderleicht," sagte der Verkäufer.*

Easy come, easy go. *Wie gewonnen, so zeronnen.*

easy to say — *gut reden können.*

That's easy for him to say because he knows nothing about it. *Der kann gut reden, weil er nichts davon versteht.*

easy to get on with — *gut auskommen mit.*

Most colleagues find they can get on with her easily. *Die meisten Kollegen finden, dass sie mit ihr gut auskommen können.*

to take it easy — *es sich gut gehen lassen.*

On vacation I took it easy, but now I've got to work hard. *Auf Urlaub ließ ich's mir gut gehen aber jetzt muss ich schuften.*

---

to eat — *essen; fressen*

to eat humble pie — *klein beigeben.*

The congressman couldn't prove his statements and had to eat humble pie. *Der Abgeordnete konnte seine Äußerungen nicht beweisen und musste klein beigeben.*

to eat one's words — *seine Worte zurücknehmen.*

He had to eat his words. *Er musste seine Worte zurücknehmen.*

to eat out of house and home — *die Haare vom Kopf fressen.*

The children are eating the old lady in the shoe out of house and home. *Die Kinder fressen der alten Dame im Schuh die Haare vom Kopf weg.*

What's eating you (her, him, them)? *Welche Laus ist dir (ihm, ihr, ihnen) über die Leber gelaufen?*

---

edge — *die Kante*

   to go over the edge — *überschnappen.*

   After his beloved's death, he went over the edge. *Nach dem Tod seiner Geliebten ist er übergeschnappt.*

   to have a competitive edge — *konkurrenzfähiger sein.*

   His firm has a competitive edge over all the others. *Seine Firma ist konkurrenzfähiger als die anderen.*

egg — *das Ei*

   to put all one's eggs in one basket — *alles auf eine Karte setzen.*

   She dared to put all her eggs in one basket and won. *Sie wagte es, alles auf eine Karte zu setzen, und gewann.*

   to teach one's grandmother to suck eggs — *klüger als die Henne sein wollen.*

   Don't teach your grandmother to suck eggs. *Da will das Ei wieder klüger als die Henne sein.*

eleventh — *elft*

   at the eleventh hour — *fünf Minuten vor zwölf.*

   At the eleventh hour the invasion was called off. *Fünf Minuten vor zwölf wurde die Invasion abgeblasen.*

empty — *leer*

   Empty vessels make the most noise. *Leere Töpfe klappern und leere Köpfe plappern am meisten.*

end — *das Ende*

   That's the living end! *Da ist ein/das Ende von weg!*

   They gave that idiot the first prize? That's the living end! *Diesem Idioten hat man den ersten Preis gegeben? Da ist ein Ende von weg!*

   to be at the end of one's rope (tether, wits) — *weder aus noch ein wissen.*

   Tormented by regret and sorrow, she was at her wits' end. *Vor Reue und Schmerz gepeinigt, wusste sie weder aus noch ein.*

to go off the deep end — *aus dem Häuschen geraten.*

When he heard the car was totaled, he went off the deep end. *Als er vom Totalschaden des Wagens hörte, geriet er aus dem Häuschen.*

to know which end is up — *wissen, wo hinten und vorn ist.*

The team became confused and didn't know which end was up anymore. *Die Mannschaft geriet in Verwirrung und wusste nicht mehr, wo hinten und vorn war.*

to make ends meet — *auskommen.*

It's difficult for them to make ends meet on 100 euros a month. *Es fällt ihnen schwer, mit monatlich hundert Euro auszukommen.*

to stand on end — *zu Berge stehen.*

Her hair stood on end when she saw the ghost. *Ihr standen die Haare zu Berge, als sie das Gespenst erblickte.*

---

to end — *enden; zu Ende gehen; ausgehen*

All's well that ends well. *Ende gut, alles gut.*

to end up — *landen.*

They ended up at our place. *Sie landeten schließlich bei uns.*

to end (up) in a stalemate —*mit einem Patt ausgehen.*

The election ended in a stalemate. *Die Wahl ging mit einem Patt aus.*

---

enemy — *der Feind*

to be one's own worst enemy — *sich selber im Weg stehen.*

If he weren't his own worst enemy, he'd make better progress. *Wenn er sich selber nicht immer im Weg stünde, würde er größere Fortschritte machen.*

---

enough — *genug*

oddly enough — *seltsamerweise.*

Oddly enough, the gambler was glad when he had no more money. *Seltsamerweise war der Spieler froh, als er kein Geld mehr hatte.*

to be enough — *reichen.*

That's enough now! *Jetzt reicht's!*

to be nowhere near enough — *von hinten und vorne nicht ausreichen.*
That's nowhere near enough. *Das reicht von hinten und vorne nicht aus.*

to establish — *gründen*
  to become established — *Fuß fassen.*
  Our firm had trouble getting established abroad. *Unsere Firma hatte Schwierigkeiten, im Ausland Fuß zu fassen.*

even — *eben; gleich*
  to be even — *quitt sein.*
  Here's your money; now we're even. *Hier hast du dein Geld; jetzt sind wir quitt.*

  evenhanded — *gerecht.*
  The government is trying to treat the minorities in an evenhanded way. *Die Regierung versucht, die Minderheiten gerecht zu behandeln.*

  to be even tempered — *ausgeglichen sein.*
  She is an even tempered person. *Sie ist ein ausgeglichener Mensch.*

  to get even — *heimzahlen.*
  The senator swore to get even with the reporter. *Der Senator schwor, es der Reporterin heimzuzahlen.*

every — *jed,- all-*
  every other day — *alle zwei Tage.*
  Every other day he eats fish. *Alle zwei Tage isst er Fisch.*

  every now and then; every so often — *hin und wieder.*
  Every now and then they drop in on us. *Hin und wieder schauen sie bei uns 'rein.*

  every Tom, Dick, and Harry — *Hinz und Kunz.*
  The snob wanted something more exclusive, not some place for every Tom, Dick, and Harry. *Der Snob wollte etwas Exklusiveres, kein Lokal für Hinz und Kunz.*

everything — *alles*
  to have everything one's heart desires — *alles haben, was man sich nur wünschen kann.*

People thought the princess had everything one's heart could desire, but she ran off with a gypsy. *Man glaubte, die Prinzessin hätte alles, was man sich nur wünschen könnte, aber sie brannte mit einem Zigeuner durch.*

to mean everything to — *ein und alles sein.*
Their little daughter meant everything to them. *Ihr Töchterchen war ihr ein und alles.*

---

eye — *das Auge*
an eagle's eye — *ein wachsames Auge.*
The miser kept an eagle's eye on his treasures. *Der Geizhals hatte ein wachsames Auge auf seine Schätze.*

as far as the eye can see — *so weit das Auge reicht.*
As far as the eye could see, everything was in ruins. *So weit das Auge reichte, lag alles in Trümmern.*

to have/keep an eye on — *auf dem Kieker haben.*
The police have been keeping an eye on him for some time. *Die Polizei hat ihn schon lange auf dem Kieker.*

to turn a blind eye — *ein Auge zudrücken.*
She knew what he was, but always turned a blind eye. *Sie wusste, was er war, aber sie drückte immer ein Auge zu.*

to be eyecatching — *die Augen aller auf sich ziehen.*
She's grown old but is still eyecatching. *Sie ist in die Jahre gekommen; zieht aber noch die Augen aller auf sich.*

---

eyebrow — *die Augenbraue*
to raise eyebrows — *Stirnrunzeln hervorrufen.*
Her behavior raised a few eyebrows. *Ihr Benehmen hat einiges Stirnrunzeln hervorgerufen.*

---

eyetooth — *der Eckzahn*
to cut one's eyeteeth — *Erfahrungen sammeln.*
The boy is cutting his eyeteeth. *Der Junge sammelt Erfahrungen.*

---

face — *das Gesicht*

  to keep a straight face — *sich das Lachen verbeißen.*
She kept a straight face and let him talk. *Sie verbiss sich das Lachen und ließ ihn reden.*

  to make faces — *Grimassen schneiden.*
Grandpa likes to make faces for his grandchildren. *Opa schneidet gern Grimassen für die Enkel.*

  to take at face value — *etwas für bare Münze nehmen.*
Few reporters took his explanations at face value. *Wenige Reporter nahmen seine Erklärungen für bare Münze.*

---

to face — *liegen*

  to face a trial — *sich vor Gericht verantworten müssen.*
She's facing a murder trial. *Wegen Mordes muss sie sich vor Gericht verantworten.*

  to face the music — *die Suppe auslöffeln.*
One day you'll have to face the music. *Eines Tages wirst du die Suppe auslöffeln müssen.*

  to face up to — *ins Auge sehen.*
He had to face up to the truth. *Er musste der Wahrheit ins Auge sehen.*

---

to fall — *fallen*

  to fall back on — *zurückgreifen auf.*
They can always fall back on their reserves. *Sie können immer auf ihre Reserven zurückgreifen.*

  to fall behind — *ins Hintertreffen geraten.*
Because it didn't adapt to new technology, our firm fell behind. *Weil sie sich der neuen Technik nicht anpasste, geriet unsere Firma ins Hintertreffen.*

  to fall by the wayside — *auf der Strecke bleiben.*
Because of the ratings, that TV program fell by the wayside. *Wegen der Einschaltquoten blieb diese Fernsehsendung auf der Strecke.*

to fall flat — *danebengehen.*

Their efforts fell flat. *Ihre Bemühungen gingen daneben.*

to fall flat on one's face — *auf die Nase fallen.*

He won't be playing the role, since he fell flat on his face again during rehearsal. *Er wird die Rolle nicht spielen, weil er bei der Probe wieder auf die Nase fiel.*

to fall for — *sich verknallen.*

She's fallen for an older man again. *Sie hat sich wieder in einen älteren Mann verknallt.*

to fall for — *hereinfallen; auf den Leim gehen.*

He fell for their propaganda. *Er ist ihrer Propaganda auf den Leim gegangen.*

to fall in love — *sich verlieben.*

He fell passionately in love with her. *Er verliebte sich leidenschaftlich in sie.*

to fall out with — *sich entzweien.*

When dividing their booty, the thieves had a falling out. *Bei der Beuteteilung entzweiten sich die Diebe.*

to fall short of expectations — *den Erwartungen nicht entsprechen.*

Production fell short of government expectations. *Die Produktion entsprach den Erwartungen der Regierung nicht.*

---

fall guy — *das Bauernopfer, der Prügelknabe*

The Secretary of Commerce was the fall guy in that affair; it's the President who should have resigned. *Der Wirtschaftsminister war das Bauernopfer in dieser Sache; eigentlich hätte der Präsident zurücktreten sollen.*

---

false — *falsch*

false teeth — *dritte Zähne.*

Grandpa refuses to wear his false teeth. *Opa weigert sich, seine dritten Zähne zu tragen.*

to play false — *ein falsches Spiel treiben.*

Frankie played false with Johnny. *Frankie hat mit Johnny ein falsches Spiel getrieben.*

to sail under false colors — *unter falscher Flagge segeln.*
The alleged missionary was sailing under false colors. *Der angebliche Missionar segelte unter falscher Flagge.*

far — *weit*

better by far — *weitaus besser.*
Their proposals were better by far. *Ihre Vorschläge waren weitaus besser.*

Far from it! — *Ganz im Gegenteil!*

a far cry from — *weit entfernt von.*
This VW is a far cry from the Porsche you promised me. *Dieser VW ist weit entfernt von dem Porsche, den du mir versprochen hattest.*

far-fetched — *weit hergeholt; an den Haaren herbeigezogen.*
Many of Rapunzel's ideas are extremely far-fetched. *Viele von Rapunzels Ideen sind an den Haaren herbeigezogen.*

to go too far — *es zu bunt treiben.*
Some said the young poet had gone too far again. *Einige sagten, der junge Dichter hätte es wieder zu bunt getrieben.*

fashion — *die Mode*

after a fashion — *schlecht und recht.*
He wasn't at all enthusiastic about the work but he did it after a fashion. *Er war von der Arbeit gar nicht begeistert, tat sie aber schlecht und recht.*

fast — *schnell*

to be fast — *vorgehen.*
His watch was fast and we arrived too early. *Seine Uhr ging vor, und wir kamen zu früh an.*

to be fast friends — *dicke Freunde sein.*
They're fast friends. *Sie sind dicke Freunde.*

to pull a fast one — *übers Ohr hauen.*
The diamond dealer tried to pull a fast one on us. *Der Diamantenhändler versuchte, uns übers Ohr zu hauen.*

fat — *das Fett*

The fat is in the fire. *Der Teufel ist los.*

to do a fat lot of good — *herzlich wenig nutzen.*
The combs did the bald man a fat lot of good. *Dem Kahlen nutzten die Kämme herzlich wenig.*

to live off the fat of the land — *wie die Made im Speck leben.*
Lenny longed to live off the fat of the land. *Lenny lechzte danach, wie die Made im Speck zu leben.*

A fat lot I care! *Das ist mir so was von egal!*

fault — *der Fehler*

to a fault — *übertrieben.*
Some Königsbergers thought Kant was punctual to a fault. *Einige Königsberger fanden Kant übertrieben pünktlich.*

feather — *die Feder*

Birds of a feather flock together. *Gleich und gleich gesellt sich gern.*

to feather one's nest — *sein Schäfchen ins Trockene bringen.*
The party boss feathered his nest and didn't bother about the members. *Der Parteibonze brachte sein Schäfchen ins Trockene und kümmerte sich nicht um die Mitglieder.*

feast — *der Schmaus, das Festmahl; der Feiertag*

a feast for the ears — *ein Ohrenschmaus.*
His new atonal music is certainly no feast for the ears. *Seine neue atonale Musik ist gewiss kein Ohrenschmaus.*

a feast for the eyes — *eine Augenweide.*
The belly dancer was a real feast for the eyes. *Die Bauchtänzerin war echt eine Augenweide.*

to feed — *füttern*

to be fed up — *die Nase voll haben.*
She was fed up with his snoring. *Sie hatte die Nase voll von seinem Schnarchen.*

to feel — *fühlen*

  to feel cold/warm — *kalt/warm sein.*

They didn't know how to set the heat, because he always feels cold and
she always feels warm. *Sie wussten nicht, wie sie die Heizung anstellen
sollten, weil ihm immer kalt und ihr immer warm ist.*

  to feel for — *Mitleid haben mit.*

He said he really felt for me but couldn't help me. *Er sagte, er hätte viel
Mitleid mit mir, könnte mir aber nicht helfen.*

  to feel like — *Lust haben.*

Do you feel like going to the fairgrounds with me? *Hätten Sie Lust, mit
mir auf den Rummelplatz zu gehen?*

  to feel on top of the world — *obenauf.*

They're healthy and feel on top of the world. *Sie sind gesund und
obenauf.*

  to feel out — *seine Fühler ausstrecken; auf den Busch klopfen.*

First we should feel out whether the undertaking is possible now. *Zuerst
sollten wir unsere Fühler ausstrecken, ob das Unternehmen jetzt
möglich ist.*

  to feel sorry for oneself — *sich bemitleiden.*

He stopped feeling sorry for himself and felt better. *Er hörte auf, sich zu
bemitleiden, und fühlte sich besser.*

  to feel the pinch of — *zu spüren bekommen.*

Retirees especially felt the pinch of inflation. *Besonders Rentner haben
die Inflation zu spüren bekommen.*

---

few — *wenig*

  few and far between — *dünn gesät.*

Such opportunities are few and far between. *Solche Gelegenheiten sind
dünn gesät.*

---

figure — *die Zahl; die Gestalt; die Figur*

  figurehead — *die Galionsfigur.*

The queen now wants to be more than a figurehead. *Die Königin will jetzt
mehr als Galionsfigur sein.*

---

to fill — *füllen*

Fill 'er up please! *Voll tanken, bitte!*

filthy — *dreckig*

   to be filthy rich — *Geld wie Dreck haben.*

Our relatives were filthy rich, but we were dirt poor. *Unsere Verwandten hatten Geld wie Dreck, wir aber waren bettelarm.*

fine — *fein*

   to be fine and dandy — *in bester Butter sein, alles paletti.*

He finally found a good job and everything's fine and dandy now. *Endlich hat er eine gute Stelle gefunden und es ist jetzt alles in bester Butter.*

finger — *der Finger*

   not to lift a finger — *keinen Finger krumm machen, keinen Schlag tun.*

He didn't lift a finger to help me with the difficult job. *Er tat keinen Schlag, mir bei der schweren Arbeit zu helfen.*

   to have a finger in the pie — *die Hand im Spiel haben.*

She's retired but still has a finger in the pie. *Sie hat sich zurückgezogen, hat aber noch die Hand im Spiel.*

   to slip through one's fingers — *durch die Lappen gehen.*

Another golden opportunity has slipped through our fingers! *Wieder ist uns eine goldene Gelegenheit durch die Lappen gegangen!*

to finish — *beenden*

   the finishing touch — *der letzte Schliff.*

He wanted to apply the finishing touch to his painting, but all he did was muck it up. *Er wollte seinem Gemälde den letzten Schliff geben, hat es aber nur vermanscht.*

fire — *das Feuer*

   to come under fire — *unter Beschuss geraten.*

Factory livestock farming has come under fire. *Die Massentierhaltung ist unter Beschuss geraten.*

to set the world on fire — *das Pulver erfinden.*
He'll never set the world on fire. *Er hat das Pulver nicht erfunden.*

first — *erst*
at first go/try — *auf Anhieb.*
She succeeded at first try. *Es gelang ihr auf Anhieb.*

First come, first served. *Wer zuerst kommt, mahlt zuerst.*

to be on a first name basis — *sich duzen.*
They were soon on a first name basis. *Bald dutzten sie sich.*

at first sight — *auf den ersten Blick.*
Don Juan spoke of love at first sight. *Don Juan sprach von Liebe auf den ersten Blick.*

fish — *der Fisch*
fishy — *nicht ganz astrein/hasenrein sein.*
There's something fishy about that. *Das ist nicht ganz astrein.*

to fix — *reparieren*
fixed prices — *Festpreise*
Some people like to haggle, but we buy only at fixed prices. *Einigen gefällt das Feilschen, aber wir kaufen nur zu Festpreisen.*

to fix dinner — *das Abendessen zubereiten.*
Her husband always fixes dinner for her. *Ihr Mann bereitet ihr immer das Abendessen zu.*

to fix a judge/jury — *den Richter (die Geschworenen) bestechen.*
The gangster tried to fix the judge. *Der Gangster versuchte, den Richter zu bestechen.*

flash — *das Aufleuchten; der Blitz*
to be over in a flash — *im Nu vorbei sein.*
Don't be frightened; it'll all be over in a flash. *Hab keine Angst; im Nu ist alles vorbei.*

to reply quick as a flash — *wie aus der Pistole geschossen antworten.*
The senator replied to the accusation quick as a flash. *Der Senator antwortete auf die Anschuldigung wie aus der Pistole geschossen.*

flash in the pan — *das Strohfeuer, die Eintagsfliege.*
Her debut was very promising, but her career was just a flash in the pan.
*Ihr Debüt war vielversprechend, ihre Karriere war aber nur eine
Eintagsfliege.*

flat — *flach; platt*
flat broke — *völlig abgebrannt, pleite.*
We wound up flat broke in Las Vegas. *Am Ende waren wir völlig
abgebrannt in Las Vegas.*

to flog — *auspeitschen*
to flog a dead horse — *offene Türen einrennen.*
Enough of that! You're flogging a dead horse. *Genug davon! Du rennst
offene Türen ein.*

fly — *die Fliege*
a fly in the ointment — *ein Haar in der Suppe.*
Unfortunately, there are too many flies in this ointment. *Leider gibt es zu
viele Haare in dieser Suppe.*

to fly — *fliegen*
to fly a kite — *einen Drachen steigen lassen.*
Go fly a kite! *Geh hin, wo der Pfeffer wächst!/Verzieh dich!/Kauf dir
einen Keks!/Back dir ein Eis!*

to fly off the handle — *in die Luft gehen.*
Don't fly off the handle right away. *Geh nicht gleich in die Luft!*

fool — *der Tor/die Törin*
There's no fool like an old fool. *Alter schützt vor Torheit nicht.*

to be nobody's fool — *nicht von gestern sein.*
Judy is nobody's fool. *Judy ist nicht von gestern.*

to make a fool of — *zum Narren halten.*
You made a fool of me with that story. *Mit dieser Geschichte hast du mich
zum Narren gehalten.*

foot — *der Fuß*

to foot the bill — *die Zeche bezahlen.*
And you expect me to foot the bill? *Und du erwartest, dass ich die Zeche bezahle?*

to get back on one's feet — *wieder auf die Beine kommen.*
We hope that grandpa gets back on his feet soon. *Wir hoffen, dass Opa bald wieder auf die Beine kommt.*

to go on foot — *zu Fuß gehen.*
Most pilgrims went on foot, but some took the bus. *Die meisten Pilger gingen zu Fuß, aber einige nahmen den Bus.*

to have a foot in both camps — *auf beiden Schultern Wasser tragen.*
He still has a foot in both camps, but neither the liberals nor the conservatives trust him. *Er trägt noch Wasser auf beiden Schultern, aber weder die Liberalen noch die Konservativen trauen ihm.*

to keep one's feet on the ground — *auf dem Teppich/Boden bleiben.*
She's inherited a lot of money, but has kept her feet on the ground. *Sie hat viel Geld geerbt, ist aber auf dem Teppich geblieben.*

to put one's feet up — *die Beine hochlegen.*
I'm going to put my feet up now and let the robot do the vacuuming. *Jetzt lege ich die Beine hoch und lasse den Roboter staubsaugen.*

to put one's best foot forward — *sich von seiner besten Seite zeigen.*
I put my best foot forward but I still didn't get the part. *Ich zeigte mich von meiner besten Seite; trotzdem bekam ich die Rolle nicht.*

to put one's foot in it — *ins Fettnäpfchen treten.*
Leave that subject alone or you'll put your foot in it again. *Laß das Thema oder du trittst wieder ins Fettnäpfchen.*

forever — *ewig*

forever and a day — *auf immer und ewig.*
The millionaire swore to his fourth bride that he would love her forever and a day. *Der Millionär schwur seiner vierten Braut, er würde sie auf immer und ewig lieben.*

forty — *vierzig*
to get 40 winks — *ein Nickerchen machen.*
On the train I managed to get 40 winks. *Im Zug gelang es mir, ein Nickerchen zu machen.*

four — *vier*
four-letter words — *Vulgärausdrücke; Kraftwörter; Kraftausdrücke.*
In school we read the bowdlerized version, without the four-letter words. *In der Schule lasen wir die zensierte Ausgabe, ohne die Vulgärausdrücke.*

fox — *der Fuchs*
to put the fox in charge of the henhouse — *den Bock zum Gärtner machen.*
If he's supposed to look after your wine cellar then you're putting the fox in charge of the henhouse. *Wenn der deinen Weinkeller überwachen soll, dann machst du den Bock zum Gärtner.*

frying pan — *die Bratpfanne*
to go from the frying pan into the fire — *vom Regen in die Traufe kommen.*
We thought we were safe but we just went from the frying pan into the fire. *Wir glaubten uns in Sicherheit, aber wir kamen nur vom Regen in die Traufe.*

fully — *völlig*
fully fledged — *flügge.*
When the kids are fully fledged I'll go to work again. *Wenn die Kinder flügge sind, geh ich wieder arbeiten.*

fun — *der Spaß*
for the fun of it — *zum Spaß.*
He did it just for the fun of it. *Er hat es nur zum Spaß gemacht.*

to make fun of — *sich lustig machen.*
He made fun of her new hat, then tried it on. *Er machte sich über ihren neuen Hut lustig, probierte ihn dann.*

fur — *der Pelz*

They quarreled and the fur really flew. *Sie stritten sich und da flogen die Fetzen.*

fuss — *das Getue*

to make a fuss — *viel Aufheben(s) machen.*

You're making too much fuss about the president's speech; no one takes it at face value. *Du machst zu viel Aufheben von der Rede des Präsidenten — niemand nimmt sie für bare Münze.*

to make a fuss over — *einen Wirbel machen.*

They made a fuss over the movie superstar in the restaurant. *Im Restaurant wurde um die Filmdiva viel Wirbel gemacht.*

fussy — *pingelig/etepetete.*

Relax and don't be so fussy. *Entspann dich und sei nicht so pingelig!*

gallery — *die (Kunst)Galerie; Empore (church); der Balkon/oberste Rang*

to play to the gallery — *sich in Szene setzen.*

Enough showing-off. You're always playing to the gallery, like some ham actor. *Genug der Effekthascherei. Du setzt dich immer in Szene, wie ein Schmierenkomödiant.*

game — *das Spiel*

The game is up. *Das Spiel ist aus.*

to beat at someone's own game — *mit seinen eigenen Waffen schlagen.*

We beat them at their own game. *Wir haben sie mit ihren eigenen Waffen geschlagen.*

gander — *der Gänserich, Ganter*

to take a gander at — *einen Blick auf etwas werfen, mal ansehen.*

Just take a gander at her last letter. *Sieh mal ihren letzten Brief an.*

What's sauce for the goose is sauce for the gander. *Was dem einen recht ist, ist dem anderen billig. Mann und Frau sollten mit gleichem Recht behandelt werden.*

garden — *der Garten*
garden-variety — *gewöhnlich, Wald-und-Wiesen.*
He's certainly not a charismatic personality, just a garden-variety politician. *Charismatiker ist er gewiss nicht, nur ein Wald-und-Wiesen-Politiker.*

to lead down the garden path — *aufs Glatteis führen.*
Don't let that broker lead you down the garden path. *Lasst euch von dem Makler nicht aufs Glatteis führen!*

gauntlet — *der Stulpenhandschuh/Fehdehandschuh*
to fling/throw down the gauntlet — *den Fehdehandschuh hinwerfen.*
Mr. Pickwick wanted to throw down the gauntlet to society. *Herr Pickwick wollte der Gesellschaft den Fehdehandschuh hinwerfen.*

to run the gauntlet — *Spießruten laufen.*
The religious fanatics were ecstatic as they ran the gauntlet through the ranks of their tormentors. *Die religiösen Fanatiker liefen mit Wonne und Wollust einen Spießrutenlauf durch die Reihen ihrer Peiniger.*

to gentrify — *luxussanieren, verbürgerlichen*
I liked the old part of town better before it was gentrified. *Die Altstadt gefiel mir besser vor der Luxussanierung.*

to get — *bekommen, kriegen*
to get — *werden.*
She got rich/tired/old/sick/smart. *Sie wurde reich/müde/alt/krank/klug.*

not to let s.t. get to you/not to let s.t. get you down — *sich nicht unterkriegen lassen.*
Like Pollyanna, grandpa always finds good in everything and doesn't let anything get to him. *Wie Pollyanna findet Opa immer Gutes in allem und lässt sich nicht unterkriegen.*

to get a move on — *sich einen Zahn zulegen.*
Get a move on, or we'll arrive too late. *Leg dir einen Zahn zu, sonst kommen wir zu spät.*

to get along with — *sich gut verstehen.*
He doesn't get along well with his partner anymore. *Er versteht sich nicht mehr gut mit seinem Partner.*

to get (around) to — *dazu kommen.*
I wanted to write them, but I didn't get to it. *Ich wollte ihnen schreiben, aber ich kam nicht dazu.*

to get back at — *auswischen, heimzahlen, sich rächen.*
The vengeful dictator wanted to get back at his enemies. *Der rachsüchtige Diktator wollte seinen Feinden eins auswischen.*

to get back to — *sich wieder in Verbindung setzen mit, darauf zurückkommen.*
After consulting with the boss, I'll get back to you on that. *Nach Rücksprache mit dem Chef komme ich darauf zurück.*

to get by — *über die Runden kommen.*
With the help of his friends Schubert got by nicely. *Mit Hilfe seiner Freunde kam Schubert gut über die Runden.*

to get going — *in Gang bringen.*
She finally got the project going. *Sie hat das Unternehmen endlich in Gang gebracht.*

to get it — *kapieren.*
Don't you get it yet? *Kapierst du's noch nicht?*

to get nowhere — *nichts erreichen.*
With methods like that, you'll get nowhere with them. *Mit solchen Methoden erreichst du nichts bei ihnen.*

to get over — *verkraften.*
She hasn't yet gotten over the death of her fiancé. *Sie hat den Tod ihres Verlobten noch nicht verkraftet.*

to get someone wrong — *jemanden falsch verstehen.*
You got me wrong. *Sie haben mich falsch verstanden.*

to get somewhere with s.o. — *bei jmdm. landen.*
All that flattery won't get you anywhere with me. *Mit solchen Schmeicheleien landest du bei mir nicht.*

get the knack/hang of — *auf den richtigen Draht kommen.*
It took a long time before he got the hang of it. *Es dauerte lange, bevor er auf den richtigen Draht kam.*

to get what one wants — *auf seine Kosten kommen.*
In her restaurant everyone gets what they want. *In ihrem Restaurant kommt jeder auf seine Kosten.*

to get off — *aussteigen*
  to get off easy — *glimpflich davonkommen.*
The big shots got off easy. *Die großen Tiere kamen glimpflich davon.*

  to get off scot free — *ungeschoren davonkommen.*
They tried to bribe the judge and get off scot free. *Sie versuchten, den Richter zu bestechen und ungeschoren davonzukommen.*

  to get off the ground — *in Gang kommen.*
Despite many efforts, the project never really got off the ground. *Trotz vieler Bemühungen ist das Projekt nie richtig in Gang gekommen.*

  to tell someone where to get off — *gehörig Bescheid stoßen.*
If he keeps on like that, I'll tell him where to get off. *Wenn er so weitermacht, stoß ich ihm gehörig Bescheid.*

to get up — *aufstehen*
  to get up on the wrong side of the bed — *mit dem linken Bein zuerst aufstehen.*
He's in a bad mood again — probably got up on the wrong side of the bed. *Er ist wieder schlechter Laune — stand wohl mit dem linken Bein zuerst auf.*

ghost — *das Gespenst*
  ghost town — *die Geisterstadt.*
The former metropolis has almost turned into a ghost town. *Aus der einstigen Metropole ist fast eine Geisterstadt geworden.*

  not to have a ghost of a chance — *nicht die geringste Aussicht haben.*
He said I didn't have a ghost of a chance, but I'm going to try anyway. *Er sagte, ich hätte nicht die geringste Aussicht darauf, aber ich will's trotzdem versuchen.*

gift — *das Geschenk*

to have the gift of gab — *ein flinkes Mundwerk haben.*

Patrick kissed the stone and now has the gift of gab. *Patrick küsste den Stein und hat jetzt ein flinkes Mundwerk.*

to look a gift horse in the mouth — *einem geschenkten Gaul ins Maul schauen.*

You don't look a gift horse in the mouth. *Geschenktem Gaul schaut man nicht ins Maul.*

---

to give — *geben*

to give a talk — *eine Rede halten.*

She gave an interesting talk. *Sie hat eine interessante Rede gehalten.*

to give (information over the telephone) — *durchgeben.*

Can you give me their number? *Können Sie mir ihre Nummer durchgeben?*

to give away — *vergeben.*

We have many prizes to give away. *Wir haben viele Preise zu vergeben.*

to give oneself away — *sich verraten.*

How did the spy give himself away? *Wie hat sich der Spion verraten?*

to give a dressing down — *abkanzeln.*

The boss gave him a real dressing down. *Die Chefin kanzelte ihn so richtig ab.*

to give the game away — *die Katze aus dem Sack lassen.*

We'd have won if you hadn't given the game away. *Wir hätten gewonnen, wenn du die Katze nicht aus dem Sack gelassen hättest.*

to have to give/grant that — *lassen müssen.*

You've got to give him that, he's generous. *Das muß man ihm lassen, er ist freigebig.*

---

glove — *der Handschuh*

to fit like a glove — *wie angegossen passen.*

Everything she wears fits like a glove. *Alles, was sie trägt, passt wie angegossen.*

to handle with kid gloves — *wie ein rohes Ei behandeln, mit Samthandschuhen/Glacéhandschuhen anfassen.*

If you want to deal with that hot potato at all, handle it with kid gloves. *Wenn Sie dieses heiße Eisen überhaupt anfassen wollen, dann aber nur mit Samthandschuhen.*

---

glue — *der Klebstoff*

to be ready for the glue factory — *zum alten Eisen gehören.*

I know you think I'm ready for the glue factory, but you're in for a big surprise. *Ich weiß, du denkst ich gehöre schon zum alten Eisen, aber bald erlebst du dein blaues Wunder.*

---

to go — *gehen*

to go all out — *alles daransetzen; alle Register ziehen.*

We must go all out to get that account. *Wir müssen alles daransetzen, diesen Auftrag zu bekommen.*

to go bust/belly up/bankrupt — *in Konkurs gehen, Pleite machen.*

Some big banks went belly up. *Einige Großbanken haben Pleite gemacht.*

to go far — *es weit bringen.*

She will go far in life. *Sie wird es im Leben weit bringen.*

to go out of one's way — *sich besondere Mühe geben.*

The teacher went out of her way to explain everything again. *Die Lehrerin gab sich besondere Mühe, uns alles nochmals zu erklären.*

to go through — *durchbringen.*

In a few years the merry widow went through the entire fortune. *In wenigen Jahren brachte die lustige Witwe das ganze Vermögen durch.*

to go without saying — *sich von selbst verstehen.*

Of course we'll invite you — that goes without saying. *Natürlich laden wir Sie ein — das versteht sich von selbst.*

to have a go at — *sein Glück versuchen.*

You could have a go at it. *Du könntest dein Glück damit versuchen.*

to have nothing to go on — *keinen Anhalt haben.*

The police still have nothing to go on. *Die Polizei hat noch keinen Anhalt.*

to make a go of s.t. — *etwas schaffen/packen.*

That actor's completely burned out and can't make a go of it anymore. *Der Schauspieler ist total verbraucht und kann's nicht mehr packen.*

not to go overboard — *die Kirche im Dorf lassen.*
Let's not go overboard! *Lassen wir doch die Kirche im Dorf!*

goat — *der Bock, die Ziege*
  to get s.o.'s goat — *auf die Palme bringen, jmdn. ärgern.*
  What really gets my goat is his high-handed manner. *Was mich wirklich auf die Palme bringt ist seine überhebliche Art.*

gold — *das Gold*
  good as gold — *bombensicher sein.*
  That affair is as good as gold. *Das ist eine bombensichere Sache.*

  goldbrick(er) — *der Drückeberger.*
  There's no room for goldbrickers in our company. *In unserer Firma ist kein Platz für Drückeberger.*

  gold-digger — *der Goldgräber; Frau, die nur aufs Geld aus ist.*
  Once she was a real little gold-digger, now, in old age, she's looking for true love. *Einst war sie nur aufs Geld aus; jetzt im Alter sehnt sie sich nach der großen Liebe.*

  to be worth one's weight in gold — *nicht mit Gold aufzuwiegen sein.*
  Your cook is worth her weight in gold! *Ihre Köchin ist nicht mit Gold aufzuwiegen!*

  golden boy — *der Goldjunge; der Zampano.*
  He's lucky in everything—a real golden boy. *Er hat in allem Glück—ein richtiger Zampano.*

good — *gut*
  to be a good-for-nothing — *ein Taugenichts sein.*
  He planted flowers instead of vegetables, and some said he was a good-for-nothing. *Er pflanzte Blumen statt Gemüse, und einige sagten er wäre ein Taugenichts.*

  to be up to no good — *nichts Gutes im Schilde führen.*
  I'm sure he's up to no good. *Ich bin sicher, er führt nichts Gutes im Schild.*

  to get on s.o.'s good side/get in good with — *sich mit jmdm. gut stellen.*
  If you want to get anywhere with the boss, you'd better get in good with his secretary. *Um beim Chef etwas zu erreichen, muss man sich mit der Sekretärin gut stellen.*

too much of a good thing — *des Guten zuviel.*
That's too much of a good thing! *Das ist des Guten zuviel!*

grain — *das Korn, Getreide*
Sometimes even a blind hen finds a grain of truth. *Manchmal findet auch eine blinde Henne ein Körnchen Wahrheit.*

against the grain — *gegen den Strich.*
Electronic bookeeping goes against grandpa's grain, but he's had to come to terms with it. *Die elektronische Buchführung geht Opa gegen den Strich, aber er musste sich damit abfinden.*

to take with a grain of salt — *mit Vorsicht genießen, etwas nicht wörtlich nehmen, nicht für bare Münze nehmen.*
Yes, that all sounds great, but it has to be taken with a grain of salt. *Ja, das hört sich alles sehr schön an, aber es ist nur mit Vorsicht zu geniesen.*

grass — *das Gras*
The grass always grows greener on the other side of the fence.
Kirschen in Nachbars Garten schmecken immer besser.

to grate — *reiben*
to grate on — *auf den Keks (auf die Nerven; auf den Geist) gehen.*
His whole manner grates on me. *Seine ganze Art geht mir auf den Geist.*

grease — *das Fett*
grease monkey — *der Mechanikerlehrling.*
Now he's an oil baron, but he started out as a grease monkey. *Jetzt ist er Ölmagnat, aber als Mechanikerlehrling hat er angefangen.*

like greased lightning — *wie ein geölter Blitz.*
The thief ran like greased lightning but was caught anyway. *Der Dieb lief wie ein geölter Blitz—wurde aber trotzdem erwischt.*

to grease — *einschmieren, fetten*
to grease s.o.'s palm — *jmdm. etwas zustecken, jdn. schmieren.*
Nothing gets done in that country if you don't grease the president's palm. *In dem Land läuft nichts, wenn man den Präsidenten nicht schmiert.*

Greek — *griechisch*
  That's Greek to me. *Das sind mir böhmische Dörfer. Das kommt mir spanisch vor.*

to grin — *grinsen*
  to grin and bear it — *gute Miene zum bösen Spiel machen.*
  He lost the lawsuit, and all he can do now is grin and bear it. *Er verlor den Prozess und kann jetzt nur gute Miene zum bösen Spiel machen.*

  to grin like a Cheshire cat — *wie ein Honigkuchenpferd grinsen/strahlen.*
  Why are you grinning like a Cheshire cat? *Warum grinst du wie ein Honigkuchenpferd?*

grind — *der Trott; die Plackerei*
  the daily grind — *der tägliche Trott.*
  She's fed up with the daily grind and is looking forward to the holidays. *Sie ist des täglichen Trotts satt und freut sich auf die Ferien.*

  to be a grind — *eine Plackerei sein.*
  She thinks her job is a real grind. *Sie hält ihre Arbeit für eine wahre Plackerei.*

to grind — *schleifen*
  to come to a grinding halt — *zum Erliegen kommen.*
  Because of the strike, all rail traffic came to a grinding halt. *Wegen des Streiks kam der Bahnverkehr zum Erliegen.*

grindstone — *der Schleifstein*
  to keep one's nose to the grindstone — *sich dahinterklemmen.*
  If he doesn't keep his nose to the grindstone the job will never get done. *Wenn er sich nicht dahinterklemmt, wird die Arbeit nie fertig.*

grip — *der Griff*
  to come to grips with something — *etwas anpacken.*
  Sooner or later you'll have to come to grips with the problem. *Früher oder später musst du das Problem anpacken.*

to get a grip on oneself — *sich am Riemen reißen.*
If we don't get a grip on ourselves, we'll lose everyhing. *Wenn wir uns nicht am Riemen reißen, verlieren wir alles.*

grist — *das Mahlgut*
be grist for the mill — *Wasser auf die Mühle.*
The latest scandal is grist for the mill of his enemies. *Der neuste Skandal ist Wasser auf die Mühle seiner Feinde.*

gun — *die Schusswaffe, das Gewehr*
Give it the gun! *Leg dich ins Zeug!*

gut — *der Darm*
to bust a gut — *sich ein Bein ausreißen.*
You didn't exactly bust a gut to help me. *Du hast dir geradezu kein Bein ausgerissen mir zu helfen.*

gutless — *feige, keinen Mumm haben.*
You like to talk big, but you're gutless. *Du nimmst gern den Mund voll, aber du hast keinen Mumm.*

gut feeling — *aus dem Bauch heraus.*
My gut feeling is that the plan is unworkable. *So aus dem Bauch heraus, halte ich den Plan für undurchführbar.*

hail — *heil*
hail-fellow-well-met — *plumpvertraulich, kumpelhaft.*
Mr. Babbitt is overfamiliar, too hail-fellow-well-met for me. *Herr Babbitt ist mir zu plumpvertraulich.*

half — *halb*
to be half the battle/half way home — *die halbe Miete sein.*
You have no contacts but you've had good training; that's half the battle. *Dir fehlen Kontakte aber du bist gut ausgebildet; das ist schon die halbe Miete.*

half-baked — *unausgegoren.*
I'm through listening to your half-baked, crackpot ideas. *Deine unausgegorenen Schnapsideen will ich mir nicht länger anhören.*

half-cocked — *vorschnell, voreilig.*
Don't go off half-cocked again. *Sei nicht wieder vorschnell.*

half-crocked — *leicht angetrunken, angeschwipst.*
I left the bar half-crocked. *Leicht angeschwipst trat ich aus der Bar.*

Well begun is half done. *Gut begonnen ist halb gewonnen.*

---

ham — *der Schinken*
ham actor — *der Schmierenkomödiant, der Klammoteur.*
The critics call him a ham actor, but he's still a favorite with audiences. *Die Kritiken halten ihn für einen Schmierenkomödianten, aber er ist nach wie vor ein Publikumsliebling.*

ham-fisted/ham-handed — *ungeschickt, tollpatschig.*
The boss was ham-handed again; tact, sensitivity were necessary. *Der Chef hat wieder ungeschickt gehandelt; Takt, Feingefühl waren nötig.*

to ham it up — *überzogen spielen, ein Schmierentheater machen; etwas dick auftragen, sich in Szene setzen.*
He really hammed it up and laid it on thick. *Er hat sich in Szene gesetzt und die Geschichte dick aufgetragen.*

---

hand — *die Hand*
Hands off! — *Hände weg!*
"Hands off the cake," mother called out. *"Hände weg vom Kuchen," rief Mutter.*

Hands up! — *Hände hoch!*
"Hands up or we'll shoot," cried the police. *"Hände hoch oder wir schießen," rief die Polizei.*

to be an old hand at — *ein alter Praktiker sein.*
He's an old hand at safecracking. *Er ist ein alter Praktiker im Panzerknacken.*

to bite the hand that feeds one — *den Ast absägen auf dem man sitzt.*
Be careful not to bite the hand that feeds you. *Pass auf, den Ast nicht abzusägen, auf dem du sitzt.*

to get one's hands on — *etwas in die Finger kriegen.*

His wife had hidden the whisky bottle well, but he got his hands on it anyway. *Seine Frau hatte die Whiskeyflasche gut versteckt, aber er kriegte sie dennoch in die Finger.*

to give a hand to/lend a helping hand — *zur Hand gehen, mit anpacken, mit Hand anlegen.*

The neighbors lent a helping hand and the barn was quickly rebuilt. *Die Nachbarn haben mit angepackt und schnell wurde die Scheune wieder aufgebaut.*

to have a hand in — *mitmischen.*

Grandpa's retired, but he still wants to have a hand in the negotiations. *Opa hat sich zurückgezogen, will aber noch bei den Verhandlungen mitmischen.*

to know like the back of one's hand — *wie seine Westentasche kennen.*

He said he knew New York like the back of his hand, but he got us lost several times. *Er sagte, er kenne New York wie seine Westentasche; trotzdem hat er uns mehrmals irregeführt.*

to live from hand to mouth — *von der Hand in den Mund leben.*

At that time we lived from hand to mouth; but we were young and in love. *Damals lebten wir von der Hand in den Mund; wir waren aber jung und verliebt.*

to work hand in glove with — *unter einer Decke stecken.*

Some thought the criminals were working hand in glove with the politicians. *Einige glaubten, die Verbrecher steckten unter einer Decke mit den Politikern.*

---

hard — *hart*

hard liquor — *der Schnaps.*

He can't handle hard liquor any more. *Schnaps kann er nicht mehr ab.*

---

harp — *die Harfe*

to harp on s.t. — *auf etwas herumreiten; über die Ohren hauen.*

Will you stop harping on that subject! *Hör doch endlich auf, mir dieses Thema um die Ohren zu hauen!*

---

hat — *der Hut*

    at the drop of a hat — *bei dem geringsten Anlass.*
    At the drop of a hat she'll sing her favorite aria. *Bei dem geringsten Anlass singt sie ihre Lieblingsarie vor.*

    to eat one's hat — *einen Besen fressen.*
    If that's true I'll eat my hat. *Wenn das stimmt, fress ich einen Besen.*

    to talk through one's hat — *dummes Zeug reden.*
    You're talking through your hat again. *Du redest wieder dummes Zeug!*

hatchet — *das Beil*

    to bury the hatchet — *das Kriegsbeil begraben.*
    Lizzie longed to bury the hatchet. *Lizzie lechzte danach, das Kriegsbeil zu begraben.*

hatter — *der Hutmacher*

    to be as mad as a hatter — *eine Meise unter dem Pony/Hut haben.*
    They found him charming precisely because he's mad as a hatter. *Man fand ihn charmant, gerade weil er eine Meise unterm Pony hat.*

to have — *haben*

    to have had it/to have had it up to here — *die Nase voll haben/es hängt einem etwas zum Halse raus.*
    I've had it up to here with your lame excuses. *Deine faulen Ausreden hängen mir zum Halse raus.*

    to have it in for — *es abgesehen haben.*
    She thinks the teacher has (got) it in for her. *Sie glaubt, die Lehrerin hat es auf sie abgesehen.*

    has-been — *eine vergangene/vergessene Größe, weg vom Fenster, abgehalftert.*
    With that role she wants to prove that she's no has-been. *Mit der Rolle will sie beweisen, dass sie noch lange keine Abgehalfterte ist.*

hay — *das Heu*

    One must make hay while the sun shines. *Man muss das Eisen schmieden, solange es heiß ist. (Man muss die Feste feiern, wie sie fallen.)*

to go haywire — *durcheinander geraten.*

During the riot everything went haywire. *Während der Meute geriet alles durcheinander.*

to hit the hay — *sich in die Falle hauen.*

If I don't hit the hay soon, I'll collapse. *Wenn ich mich nicht bald in die Falle haue, fall ich um.*

---

head — *der Kopf*

head and shoulders above — *haushoch überlegen.*

She is head and shoulders above the competition. *Sie ist der Konkurrenz haushoch überlegen.*

to be head over heels in love — *bis über beide Ohren verliebt sein.*

The student at Heidelberg was head over heels in love. *Der Heidelberger Student war bis über beide Ohren verliebt.*

heads or tails — *Kopf oder Zahl.*

Heads we go, tails we stay. *Bei Kopf gehen wir, bei Zahl bleiben wir.*

to make heads or tails of — *aus etwas klug werden.*

I couldn't make heads or tails of the whole story. *Aus der ganzen Geschichte konnte ich nicht klug werden.*

---

to hear — *hören*

to be hard of hearing — *schlecht hören.*

Grandpa is hard of hearing, but he won't wear a hearing aid. *Opa hört schlecht, will aber kein Hörgerät tragen.*

to hear about — *zu Ohren kommen.*

I heard about that matter recently. *Diese Geschichte ist mir vor Kurzem zu Ohren gekommen.*

---

heart — *das Herz*

to learn by heart — *auswendig lernen.*

Our daughter has learned many poems by heart. *Unsere Tochter hat viele Gedichte auswendig gelernt.*

to take to one's heart — *sich ins Herz schließen.*

I couldn't stand them at first, but now I've taken them to my heart. *Zuerst konnte ich sie nicht leiden aber jetzt hab ich sie ins Herz geschlossen.*

heat — *die Hitze*
  If you can't stand the heat, stay out of the kitchen. *Wer den Wind nicht verträgt, hat auf dem Gipfel nichts zu suchen.*

heaven — *der Himmel*
  to be heaven-sent — *wie gerufen kommen.*
  That was a heaven-sent opportunity. *Die Gelegenheit kam wie gerufen.*

  Heavens to Betsy! *Ach, du dickes Ei!*

heel — *die Ferse; der Absatz*
  to dig in one's heels — *sich stur stellen.*
  I tried to persuade him, but he dug in his heels. *Ich versuchte ihn zu überreden, aber er stellte sich stur.*

  to let someone cool his heels — *jemanden zappeln lassen.*
  They let him cool his heels before they admitted him. *Sie ließen ihn zappeln, bevor sie ihn zuließen.*

  to take to one's heels — *Fersengeld geben.*
  The police came, and the looters took to their heels. *Die Polizei kam und die Plünderer gaben Fersengeld.*

hell — *die Hölle*
  Hells bells!/Holey Moley! — *Ach, du heiliger Bimbam!*

  All hell broke loose. *Da gab es Mord und Todschlag.*

  to give someone hell — *jemandem die Hölle heiß machen.*
  The boss's wife gave him hell again. *Die Frau des Chefs machte ihm wieder die Hölle heiß.*

  hell-bent on — *auf Teufel komm raus.*
  The Dutch sea-captain was hell-bent on rounding the Cape of Good Hope. *Auf Teufel komm raus wollte der holländische Kapitän den Kap der Guten Hoffnung umfahren.*

  to run like hell — *wie der Teufel laufen.*
  They ran like hell. *Sie liefen wie der Teufel.*

  till hell freezes over — *bis zum Sankt-Nimmerleins-Tag.*
  He can wait till hell freezes over before I apologize to him. *Er kann bis zum Sankt-Nimmerleins-Tag warten, bevor ich mich bei ihm entschuldige.*

high — *hoch*

highfalutin — *hochtrabend.*

The professor dismissed the dissertation as a jumble of highfalutin words. *Der Professor tat die Dissertation als ein Gewirr von hochtrabenden Worten ab.*

to be high time — *die höchste Zeit sein.*

It's high time for the children to go to bed. *Es ist die höchste Zeit, dass die Kinder ins Bett gehen.*

to be left high and dry — *festsitzen.*

He drove off and left us high and dry. *Er fuhr ab, und ließ uns festsitzen.*

hill — *der Hügel*

to go downhill/uphill — *bergab/bergauf gehen.*

The economists declared the economy was going downhill (uphill). *Die Wirtschaftswissenschaftler behaupteten, es ginge mit der Wirtschaft bergab (bergauf).*

to be over the hill — *die besten Jahre hinter sich haben.*

It's not true that she's over the hill. *Es stimmt nicht, dass sie die besten Jahre hinter sich hat.*

to head for the hills — *sich aus dem Staub machen.*

Instead of fighting, the army headed for the hills. *Statt zu kämpfen, machte sich die Armee aus dem Staub.*

hint — *der Hinweis, der Wink*

to drop a broad hint — *einen Wink mit dem Zaunpfahl geben.*

She dropped many broad hints. *Sie gabe viele Winke mit dem Zaunpfahl.*

hit — *der Schlag*

to be a big hit — *ein Renner sein.*

The exposition was a big hit with the public. *Die Ausstellung war ein Publikumsrenner.*

to be hit or miss — *aufs Geratewohl gehen.*

It was all hit or miss. *Es ging alles aufs Geratewohl.*

to hit — *schlagen, treffen*

to hit where it hurts — *an den Kragen gehen.*

The new budget cuts hit the bureaucrats where it hurts. *Die neuen Haushaltskürzungen gingen den Beamten an den Kragen.*

to hit home — *an die Nieren gehen.*

That sad story really hit home. *Diese traurige Geschichte ging mir an die Nieren.*

to hit back at — *Kontra geben.*

The senator hit back at his opponents. *Der Senator gab seinen Gegnern Kontra.*

to hit it off — *sich gut verstehen.*

We didn't hit it off right at first, but now we get along long fine. *Wir hatten uns zuerst nicht richtig verstanden, aber jetzt kommen wir gut mit einander aus.*

---

hitch — *der Haken*

to go off without a hitch — *reibungslos über die Bühne gehen.*

Everything went off without a hitch. *Alles ging reibungslos über die Bühne.*

---

hog — *das Schwein*

to go whole hog — *aufs Ganze gehen.*

It wouldn't be advisable to go whole hog now. *Jetzt wär's nicht ratsam aufs Ganze zu gehen.*

to live high on the hog — *wie die Made im Speck leben.*

Ulf won big in the lottery and is now living high on the hog. *Im Lotto zog Ulf das große Los und lebt jetzt wie die Made im Speck.*

to hog — *sich aneignen, für sich beanspruchen, in Beschlag nehmen.*

My brother always hogs the bathroom. *Mein Bruder nimmt immer das Badezimmer in Beschlag.*

---

to hold — *halten*

to get hold of — *erreichen.*

I tried all day to get hold of her on the telephone. *Ich versuchte den ganzen Tag, sie telefonisch zu erreichen.*

to hold forth — *sich auslassen.*

He held forth about his favorite subject again. *Er ließ sich wieder über sein Lieblingsthema aus.*

to hold tight — *festhalten.*

"Hold tight!" said the teacher to the children in the subway. *"Haltet euch fest!" sagte die Lehrerin den Kindern in der Untergrundbahn.*

to hold up as an example — *als Beispiel hinstellen.*

His mother always held up the boy next door as a shining example. *Seine Mutter stellte immer den Jungen nebenan als leuchtendes Vorbild hin.*

to hold up to ridicule — *dem Spott preisgeben.*

The miser held up the poor to ridicule. *Der Geizhals gab die Armen dem Spott preis.*

to hold water — *stichhaltig sein.*

His arguments don't hold water. *Seine Argumente sind nicht stichhaltig.*

---

home — *das Heim*

homespun — *hausbacken.*

That style seems rather homespun today. *Heute findet man diesen Stil ziemlich hausbacken.*

---

hook — *der Haken*

by hook or by crook — *auf Biegen oder Brechen.*

He wanted to win the game by hook or by crook. *Er wollte das Spiel auf Biegen oder Brechen gewinnen.*

on one's own hook — *auf eigene Faust.*

We left the group and visited the mosque on our own hook. *Wir verließen die Gruppe und besuchten die Moschee auf eigene Faust.*

to fall for hook, line, and sinker — *ganz schön reinfallen.*

We fell for it hook, line and sinker. *Wir sind ganz schön reingefallen.*

to get off the hook — *den Kopf aus der Schlinge ziehen.*

It wasn't easy for him to get off the hook. *Es war ihm nicht leicht, den Kopf aus der Schlinge zu ziehen.*

---

hoot — *das Hupen*
(to be) a hoot — *zum Schießen sein.*
What a hoot! *Das ist zum Schießen!*

to not give a hoot (two hoots, a hoot in Hades/hell) — *einem (völlig) schnuppe sein.*
We don't give a hoot! *Das ist uns völlig schnuppe!*

hop — *der Sprung*
a short hop/a hop, skip, and a jump — *ein kleiner Satz, ein Katzensprung.*
From here to the station it's just a short hop. *Von hier zum Bahnhof ist's nur ein Katzensprung.*

to hop — *hüpfen*
hopping mad — *fuchsteufelswild.*
Bette was hopping mad. *Bette war fuchsteufelswild.*

to hop about — *ständig unterwegs sein.*
Europe, Asia, Africa—she's always hopping about. *Europa, Asien, Afrika—sie ist ständig unterwegs.*

horn — *das Horn*
to lock horns — *die Klingen kreuzen.*
That's not the first time I've locked horns with him. *Das ist nicht das erste Mal, das ich mit ihm die Klingen kreuze.*

horse — *das Pferd*
You can lead a horse to water, but you can't make him drink. *Man kann niemand zu seinem Glück zwingen.*

to be hungry enough to eat a horse — *einen Bärenhunger haben.*
I could eat a horse. *Ich habe einen Bärenhunger.*

horse sense — *der gesunde Menschenverstand.*
Yes, he's an intellectual, but he lacks horse sense. *Ja, er ist ein Intellektueller, aber ihm fehlt der gesunde Menschenverstand.*

one-horse town — *das Kuhdorf/Kaff.*
We're happy in our one-horse town. *Wir leben glücklich in unserem Kaff.*

to bet on the wrong horse — *aufs falsche Pferd setzen.*

The boss bet on the wrong horse and is broke now. *Der Chef hat aufs falsche Pferd gesetzt und ist jetzt pleite.*

Hold your horses! — *Immer mit der Ruhe! Immer sachte mit den jungen Pferden. Nur nicht so hastig!*

Hold your horses! We'll have to think about that carefully. *Nur nicht so hastig! Das muss sorgfältig überlegt werden.*

straight from the horse's mouth — *aus erster Hand.*

I have it straight from the horse's mouth that the firm will soon declare bankruptcy. *Ich hab's aus erster Hand, dass die Firma bald Konkurs anmeldet.*

hot — *heiß*

to get into hot water — *in Teufels Küche kommen.*

If your son keeps on like that. he's going to get into hot water. *Wenn Ihr Sohn so weitermacht, kommt er in Teufels Küche.*

to make things hot for s.o. — *jmdm. einheizen.*

If you don't play ball, we'll make things really hot for you. *Wenn du nicht mitspielst, heizen wir dir tüchtig ein.*

hour — *die Stunde*

every hour on the hour — *zu jeder vollen Stunde.*

There's news every hour on the hour. *Nachrichten gibt's zu jeder vollen Stunde.*

househusband — *der Hausmann*

I'm a househusband, do all the housework and cook plain, hearty fare like pig's knuckles and sauerkraut. *Ich bin Hausmann, mache alle Hausarbeiten, und koche Hausmannskost wie etwa Eisbein mit Sauerkraut.*

howler — *der Schnitzer*

to make a howler — *sich einen Schnitzer leisten.*

They laughed at Mrs. Stöhr's linguistic howlers, but they made several gross howlers themselves. *Sie lachten über Frau Stöhrs Sprachschnitzer, aber sie leisteten sich selbst einige grobe Schnitzer.*

hue — *der Farbton; ein lautes Geschrei*
  to raise a hue and cry — *Zeter und Mordio schreien.*
  He's raised a hue and cry too often. *Zu oft hat er Zeter und Mordio geschrieen.*

humble — *demütig*
  to eat humble pie — *einen Kanossagang machen.*
  Like kings and emperors before him, the president decided to eat humble pie, the better to prepare for a counterattack. *Wie Kaiser und Könige vor ihm, beschloss der Präsident einen Kanossagang zu machen, umso besser zum Gegenschlag auszuholen.*

hump — *der Buckel*
  dowager's hump — *die Witwenbuckel.*
  Lack of calcium can lead to a dowager's hump. *Kalziummangel kann eine Witwenbuckel verursachen.*

hungry — *hungrig*
  to be hungry — *hungrig sein; Hunger haben.*
  "We Englishmen are never hungry, only thirsty," says a guest of the prince in *Die Fledermaus*. *"Wir Engländer haben nie Hunger, nur Durst," sagt ein Gast des Prinzen in* Die Fledermaus.

  to be hungry for — *Hunger auf etwas haben.*
  He was hungry for snails and frogs' legs. but he had to make do with pigs' knuckles. *Er hatte Hunger auf Schnecken und Froschschenkel, aber er musste mit Eisbein vorliebnehmen.*

ice — *das Eis*
  to break the ice — *das Eis brechen.*
  Fritz cracked a few jokes, and that broke the ice. *Fritz riss einige Witze and brach damit das Eis.*

to cut no ice — *nicht imponieren.*

She said the billionaire cut no ice with her, because he had no spiritual riches. *Sie sagte, der Milliardär imponiere ihr nicht, weil ihm der innere Reichtum fehle.*

icing — *der Zuckerguss*
    the icing on the cake (crowning touch) — *das Sahnehäubchen, die Krönung des Ganzen.*

The house is beautiful, but the gardens are really the icing on the cake. *Das Haus ist schön, aber die Gärten sind wirklich das Sahnehäubchen.*

idea — *die Idee; die Vorstellung.*
    What's the big idea? *Was soll denn das?*

    to put ideas into someone's head — *jemandem einen Floh ins Ohr setzen.*

Who's been putting ideas like that into your head? *Wer hat dir solche Flöhe ins Ohr gesetzt?*

in — *in*
    to be in for it — *es kriegen.*

If mother finds out, you'll be in for it. *Wenn Mutter das erfährt, kriegst du's.*

    to have it in for — *es abgesehen haben.*

She thinks the teacher has got it in for her. *Sie denkt, die Lehrerin hat es auf sie abgesehen.*

    to let in on — *in etwas einweihen.*

For a small fee I'll let you in on the secret. *Gegen ein geringes Entgelt weih ich euch in das Geheimnis ein.*

    to know all the ins and outs — *alle Schliche kennen.*

He knows all the ins and outs of the advertising business. *Er kennt alle Schliche der Werbebranche.*

Indian — *indianisch (Amerindian); indisch (Indian)*
Indian summer — *der Altweibersommer.*

In the Rhineland we enjoyed Indian summer and drank golden wine. *Im Rheinland genossen wir den Altweibersommer und tranken goldenen Wein.*

infancy — *die frühe Kindheit*
    to be in its infancy — *in den Kinderschuhen stecken.*
    Microtechnology is still in its infancy. *Die Mikrotechnik steckt noch in den Kinderschuhen.*

inside — *innen*
    to know inside out — *in- und auswendig kennen.*
    He said he knew the city inside out; nevertheless, we got lost. *Er sagte, er kannte die Stadt in- und auswendig — trotzdem verliefen wir uns.*
    to turn inside out — *auf den Kopf stellen.*
    Bluebeard's new wife wanted to turn the whole house inside out. *Blaubarts neue Frau wollte das ganze Haus auf den Kopf stellen.*
    to wear inside out — *falsch herum tragen.*
    He often thinks of yin and yang and wears his sweater inside out. *Er denkt oft an Jinjang und trägt seinen Pullover falsch herum.*

insult — *die Beleidigung*
    to add insult to injury — *noch eins/noch einen draufsetzen.*
    You've already done us much injustice and now you're adding insult to injury. *Sie haben uns schon viel Unrecht getan und jetzt setzen Sie noch einen drauf.*

ivory — *das Elfenbein*
    ivory tower — *der Elfenbeinturm.*
    Those who spend some time in an ivory tower are better able to cope with life. *Diejenigen, die sich zeitweilig im Elfenbeinturm aufhalten, werden besser mit dem Leben fertig.*

Jack —*der Bube; Hans*
    I'm all right, Jack. *Ich kümmere mich um mich, nicht um die anderen.*
    cheap-jack — *der billige Jakob.*
    The millionaire buys cheap-jack clothes/buys his clothes at the thrift shop. *Der Millionär kleidet sich beim billigen Jakob.*

Jack Frost — *Väterchen Frost.*
Jack Frost has already put in an appearance here. *Väterchen Frost hat sich schon bei uns gemeldet.*

to be a jack of all trades — *ein Tausendsassa, Hansdampf in allen Gassen sein.*
In my mountain cabin I had to be a jack of all trades. *In meiner Berghütte musste ich Hansdampf in allen Gassen sein.*

to be a jack of all trades and master of none — *von allem ein bisschen verstehen, aber von nichts sehr viel.*
Peter is a Jack of all trades and master of none — yet, he's a happy dilettant. *Peter versteht von allem ein bisschen, aber von nichts sehr viel — dennoch ist er ein glücklicher Dilettant.*

jack-in-the-box — *der Schachtelteufel.*
The children had fun with the little jack-in-the-box. *Die Kinder amüsierten sich mit dem Schachtelteufelchen.*

---

jam — *die Klemme; die Marmelade*
to be in a jam — *in der Klemme stecken.*
When he was in a jam his friend helped him. *Als er in der Klemme steckte, half ihm sein Freund.*

jam tomorrow — *schöne Zukunftsverheißungen; heile Welt von morgen.*
The president promised jam tomorrow. *Der Präsident versprach eine heile Welt von morgen.*

---

jay(bird) — *der Häher*
naked as a jaybird — *ganz nackt, splitternackt, splitterfasernackt.*
Naked as a jaybird, he sunbathed on the balcony. *Splitterfasernackt sonnte er sich auf dem Balkon.*

to jaywalk — *als Fußgänger im Straßenverkehr unachtsam sein, bei Rot über die Straße gehen.*
Don't jaywalk! That can be dangerous. *Geh nicht bei Rot über die Straße! Das kann gefährlich sein.*

---

to jilt — *sitzenlassen*
Miss Havisham's fiancé jilted her. *Fräulein Havisham's Verlobter ließ sie sitzen.*

John Hancock — *Friedrich Wilhelm*
If we could get his John Hancock on the petition, it would be a big help. *Wenn wir seinen Friedrich Wilhelm auf der Unterschriftenliste bekommen könnten, wäre es von großem Nutzen.*

John Q. Public — *Otto Normalverbraucher; Lieschen Müller*
John Q. Public wouldn't understand such behavior. *Otto Normalverbraucher hätte kein Verständnis für solches Benehmen.*

joke — *der Witz*
to play a joke on — *einen Streich spielen.*
Till played many jokes on them. *Till spielte ihnen viele Streiche.*

to take a joke — *Spaß verstehen.*
He can't take a joke. *Der versteht keinen Spaß.*

joker — *der Witzbold; der Spaßvogel; der Joker*
the joker in the pack — *der Unsicherheitsfaktor.*
Maybe there's a joker in the pack, a hidden clause. *Es gibt vielleicht einen Unsicherheitsfaktor — vielleicht eine versteckte Klausel.*

joy — *die Freude*
joyride — *die Spritztour.*
The boy alleged that he'd stolen the car just to go for a joyride. *Der Junge behauptete, er hätte den Wagen gestohlen, nur um eine Spritztour zu machen.*

jugular vein — *die Drosselvene*
to go for the jugular — *versuchen, den Lebensnerv zu treffen.*
During the interview the reporter went for the jugular. *Während des Interviews versuchte der Reporter den Lebensnerv zu treffen.*

to jump — *springen*
to go jump in the lake — *sich zum Teufel scheren.*
"Go jump in the lake," she told him angrily. *"Scher dich zum Teufel," sagte sie ihm zornig.*

to jump for joy — *Freudentänze vollführen.*

She won the lottery and jumped for joy. *Sie zog das große Los und führte Freudentänze voll.*

to jump out of one's skin — *aus der Haut fahren.*

When I tell him, he'll jump out of his skin. *Wenn ich's ihm sage, fährt er gleich aus der Haut.*

---

just — *gerecht*

Just a moment, please. *(Einen) Moment mal.*

just as — *gerade als.*

Just as Vronsky was getting off the train, Anna caught sight of him. *Gerade als Vronsky aus dem Zug ausstieg, erblickte ihn Anna.*

just as — *genauso.*

But the salesman said these were just as good. *Aber der Verkäufer sagte, diese wären genauso gut.*

Just Married! *Frisch Verheiratet!*

"Just Married!" was written on the car. *Auf dem Wagen stand "Frisch Verheiratet!"*

to be just like someone — *jemandem ähnlich sehen.*

You lost it? — That's just like you. *Du hast es verloren? Das sieht dir ähnlich!*

just like that — *mir nichts, dir nichts.*

Just like that you want to abandon me now? *Mir nichts, dir nichts willst du mich jetzt verlassen?*

just the same — *trotzdem.*

Just the same, I'd rather go away. *Trotzdem möchte ich lieber weggehen.*

---

justice — *die Gerechtigkeit*

to bring to justice — *vor Gericht stellen.*

He was finally brought to justice. *Er wurde endlich vor Gericht gestellt.*

to do justice to — *gebührend zusprechen.*

They all did justice to my roast goose. *Alle sprachen meinem Gänsebraten gebührend zu.*

---

kangaroo — *der Kanguru*
  kangaroo court — *das Scheingericht, die Lynchjustiz.*
  The kangaroo court sentenced them to death. *Das Scheingericht verurteilte sie zum Tode.*

---

to keep — *behalten*
  to keep abreast of — *auf dem Laufenden bleiben.*
  I doubt that our old dentist keeps abreast of the new procedures. *Ich bezweifle, dass unser alter Zahnarzt mit den neuen Verfahren auf dem Laufenden bleibt.*

  to keep at it — *bei der Stange bleiben.*
  She kept at it and finally found a nice apartment. *Sie blieb bei der Stange und fand endlich eine schöne Wohnung.*

  to keep in good with — *sich warmhalten.*
  He still keeps in good with his ex-boss. *Er hält sich seinen ehemaligen Chef noch warm.*

  to keep in mind — *im Auge behalten.*
  One should keep that difficulty in mind. *Diese Schwierigkeit sollte man im Auge behalten.*

  to keep in good repair — *in Schuss halten.*
  Keeping the house in good repair is expensive. *Es kostet viel, das Haus in Schuss zu halten.*

  to keep one's calm/cool/composure — *Fassung behalten/sich nicht aus der Ruhe bringen lassen.*
  Despite many provocations the Buddhist kept his cool. *Trotz vieler Provokationen behielt der Buddhist Fassung.*

  to keep pace — *Schritt halten.*
  We can scarcely keep pace with all the new changes. *Mit all den neuen Änderungen können wir kaum Schritt halten.*

to keep up appearances — *den Stil wahren.*

It's getting more and more difficult to keep up appearances. *Es wird immer schwieger den Stil zu wahren.*

to keep up with — *mithalten.*

At sports Grandpa could keep up fairly well with his grandchildren. *Beim Sport konnte Opa mit den Enkeln ziemlich gut mithalten.*

to keep up with (supply) — *nachkommen.*

We can't keep up with the demand anymore. *Wir können der Nachfrage nicht mehr nachkommen.*

to keep up with the Joneses — *mit den Nachbarn gleichziehen.*

They're wasting time and money trying to keep up with the Joneses. *Sie verschwenden Zeit und Geld, indem sie versuchen, mit den Nachbarn gleichzuziehen.*

kick — *der Tritt*

to do for kicks — *aus Spaß machen.*

They did it just for kicks. *Sie haben es nur aus Spaß gemacht.*

to get a kick out of — *einen Riesenspaß haben.*

He gets a kick out of his old Cole Porter records. *Er hat einen Reisenspaß an seinen alten Cole Porter Platten.*

to have a kick — *es in sich haben.*

Your homemade elixir has got quite a kick. *Dein hausgebranntes Elixir hat's in sich.*

to kick — *treten*

to kick a habit — *aufstecken.*

She was a drug addict, but she's kicked the habit. *Sie war drogensüchtig, aber sie hat es aufgesteckt.*

to kick in — *greifen.*

The drug didn't kick in till a few hours later. *Erst einige Stunden später griff das Medikament.*

to kick oneself — *sich in den Hintern beißen.*

I could kick myself for having missed it. *Ich könnte mir in den Hintern beißen, dass ich's versäumt habe.*

to kick over the traces — *über die Stränge schlagen.*
Even pillars of the community like to kick over the traces occasionally.
*Selbst Stützen der Gesellschaft schlagen manchmal gern über die
Stränge.*

to kick the bucket — *abkratzen.*
Jenny kicked the bucket at 76. *Mit 76 Jahren kratzte Jenny ab.*

to kill — *töten*
    dress to kill — *sich herausputzen.*
    She dressed to kill because she knew that he would be there. *Sie putzte
    sich heraus, weil sie wusste, dass er da sein würde.*

    to kill time — *die Zeit totschlagen.*
    "Use and experience time intensely, instead of killing it," counseled the
    philosopher. *"Nutzt und erlebt die Zeit, statt sie totzuschlagen," riet die
    Philosophin.*

    to kill two birds with one stone — *zwei Fliegen mit einer Klappe
    schlagen.*
    By skillful maneuvering she hoped to kill two birds with one stone. *Durch
    geschicktes Lavieren hoffte sie, zwei Fliegen mit einer Klappe zu
    schlagen.*

    contract killer — *gedungener Mörder.*
    The movie was about a school for contract killers. *Der Film handelte von
    einer Schule für gedungene Mörder.*

    to make a killing — *einen Reibach machen.*
    Gary made a killing on the stock market. *Im Börsenhandel machte Gary
    einen Reibach.*

to kiss — *küssen*
    to kiss and make up — *sich mit einem Kuss versöhnen.*
    They kissed and made up again. *Sie versöhnten sich wieder mit einem
    Kuss.*

kite — *der Drachen*
Go fly a kite! *Back dir ein Eis!/Kauf dir einen Keks!*

kitten — *das Kätzchen*

  to have kittens — *zum Junge-Hunde-Kriegen sein/zum Kinderkriegen sein.*

My husband lost everything on the stock market. I'm furious. It's enough
to have kittens! *Mein Mann hat alles an der Börse verloren. Ich bin
wütend. Es ist zum Junge-Hunde-Kiregen!*

---

to knit — *stricken*

  to knit one's brow — *die Stirn runzeln.*

The philosopher has deep wrinkles in his face because he often knits his
brow. *Der Philosoph hat tiefe Falten im Gesicht, weil er oft die Stirn
runzelt.*

---

to knock — *klopfen*

  knocked over with a feather — *einfach platt.*

When I found out about his secret life you could have knocked me over
with a feather. *Als ich von seinem Geheimleben erfuhr, da war ich
einfach platt.*

---

to knock — *klopfen*

  to knock off from work — *Feierabend machen.*

We're tired and are going to knock off from work now. *Wir sind müde und
machen jetzt Feierabend.*

  to knock off — *hinhauen.*

Knock off your doctoral dissertation first, then write your novel. *Hauen
Sie zuerst Ihre Doktorarbeit hin, dann schreiben Sie Ihren Roman!*

  to knock off — *umlegen; umbringen.*

The gangster tried to knock off all his enemies. *Der Gangster versuchte,
alle seine Feinde umzubringen.*

---

knot — *der Knoten*

  to tie the knot — *heiraten, sich das Jawort geben.*

They finally tied the knot. *Endlich haben sie geheiratet.*

---

to know — *wissen; kennen; können*

  to know backwards and forwards — *aus dem Effeff verstehen.*

She knows her profession backwards and forwards. *Ske versteht ihren
Beruf aus dem Effeff.*

to know by sight — *vom Sehen kennen.*

I know her by sight, but I don't know if she knows Greek. *Ich kenne sie vom Sehen, aber ich weiß nicht, ob sie Griechisch kann.*

to know the ropes — *den Rummel kennen.*

Why don't you talk with someone who knows the ropes? *Warum sprichst du nicht mit jemand, der den Rummel kennt?*

to know the score — *wissen wo's lang geht.*

We've known the score for some time. *Längst schon wissen wir wo's lang geht.*

to know with whom one is dealing — *seine Pappenheimer kennen.*

They won't leave me in the lurch, I know with whom I'm dealing. *Sie werden mich nicht im Stich lassen. Ich kenne meine Pappenheimer.*

not to know from Adam — *keine Ahnung haben.*

I didn't know him from Adam. *Ich hatte keine Ahnung, wer er war.*

know-it-all — *der Besserwisser.*

He should make an effort not to appear to be a know-it-all. *Er sollte sich Mühe geben, nicht als Besserwisser aufzutreten.*

knuckle — *der Knöchel*

to knuckle down — *sich ins Zeug legen.*

We can win if we knuckle down. *Gewinnen können wir, wenn wir uns ins Zeug legen.*

lady — *die Dame*

ladies' man — *der Frauenheld.*

Uncle Otto is still a ladies' man. *Onkel Otto is noch ein Frauenheld.*

lake — *der See*

to go jump in the lake — *hingehen, wo der Pfeffer wächst.*

I told him to go jump in the lake. *Ich sagte ihm, er sollte hingehen, wo der Pfeffer wächst.*

lamb — *das Lamm*

in two shakes of a lamb's tail — *im Nu, im Handumdrehen, gleich.*
I'll be with you it two shakes of a lamb's tail. *Gleich bin ich wieder da.*

large — *groß*

at large — *auf freiem Fuß.*
The gangster is at large again. *Der Gangster ist wieder auf freiem Fuß.*

taking the large view — *im Großen und Ganzen gesehen.*
Taking the large view, our situation isn't so bad. *Im Großen und Ganzen gesehen ist unsere Lage nicht so schlimm.*

lark — *die Lerche*

to be merry (happy) as a lark — *sich wie ein Schneekönig freuen.*
When the boy opened the presents, he was merry as a lark. *Als der Junge die Geschenke öffnete, freute er sich wie ein Schneekönig.*

as a lark — *aus Spaß/Jux.*
He spoke to her as a lark, but he wound up falling in love with her. *Aus Jux sprach er sie an, aber letztendlich verliebte er sich in sie.*

to go for a lark — *sich einen Jux machen.*
Incognito, he went to Vienna to go for a lark. *Inkognito fuhr er nach Wien, um sich einen Jux zu machen.*

last — *letzt*

at last — *endlich.*
At last I've found a barman who can make a real zombie. *Endlich hab ich einen Barmann gefunden, der einen echten Zombie mixen kann.*

last night — *gestern Abend.*
Last night she sang *Tosca. Gestern Abend hat sie* Tosca *gesungen.*

to laugh — *lachen*

to make o.s. a laughing stock — *sich lächerlich machen.*
If I came out for your project I'd make a laughing stock of myself. *Wenn ich mich für Ihr Projekt einsetzte, würde ich mich lächerlich machen.*

law — *das Gesetz*

to lay down the law — *ein Machtwort sprechen.*
The children carried on until mother laid down the law. *Die Kinder tobten, bis Mutter ein Machtwort sprach.*

to take the law into one's own hands — *sich selbst Recht verschaffen.*
The cattle raisers tried to take the law into their own hands. *Die Viehzüchter versuchten, sich selbst Recht zu verschaffen.*

lawyer — *der Rechtsanwalt*

shyster lawyer — *der Winkeladvokat/Rechtsverdreher/Scheißadvokat.*
If you call me a shyster again, I'll sue you. *Wenn Sie mich wieder einen Rechtsverdreher nennen, verklage ich Sie.*

lazy — *faul*

lazybones — *der Faulenzer.*
He's already had a job offer, but that lazybones isn't interested. *Er hat schon ein Stellenangebot bekommen aber dieser Faulenzer will nichts davon wissen.*

to lead — *führen*

to lead by the nose — *an der Nase herumführen.*
The con man led them by the nose. *Der Betrüger führte sie an der Nase herum.*

to lead down the garden path — *aufs Glatteis führen.*
The real-estate agent led them down the garden path. *Der Immobilienmakler hat sie aufs Glatteis geführt.*

leading lady/leading man — *der Hauptdarsteller/die Hauptdarstellerin.*
The leading man was nothing special, but the leading lady was splendid. *Der Hauptdarsteller war nichts Besonderes; die Hauptdarstellerin hingegen war großartig.*

lead story — *der Aufmacher.*
We'll use this report on the rain forest as the lead story. *Diese Reportage über den Regenwald benutzen wir als Aufmacher.*

leaf — *das Blatt*

to take a leaf out of s.o.'s book — *von jmdm. eine Scheibe abschneiden.*

Your cousin Al studies hard; you should take a leaf from his book. *Dein Vetter Al lernt fleißig; von ihm solltest du dir eine Scheibe abschneiden.*

leap — *der Sprung*
  by leaps and bounds — *mit Riesenschritten; sprunghaft.*
  The economy is advancing by leaps and bounds. *Die Wirtschaft geht mit Riesenschritten vorwärts.*

to learn — *lernen*
  to learn from the bottom up — *von der Pike auf lernen.*
  She has learned her job from the bottom up. *Sie hat ihren Beruf von der Pike auf gelernt.*

to leave — *(ver)lassen*
  to leave alone (in peace) — *in Ruhe lassen.*
  Leave the child alone! *Lass doch das Kind in Ruhe!*

  to leave in the lurch — *im Stich lassen.*
  Despite his promises, he left us in the lurch. *Trotz seiner Versprechungen hat er uns im Stich gelassen.*

  to leave no stone unturned — *nichts unversucht lassen.*
  He left no stone unturned but he couldn't save his business. *Er ließ nichts unversucht, konnte aber sein Geschäft nicht retten.*

  to leave out — *auslassen.*

  to be left out in the cold/left standing in the rain — *in die Röhre kucken, außen vor bleiben.*
  They lived it up and left me out in the cold. *Sie lebten sich aus, und ließen mich in die Röhre gucken.*

leg — *das Bein*
  to be on one's last legs — *auf dem letzten Loch pfeifen.*
  He seemed to be on his last legs, but he surprised us all. *Er schien, auf dem letzten Loch zu pfeifen, aber er überraschte uns alle.*

  to give a leg up — *unter die Arme greifen.*
  His uncle gave him a leg up. *Sein Onkel griff ihm unter die Arme.*

leopard — *der Leopard*

A leopard can't change its spots. *Niemand kann aus seiner Haut heraus. (Über seinen Schatten kann man nicht springen.)*

to let — *lassen*

to let it all hang out — *die Kuh fliegen lassen.*
Tonight we're going to let it all hang out. *Heute abend wollen wir die Kuh fliegen lassen.*

to let it go at that — *es dabei bewenden lassen.*
Let's let it go at that. *Lassen wir's dabei bewenden.*

liar — *der Lügner*

to be an out-and-out liar — *wie gedruckt lügen.*
He's an out-and-out liar. *Er lügt wie gedruckt.*

lid — *der Deckel*

Put a lid on it! *Schwamm drüber!*

lie — *die Lüge*

to be a pack of lies — *erstunken und erlogen sein.*
Everything said against her is a pack of lies. *Alles, was gegen sie gesagt wurde, ist erstunken und erlogen.*

to lie through one's teeth/like a trooper/like all get out — *lügen, dass sich die Balken biegen/wie gedruckt lügen.*
You know he lies like a trooper yet you believed his story. *Du weißt er lügt, dass sich die Balken biegen, trotzdem hast du ihm seine Geschichte geglaubt.*

to lie — *liegen*

to lie low — *sich versteckt halten.*
The criminals are still lying low. *Die Verbrecher halten sich noch versteckt.*

life — *das Leben*

It's a matter of life and death. *Es geht um Kopf und Kragen.*

to be the life of the party — *strahlender Mittelpunkt sein, Leben in eine Party bringen.*

Tim is the life of every party. *Tim bringt Leben in jede Fete.*

to live the life of Riley — *wie Gott in Frankreich leben.*

He inherited a lot of money from his aunt and for a while lived the life of Riley. *Von seiner Tante erbte er viel Geld, und eine Zeitlang lebte er wie Gott in Frankreich.*

to risk life and limb — *Kopf und Kragen riskieren.*

As a stuntman I often risk life and limb for the stars. *Als Kaskadeur riskiere ich oft Kopf und Kragen für die Stars.*

You can bet your life on it! — *Darauf kannst du Gift nehmen.*

light — *das Licht*

according to one's lights — *nach bestem Wissen und Gewissen.*

I acted honorably according to my lights. *Ich habe ehrlich, nach bestem Wissen und Gewissen gehandelt.*

to have a light — *Feuer haben.*

Do you have a light, please? *Haben Sie Feuer, bitte?*

lit up (drunk) — *sternhagelvoll/blau.*

He drank too much mulled wine during the Yule feast and was soon all lit up. *Beim Julfest trank er zu viel Glühwein und wurde schnell blau.*

to light into s.o./s.t. — *über jmdn./etwas herfallen, beschimpfen.*

Why did he light into us like that? *Warum ist er über uns so hergefallen?*

like — *wie*

like all get out — *was das Zeug hält.*

Rhinelanders go all out celebrating carnival season. *Im Karneval feiern die Rheinländer was das Zeug hält.*

limelight — *das Kalklicht*

to be in the limelight — *im Rampenlicht stehen.*

Once she was in the limelight. *Einst stand sie im Rampenlicht.*

limit — *die Grenze*

That's the absolute limit! *Das ist der absolute Hammer!*

line — *die Linie*

One must draw the line somewhere! — *Alles hat seine Grenzen!*

the line of least resistance — *der Weg des geringsten Widerstandes.*
The line of least resistance isn't always the best line. *Der Weg des geringsten Widerstandes ist nicht immer der beste.*

line of work — *der Beruf, die Berufstätigkeit.*
What line of work are you in? I'm a mechanic by trade. *Was sind Sie von Beruf? Ich bin Mechaniker von Beruf.*

---

to line — *füttern; säumen; auskleiden*

to line one's pockets — *in die eigene Tasche wirtschaften.*
The CEO just lined his own pockets. *Der Generaldirektor hat nur in die eigene Tasche gewirtschaftet.*

---

lip — *die Lippe*

Let's have none of your lip! *Keine frechen Bemerkungen!*

to be on everybody's lips — *in aller Munde sein.*
After that movie, her name was on everybody's lips. *Nach dem Film war ihr Name in aller Munde.*

to keep a stiff upper lip — *Haltung bewahren.*
Despite everything she kept a stiff upper lift. *Trotz allem bewahrte sie Haltung.*

to pay lip service — *Lippenbekenntnisse ablegen.*
The Senator just paid lip service to environmental protection. *Der Senator hat nur Lippenbekenntnisse für den Umweltschutz abgelegt.*

---

to live — *leben*

to live and let live — *leben und leben lassen.*
He often says, "Live and let live," but he still goes hunting. *Er sagt oft: "Leben und leben lassen," trotzdem geht er noch auf die Jagd.*

to live high on the hog — *in Saus und Braus leben.*
With his aunt's fortune he lived high on the hog. *Mit dem Vermögen seiner Tante lebte er in Saus und Braus.*

to live it up — *sich ausleben.*
For years he lived it up; now he has to rest frequently. *Jahrelang hat er sich ausgelebt; jetzt muss er sich oft ausruhen.*

all the livelong day — *den lieben langen Tag.*
He lounges around all the livelong day, while I have to work my fingers
to the bone. *Den lieben langen Tag liegt er auf der Bärenhaut, wähend
ich schuften muss.*

---

load — *die Last*
loads of — *jede Menge.*
There are loads of plays we'd like to see. *Es gibt jede Menge
Theaterstücke, die wir uns gern ansehen möchten.*

---

loaf — *der Brotlaib*
Half a loaf is better than none. *Wenig ist besser als gar nichts.*

to use one's loaf/noodle/head — *seinen Grips anstrengen.*
Instead of loafing around the house, he should use his loaf and get down
to work. *Statt zu Hause herumzulungern, sollte er seinen Grips
anstrengen und an seine Arbeit gehen.*

---

lock — *das Schloss; die Schleuse*
lock, stock, and barrel — *voll und ganz/total/ ganz und gar/ in Bausch
und Bogen/ mit allem Drum und Dran.*
We lost everything—lock, stock and barrel. *Alles haben wir verloren, voll
und ganz.*

---

to lock — *schließen*
to lock the barn door after the horse has been stolen — *den Brunnen
zudecken, wenn das Kind ertrunken ist.*
What's the use of locking the barn door after the horse has been stolen?
Was nutzt es den Brunnen zuzudecken, wenn das Kind ertrunken ist?

---

log — *der Klotz*
to sleep like a log — *wie ein Bär schlafen.*
Even if atom bombs fell around him, he'd still sleep like a log. *Selbst wenn
Atombomben um ihn her fielen, würde er noch wie ein Bär schlafen.*

---

long — *lang*
Long live the queen! *Es lebe die Königin!*

long-running (success) — *der Dauerbrenner.*

The critics panned it, but it became a long running success anyway. *Die Kritiker hauten es in die Pfanne, trotzdem wurde es zu einem Dauerbrenner.*

---

to look — *schauen*

Look before you leap! *Erst wägen, dann wagen!*

to look nice on — *gut stehen.*

Annie's hat looked so nice on her. *Annies Hut stand ihr so gut.*

Look out! — *Vorsicht!*

lookout — *der Ausguck; die Aussicht.*

You can't pay for the car? That's your lookout! *Den Wagen kannst du nicht bezahlen? Das ist dein Problem!*

to look out — *heraussehen.*

to look out on — *zu etwas gehen/zu etwas hin liegen.*

This room overlooks the Rhine, the other one looks out on the vineyards. *Dieses Zimmer liegt zum Rhein hin, das andere geht zu den Weinbergen.*

to look out for number one — *sein Schäfchen ins Trockene bringen.*

The boss looked out for number one without concern for the others. *Der Chef brachte sein Schäfchen ins Trockene, ohne sich um die anderen zu kümmern.*

---

to lose — *verlieren*

to lose heart — *den Mut verlieren.*

Don't lose heart; things will get better again. *Nur nicht den Mut verlieren—es wird ja alles wieder besser.*

---

loss — *der Verlust*

to be at a loss for — *verlegen sein um.*

Her husband is never at a loss for an excuse. *Ihr Mann ist nie um eine Ausrede verlegen.*

not to be at a loss for words — *nicht auf den Mund gefallen sein.*

Why didn't you open your mouth? You're usually not at a loss for words. *Warum hast du den Mund nicht aufgetan? Sonst bist du nicht auf den Mund gefallen.*

to cut one's losses — *die Verluste begrenzen.*

They sold the stocks to cut their losses. *Sie verkauften die Aktien, um ihre Verluste zu begrenzen.*

---

lost — *verloren*

Get lost! *Zieh Leine! (Geh hin, wo der Pfeffer wächst.)*

to get lost driving — *sich verfahren.*

They got lost driving on the autobahn. *Sie haben sich auf der Autobahn verfahren.*

to get lost in an airplane — *sich verfliegen.*

The aviator Corrigan got lost. *Der Pilot Corrigan verflog sich.*

to get lost walking — *sich verlaufen.*

We got lost walking in the Vienna Woods. *Wir verliefen uns im Wiener Wald.*

---

to lounge about — *faulenzen; auf der Bärenhaut liegen*

His wife is too industrious to lounge about with him for very long. *Seine Frau ist zu fleißig, um lange mit ihm auf der Bärenhaut zu liegen.*

---

lousy — *verlaust, lausig*

Kiddos get ahold of combs; times are lousy and the lice are loose. *Kinder kauft euch Kämme — die Zeit wird lausig.*

lousy with money — *im Geld schwimmen, Geld wie Dreck haben.*

The neighbors are lousy with money. *Die Nachbarn schwimmen im Geld.*

---

love — *die Liebe*

Love is blind. *Die Liebe macht blind.*

not for love or money — *nicht für Geld und gute Worte.*

Not for love or money could we get tickets to the opera. *Nicht für Geld und gute Worte konnten wir Karten für die Oper bekommen.*

Love me, love my dog. *Man muss mich so nehmen, wie ich bin.*

---

luck — *das Glück*

to be lucky — *Glück haben.*

At first he was lucky. *Zuerst hatte er Glück.*

to be a lucky dog/devil. *Ein Glückspilz sein.*

You won first prize? Man, you're some lucky dog! *Den ersten Preis hast du gewonnen? Mensch, bist du aber ein Glückspilz!*

Good luck! — *Viel Glück!*

Best of luck! — *Hals- und Beinbruch!*

Lots of luck! — *Toi, toi, toi!*

---

to lump — *zusammentun*

to like it or lump it — *sich wohl oder übel abfinden müssen.*

If he doesn't like it, he can lump it. *Er wird sich wohl oder übel damit abfinden müssen.*

to lump everything together — *alles über einen Kamm scheren; alles über einen Leisten schlagen.*

The professor has an interesting theory, but too often everything is lumped together (to fit the theory). *Der Professor hat eine interessante Theorie, aber zu oft wird alles über einen Leisten geschlagen.*

---

lunch — *das Mittagessen*

to have lunch — *zu Mittag essen.*

We didn't have lunch today. *Heute haben wir nicht zu Mittag gegessen.*

to have someone for lunch — *kurzen Prozess machen.*

The tennis champion had her opponents for lunch. *Die Tennis-Weltmeisterin machte kurzen Prozess mit ihren Gegnerinnen.*

There's no free lunch. — *Es wird einem nichts geschenkt.*

---

mad — *verrückt; böse*

mad about — *wild auf.*

He's quite mad about old Noel Coward records. *Er ist ganz wild auf alte Noel Coward-Platten.*

---

to make — *machen*

to make an effort — *sich Mühe geben.*

Mother made an effort to divide the cake fairly. *Mutter gab sich Mühe, den Kuchen gerecht zu verteilen.*

to make the best of a bad bargain — *gute Miene zum bösen Spiel machen.*

I didn't like the terms of the contract, but tried to make the best of a bad bargain. *Die Vertragsbedingungen gefielen mir nicht, aber ich versuchte gute Miene zum bösen Spiel zu machen.*

to make do with — *sich behelfen; vorliebnehmen.*

There's no more champagne, so we'll have to make do with mineral water. *Leider ist kein Sekt mehr da, so werden wir uns mit Mineralwasser behelfen müssen.*

to make do with less — *sich nach der Decke strecken.*

In the recession we had to make do with less. *In der Rezession mussten wir uns nach der Decke strecken.*

to make no headway — *nicht vom Fleck kommen.*

Despite all their efforts, they made no headway. *Trotz aller Bemühungen kamen sie nicht vom Fleck.*

to make out — *abschneiden.*

Our party hopes to make out better in the next elections. *Die Partei hofft, bei den nächsten Wahlen besser abzuschneiden.*

to make out — *entziffern.*

We couldn't make out his handwriting. *Seine Handschrift konnten wir nicht entziffern.*

to make up a story — *eine Geschichte erfinden.*

The reporter made up the whole story. *Der Reporter hat die ganze Geschichte erfunden.*

to make up for — *wettmachen.*

Today's exchange rate more than makes up for yesterday's losses. *Der heutige Wechselkurs hat die gestrigen Verluste mehr als wettgemacht.*

marble — *der Marmor (stone); die Murmel, der Klicker*
not to have all one's marbles — *nicht alle Tassen im Schrank haben.*
Lenny hasn't got all his marbles. *Lenny hat nicht alle Tassen im Schrank.*

to pick up one's marbles and go home — *Koffer packen und nach Hause gehen.*
There's nothing left for us to do but to pick up our marbles and go home.
Uns bleibt nichts anderes übrig als Koffer packen und nach Hause gehen.

---

mark — *die Spur*
to be on the mark — *richtig liegen, zutreffend sein.*
You're right on the mark there. *Da liegst du genau richtig.*

to be off the mark — *daneben liegen.*
I think you're off the mark this time. Ich glaube, diesmal liegst du daneben.

to overstep the mark — *zu weit gehen.*
Some think our ad's offensive. Maybe we've overstepped the mark.
Einige finden unsere Werbung anstößig. Vielleicht sind wir zu weit gegangen.

to be wide of the mark — *sich gewaltig irren; daneben sein.*
I didn't say that; you're wide of the mark. *Das hab ich gar nicht gesagt; du irrst dich gewaltig.*

to hit the mark — *ins Schwarze treffen.*
Her arguments hit the mark. *Ihre Argumente trafen ins Schwarze.*

to make one's mark — *sich einen Namen machen.*
She has made her mark in painting. *Sie hat sich in der Malerei einen Namen gemacht.*

On your marks! Ready! Go! *Auf die Plätze! Fertig! Los!*

---

matter — *die Sache*
a matter of course — *eine Selbstverständlichkeit.*
Certainly we want to do our part; that's a matter of course. *Gewiss wollen wir mithelfen — das ist eine Selbstverständlichkeit.*

as a matter of fact — *tatsächlich.*
As a matter of fact, I've known them for some time. *Tatsächlich kenn ich sie seit langem.*

to mean — *bedeuten*
Do you really mean that? *Ist das wohl Ihr Ernst?*

to mean everything to — *ein und alles sein.*
"You mean everything to me," declared Casanova. *"Du bist mein ein und alles," erklärte Casanova.*

means — *das Mittel*
by no means — *keineswegs; auf keinen Fall.*
By no means would I recommend that. *Das würde ich keineswegs empfehlen.*

to live beyond one's means — *über seine Verhältnisse leben.*
For years they've lived beyond their means. *Jahrelang haben sie über ihre Verhältnisse gelebt.*

meat — *das Fleisch*
One man's meat is another man's poison. *Was den einen freut, ist dem anderen leid. (Was dem einen sin Uhl, ist dem andern sin Nachtigall.)*

medicine — *die Medizin; das Medikament*
to give someone a taste of his own medicine — *Gleiches mit Gleichem vergelten.*
He thinks he's a saint, yet he wants to give his opponents a taste of their own medicine. *Er hält sich für einen Heiligen; trotzdem will er seinen Gegnern Gleiches mit Gleichem vergelten.*

to meet — *treffen*
to meet one's match — *seinen Meister finden.*
One day he'll meet his match. *Eines Tages wird er seinen Meister finden.*

to meet the deadline — *den Termin einhalten.*
She tried to meet the deadline. *Sie versuchte, den Termin einzuhalten.*

to mend — *reparieren*
  on the mend — *auf dem Wege der Besserung.*
  Uncle Otto is on the mend. *Onkel Otto ist auf dem Wege der Besserung.*

merry — *lustig*
  the more the merrier — *je mehr desto besser.*
  Of course they should come — the more the merrier! *Natürlich sollen sie kommen — je mehr desto besser!*

mess — *das Durcheinander*
  to be in a mess — *in der Patsche sitzen.*
  If we come too late, we'll be in a mess. *Wenn wir zu spät kommen, sitzen wir in der Patsche.*

  to make a mess of — *verpfuschen.*
  He's made a mess of everything. *Er hat alles verpfutscht.*

mile — *die Meile*
  A miss is as good as a mile. *Dicht vorbei ist auch daneben.*

milk — *die Milch*
  There's no use crying over spilled milk. *Hin ist hin und vorbei ist vorbei./Was geschehen ist, ist geschehen.*

mill — *die Mühle*
  run of the mill — *nullachtfünfzehn*
  The last performances were rather run of the mill. *Die letzten Aufführungen waren ziemlich nullachtfünfzehn.*

  to have been through the mill — *viel durchgemacht haben.*
  These poor refugees have been through the mill. *Diese armen Flüchtlinge haben viel durchgemacht.*

  to put through the mill — *in die Mangel nehmen.*
  The sergeant put the recruits through the mill. *Der Feldwebel nahm die Rekruten in die Mangel.*

millstone — *der Mühlstein*
  to be a millstone around someone's neck — *ein Klotz am Bein sein.*

I don't know how I can get rid of that millstone around my neck. *Ich weiß nicht, wie ich mir diesen Klotz am Bein loswerden kann.*

to mince — *zuhacken*
not to mince words — *kein Blatt vor den Mund nehmen.*
She didn't mince words when she told the boss she wouldn't put up with harassment anymore. *Sie nahm kein Blatt vor den Mund, als sie dem Chef sagte, sie würde sich keine weitere Belästigung gefallen lassen.*

mind — *der Sinn; der Verstand*
to be out of one's mind — *den Verstand verloren haben.*
I think he's out of his mind. *Ich glaube er hat den Verstand verloren.*

to bear/keep in mind — *nicht vergessen.*
Bear in mind that he's already betrayed us once. *Vergessen sie nicht, dass er uns schon einmal betrogen hat.*

to have an open mind — *unvoreingenommen sein.*
He says he has an open mind. *Er sagt, er sei unvoreingenommen.*

to have in mind — *vorhaben.*
We have in mind buying a little restaurant. *Wir haben vor, ein kleines Restaurant zu kaufen.*

to know one's own mind — *wissen was man will.*
He often doesn't know his own mind. *Oft weiß er nicht, was er will.*

a load off one's mind — *ein Stein vom Herzen.*
You'll help me? That's a load off my mind. *Du willst mir helfen? Da fällt mir ein Stein vom Herzen.*

Out of sight, out of mind. *Aus den Augen, aus dem Sinn.*

to put out of one's mind — *aus dem Kopf schlagen.*
Just put that out of your mind; you're not driving my car! *Schlag dir das nur aus dem Kopf; meinen Wagen fährst du nicht!*

minor — *minderjährig*
In that country one is no longer a minor at 16. *In dem Land ist man mit sechzehn Jahren nicht mehr minderjährig.*

minor — *geringfügig.*
The damage was minor. *Der Schaden war geringfügig.*

Asia Minor — *(das) Klein Asien; kleinasiatisch.*
Sie is interested in the art and religions of Asia Minor. *Sie interessiert sich für kleinasiatische Kunst und Religionen.*

to minor in — *als Nebenfach haben/studieren.*
She's majoring in German and minoring in art history. *Sie studiert Deutsch als Hauptfach und Kunstgeschichte als Nebenfach.*

---

mint — *die Münze; die Münzanstalt*
to make a mint — *einen Haufen Geld machen.*
Hedi made a mint with her inventions. *Mit ihren Erfindungen hat Hedi einen Haufen Geld gemacht.*

---

minute — *die Minute*
Just a minute! — *Einen Augenblick!*

to take the minutes — *das Protokoll führen.*
He was supposed to be taking the minutes, but he fell asleep. *Er sollte das Protokoll führen, aber er schlief dabei ein.*

---

to miss — *verpassen*
to not miss out on anything — *nichts anbrennen lassen.*
She didn't want to miss out on anything. *Sie wollte nichts anbrennen lassen.*

---

to misplace — *abhanden kommen*
The professor misplaces quantities of pens, gloves, and umbrellas. *Unmengen von Kugelschreibern, Handschuhen und Regenschirmen kommen dem Professor ab.*

---

model — *das Modell; das Vorbild; das Muster*
to be a painter's model — *Modell stehen.*
He was a model for many painters. *Er stand vielen Malerinnen Modell.*

to take as a model — *zum Vorbild nehmen.*
They thought the hypocrite was a paragon (model) of virtue and took him for a model. *Man hielt den Heuchler für einen Ausbund aller Tugenden und nahm ihn zum Vorbild.*

Monday — *der Montag*

Monday morning quarterback — *einer der im Nachhinein klug ist.*
Yes, after the game, everyone's a Monday morning quarterback. *Ja, nach dem Spiel, im Nachhinein, ist jeder klug.*

money — *das Geld*

for my money — *für meine Begriffe.*
For my money, it's the best restaurant in town. *Für meine Begriffe ist es das beste Restaurant der Stadt.*

Money is no object. — *Geld spielt keine Rolle.*

Money makes the world go round. — *Geld regiert die Welt.*

to be rolling in money — *Geld wie Heu haben; steinreich sein.*
The rock singer was rolling in money. *Der Rocksänger war steinreich.*

monkey — *der Affe*

I'll be a monkey's uncle! — *Mich laust der Affe!*

to make a monkey of — *zum Affen halten.*
He tried to make a monkey out of me. *Er versuchte, mich zum Affen zu halten.*

monopoly — *das Monopol*

to act as if one had a monopoly on — *tun, als ob man etwas gepachtet hätte.*
This politician acts as if he and his party had a monopoly on social justice and virtue. *Dieser Politiker tut so, als hätten er und seine Partei die soziale Gerechtigkeit und die Tugend gepachtet.*

moon — *der Mond*

once in a blue moon — *alle Jubeljahre.*
Once in a blue moon she calls us up. *Alle Jubeljahre ruft sie uns an.*

to promise the moon — *das Blaue vom Himmel versprechen.*
He promised the voters the moon. *Er versprach den Wählern das Blaue vom Himmel.*

to reach for the moon — *nach den Sternen greifen.*
She tried to reach for the moon. *Sie versuchte, nach den Sternen zu greifen.*

to moonlight — *nebenberuflich arbeiten.*

He moonlights playing the piano in a bar. *Nebenberuflich spielt er Klavier in einer Bar.*

moonshine — *der Mondschein; schwarzgebrannter Alkohol.*

He got sick on his own moonshine. *Er erkrankte an seinem eigenen schwarzgebrannten Alkohol.*

moral — *sittlich*

to stand by with moral and practical support — *mit Rat und Tat zur Seite stehen.*

They stood by us with moral and practical support. *Sie standen uns mit Rat und Tat zur Seite.*

moss — *das Moos*

A rolling stone gathers no moss. *Rollender Stein wird nicht moosig./Wer rastet, rostet.*

A rolling stone gathers no moss, but sometimes one has to rest and let a little moss gather. *Ja, wer rastet rostet, aber manchmal muss man sich ein bisschen ausruhen.*

motion — *die Bewegeung*

in slow motion — *in Zeitlupe.*

It took slow motion to determine the winner. *Erst in Zeitlupe konnte man den Gewinner feststellen.*

mountain — *der Berg*

to make a mountain out of a molehill — *aus einer Mücke einen Elefanten machen.*

You don't have to make a mountain out of every molehill. *Du brauchst nicht aus jeder Mücke einen Elefanten zu machen.*

mouth — *der Mund*

to make one's mouth water — *einem das Wasser im Munde zusammenlaufen.*

The chef talked of his recipes and made our mouths water. *Der Küchenchef sprach von seinen Rezepten und uns lief das Wasser im Munde zusammen.*

to put one's money where one's mouth is — *Taten auf Worte folgen lassen.*

That all sounds great, but are you prepared to put your money where your mouth is? *Das hört sich alles schön an, aber bist du bereit Taten auf Worte folgen zu lassen?*

to talk out of both sides of one's mouth — *Widersprechendes reden; einmal hü, einmal hott sagen.*

Nobody knows if the firm's going to expand or downsize; the boss blows hot and cold. *Keiner weiß, ob die Firma aus- oder abbaut; der Chef sagt einmal hü, einmal hott.*

---

to move — *bewegen*

to get a move on — *sich auf die Socken machen.*

We got a move on and achieved almost all of our goals. *Wir machten uns auf die Socken und erreichten fast alle unsere Ziele.*

to move mountains — *Berge versetzen.*

By zeal and idealism she thought she could move mountains. *Durch Eifer und Idealismus glaubte sie, Berge versetzen zu können.*

---

mud — *der Schlamm*

Here's mud in your eye! *Zum Wohl!, Prösterchen!*

His name is mud. *Er ist unten durch.*

to be as clear as mud — *völlig unklar sein, nur Bahnhof verstehen.*

That's as clear as mud to me. *Davon verstehe ich nur Bahnhof.*

---

naked — *nakt*

visible to the naked eye — *mit bloßem Auge sichtbar.*

Jupiter isn't visible to the naked eye tonight. *Mit bloßem Auge ist der Jupiter heute abend nicht sichtbar.*

---

name — *der Name*

What's your name? *Wie heißen Sie?*
What's your first name? *Wie heißen Sie mit Vornamen?*
What's your last name? *Wie heißen Sie mit Nachnamen?*
What was your name again? *Wie war gleich Ihr Name?*
What's the dog's name? *Wie heißt der Hund?*

to name names — *Ross und Reiter nennen.*
In her memoirs the actress didn't always name names. *In ihren Memoiren nannte die Schauspielerin nicht immer Ross und Reiter.*

---

nap — *das Nickerchen*

to catch napping — *überrumpeln.*
The enemy army caught us napping. *Das feindliche Heer überrumpelte uns.*

to take a nap — *ein Nickerchen machen.*
She was tired and took a nap. *Sie war müde und machte ein Nickerchen.*

---

necessity — *die Not*

Necessity is the mother of invention. *Die Not macht erfinderisch/Die Not bricht Eisen.*

---

neck — *der Hals*

to be breathing down someone's neck — *jemandem im Nacken sitzen; jemandem ständig auf die Finger sehen.*
The crooks want their money and are breathing down his neck. *Die Gauner wollen ihr Geld und sitzen ihm im Nacken.*
When painting her landscapes, she doesn't like anyone breathing down her neck. *Wenn sie ihre Landschaftsbilder malt, hat sie es nicht gern, wenn man ihr ständig auf die Finger sieht.*

to give a pain in the neck — *auf den Wecker gehen.*
Unwanted telephone calls give us a pain in the neck. *Unerwünschte Telefonanrufe gehen uns auf den Wecker.*

to risk one's neck — *Kopf und Kragen riskieren.*
As a racing driver, he often had to risk his neck. *Als Rennfahrer musste er oft Kopf und Kragen riskieren.*

to run neck and neck — *Kopf an Kopf rennen/laufen.*

Almost to the last moment the two ran neck and neck. *Fast bis zum letzten Augenblick liefen die beiden Kopf an Kopf.*

to save one's neck — *seinen Kopf retten.*

To save his own neck, he turned state's evidence. *Um den eigenen Kopf zu retten, trat er als Kronzeuge auf.*

to stick one's neck out — *die Hand ins Feuer legen.*

I've stuck my neck out for him and now he leaves me in the lurch. *Für ihn hab ich die Hand ins Feuer gelegt, und jetzt lässt er mich im Stich.*

---

to need — *brauchen*

That's all I (she, he, we, they) needed! — *Das fehlte nur noch! (Auch das noch!)*

---

needle — *die Nadel, die Stecknadel*

to be on pins and needles — *wie auf glühenden Kohlen sitzen.*

The whole time I was on pins and needles. *Die ganze Zeit war ich wie auf glühenden Kohlen.*

to look for a needle in a haystack — *die (Steck)Nadel im Heuhaufen/im Heuschober suchen.*

In that town clean, cheap hotels are as rare as a needle in a haystack. *In der Stadt sind billige, saubere Hotels so selten wie die Nadel im Heuhaufen.*

to needle — *fuchsen.*

Will you stop needling the little boy! *Hört doch auf, den Kleinen zu fuchsen!*

---

neither . . . nor — *weder . . . noch.*

neither here nor there — *nichts zur Sache tun.*

That objection is neither here nor there. *Dieser Einwand tut nichts zur Sache.*

That is neither fish nor fowl. — *Das ist weder Fisch noch Fleisch.*

---

network — *das Netz, Netzwerk*

old-boy network — *die Seilschaft/Klüngelei.*

The old-boy network protected him. *Die Seilschaft hat ihn in Schutz genommen.*

---

next — *nächst*
next door — *nebenan.*
She didn't want to marry the nice boy next door. *Sie wollte den netten Jungen von nebenan nicht heiraten.*

night — *die Nacht*
to make a night of it — *die ganze Nacht durchfeiern.*
We made a night of it. *Wir haben die ganze Nacht durchgefeiert.*

to nip — *kneifen*
to nip in the bud — *im Keim ersticken.*
The general wanted to nip the revolt in the bud. *Der General wollte den Aufstand im Keim ersticken.*

norm — *die Norm*
to depart from the norm — *aus der Reihe tanzen.*
Udo departed from the norm too often and was dismissed. *Udo tanzte zu oft aus der Reihe und wurde entlassen.*

nose — *die Nase*
to cut off one's nose to spite one's face — *sich ins eigene Fleisch schneiden.*
Full of pride and presumption, he cut off his nose to spite his face. *Voll Hoch- und Übermut schnitt er sich ins eigene Fleisch.*

as plain as the nose on your face — *sonnenklar; klar wie Klärchen.*
The lawyer engaged in shady deals — that's as plain as the nose on your face. *Der Anwalt hat dunkle Geschäfte gemacht — das ist sonnenklar.*

not to be able to see beyond the end of one's nose — *nicht fähig sein, über den eigenen Tellerrand zu blicken.*
Ute's the only one with vision; the others can't seen beyond the end of their noses. *Ute ist die einizge mit Weitblick; die anderen sind nicht fähig, über den eigenen Tellerrand zu blicken.*

to pay through the nose — *schwer draufzahlen.*
He knew we wanted the property and made us pay through the nose. *Er wusste, dass wir das Grundstück wollten, und zwang uns schwer draufzuzahlen.*

to put one's nose to the grindstone — *sich ins Zeug legen.*
We put our noses to the grindstone to meet the deadline. *Wir haben uns ins Zeug gelegt, um den Termin einzuhalten.*

not — *nicht*

Not on your life!/Not for love or money!/Not at any price/Not for all the tea in China! *Nie im Leben!/Um keinen Preis der Welt!/Nicht um alles in der Welt!*

Not up to par/snuff. *Nicht auf der Höhe sein.*
I'm not feeling quite up to snuff; I'll mow the lawn tomorrow. *Heute fühl ich mich nicht ganz auf der Höhe; morgen mäh ich den Rasen.*

note — *der Vermerk*

to be of note — *von Bedeutung sein.*
Since you left, nothing of note has happened. *Seit du fort bist, ist nichts von Bedeutung geschehen.*

to take due note of — *sich hinter die Ohren schreiben.*
Her suggestions are well thought through, and I've taken due note of them. *Ihre Ratschläge sind gut durchdacht und ich hab sie mir hinter die Ohren geschrieben.*

nothing — *nichts*

to come to nothing — *ausgehen wie das Hornberger schießen.*
For weeks on end they made a lot of fuss about it, but it all came to nothing. *Wochenlang machte man viel Wirbel darüber doch schließlich ging alles wie das Hornberger Schießen aus.*

nothing at all — *gar nichts; Null Komma nichts.*
We want nothing at all from you. *Wir wollen gar nichts von Ihnen.*

Nothing of the sort! — *Mitnichten!*

notice — *die Bekanntmachung*

at (on) short notice — *von heute auf morgen.*
I can't arrange that at such short notice. *Das kann ich nicht so von heute auf morgen veranstalten.*

to give notice — *kündigen.*

She thought she had job security, but they gave her a week's notice. *Sie glaubte, einen sicheren Arbeitsplatz zu haben, aber man hat ihr mit einer Frist von einer Woche gekündigt.*

nowhere — *nirgends; nirgendwo*

    to come from nowhere — *wie aus dem Nichts auftauchen; wie Zieten aus dem Busch auftauchen.*

You always come from nowhere; I think you're a ghost. *Du tauchst immer wie aus dem Nichts auf; ich glaube du bist ein Gespenst.*

    to get nowhere — *Null Komma nichts erreichen.*

He tried everything but he got nowhere with me. *Er hat alles versucht aber bei mir hat er Null Komma nichts erreicht.*

number — *die Nummer; die Zahl*

    any number of times — *zigmal.*

I've told him any number of (umpteen) times, but he's forgotten it again. *Zigmal hab ich's ihm gesagt, aber er hat's wieder vergessen.*

    to do a number on — *verarschen/auf den Arm nehmen.*

1000 dollars for that? They did a number on you! *Tausend Dollar dafür? Da hast du dich verarschen lassen!*

    to do by the numbers — *mechanisch erledigen.*

His heart wasn't in it; he just did it by the numbers. *Mit dem Herzen war er nicht dabei; er hat's nur mechanisch erledigt.*

    to do number one — *klein machen (baby talk).*

    to do number two — *groß machen, Aa machen.*

Do you have to do number one or number two? *Musst du klein oder gross machen?*

    to have got someone's number — *jemanden durchschaut haben.*

You're trying to make a sucker of me, but I've got your number. *Du versuchst mich zu verarschen, aber dich hab ich längst durchschaut.*

    to look out for number one — *egoistisch handeln, nur an sich denken.*

Uncle Fritz never helps us; he just looks out for number one. *Uns hilft Onkel Fritz nie; er handelt immer nur egoistisch.*

nut — *die Nuss*

to be nuts — *verrückt sein*

They're all nuts! *Die sind alle verrückt!.*

to be nuts about — *wild auf.*

All the men were nuts about the belly dancer. *Alle Männer waren ganz wild auf die Bauchtänzerin.*

to go nuts — *durchdrehen.*

He was under constant pressure and went nuts. *Er stand ständig unter Druck und drehte durch.*

Nuts to you! — *Du kannst (ihr könnt) mir den Buckel runterrutschen!*

The general really used a stronger expression than "nuts to you." *Der General benutzte eigentlich einen derberen Ausdruck als: "Ihr könnt mir den Buckel runterrutschen."*

nutshell — *die Nussschale*

in a nutshell — *kurz gesagt.*

In a nutshell, we don't want it. *Kurz gesagt, wir wollen's nicht.*

to put in a nutshell — *auf den Punkt bringen.*

Could you make an attempt to put your arguments in a nutshell? *Könnten Sie den Versuch machen, Ihre Argumente auf den Punkt zu bringen?*

oar — *das Ruder*

to put an oar in — *seinen Senf dazu geben.*

Of course, he had to put an oar in. *Natürlich musste er seinen Senf dazu geben.*

oats — *der Hafer*

to sow one's wild oats — *sich die Hörner abstoßen.*

The boy is still sowing his wild oats, unfortunately. *Der Junge stößt sich noch die Hörner ab, leider.*

to observe — *beobachten*
   to observe closely — *auf die Finger sehen.*
   We observed the magician closely. *Wir sahen dem Zauberer auf die Finger.*

obvious — *offenkundig; auf der Hand liegen*
   The answer is obvious. — *Die Antwort liegt auf der Hand.*

   the obvious thing to do — *das Naheliegende.*
   He did everything except the obvious. *Er hat alles, nur nicht das Naheliegende getan.*

off — *entfernt; weg*
   off and on — *dann und wann.*
   Off and on he's in a good mood. *Dann und wann ist er gut gelaunt*

   off day — *nicht auf der Höhe sein; nicht auf dem Damm/Posten sein.*
   I missed the error. We all have our off days. *Den Fehler hab ich übersehen. Jeder ist mal nicht auf dem Posten.*

   off limits — *gesperrt, tabu.*
   The bar was off limits to the sailors, but they went in anyway. *Die Bar war den Matrosen gesperrt; trotzdem gingen sie hinein.*

   off the top of my head — *spontan; aus dem Handgelenk; aus dem hohlen Bauch; aus dem Stegreif.*
   Off the top of my head, I think it's a good idea. *Spontan halt ich das für eine gute Idee.*

   off-color — *anzüglich.*
   Schiller didn't always like it when Goethe told off-color jokes. *Schiller gefiel es nicht immer, wenn Goethe anzügliche Witze riss.*

to offend — *Anstoß erregen*
   Goethe's and Mozart's strong language offended some. *Die von Goethe und Mozart benutzten Kraftausdrücke erregten bei einigen Anstoß.*

   to feel offended — *sich verletzt/beleidigt fühlen.*
   He thought the exhibition terrible and felt offended as a patriot. *Er fand die Ausstellung scheußlich, und fühlte sich als Patriot beleidigt.*

office — *das Büro*
   office hours — *die Sprechstunden.*
   The mayor has office hours tomorrow. *Die Bürgermeisterin hat morgen Sprechstunden.*

old — *alt*
   old-boy network — *die Kumpanei, die Männerklüngel.*
   The new boss is fighting against the old-boy network. *Die neue Chefin kämpft gegen Männerklüngelei.*

   old hat — *ein alter Zopf.*
   His entire way of thinking is old hat. *Seine ganze Denkweise ist nur ein alter Zopf.*

omelette — *das Omelett, die Omelette*
   You can't make an omelette without breaking eggs. — *Wo gehobelt wird, da fallen Späne.*

on — *auf*
   to be on — *gespielt werden.*
   What's on at the theater tonight? *Was wird heute Abend im Theater gespielt?*

   to have on — *vorhaben.*
   If you've nothing on for tonight, come with us. *Wenn Sie heute abend nichts vorhaben, kommen Sie mit uns!*

   on the scene/spot — *vor Ort.*
   On television they reported on the spot about the floodings. *Im Fernsehen wurde vor Ort über die Überschwemmungen berichtet.*

once — *einmal*
   Once is not enough. — *Einmal ist keinmal.*

   once again — *abermals.*
   The union didn't want to give up on a wage raise once again. *Die Gewerkschaft wollte nicht abermals auf eine Tariferhöhung verzichten.*

   once upon a time — *es war einmal.*
   Once upon a time, there was a golden age that they often recalled. *Es war einmal ein goldenes Zeitalter, an das sie oft zurückdachten.*

one — *eins*

    to be (have) one up on — *um eine Nasenlänge voraus sein.*

    The blackmailer was one up on his victim. *Der Erpresser war seinem Opfer um eine Nasenlänge voraus.*

    I, for one — *ich meinerseits.*

    I, for one, think the idea might be useful. *Ich meinerseits finde, die Idee könnte nützlich sein.*

    one of these days — *bei Gelegenheit.*

    One of these days we could look at the matter more closely. *Bei Gelegenheit könnten wir die Sache näher untersuchen.*

to open — *öffnen*

    to open the door wide — *Tür und Tor öffnen.*

    Measles can open the door wide to other viruses. *Die Masernkrankheit kann anderen Viren Tür und Tor öffnen.*

open — *offen*

    open-air (theater, concert, etc.) — *Freilicht.*

    In the summer we like to go to open-air concerts. *Im Sommer gehen wir gern in Freilichtkonzerte.*

    in the open air — *unter freiem Himmel.*

    We danced in the open air. *Wir tanzten unter freiem Himmel.*

    opening hours; hours of business — *die Öffnungszeiten.*

    Can you tell me the museum's opening hours? *Können Sie mir die Öffnungszeiten des Museums sagen?*

order — *der Befehl*

    to be made to order — *auf den Leib geschnitten sein.*

    The role of Medea is made to order for her. *Die Rolle der Medea ist ihr auf den Leib geschnitten.*

out — *aus*

    to be out for a buck — *hinter dem Geld her sein.*

    He's always out for a buck. *Er ist immer hinter dem Geld her.*

to be out for all one can get — *vom Stamme Nimm sein.*

The lawyer is out for all he can get. *Der Rechtsanwalt ist vom Stamme Nimm.*

to be out to get — *scharf auf.*

The widow is out to get uncle Otto. *Die Witwe ist scharf auf Onkel Otto.*

to go all out — *alle Minen springen lassen.*

They went all out to get the contract. *Sie ließen alle Minen springen, um den Auftrag zu bekommen.*

out and out — *ausgemacht.*

The president and the whole board are all out and out liars. *Der Präsident und der ganze Vorstand sind alle ausgemachte Lügenbolde.*

---

outset — *der Anfang*

at the outset — *von Anfang an; von vornherein.*

We didn't like the scheme at the very outset. *Schon von vornherein gefiel uns das Konzept nicht.*

---

to outsmart — *überlisten*

The soldier succeeded in outsmarting the devil. *Es gelang dem Soldaten, den Teufel zu überlisten.*

---

over — *über*

to be over (with) — *aus sein.*

Despite all that, our love can never be totally over. *Trotz allem kann es mit unserer Liebe niemals ganz aus sein.*

to be over and done with — *aus und vorbei sein.*

Our friendship is over and done with. *Unsere Freundschaft ist aus und vorbei.*

---

to overdo — *es übertreiben*

Just tell the true story, and don't overdo it. *Erzähl nur die wahre Geschichte und übertreib's nicht.*

to overdo — *sich übernehmen.*

She's often tired because she overdoes it at work. *Sie ist oft müde, weil sie sich bei der Arbeit übernimmt.*

overdone — *verkocht; verbraten.*
The tenderloin is overdone. *Der Lendenbraten ist verbraten.*

oyster — *die Auster*
    the world is one's oyster — *die Welt steht einem offen/die Welt liegt einem zu Füßen.*
    There you sit moping about busted love—yet you're young, healthy, and intelligent. The world is your oyster! *Da verzehrst du dich vor Liebeskummer; aber du bist jung, gesund und gescheit. Die Welt steht dir offen!*

to pack — *packen*
    to pack quite a punch — *ganz schön zuschlagen können.*
    This boxer packs quite a punch, but he still loses most of the time. *Dieser Boxer kann ganz schön zuschlagen; trotzdem verliert er meistens.*

    to pack quite a wallop — *ganz schön reinhauen.*
    Your home-brewed elixir packs quite a wallop. *Dein hausgebrautes Elixir haut ganz schön rein.*

    to send packing — *fortjagen; zum Teufel schicken.*
    He sent the door-to-door salesman packing. *Den Klinkenputzer hat er fortgejagt.*

pain — *der Schmerz*
    to be a pain (in the neck) — *eine richtige Nervensäge sein.*
    Fritz is a real pain. *Fritz ist eine richtige Nervensäge.*

to paint — *malen; anstreichen*
    to paint oneself into a corner — *sich selbst in die Bredouille bringen.*
    By lying a lot he painted himself into a corner. *Durch viel Lügen brachte er sich selbst in die Bredouille.*

to paint the town red — *auf die Pauke hauen.*

In his student days he often painted the town red. *In seiner Studentenzeit haute er oft auf die Pauke.*

---

pale — *der Pfahl*

to be beyond the pale — *die Grenze des Schicklichen überschreiten.*

His behavior was beyond the pale. *Sein Benehmen überschritt die Grenze des Schicklichen.*

---

palm — *die Handfläche; der Handteller*

to grease someone's palm — *jemanden schmieren/bestechen.*

He tried to grease my palm, but I don't accept bribes. *Er versuchte, mich zu bestechen, aber Schmiergelder nehm ich nicht an.*

to have an itching palm — *sich schmieren lassen.*

In Brecht's play the judge had an itchy palm, but he was just to the poor. *In Brechts Stück ließ sich der Richter schmieren; trotzdem ließ er den Armen Gerechtigkeit widerfahren.*

to have in the palm of one's hand — *in der Hand haben.*

The gangster had the mayor in the palm of his hand. *Der Gangster hatte den Bürgermeister in der Hand.*

to palm off — *andrehen.*

The pastry cook tried to palm off on me his tarts from the day before yesterday. *Der Konditor versuchte, mir seine Torten von vorgestern anzudrehen.*

---

to pan — *in die Pfanne hauen*

Because the critic had panned his play, the author belted him in the face. *Weil der Kritiker sein Stück in die Pfanne gehauen hatte, haute ihm der Autor ins Gesicht.*

to pan out — *gut laufen; sich verwirklichen; klappen.*

The prospector thought he'd found gold and made great plans but they didn't pan out. *Der Goldsucher glaubte Gold gefunden zu haben und machte große Pläne, die sich aber nicht verwirklichten.*

---

parade — *die Parade*
   to rain on someone's parade — *jmdm. die Petersilie/das Geschäft verhageln.*
   The new competition rained on our parade. *Die neue Konkurrenz hat uns das Geschäft verhagelt.*

part — *der Teil*
   I'm a stranger in these parts. *Ich kenne mich hier nicht aus.*

   foreign parts — *das Ausland.*
   He's now in foreign parts. *Er befindet sich jetzt im Ausland.*

   to be part and parcel of — *einen wesentlichen Bestandteil bilden.*
   The right of way is part and parcel of the agreement. *Das Durchfahrtsrecht bildet einen wesentlichen Bestandteil des Abkommens.*

   to take part in — *teilnehmen an.*
   We also want to take part in the celebration. *Wir wollen auch an der Feier teilnehmen.*

   to take someone's part — *Partei ergreifen.*
   Why do you always have to take his part? *Warum musst du immer für ihn Partei ergreifen?*

to part — *trennen*
   A fool and his money soon are parted. — *Wer nicht aufpasst, dem rinnt das Geld durch die Finger.*

   This is where we part company. — *Hier trennen sich unsere Wege.*

party — *die Partei*
   across party lines — *quer durch die Parteien; Partei übergreifend.*
   There was discontent across all party lines. *Quer durch die Parteien herrschte Unzufriedenheit.*

to pass — *bestehen*
   She passed the exam with flying colors. *Sie hat das Examen glänzend bestanden.*

   to pass — *überholen.*
   He tried to pass the Porsche with his Mercedes. *Mit seinem Mercedes versuchte er, den Porsche zu überholen.*

to pass by — *vorbeigehen.*

She passed by without saying a word. *Sie ging vorbei, ohne ein Wort zu sagen.*

to pass the buck — *den schwarzen Peter zuschieben.*

The Foreign Minister tried to pass the buck to the Minister of the Interior. *Der Außenminister versuchte, dem Innenminister den schwarzen Peter zuzuschieben.*

pass — *der Pass*

to cut s.o. off at the pass — *jmdm. das Wasser abgraben.*

The competition is trying to cut us off at the pass. *Die Konkurrenz versucht uns das Wasser abzugraben.*

pat — *der Klaps*

to have down pat — *wie am Schnürchen können.*

I've got everything I'm supposed to tell the boss tomorrow down pat. *Alles, was ich morgen dem Chef sagen soll, kann ich wie am Schnürchen.*

to pat on the back — *auf die Schulter klopfen.*

After his success, he patted himself on the back. *Nach dem Erfolg klopfte er sich auf die Schulter.*

patience — *die Geduld*

He would try the patience of Job. *Bei ihm braucht man eine Engelsgeduld.*

to pave — *plfastern; betonieren*

The world is getting paved over. *Die Welt wird zubetoniert.*

to pave the way for s.o. — *jmdm. den Weg ebnen.*

She paved the way for us and we think the world of her. *Sie hat uns den Weg geebnet und wir halten große Stücke auf sie.*

to pay — *zahlen*

It doesn't pay to work on that anymore. *Es lohnt sich nicht, mehr darüber zu arbeiten.*

to pay attention — *achten auf.*

Edgar didn't pay attention to the quicksand. *Edgar achtete nicht auf den Treibsand.*

to pay a dividend — *eine Dividende ausschütten.*
Last year that steel company didn't pay a dividend. *Letztes Jahr schüttete dieser Stahlkonzern keine Dividende aus.*

to pay off — *auszahlen; sich bezahlt machen.*
The boss paid off the workers. *Der Chef zahlte die Arbeiter aus.*
Our tenacity paid off. *Unsere Beharrlichkeit hat sich bezahlt gemacht.*

to pay off — *schmieren; Schweigegeld zahlen.*
Before she murdered him, she paid off (paid hush money) to the blackmailer for many years. *Lange Jahre zahlte sie dem Erpresser Schweigegeld, bevor sie ihn ermordete.*

---

pea — *die Erbse*
as alike as two peas in a pod — *sich gleichen wie ein Ei dem anderen.*
They are as alike as two peas in a pod. *Sie gleichen sich wie ein Ei dem anderen.*

---

peg — *der Pflock*
to take s.o. down a peg or two — *jmdn. herunterputzen; jmdm. einen Dämpfer aufsetzen.*
Someone should have taken down that conceited fop a peg or two long ago. *Diesem eingebildeten Geck hätte man längst einen Dämpfer aufsetzen müssen.*

---

phony — *falsch; getürkt*
He fell for the phony advertising. *Er ist auf die getürkte Werbung reingefallen.*

to be as phony as a three-dollar bill — *ein falscher Fünfziger sein.*
Don't trust him; he's as phony as a three-dollar bill. *Trau ihm nicht; er ist ein falscher Fünfziger!*

---

to pick — *pflücken; wählen*
to pick a fight/argument — *einen Streit vom Zaun brechen.*
He was drunk and wanted to take on everyone. He tried to pick a fight with me too. *Er war besoffen, wollte sich mit allen anlegen und versuchte auch mit mir einen Streit vom Zaun zu brechen.*

---

to pick up — *aufheben*

The witch picked up the stones. *Die Hexe hob die Steine auf.*

to pick up — *abholen.*

I'll pick you up at the station. *Ich hole Sie am Bahnhof ab.*

to pick up (speed) — *durchstarten.*

The business was in difficulty, but now it's picking up (speed) again. *Sein Geschäft hatte Schwierigkeiten, aber jetzt startet es wieder durch.*

picnic — *das Picknick*

to have a picnic — *ein Picknick machen.*

We had a marvelous picnic yesterday. *Wir haben gestern ein wunderschönes Picknick gemacht.*

to be no picnic — *kein Zuckerlecken sein; kein Honig(sch)lecken sein.*

Spending eighteen hours in the airplane to Australia is no picnic. *Achtzehn Stunden im Flugzeug nach Australien ist kein Honiglecken.*

piece — *das Stück*

to give a piece of one's mind — *gründlich seine Meinung sagen; jemandem den Kopf waschen.*

He was impertinent and stupid, and I gave him a piece of my mind. *Er benahm sich dummdreist, und ich sagte ihm gründlich meine Meinung.*

to go to pieces — *die Fassung verlieren*

If something goes wrong, he goes to pieces easily. *Wenn etwas schief geht, verliert er leicht die Fassung.*

pig — *das Schwein*

to buy/sell a pig in a poke — *die Katze im Sack kaufen/verkaufen.*

We don't want to sell you a pig in a poke. *Wir wollen Ihnen keine Katze im Sack verkaufen.*

to eat like a pig — *den Wanst vollschlagen.*

It's no pleasure watching while he eats like a pig. *Es ist keine Freude zuzusehen, während er sich den Wanst vollschlägt.*

pillar — *die Säule*
from pillar to post — *von Pontius zu Pilatus.*
At City Hall they sent me from pillar to post. *Im Rathaus hat man mich von Pontius zu Pilatus geschickt.*

pin — *die Stecknadel*
One could have heard a pin drop. *Man hätte eine Stecknadel fallen hören können.*

to pin down — *festnageln; festlegen.*
They promised to come tomorrow, but I couldn't pin them down to a definite time. *Sie versprachen, morgen zu kommen, aber ich konnte sie auf keine bestimmte Zeit festnageln.*

pinch — *der Kniff*
in a pinch — *zur Not.*
In a pinch we could use it. *Zur Not könnte wir's benutzen.*

to feel the pinch — *knapp bei Kasse sein.*
They go to the theater less, because they're feeling the pinch.
Sie gehen seltener ins Theater, weil sie knapp bei Kasse sind.

to pinch — *kneifen.*
That's where the shoes pinches. *Da liegt der Hase im Pfeffer.*

to pinch pennies — *jeden Pfennig (zweimal/dreimal) umdrehen.*
You won't get the money from him; he'll pinch a penny twice before he spends it. *Von ihm kriegst du das Geld nicht; er dreht jeden Pfennig um, bevor er ihn ausgibt.*

place — *die Stelle; der Platz; der Ort*
all over the place — *wie Kraut und Rüben.*
Clothes and toys were scattered all over the place. *Kleider und Spielsachen lagen wie Kraut und Rüben herum.*

plain — *einfach*
as plain as the nose on one's face — *sonnenklar sein.*
It's as plain as the nose on your face that you've started drinking again.
Es ist sonnenklar, dass du mit dem Trinken wieder angefangen hast.

in plain language — *im Klartext.*

In plain language that means we'll have to come up with more money. *Im Klartext heißt es, dass wir mehr Geld berappen müssen.*

---

plan — *der Plan*

to plan on — *rechnen mit.*

We hadn't planned on that. *Damit hatten wir nicht gerechnet.*

---

to plaster — *verputzen, vergipsen*

to get plastered — *sich einen andudeln, sich besaufen.*

The bagpiper always gets plastered during the folk festival. *Während des Volksfestes dudelt sich der Dudelsackpfeifer immer einen an.*

---

plate — *der Teller*

to have a lot (of work) on one's plate — *viel am Hals/viel um die Ohren haben.*

During our absence lots of mail piled up. Lots on our plate; we've got our work cut out for us. *Während unserer Abwesenheit hat sich viel Post angehäuft. Wir haben jetzt viel um die Ohren.*

---

to play — *spielen*

to have played all one's cards — *seinen letzten Trumpf ausgespielt haben.*

We don't have to worry about him anymore; he's played all his cards. *Wir brauchen uns nicht mehr um ihn zu kümmern; er hat nun seinen letzten Trumpf ausgespielt.*

to play by ear — *nach dem Gehör spielen.*

She played the song by ear. *Sie hat das Lied nach dem Gehör gespielt.*

to play it by ear — *es der Situation überlassen.*

As to how we act in the future, we'll have to play it by ear. *Wie wir uns in Zunkunft verhalten, müssen wir es der Situation überlassen.*

to play down — *verharmlosen.*

He tried to play down his participation in the conspiracy. *Er versuchte, seine Teilnahme an der Verschwörung zu verharmlosen.*

to play for time — *versuchen Zeit zu gewinnen.*
Just play for time; we've got to play it cool. *Versuch nur Zeit zu gewinnen; wir müssen auf cool machen.*

to play hooky — *schwänzen.*
She often played hooky from school, nevertheless she was very successful in life. *Die Schule hat sie oft geswänzt; trotzdem hatte sie viel Erfolg im Leben.*

to play into someone's hands — *jemandem in die Hände arbeiteten.*
With his thoughtless remarks he played into the opposition's hands. *Mit seinen unbedachten Äußerungen arbeitete er der Opposition in die Hände.*

to play it safe — *auf Nummer Sicher gehen.*
She'd like to work on her novel, but she's playing it safe and works as an advertising copy writer. *Sie würde gern an ihrem Roman schreiben, aber sie geht auf Nummer Sicher und arbeitet als Werbetexterin.*

to play second fiddle — *Zweite Geige spielen.*
We've played second fiddle long enough. *Wir haben lange genug die Zweite Geige gespielt.*

to play small-time theaters/clubs — *tingeln.*
Once he was a great star; now he plays small-time clubs in the provinces. *Einst war er ein großer Star; jetzt tingelt er durch die Provinz.*

to play up — *hochspielen.*
The demonstration was played up by the media. *Die Demonstration wurde von den Medien hochgespielt.*

---

plunge — *der Sprung, der Sturz*
to take the plunge — *den Sprung wagen; Augen zu und durch!*
Forget your fear. Just close your eyes and take the plunge! *Vergiss die Bange. Augen zu und durch!*

---

to poach — *wildern*
to poach on someone's preserve — *jemandem ins Gehege kommen.*
Take care not to poach on the director's prepreserve. *Gib acht, dem Abteilungsleiter nicht ins Gehege zu kommen.*

---

point — *der Punkt*

    to be beside the point — *nicht zur Sache gehören.*

    That's all very interesting, but it's beside the point. *Das ist alles sehr interessant, gehört aber nicht zur Sache.*

    to get to the point — *zu Potte kommen.*

    It took a long time for him to get to the point. *Es dauerte lange, bevor er zu Potte kam.*

    to make points with s.o. — *bei jmdm. ankommen; punkten.*

    He's still trying to make points with me, but I can't stand him. *Er versucht noch, bei mir anzukommen, aber ich kann ihn nicht leiden.*

pole — *die Stange*

    to trust s.o. as far as one could throw a 10-foot pole. — *jmdm. nicht um die Ecke trauen.*

    I trust that supposed finance expert about as far as I can throw a 10-foot pole. *Diesem vermeintlichen Finanzexperten traue ich nicht um die Ecke.*

to pop — *knallen*

    to pop the question — *einen Heiratsantrag machen.*

    When he finally popped the question, she said no. *Als er endlich einen Heiratsantrag machte, sagte sie nein.*

    to pop up out of nowhere — *wie Ziethen aus dem Busch erscheinen.*

    That fellow's uncanny; he's always popping up out of nowhere. *Der Kerl ist unheimlich; er erscheint immer wie Ziethen aus dem Busch.*

posh — *piekfein*

    We wanted something more homey, less posh. *Wir wollten etwas Gemütlicheres, weniger Piekfeines.*

pot — *der Topf*

    That's a case of the pot calling the kettle black. — *Das ist ein Fall von einem Esel, der den anderen Langohr schilt.*

    to go to pot — *auf den Hund kommen.*

    He gambled away his money, and his business went to pot. *Er verspielte sein Geld, und sein Geschäft kam auf den Hund.*

to take potluck — *aufs Geratewohl gehen; sich überraschen lassen.*
I don't know what my husband cooked for tonight. Do you want to take
potluck? *Ich weiß nicht was mein Mann für heute Abend gekocht hat.
Willst du dich überraschen lassen?*

to pour — *gießen*
    to pour oil on troubled waters — *Öl auf die Wogen gießen; die Wogen
    glätten.*
During the peace negotiations the ambassador tried to pour oil on troubled
waters. *Während der Friedensverhandlungen versuchte die
Botschafterin, Öl auf die Wogen zu gießen.*

    to pour (rain) — *in Strömen gießen.*
It's pouring again. *Es gießt wieder in Strömen.*

powder — *der Puder; das Pulver*
    to not be worth the powder to blow it to hell — *keinen Pfifferling wert
    sein; vollkommen wertlos sein.*
His suggestions weren't worth the powder to blow them to hell. *Seine
Vorschläge waren keinen Pfifferling wert.*

    to powder one's nose — *sich die Nase pudern; kurz verschwinden.*
I've got to powder my nose. *Ich muss mal kurz verschwinden.*

    to take a powder — *die Flatter machen; abhauen; verschwinden.*
Take a powder, creep! *Hau ab, Fiesling!*

practice — *die Übung*
    Practice makes perfect. *Übung macht den Meister. (Es ist noch kein
    Meister vom Himmel gefallen.)*

to preach — *predigen*
    to preach a sermon — *eine Predigt halten.*
He preached many sermons and converted others — but not himself. *Er
hielt viele Predigten, bekehrte andere, aber nicht sich selbst.*

    to preach to the converted — *offene Türen einrennen.*
We've already said yes, so save your efforts; you're only preaching to the
converted. *Wir haben schon ja gesagt, so kannst du dir deine Mühe
ersparen; du rennst nur offene Türen ein.*

present — *gegenwärtig*
at present — *derzeit.*
At present we're not hiring any additional staff. *Derzeit stellen wir kein zusätzliches Personal ein.*

---

presentable — *ansehnlich*
Her water colors are quite presentable. *Ihre Aquarelle können sich sehen lassen.*

---

pretentious — *großspurig; hochtrabend*
Her pantheistic-polytheistic epic:Accessing and Keeping Company with the Ongoing Gods, is a bit pretentious. *Ihr pantheistisch-polytheistisches Epos Zu- und Umgang mit den Andauernden Göttern ist etwas großspurig.*

---

pretty — *hübsch*
to be sitting pretty — *reich, zahlungskräftig sein; in Geld schwimmen.*
They won a lot of money and are sitting pretty—for the moment. *Sie haben viel Geld gewonnen und sind im Moment zahlungskräftig.*

---

to prick — *stechen*
Goethe's conscience pricked him, but he abandoned the girl anyway. *Goethe hatte Gewissensbisse; trotzdem verließ er das Mädchen.*

to prick up one's ears — *die Ohren spitzen.*
The boy pricked up his ears when his parents were talking about possible birthday presents. *Der Junge spitzte die Ohren, als seine Eltern von möglichen Geburtstagsgeschenken redeten.*

---

principle — *das Prinzip*
to be a stickler for principles — *ein Prinzipienreiter sein.*
As a stickler for principles, it was difficult for him to have to make compromises. *Als Prinzipienreiter fiel es ihm schwer, Kompromisse schließen zu müssen.*

---

private — *privat*
a private party — *eine geschlossene Gesellschaft.*

Unfortunately, there was a private party in the restaurant's nicest room. *Leider gab es eine geschlossene Gesellschaft im schönsten Saal des Restaurants.*

---

pro — *für*

the pros and cons — *das Für und Wider.*

Before we decide, we'll have to consider the pros and cons carefully. *Bevor wir uns entscheiden, müssen wir das Für und Wider sorgfältig abwägen.*

---

proof — *der Beweis*

The proof of the pudding is in the eating. *Probieren geht über studieren.*

to prove one's worth — *seinen Mann stehen.*

The new boss proved her worth from the very beginning. *Gleich von Anfang an stand die neue Chefin ihren Mann.*

to prove someone right — *jemandem recht geben.*

Success proved her right. *Der Erfolg gab ihr recht.*

---

proud — *stolz*

nothing to be proud of — *kein Ruhmesblatt sein.*

This agreement is nothing for us to be proud of. *Dieses Abkommen ist für uns kein Ruhmesblatt.*

---

to pull — *ziehen*

pull — *Beziehungen; Vitamin B.*

Without pull he wouldn't have made it. *Ohne Vitamin B hätte er es nicht geschafft.*

to pull a fast one — *reinlegen.*

You pulled a fast one on me, and I'll never forgive you for it. *Du hast mich reingelegt und das verzeih ich dir nie.*

to pull out all the stops — *alle Hebel in Bewegung setzen.*

We must pull out all the stops to protect the environment. *Wir müssen alle Hebel in Bewegung setzen, um die Umwelt zu schützen.*

to **pull oneself together** — *sich zusammennehmen.*

She felt weak, but she pulled herself together and won the race. *Ihre Kräfte ließen nach, aber sie nahm sich zusammen und machte das Rennen.*

to **pull someone's leg** — *jemanden verkohlen.*

I mistakenly believed that he was just pulling my leg again. *Irrtümlicherweise glaubte ich, dass er mich nur wieder verkohlte.*

to **pull strings** — *Beziehungen spielen lassen.*

Couldn't you pull strings so that we too get an invitation to the reception? *Könntest du deine Beziehungen nicht spielen lassen, damit auch wir eine Einladung zum Empfang bekommen?*

to **pull the rug out from under someone** — *den Boden unter den Füßen wegziehen.*

Slowly, logically I explained the plan; then the boss pulled the rug out from under me. *Langsam, logisch legte ich den Plan aus, dann zog der Chef mir den Boden unter den Füßen weg.*

to **pull through** — *durchkommen.*

The doctors think he'll pull through. *Die Ärzte glauben, er wird durchkommen.*

to **pull together** — *an einem Strang ziehen.*

Industry and labor should all pull together to protect the environment. *Arbeitgeber und Arbeitnehmer sollten alle an einem Strang ziehen, um die Umwelt zu schützen.*

to **pull the wool over someone's eyes** — *blauen Dunst vormachen.*

I think you want to pull the wool over our eyes. *Ich glaube, du willst uns blauen Dunst vormachen.*

---

to **push** — *schieben*

to **push off** — *abschieben; Leine ziehen, sich verziehen.*

Push off! *Verzieh dich!*

to **push up daisies** — *sich die Radieschen von unten angucken.*

The old gardener is now pushing up daisies. *Der alte Gärtner guckt sich jetzt die Radieschen von unten an.*

---

to **put** — *setzen*

to **put down** — *jmdn. heruntermachen, abwerten, schlechtmachen.*

Your constantly putting everything and everybody down isn't very edify-ing of you. *Dass du alles und alle immer wieder nur heruntermachst, ist nicht sehr erbaulich von dir.*

to put it mildly — *gelinde gesagt.*
To put it mildly, he behaved badly. *Gelinde gesagt, hat er schlecht gehandelt.*

to put (nothing) past someone — *jemandem alles zutrauen.*
I put no lie past him. *Ich traue ihm jede Lüge zu.*

to put on the back burner — *zurückstellen; auf Eis legen; auf die Wartebank schieben.*
They've put problems like global warming on the back burner. *Probleme wie die Erderwärmung haben sie auf Eis gelegt. Aber das Eis schmilzt ständig.*

to put one's life on the line — *sein Leben aufs Spiel setzen.*
As a stuntman in many movies, he often put his life on the line. *Als Kaskadeur in vielen Filmen setzte er oft sein Leben aufs Spiel.*

to put one over on — *ein Schnippchen schlagen.*
In some fairy tales, humans sometimes succeed in putting one over on the devil. *In einigen Märchen schlagen Menschen manchmal dem Teufel ein Schnippchen.*

to put over successfully — *etwas über die Bühne bringen.*
Money was short, but we managed to put the festival over successfully. *Trotz knapper Kasse gelang es uns, die Festspiele über die Bühne zu bringen.*

to put a price on someone's head — *ein Kopfgeld aussetzen.*
The fundamentalists put a price on the writer's head. *Die Fundamentalisten haben ein Kopfgeld auf die Schriftstellerin ausgesetzt.*

to put on — *sich anziehen.*

to put someone on — *jemanden auf den Arm nehmen.*
When his colleagues told him he had won the lottery, he thought they were putting him on. *Als die Kollegen ihm sagten, er hätte das große Los gezogen, glaubte er, sie nahmen ihn auf den Arm.*

to put off — *aufschieben; vertrösten.*
With the help of modern medicine humans are trying to put off death. *Durch Hilfe der modernen Medizin versucht der Mensch, den Tod zu vertrösten.*

to put off indefinitely — *auf die lange Bank schieben.*
Important decisions were put off indefinitely. *Wichtige Entscheidungen wurden auf die lange Bank geschoben.*

a put-up job — *ein abgekartetes Spiel.*
The whole thing was just a put-up job. *Das Ganze war nur ein abgekartetes Spiel.*

to put up with — *sich gefallen lassen; hinnehmen.*
We don't want to put up with propaganda like that any more. *Solche Propaganda wollen wir nicht mehr hinnehmen.*

quality — *die Qualität*
people of quality — *die Leute von Rang und Namen.*
In Moliere's play, Mr. Jourdain is interested only in people of quality. *In Molieres Stück interessiert sich Herr Jourdain nur für die Leute von Rang und Namen.*

question — *die Frage*
Ask a silly question and you get a silly answer. — *Wie die Frage, so die Antwort.*
$64,000 (crucial/all important) question — *die Gretchenfrage.*
Will the experiment succeed, that's the crucial question. *Ob der Versuch gelingt, das ist die Gretchenfrage.*

quiet — *ruhig*
Keep quiet! *Halt's Maul!*

to keep something quiet — *etwas geheimhalten.*
He tried to keep things quiet about his connections to the Stasi. *Er versuchte, seine Beziehungen zur Stasi geheimzuhalten.*

to keep quiet/silent — *schweigen.*
Why did you keep quiet? *Warum hast du geschwiegen?*

quick — *schnell*

Be quick! — *Mach schnell!*

Be quick about it! — *Mach ein bisschen dalli!*

to cut to the quick — *tief getroffen sein.*
His callous attitude cut her to the quick. *Seine gefühllose Haltung traf sie tief.*

to be quick on the comeback — *schlagfertig sein.*
She didn't let his insults go unchallenged, because she's quick on the comeback. *Seine Beleidigungen ließ sie nicht sitzen, denn sie ist schlagfertig.*

to be quick on the uptake — *schnell von Begriff sein.*
I don't have to tell you that twice, for you're quick on the uptake. *Das brauch ich dir nicht zweimal zu sagen, denn du bist schnell von Begriff.*

to be quick-tempered — *hitzig sein; leicht aufbrausen.*
He's grown older, but he's still quick-tempered. *Er ist älter geworden, aber er braust noch leicht auf.*

to be quick-witted — *Köpfchen haben.*
To get ahead you have to be quick-witted. *Um vorwärts zu kommen, muß man Köpfchen haben.*

---

to quit — *kündigen*
Quit kidding around! — *Lass doch deine Anpflaumereien!*

---

race — *das Rennen*

to win the race — *das Rennen machen*
Till the last minute no one knew who would win the electoral race. *Bis zum letzten Augenblick wußte keiner, wer das Wahlrennen machen würde.*

---

rack — *die Folter*

to be on the rack — *Folterqualen leiden,*
I was on the rack till he told me the truth. *Ich litt Folterqualen, bis er mir die Wahrheit sagte.*

to go to rack and ruin — *zugrunde gehen.*
He went to rack and ruin because of his passion for gambling. *Er ist an seiner Spielleidenschaft zugrunde gegangen.*

to put/keep someone on the rack — *auf die Folter spannen,*
Don't keep me on the rack any longer; tell me everything! *Spann mich nicht länger auf die Folter; sag mir alles!*

rack of lamb — *vorderes Rippenstück.*
With our rack of lamb we enjoyed a rosé wine from Baden. *Zu unserem vorderen Rippenstück vom Lamm genossen wir einen badischen Schillerwein.*

to rack — *plagen; quälen*

Joe's body was all aching and racked with pain. *Joes Körper war ganz von Schmerzen gequält und geplagt.*

to rack one's brains — *sich den Kopf zerbrechen.*
I racked my brains, but I couldn't come up with an anwer. *Ich zerbrach mir den Kopf aber ich konnte keine Antwort hervorbringen.*

rag — *der Fetzen*

to go from rags to riches — *sich aus der Armut zum Reichtum empor arbeiten; vom Tellerwäscher zum Millionär.*
Horatio went from rags to riches. *Horatio arbeitete sich aus der Armut zum Reichtum empor.*

rag — *das Käseblatt.*
He believes everything he reads in that rag. *Er glaubt alles, was er in dem Käseblatt liest.*

rage — *die Wut*

to be all the rage — *um sich reißen; der letzte Schrei sein.*
This punk hairstyle is all the rage now. *Diese Punkfrisur ist jetzt der letzte Schrei.*

rain — *der Regen*
  rain or shine — *bei jedem Wetter.*
  We take a walk ever day, rain or shine. *Wir machen täglich einen Spaziergang, bei jedem Wetter.*

  to rain — *regnen.*
  It's raining cats and dogs. — *Es regnet Bindfäden/junge Hunde.*

  When it rains it pours. — *Ein Unglück kommt selten allein.*

  Now she's happy but last year she lost her fortune, her husband, and got sick—oh, when it rains it pours. *Jetzt ist sie glücklich, aber letztes Jahr verlor sie ihr Vermögen, ihren Mann und wurde auch krank—ach, ein Unglück kommt selten allein.*

rainy — *regnerisch*
  to save for a rainy day — *einen Notgroschen zurücklegen; etwas auf die hohe Kante legen.*
  In the fable the grasshopper didn't save for a rainy day. *In der Fabel hatte sich die Grille keinen Notgroschen zurückgelegt.*

to raise — *aufheben*
  to raise hell — *einen Mordskrach schlagen.*
  He forgot the appointment, and she raised hell. *Er hatte den Termin vergessen, und sie schlug einen Mordskrach.*

to rake — *harken*
  to rake in — *scheffeln.*
  Despite the economic crisis, he's still raking in big profits. *Trotz der Wirtschaftskrise scheffelt er noch große Gewinne.*

  to rake over the coals — *die Hölle heiß machen.*
  She really raked him over the coals. *Sie hat ihm ganz richtig die Hölle heiß gemacht.*

ramrod — *der Ladestock*
  to stand ramrod-straight — *wie eine Eins stehen; stocksteif stehen.*
  The sentry stood ramrod-straight before the embassy. *Der Wachtposten stand wie eine Eins vor der Botschaft.*

at random — *aufs Geratewohl; auf gut Glück*
She chose a chocolate at random. *Sie wählte eine Praline auf gut Glück.*

rank — *der Rang*
to rank high with — *eine gute Nummer haben.*
She ranks high in our books. *Sie hat bei uns eine gute Nummer.*

rat — *die Ratte*
to look like a drowned rat — *wie eine gebadete Maus aussehen.*
He got caught in the storm and looked like a drowned rat. *Der Sturm hatte ihn erwischt, und er sah wie eine gebadete Maus aus.*

to smell a rat — *Lunte (den Braten) riechen.*
When the package with the bomb arrived, she smelled a rat and didn't open it. *Als das Paket mit der Bombe ankam, roch sie Lunte und öffnete es nicht.*

to rat on — *verpfeifen; anschwärzen.*
You want me to rat on my old friends now? *Du willst, dass ich meine alten Freunde jetzt verpfeife?*

raw — *roh*
to give a raw deal to — *übel mitspielen.*
The widow was given a raw deal. *Der Witwe wurde übel mitgespielt.*

to read — *lesen*
to read the riot act — *die Leviten lesen.*
If he really did it, I'll read the riot act to him. *Wenn er's wirklich getan hat, werde ich ihm die Leviten lesen.*

to read into — *hineingeheimnissen.*
You're reading too much into her letter—but if it amuses you…. *In ihren Brief geheimnisst du zu viel hinein—aber wenn's dir Spaß macht...*

ready — *bereit*
ready-made — *fertig; von der Stange, prêt à porter.*
Do you sell ready-made window frames? *Verkaufen Sie fertige Fensterrahmen?*

He's obese but can still buy many ready-made clothes. *Er ist sehr dick, kann aber noch vieles von der Stange kaufen.*

rear — *hinten*
   to bring up the rear — *den Schluss/die Nachhut bilden; Schlusslicht sein.*
   Once we were avant-garde; now we're bringing up the rear. *Einst waren wir Vorreiter; jetzt sind wir Schlusslicht.*

reason — *der Grund; die Vernunft*
   There's a reason for that. *Das hat seinen Grund.*

   for no reason at all — *für nichts und wieder nichts.*
   For no reason at all he backed out. *Für nichts und wieder nichts sagte er ab.*

   to see reason — *Vernunft annehmen.*
   When will you see reason and realize that you can't continue to smoke and drink like that? *Wann wirst du Vernunft annehmen und einsehen, dass du nicht weiter so rauchen und trinken kannst?*

record — *die Schallplatte*
   to put on (play) the same broken record — *die alte Platte laufen lassen.*
   It's sad that he always has to put on the same broken record. *Es ist traurig, dass er immer die alte Platte laufen lassen muss.*

red — *rot*
   to be caught red-handed — *auf frischer Tat ertappt werden.*
   The burglars were caught red-handed. *Die Einbrecher wurden auf frischer Tat ertappt.*

   to be in the red — *in den roten Zahlen stehen.*
   Despite economy measures, they're still in the red. *Trotz Sparmaßnahmen stehen sie noch in den roten Zahlen.*

   red tape — *der Amtsschimmel.*
   The red tape was too much for me, and I let the matter drop. *Der Amtsschimmel war mir zu viel und ich ließ die Sache fallen.*

   to see red — *wie ein rotes Tuch wirken.*
   When he gets drunk and I see his red nose, it makes me see red. *Wenn er sich betrinkt und ich seine rote Nase sehe, wirkt es wie ein rotes Tuch auf mich.*

rein — *der Zügel*
> **to give free rein to** — *freien Lauf lassen.*
> After years of tension and bitterness, he gave free rein to his emotions and wept loudly. *Nach Jahren der Verkrampfung und Erbitterung ließ er seinen Gefühlen freien Lauf und weinte laut.*
>
> **to keep a tight rein on** — *sehr streng halten.*
> His children turned out badly despite his always having kept a tight rein on them. *Ihm sind die Kinder missraten, trotzdem er sie immer sehr streng hielt.*

to reproach — *Vorwürfe machen; vorwerfen*
> **to be above reproach** — *über jeden Vorwurf erhaben sein.*
> The dictator was a bad human being, and his wife wasn't above reproach either. *Der Diktator war ein schlechter Mensch, und seine Frau war auch nicht über jeden Vorwurf erhaben.*
>
> **to have nothing to reproach oneself for** — *sich nichts vorzuwerfen haben.*
> I did my best and have nothing to reproach myself for. *Ich habe mein Bestes getan und habe mir nichts vorzuwerfen.*

resistance — *der Widerstand*
> **to take the line of least resistance** — *das Brett bohren, wo es am dünnsten ist.*
> He does as little as possible and always takes the line of least resistance. *Er tut so wenig wie möglich und bohrt das Brett immer, wo es am dünnsten ist.*

rest — *die Ruhe*
> **to get a good night's rest** — *sich ordentlich ausschlafen.*
> Klytemnestra complained that she could never get a good night's rest. *Klytemnestra klagte, dass sie sich nie ordentlich ausschlafen konnte.*
>
> **to set someone's mind at rest** — *beruhigen.*
> The doctor set his mind at rest by speaking openly with him. *Die Ärztin beruhigte ihn, indem sie offen mit ihm sprach.*

revenge — *die Rache*
> Revenge is sweet. *Rache ist süß/Blutwurst.*

rhyme — *der Reim*

    to find no rhyme or reason for — *sich keinen Reim machen können.*

She could find no rhyme or reason for his crazy behavior. *Auf sein verrücktes Benehmen konnte sie sich keinen Reim machen.*

    without rhyme or reason — *ohne Sinn und Verstand.*

His arguments are without rhyme or reason. *Seine Argumente sind ohne Sinn und Verstand. (Seine Argumente haben weder Hand noch Fuß.)*

ride — *der Ritt; die Fahrt*

    to take someone for a ride — *verschaukeln; übers Ohr hauen.*

The real estate agent took us for a ride. *Der Immobilienmakler hat uns übers Ohr gehauen.*

right — *richtig*

    right away — *sofort.*

"I'll do it right away," is what you said an hour ago. *"Ich mach's sofort" hast du vor einer Stunde gesagt.*

    to be all right — *in Ordnung gehen.*

Don't worry. Everything will be all right soon. *Keine Bange! Bald wird alles in Ordnung gehen.*

    to be right — *recht haben.*

He thinks he's always right. *Er glaubt, er hat immer recht.*

    right now — *gleich jetzt; auf der Stelle.*

I want it right now. *Ich will's auf der Stelle!*

    right now — *im Moment.*

Right now she's working on her novel. *Im Moment schreibt sie an ihrem Roman.*

riot — *der Aufruhr*

    to be a riot/riotously funny — *zum Schießen/zum Schreien sein.*

Some found the comic a riot, others wanted to take a shot at him. *Einige fanden den Komiker zum Schießen, andere hätten gern auf ihn geschossen.*

to rip off — *abreißen*

to get ripped off — *sich neppen lassen.*
We don't want to get ripped off by anyone. *Wir wollen uns von niemand neppen lassen.*

rip-off joint — *der Neppladen.*
That's a real rip-off joint. *Das ist ein richtiger Neppladen.*

---

to rise — *aufstehen*
Rise and shine, you lazybones! *Raus aus den Federn, ihr Faulpelze!*

to look as if one had risen from the grave — *wie eine lebende Leiche aussehen.*
When he came back from the war and imprisonment, he looked as if he'd risen from the grave. *Nachdem er aus der Kriegsgefangenschaft zurückkehrte, sah er wie eine lebende Leiche aus.*

to rise from the ashes — *aus den Trümmern wiedererstehen.*
After the war the steel industry rose from the ashes. *Nach dem Krieg ist die Stahlindustrie aus den Trümmern wiedererstanden.*

to rise to the bait — *sich ködern lassen.*
I rose to the bait because I was curious and anxious for adventure. *Ich ließ mich ködern, weil ich neugierig und abenteurlustig war.*

to rise to the occasion — *sich der Lage gewachsen zeigen.*
He was tired and couldn't rise to the occasion. *Er war müde und konnte sich der Lage nicht gewachsen zeigen.*

---

road — *die Straße*

to be on the road — *unterwegs sein.*
Bing and Bob were on the road a lot. *Bing und Bob waren viel unterwegs.*

to be on the road to recovery — *auf dem Wege der Besserung sein.*
He was very sick, but now he's on the road to recovery. *Er war schwer krank, aber jetzt ist er auf dem Wege der Besserung.*

to have one for the road — *noch einen zum Abschied trinken.*
She forbade her tipsy fiancé to have one for the road. *Sie verbot es ihrem angetrunkenen Verlobten, noch einen zum Abschied zu trinken.*

to rob — *rauben*

  to rob Peter to pay Paul — *ein Loch aufmachen, um ein anderes*
    zuzustopfen.
  For years Charles robbed Peter to pay Paul but finally he had to declare
  bankruptcy. *Jahrelang machte Charles ein Loch auf, um ein anderes*
  zuzustopfen, aber schließlich musste er Konkurs anmelden.

rock — *der Fels*

  at rock-bottom — *auf Null/Nullpunkt; im Keller.*
  The desperate refugees are at rock-bottom. *Die verzweifelten Flüchtlinge*
  sind auf den Nullpunkt angelangt.

rocker — *der Schaukelstuhl*

  to be off one's rocker — *einen Klaps haben.*
  He's off his rocker. *Der hat einen Klaps.*

to roll — *rollen*

  to roll up one's sleeves — *die Ärmel hochkrempeln.*
  We'll have to roll up our sleeves to get the work done on time. *Wir*
  müssen die Ärmel hochkrempeln, um die Arbeit rechtzeitig zu vollenden.

Rome — *Rom*

  Rome wasn't built in a day. — *Rom ist nicht an einem Tage erbaut*
  worden.

  When in Rome, do as the Romans do. — *mit den Wölfen heulen.*
  She wanted to go it alone but realized that when in Rome it would be more
  advisable to do as the Romans do. *Sie wollte einen Alleingang machen,*
  aber sie sah ein, dass es ratsamer wäre, mit den Wölfen zu heulen.

root — *die Wurzel*

  to put down roots — *Wurzeln schlagen.*
  He dreamt of putting down roots on the planet Venus. *Er träumte davon,*
  auf dem Planeten Venus Wurzeln zu schlagen.

  to root out — *ausrotten.*
  While he thought he was rooting out sin, he did much evil. *Während er*
  glaubte, die Sünde auszurotten, tat er viel Böses.

with root and branch — *mit Stumpf und Stiel.*

The tyrant wanted to destroy his enemies with root and branch. *Der Tyrann wollte seine Feinde mit Stumpf und Stiel ausrotten.*

---

rose — *die Rose*

The bloom is off the rose. *Der Lack ist ab.*

no bed of roses — *nicht auf Rosen gebettet; kein Honiglecken.*

They didn't believe her when she declared her life in the harem was no bed of roses. *Man glaubte es ihr nicht, als sie behauptete, ihr Leben im Harem wäre nicht auf Rosen gebettet.*

to see the world through rose-colored glasses — *die Welt durch eine rosarote Brille sehen.*

Although he drank the whole bottle of rosé, he was disappointed in his hope to see the world through rose-colored glasses. *Obwohl er die ganze Flasche Rosé austrank, täuschte er sich in der Hoffnung, die Welt durch eine rosarote Brille zu sehen.*

---

rough — *rauh; schwer*

a rough draft — *der Rohentwurf.*

In his tipsy condition he couldn't even work up a rough draft. *In seinem angetrunkenen Zustand konnte er nicht einmal einen Rohentwurf erarbeiten.*

to be a diamond in the rough — *eine rauhe Schale haben, ein Rauhbein sein.*

He's a diamond in the rough, but we're fond of him. *Er hat eine rauhe Schale aber wir mögen ihn gern.*

rough-and-ready — *rauhbeinig.*

Richard's rough and ready but good natured. *Richard ist rauhbeinig aber gutmütig.*

to rough it — *auf primitive Art im Freien leben.*

The poet wanted to rough it, but he soon returned to his ivory tower. *Der Dichter wollte auf primitive Art im Freien leben, aber bald kehrte er in seinen Elfenbeinturm zurück.*

---

round — *rund*

   round the clock — *rund um die Uhr.*

   The rescue teams worked round the clock. *Die Rettungsmannschaften arbeiteten rund um die Uhr.*

to rub — *reiben*

   to rub it in — *unter die Nase reiben; aufs Butterbrot schmieren.*

   Yes, we made mistakes, but you don't have to keep rubbing it in. *Ja, wir haben Fehler gemacht, aber das brauchst du uns nicht immer wieder unter die Nase zu reiben.*

   to rub shoulders with — *verkehren mit.*

   He saved his money so that he could rub shoulders with royalty in a posh hotel. *Er sparte sein Geld, damit er in einem Nobelhotel mit dem Hochadel verkehren konnte.*

   to rub the wrong way — *anecken; gegen den Strich gehen.*

   I don't know why Dr. Fell rubs me the wrong way. *Ich weiß nicht, warum Dr. Fell bei mir so aneckt.*

rubber — *das/der Gummi*

   rubber check — *der ungedeckte Scheck.*

   He paid with a rubber check again. *Er hat wieder mit einem ungedeckten Scheck bezahlt.*

   to rubber-stamp — *ja und Amen sagen.*

   The dictator expected Parliament to rubber-stamp all his decisions. *Der Diktator erwartete, dass das Parlament zu all seinen Beschlüssen Ja und Amen sagen würde.*

to ruffle — *kräuseln; verkrumpeln*

   to ruffle s.o.'s feathers — *kränken, beleidigen; jemandem auf den Schlips treten.*

   Be careful! His feathers are easily ruffled. *Sei vorsichtig! Er fühlt sich sehr leicht auf den Schlips getreten.*

rug — *der Teppich*
    to cut a rug — *das Tanzbein schwingen.*
    Let's go cut a rug, honey! *Gehen wir das Tanzbein schwingen, Schatzi!*

    to pull the rug out from — *Jmdm. den Boden unter den Füssen wegziehen; einer Sache den Boden entziehen.*
    The new revelations have pulled the rug out from under the senator's earlier statements. *Die neuen Enthüllungen haben den früheren Erklärungen des Senators den Boden entzogen.*

to rule — *regieren; beherrschen*
    to rule out — *ausschließen.*
    Factory closings aren't ruled out in the recovery plan. *Im Sanierungsplan sind Werkschließungen nicht ausgeschlossen.*

rumor — *das Gerücht*
    rumor mill — *die Gerüchteküche.*
    Ever since the chairman's disappearance, the rumor mill's been working overtime. *Seit der Vorsitzende verschwunden ist, kocht die Gerüchteküche über.*

run — *der Lauf*
    long/short run — *eine lange/kurze Laufzeit.*
    Tennessee Williams' last plays had only a short run. *Die letzten Stücke von Tennessee Williams hatten nur eine kurze Laufzeit.*

    in the long run — *auf die Dauer.*
    In the long run it's not worth continuing to rent the apartment in the city. *Auf die Dauer lohnt es sich nicht, die Wohnung in der Stadt weiter zu mieten.*

    on the run — *auf der Flucht.*
    The clairvoyant said she'd seen Elvis and the elves on the run in many supermarkets. *Die Hellseherin sagte, sie hätte Elvis und die Elfen in vielen Supermärkten auf der Flucht gesehen.*

to run — *laufen; rennen*

   to run at full volume/speed/force/capacity — *auf Hochtouren laufen.*
The machines are running at full capacity. *Die Maschinen laufen auf Hochtouren.*

   to run away from someone — *vor jemandem ausbüxen.*
When Bach saw Buxtehude's daughter, he ran away from her. *Als Bach Buxtehudes Tochter sah, büxte er vor ihr aus.*

   to run errands for — *Besorgungen machen.*
The janitor also runs errands for elderly tenants. *Der Hausmeister macht auch Besorgungen für ältere Mieter.*

   to run low on — *zur Neige gehen.*
Lucrezia was running low on poison. *Das Gift ging Lucrezia zur Neige.*

   to run down — *schlechtmachen.*
It's sad having to listen to him run down his former friend. *Es ist traurig, mitanhören zu müssen, wie er seinen ehemaligen Freund schlechtmacht.*

   to run down (over) — *überfahren.*
The drunk almost ran us down. *Der Betrunkene hatte uns beinahe überfahren.*

   run-off election — *die Stichwahl.*
He hopes to do better in the run-off election. *Bei der Stichwahl hofft er besser abzuschneiden.*

   to run off with — *durchbrennen.*
She ran off with a highwire artist. *Sie brannte mit einem Drahtseilartist durch.*

   to run out of — *ausgehen.*
She and her husband had run out of conversation. *Ihrem Mann und ihr ging der Gesprächsstoff aus.*

   to run out of patience — *die Geduld reißen.*
Finally she ran out of patience. *Endlich riss ihr die Geduld.*

   to run out on — *im Stich lassen; sich auf und davon machen.*
Now that I'm in a crisis, that scoundrel is running out on me! *Jetzt in der Not lässt mich der Schuft im Stich!*

to run with the pack — *mit den Wölfen heulen.*
At first she wanted to go it alone, but finally she had run with the pack. *Zuerst wollte sie einen Alleingang machen aber schließlich heulte sie doch mit den Wölfen.*

to sabotage — *sabotieren*
   to sabotage one's own interests — *sich in den Rücken fallen.*
   With its internal squabbling the party sabotaged its own interests. *Mit ihrem innerparteilichen Hickhack fiel sich die Partei in den Rücken.*

sack — *der Sack*
   to give s.o. the sack — *jmdn. feuern; rausschmeißen; rausfliegen lassen.*
   The boss is threatening to give us all the sack. *Die Chefin droht, uns alle zu feuern.*

   to hit the sack — *sich in die Falle/Klappe hauen.*
   I've got to hit the sack now. *Ich muss mich jetzt in die Falle hauen.*

   to sack — *in Schutt und Asche legen.*
   The soldiers sacked the city. *Die Soldaten legten die Stadt in Schutt und Asche.*

to saddle — *satteln*
   to saddle with — *aufhalsen.*
   He always saddles me with the most difficult tasks. *Die schwierigsten Aufgaben halst er immer mir auf.*

safe — *sicher*
   to be on the safe side — *um ganz sicherzugehen.*
   To be on the safe side, he joined several religions. *Um ganz sicherzugehen, trat er mehreren Religionen bei.*

   to play it safe — *auf Nummer Sicher gehen.*
   The former revolutionary now just wants to play it safe. *Der einstige Revolutionär will jetzt nur auf Nummer Sicher gehen.*

to sail — *segeln*
  Smooth sailing! *Mast- und Schotbruch!*

salt — *das Salz*
  an old salt — *ein alter Seebär.*
  It's amazing that an old salt like him could be so naive. *Erstaunlich, daß ein alter Seebär wie er so naiv sein konnte.*

  to rub salt into the wound — *Salz in die Wunde streuen.*
  Did you have to rub salt into the wound too? *Musstest du noch dazu mir Salz in die Wunde streuen?*

  to not be worth one's salt — *zu nichts taugen; keinen Schuss Pulver wert sein.*
  We had hoped for great things from him, but he's not worth his salt. *Wir hatten Großes von ihm erhofft, aber er ist keinen Schuss Pulver wert.*

  to take with a grain/pinch of salt — *nicht ganz für bare Münze nehmen, mit Vorsicht genießen.*
  Everything he said about his role in the conspiracy should be taken with a grain of salt. *Alles, was er über seine Rolle in der Verschwörung gesagt hat, ist nur mit Vorsicht zu genießen.*

sardine — *die Sardine*
  packed in like sardines — *gedrängt wie die Sardinen/Heringe.*
  In the subway we were packed in like sardines. *In der U-Bahn standen wir gedrängt wie die Heringe.*

sauce — *die Soße*
  to be on the sauce — *saufen.*
  He was a teetotaler for years, but he's really back on the sauce again now. *Jahrelang war er Abstinenzler, jetzt säuft er wieder, und wie!*

  What's sauce for the goose is sauce for the gander. *Was dem einen recht ist, ist dem anderen billig; was gilt für die Frau gilt auch für den Mann.*
  Most perfume makers don't believe in the proverb, "What's sauce for the goose is sauce for the gander." *Die meisten Parfümeure glauben nicht an das Sprichwort: "Was dem einen Geschlecht recht ist, ist dem anderen billig."*

to save — *retten*

to save face — *das Gesicht wahren.*

He more or less saved face. *Einigermaßen hat er das Gesicht gewahrt.*

saved by the bell — *gerade davonkommen.*

We were in a very embarrassing situation, but once again we were saved by the bell. *Wir waren in größter Verlegenheit, sind aber gerade noch einmal davongekommen.*

to be saved from oneself — *sich schützen.*

His son is a drug addict and needs to be saved from himself. *Sein Sohn ist rauschgiftsüchtig und muss vor sich selbst geschützt werden.*

to say — *sagen*

You can say that again! — *Das kannst du laut sagen!*

Yes that's right, the trip was badly organized; you can say that again! *Ja, das stimmt, die Reise war schlecht organisiert; das kannst du laut sagen!*

to say goodbye to something — *etwas in den Wind schreiben.*

You can say goodbye to the money you lent him. *Das Geld, das du ihm geliehen hast, kannst du in den Wind schreiben.*

to say what goes — *das Sagen haben.*

On one day in the year the fool, not the mayor. says what goes. *An einem Tag im Jahr hat der Narr, nicht die Bürgermeisterin das Sagen.*

scale — *die Schuppe; die Waage; die Skala*

(on a) large scale — *in großem Stil.*

The boss isn't planning large-scale layoffs. *Die Chefin sieht keine Entlassungen in großem Stil vor.*

scandal — *der Skandal*

scandal sheets — *die Regenbogenpresse.*

The professor said he read scandal sheets only for scientific reasons. *Der Professor behauptete, er lese die Regenbogenpresse nur aus wissenschaftlichen Gründen.*

scarce — *knapp*
   to make oneself scarce — *verduften.*
   When the others arrived, I made myself scarce. *Als die anderen ankamen, verduftete ich.*

scene — *die Szene*
   to appear on the scene — *auf den Plan treten.*
   A new viral disease has appeared on the scene. *Eine neue Viruskrankheit ist auf den Plan getreten.*

   change of scene(ry) — *der Tapetenwechsel.*
   He was sick of housework and needed a change of scenery. *Die Hausarbeit hing ihm zum Halse raus, und er brauchte Tapetenwechsel.*

   on-the-scene/spot — *vor Ort.*
   On television there are many on-the-scene reports. *Im Fernsehen gibt's viele Berichte vor Ort.*

   the scene of the crime — *der Tatort.*
   She didn't believe the murderer returned to the scene of the crime. *Sie glaubte nicht, dass der Mörder zum Tatort zurückkam.*

score — *der Spielstand*
   What's the score? — *Wie steht es?*

   to know the score — *wissen, was läuft; wissen, wie der Hase läuft.*
   Through bitter experience he now knows what the score is here. *Durch bittere Erfahrung weiß er jetzt, wie hier der Hase läuft.*

   to settle old scores — *Abrechnung halten.*
   He thought the moment was right to settle old scores. *Er hielt den Moment für geeignet, Abrechnung zu halten.*

scrap — *der Fetzen; der Schutthaufen*
   to throw (put) on the scrap heap — *zum alten Eisen werfen.*
   Through new technology traditional ways of working are being put on the scrap heap. *Durch neue Technik werden herkömmliche Arbeitsmethoden zum alten Eisen geworfen.*

scratch — *die Schramme; der Riss*

to be up to scratch — *nichts zu wünschen übriglassen.*

Her work was right up to scratch. *Ihre Arbeit ließ nichts zu wünschen übrig.*

to bring up to scratch — *auf Zack/Vordermann bringen.*

The new coach tried to bring the team up to scratch fast. *Der neue Trainer versuchte, die Mannschaft schnell auf Zack zu bringen.*

to start from scratch — *bei Null anfangen.*

Unfortunately, we'll have to start from scratch. *Leider müssen wir bei Null anfangen.*

to scratch — *kratzen.*

You scratch my back and I'll scratch yours. — *Eine Hand wäscht die andere.*

---

scream — *der Schrei*

to be a scream — *zum Totlachen/zum Schreien sein.*

The movie was a scream. *Der Film war zum Totlachen.*

---

screw — *die Schraube*

a screw loose — *eine Schraube locker/lose.*

He has a screw loose. *Bei ihm ist eine Schraube lose.*

to put the screws on someone — *den Daumen aufs Auge drücken.*

OK, I'll lend you my car; quit putting the screws on me. *Hör auf, mir den Daumen aufs Auge zu drücken, ich leih dir schon meinen Wagen.*

to screw up — *Mist bauen; verpatzen.*

You've screwed everything up for me. *Du hast mir alles verpatzt.*

---

sea — *das Meer*

to be all at sea — *ins Schwimmen kommen.*

He got nervous and soon was all at sea. *Er wurde nervös und kam bald ins Schwimmen.*

seadog — *der Seebär.*

His brothers are all seadogs, but he's a landlubber. *Seine Brüder sind alle Seebären, nur er ist Landratte.*

---

seam — *die Naht*

to be bursting at the seams — *aus allen Nähten platzen.*

Many students go abroad because our universities are bursting at the seams. *Viele Studenten gehen ins Ausland, denn unsere Universitäten platzen aus allen Nähten.*

second — *zweit*

on second thought — *bei näherer Überlegung.*

On second thought, I will go to the movies with you. *Bei näherer Überlegung geh ich doch mit euch ins Kino.*

second string — *aus der zweiten Wahl/Garnitur.*

The second string players won after all. *Die Spieler aus der zweiten Garnitur haben doch gewonnen.*

to sell — *verkaufen*

to sell down the river — *verraten und verkaufen.*

He sold his business partners down the river. *Er hat seine Geschäftspartner verraten und verkauft.*

to sell like hotcakes — *wie warme Semmeln weggehen.*

She hoped her novel would sell like hotcakes. *Sie hoffte, dass ihr Roman wie warme Semmeln weggehen würde.*

to sell s.o. a gold brick/the Brooklyn Bridge — *jmdm. etwas andrehen; jmdm. ein Schnippchen schlagen.*

In the movie they kept arresting Mae West because she was allegedly trying to sell men the Brooklyn Bridge. *Im Film verhaftete man Mae West immer wieder, weil sie angeblich den Männern was andrehen wollte.*

to send — *schicken*

to do a sendup of — *parodieren.*

The cabaret performers did a sendup of many politicians. *Die Kabarettisten parodierten viele Politiker.*

to give someone a good sendoff — *groß verabschieden.*

We gave her a good sendoff before she went to college. *Wir haben sie groß verabschiedet, bevor sie auf die Universität ging.*

to have sent — *(zu)kommen lassen.*
Can we have our breakfast sent up to our room? *Können wir unser Frühstück aufs Zimmer kommen lassen?*

serious(ly) — *ernst*
    to takes seriously — *ernst nehmen; für voll ansehen/ nehmen.*
    After such a childish reaction, who can still take him seriously? *Nach einer so kindischen Reaktion, wer kann ihn noch für voll ansehen?*

to serve — *servieren*
    to serve someone right — *jemandem recht geschehen.*
    The con man was himself taken in; it served him right. *Es geschah dem Trickbetrüger recht, dass er selbst betrogen wurde.*

    to serve up — *auftischen.*
    He served up a load of lies to us. *Er hat uns nur Lügen aufgetischt.*

to set — *stellen; legen; setzen*
    At what time does the sun set today? *Um wieviel Uhr geht heute die Sonne unter?*

    to set one's mind on something— *sich etwas in den Kopf setzen.*
    If she sets her mind on something, she follows through on it. *Wenn sie sich etwas in den Kopf setzt, dann führt sie es auch durch.*

    to set out — *sich auf den Weg machen.*
    The caravan set out for Samarkand. *Die Karawane machte sich auf den Weg nach Samarkand.*

    to set one's sights on — *absehen auf.*
    The rabbits have set their sights on our garden. *Die Kaninchen haben es auf unseren Garten abgesehen.*

    to set to work — *sich daran machen.*
    When I finally set to work, I took care of everything fairly easily. *Als ich mich endlich daran machte, erledigte ich alles ziemlich leicht.*

shadow — *der Schatten*

to be beyond the shadow of a doubt — *ohne jeden Zweifel sein.*

The eyewitness reports are certainly not beyond the shadow of a doubt, because they're contradictory. *Die Augenzeugenberichte sind beileibe nicht ohne jeden Zweifel, denn sie widersprechen sich.*

the shadowy (dark) aspects — *die Schattenseiten.*

The psychiatrist helped him to understand shadowy aspects of his past. *Die Psychiaterin half ihm, die Schattenseiten seiner Vergangenheit zu verstehen.*

shaggy — *zottelig; struppig*

shaggy dog story — *langer uninteressanter Witz ohne richtige Pointe.*

Nobody understands his shaggy dog stories. *Keiner versteht seine endlosen blöden Witze.*

to shake — *schütteln*

to be no great shakes — *nicht umwerfend sein.*

The play was no great shakes but at least the actors enjoyed themselves. *Das Stück war nicht umwerfend, aber wenigstens amüsierten sich die Schauspieler.*

to give s.o. a fair shake — *jemanden gerecht behandeln.*

She was the sheik's favorite belly-dancer because she always gave him a fair shake. *Weil sie den Scheich immer gerecht behandelte, war sie seine Lieblingsbauchtänzerin.*

to have the shakes — *den Tatterich haben.*

The old man's got the shakes. *Der Alte hat den Tatterich.*

to shake hands — *sich die Hand geben.*

In many countries people shake hands when they are introduced. *In vielen Ländern gibt man sich die Hand, wenn man sich kennenlernt.*

to shake one's dancing legs — *das Tanzbein schwingen.*

Grandpa still likes to shake his dancing legs. *Opa schwingt noch gern das Tanzbein.*

shank — *der Unterschenkel*
  on shank's mare — *auf Schusters Rappen.*
  We climbed Mount Fujiyama on shank's mare. *Wir haben den Fudschijama auf Schusters Rappen bestiegen.*

shape — *die Gestalt*
  to get into shape — *auf Trab/auf Vordermann bringen.*
  The new boss wants to get the firm into shape again. *Die neue Chefin will die Firma wieder auf Trab bringen.*

  to keep/stay in shape — *sich fit halten; die Form behalten.*
  We stay in great shape with yoga. *Mit Jogaübungen halten wir uns topfit.*

  Shape up or ship out! — *Nimm dich zusammen oder zieh Leine!*

sheet — *das Laken, das Bettuch; die Seite*
  to be three sheets to the wind — *Schlagseite haben; voll sein.*
  Uncle Otto's already three sheets to the wind but he wants to keep on boozing. *Onkel Otto hat schon Schlagseite, will aber noch mehr saufen.*

ship — *das Schiff*
  When my ship comes in, there'll be no more slaving away. *Wenn ich das große Los ziehe, ist's mit dem Schuften aus.*

  shipshape — *in tadelloser Ordnung; pikobello.*
  Everything's shipshape again at our place now. *Bei uns ist wieder alles pikobello.*

shock — *der Schock*
  to get the shock of one's life — *sein blaues Wunder erleben.*
  When she opened the door she got the shock of her life. *Als sie die Tür aufmachte, erlebte sie ihr blaues Wunder.*

shoe — *der Schuh*
  If the shoe fits, wear it. *Wem die Jacke passt, der zieht sie sich an.*
  "Are you saying, I'm one of them?"—"If the shoe fits, wear it." *"Meinst du, ich sei einer von denen?"—"Wem die Jacke passt, der zieht sie sich an."*

to be in someone's shoes — *in jemandes Haut stecken.*

He's unemployed and his wife and children left him; I wouldn't like to be in his shoes. *Er ist arbeitslos und seine Frau und Kinder haben ihn verlassen. Ich möchte nicht in seiner Haut stecken.*

to shoot — *schießen*

to shoot one's mouth off — *das Maul aufreißen.*

Why did you have to keep shooting your mouth off? *Warum musstest du immer wieder das Maul aufreißen?*

to shoot o.s. in the foot — *sich selber ein Bein stellen; sich selber in den Rücken fallen; sich ins Knie schießen.*

He should have had the job but he shot h.s. in the foot. *Er hätte den Posten bekommen sollen, aber er stellte sich selbst ein Bein.*

short — *kurz*

in short order — *auf der Stelle; sofort; gleich.*

I'll settle that in short order. *Das erledige ich sofort.*

short order — *das Schnellgericht.*

Tim's working as a short-order cook in a snack bar but he dreams of becoming a great chef. *Tim arbeitet als Schnellgericht-Koch in einer Imbissstube, träumt aber davon, ein großer Küchenchef zu werden.*

to cut short — *über den Mund fahren.*

The senator tried to cut her short and not let her finish speaking. *Der Senator versuchte, ihr über den Mund zu fahren, und sie nicht ausreden zu lassen.*

to get the short end of — *den Kürzeren ziehen.*

She had a heart for the poor, for all who got the short end of it in life. *Sie hatte ein Herz für die Armen, für alle die im Leben den Kürzeren gezogen hatten.*

to make short work of — *kurzen Prozess machen.*

She made short work of her rival. *Mit ihrer Rivalin machte sie kurzen Prozess.*

to sell oneself short — *sich unter Wert verkaufen; sein Licht unter den Scheffel stelln.*

Have confidence and don't sell yourself short. *Hab Vertrauen und verkauf dich nicht unter Wert.*

to shortchange — *übers Ohr hauen.*

Don't let that crook shortchange you again. *Lass dich nicht wieder von diesem Gauner übers Ohr hauen.*

shot — *der Schuss*

a shot in the head — *eins auf die Mütze.*

His father gave him a shot in the head. *Sein Vater gab ihm eins auf die Mütze.*

to be a big shot — *ein großes Tier sein.*

Once he was a big shot in the city administration, but now he's a town tramp. *Einst war er ein großes Tier bei der Stadtverwaltung, jetzt aber ist er Stadtstreicher.*

to shout — *schreien*

to shout something from the housetops (rooftops) — *etwas an die große Glocke hängen.*

They're engaged, but don't shout it from the housetops. *Sie sind verlobt aber das brauchst du nicht an die große Glocke zu hängen.*

show — *das Zeigen; die Schau*

to make a show of force — *die Muskeln spielen lassen.*

The dictator spoke of peace but made a show of force. *Der Diktator sprach von Frieden, ließ aber die Muskeln spielen.*

to make a show of — *zur Schau tragen.*

The hypocrite made a show of his piety. *Der Heuchler trug seine Frömmigkeit zur Schau.*

to shut — *schließen*

to shut down — *stilllegen; dichtmachen.*

The nuclear energy plant had to be shut down. *Das Kernkraftwerk musste stillgelegt werden.*

to shut one's mouth (trap) — *den Mund (das Maul, die Fresse) halten.*

Papageno couldn't keep his mouth shut. *Papageno konnte den Mund nicht halten.*

to shut up shop — *Schluss machen; den Laden dichtmachen.*
That's enough work. We're going to shut up shop and go home now.
*Genug gearbeitet! Wir wollen jetzt den Laden dichtmachen und nach
Hause gehen.*

sick — *krank*
  to be sick and tired — *zum Halse raushängen.*
  I'm sick and tired of his arrogance. *Seine Überheblichkeit hängt mir zum
  Halse raus.*

side — *die Seite*
  to take sides — *Partei ergreifen.*
  We refused to take sides and got caught in the crossfire. *Wir weigerten
  uns, Partei zu ergreifen, und gerieten dadurch zwischen die Fronten.*

sight — *die Sicht; die Sehkraft*
  to lose sight of — *aus den Augen verlieren.*
  She's never lost sight of her ideals. *Ihre Ideale hat sie nie aus den Augen
  verloren.*

  to set one's sights on — *ins Visier nehmen; etwas anpeilen.*
  The police have now set their sights on the Senator; they've had their eye
  on him for some time. *Die Polizei hat den Senator jetzt ins Visier
  genommen; sie haben ihn längst schon im Visier.*

  hindsight — *nachträgliche Einsicht; im Nachhinein.*
  Hindsight is easier than foresight. *Hinterher ist man fast immer klüger als
  vorher.*

sign — *das Zeichen; das Schild*
  sign language — *die Fingersprache.*
  She has much sensitivity and tact, and also knows sign language. *Sie hat
  viel Fingerspitzengefühl; auch kann sie die Fingersprache.*

to sign — *unterzeichnen, unterschreiben*
  signed, sealed, and delivered — *unter Dach und Fach.*
  The job's finally done; everything's now signed, sealed, and delivered.
  Die Arbeit ist endlich fertig; alles ist jetzt unter Dach und Fach.

to sink — *sinken*

He had to accept the job; it was sink or swim. *Er musste die Arbeit annehmen — friss Vogel oder stirb!*

to be sunk — *geliefert sein.*

If we can't come up with the money, we're sunk. *Wenn wir das Geld nicht aufbringen können, sind wir geliefert.*

six — *sechs*

to be at sixes and sevens — *ganz durcheinander sein.*

I was at sixes and sevens. *Ich war ganz durcheinander.*

Six of one, a half dozen of the other. *Das ist Jacke wie Hose; das ist gehüpft wie gesprungen; dasselbe in Grün.*

skeleton — *das Skelett*

to have a skeleton in the closet — *eine Leiche im Keller haben.*

The senator said there were no skeletons in his closet. *Der Senator behauptete, es gäbe keine Leichen bei ihm im Keller.*

skin — *die Haut*

by the skin of one's teeth — *mit Hängen und Würgen.*

We made it by the skin of our teeth. *Mit Hängen und Würgen haben wir's geschafft.*

That's no skin off my nose! *Das juckt/kratzt/stört mich nicht.*

He's gone bust? That's no skin off my nose. *Er macht Pleite? Das juckt micht nicht!*

skinflint — *der Geizkragen.*

You won't get much from that skinflint. *Von dem Geizkragen bekommst du nicht viel.*

skinny — *mager*

to skinny dip — *nackt schwimmen.*

You can't skinny dip here. This isn't a nudist beach. *Hier dürft ihr nicht nackt schwimmen. Das ist kein FKK (Freikörperkultur) Strand.*

the skinny/the straight skinny — *die Wahrheit, die nackte Wahrheit.*
I'm giving you the straight skinny, I swear it. *Ich sag dir die nackte Wahrheit, ich schwör's.*

sky — *der Himmel*
  to praise to the skies — *über den grünen Klee loben.*
  The critics praised Klee and Kandinsky to the skies. *Die Kritiker lobten Klee und Kandinsky über den grünen Klee.*

sleaze — *die Verdorbenheit; die Korruption*
  sleazebag — *der Stinkstiefel; der Dreckskerl.*
  He called the cop a sleazebag and had to pay a fine. *Er schimpfte den Polizisten einen Stinkstiefel und musste ein Strafgeld bezahlen.*

sleeve — *der Ärmel*
  to have something up one's sleeve — *etwas im Ärmel haben.*
  Merlin still has a lot of tricks up his sleeve for us. *Merlin hat noch viel im Ärmel für uns.*

  to laugh up one's sleeve — *sich ins Fäustchen lachen.*
  The con man laughed up his sleeve. *Der Hochstapler lachte sich ins Fäustchen.*

slim — *schlank*
  to slim down — *abspecken.*
  After eating up the whole cake, he resolved to slim down. *Nachdem er den ganzen Kuchen aufgegessen hatte, fasste er den Vorsatz, abzuspecken.*

to slip — *ausrutschen*
  to slip up — *patzen.*
  During the Scriabin sonata the pianist slipped up considerably. *Während der Skrjabin Sonate patzte der Pianist erheblich.*

  to slip away — *sich verkrümeln; sich in die Büsche schlagen.*
  I suddenly noticed that he'd slipped away. *Plötzlich merkte ich, dass er sich verkrümelt hatte.*

slow — *langsam*
My watch is slow. — *Meine Uhr geht nach.*

to be slow on the uptake — *eine lange Leitung haben; schwer von Begriff sein.*
He pretended to be slow on the uptake. *Er tat, als ob er eine lange Leitung hätte.*

sly — *schlau*
to be a sly old fox — *es faustdick hinter den Ohren haben.*
The old farmer's no fool; he's a sly old fox. *Der alte Bauer ist nicht doof; der hat es faustdick hinter den Ohren.*

small — *klein*
small fry, small potatoes — *kleine Fische, kleine Würstchen.*
They let the sharks escape and just arrested the small fry. *Die großen Haie ließ man laufen und nahmen nur die kleinen Fische fest.*

smart — *klug*
the smart set — *die Schickeria.*
In their expensive clothes they thought they belonged to the smart set. *In ihren teuren Kleidern glaubten sie der Schickeria anzugehören.*

to smash — *schmettern*
smash hit — *der Bombenerfolg, Superhit, Knüller.*
All her films were smash hits, but her last play bombed on Broadway. *Alle ihre Filme waren Bombenerfolge aber ihr letztes Stück war ein totaler Reinfall auf dem Broadway.*

smoke — *der Rauch*
Where there's smoke, there's fire. *Wo Rauch ist, ist auch Feuer.*

smoking gun — *schlagender Beweis.*
The investigation hasn't yet come up with a smoking gun. *Die Ermittlung hat bisjetzt keinen schlagenden Beweis erbracht.*

smoke and mirrors — *Schall und Rauch; eine Luftnummer*
His promises are merely smoke and mirrors. *Seine Versprechen sind nur Schall und Rauch.*

to smooth — *glätten*
to smooth over — *ausbügeln.*
She helped them to smooth over all difficulties. *Sie half ihnen, alle Schwierigkeiten auszubügeln.*

snake — *die Schlange*
snake in the grass — *heimtückische hinterlistige Person, Giftschlange.*
You sold me out, you snake in the grass, you! *Du hast mich betrogen, du Giftschlange, du!*

to sneeze — *niesen*
not to be sneezed at — *nicht zu verachten sein.*
Their offer is not to be sneezed at. *Ihr Angebot ist nicht zu verachten.*

snowball — *der Schneeball*
a snowball's chance in hell — *nicht die Spur einer Chance; Chancen gleich null.*
He doesn't stand a snowball's chance in hell of winning the race. *Seine Chancen sind gleich null, das Rennen zu machen.*

to have a snowball effect — *eine Kettenreaktion auslösen.*
His partner's defection had a snowball effect. *Der Abfall seines Partners löste eine Kettenreaktion aus.*

snug — *gemütlich*
snug as a bug in a rug — *urgemütlich; sauwohl; pudelwohl.*
We're snug as a bug in a rug in our new apartment. *In unserer neuen Wohnung fühlen wir uns pudelwohl.*

soap — *die Seife*
soapbox oratory — *die Sonntagsreden/Schönwetterreden.*
Despite all the soapbox oratory, no politician knows how to solve this problem. *Trotz aller Sonntagsreden weiß kein Politiker dieses Problem zu lösen.*

soft — *weich*
a soft drink — *ein alkoholfreies Getränk; Limonade.*

She ordered Schnapps for herself and a soft drink for her husband. *Sie bestellte Schnaps für sich und ein alkoholfreies Getränk für ihren Mann.*

song — *das Lied*
for a song — *für einen Pappenstiel; spottbillig.*
She bought the fur coat for a song. *Sie kaufte den Pelzmantel für einen Pappenstiel.*

to make a song and dance — *viel Aufhebens machen.*
It wasn't necessary to make such a song and dance about it. *Es war nicht nötig so viel Aufhebens davon zu machen.*

soon — *bald*
No sooner said than done. — *Gesagt, getan.*

sooner or later — *früher oder später; über kurz oder lang.*
Sooner or later he'll have to give in. *Früher oder später wird er nachgeben müssen.*

so-so — *so lala*
At the opera gala I only felt so-so. *Bei der Operngala fühlte ich mich nur so lala.*

to be sorry — *es einem leid tun*
We're sorry but we can't come. *Es tut uns leid, aber wir können nicht kommen.*

to be in a sorry state — *am Boden liegen.*
The newly created state's economy is in a sorry state. *Die Wirtschaft des neu geschaffenen Staates liegt am Boden.*

to sound — *tönen*
to sound off — *schwadronieren; sich aufspielen.*
Don't listen to him, he just sounds off all the time! *Hör nicht auf ihn, er schwadroniert nur immer!*

to sound out — *auf den Busch klopfen.*
Couldn't you sound him out; maybe he'll help us. *Könntest du nicht bei ihm auf den Busch klopfen; vielleicht hilft er uns.*

south — *der Süden*
to go/head south — *auf Talfahrt sein.*
Our stocks are still headed south. *Unsere Aktien sind noch auf Talfahrt.*

soup — *die Suppe*
to soup up — *aufmotzen.*
The boy's trying to soup up his old jalopy now. *Der Junge versucht jetzt seinen alten Klapperkasten aufzumotzen.*

space — *der Raum; der Platz*
to invade s.o.'s space — *jemandes Kreise stören.*
Alfie thinks he's a genius, another Archimedes, and won't let anyone invade his space. *Alfie hält sich für ein Genie, ein neuer Archimedes, und lässt seine Kreise von niemandem stören.*

spade — *der Spaten*
to call a spade a spade — *das Kind beim rechten Namen nennen.*
Why are you afraid of calling a spade a spade? *Warum hast du Angst, das Kind beim rechten Namen zu nennen?*

to spare — *schonen*
to spare no expense — *keine Kosten scheuen.*
He wanted to make a good impression and spared no expense. *Er wollte einen guten Eindruck machen und scheute keine Kosten*

spare tire — *Ersatzreifen; Bauchspeck/Fettansatz.*
The mechanic's spare tire was so huge that he had trouble changing the tires. *Der Mechaniker hatte so viel Bauchspeck, dass es ihm schwer war die Reifen auszuwechseln.*

speed — *die Geschwindigkeit.*
to put on some speed — *Tempo machen; dalli machen.*
Tell him to please put on some speed because I need him. *Sag ihm, er soll bitte Tempo machen, denn ich brauche ihn.*

spin — *der Spin*
to go for a spin in a car — *eine Spritztour machen.*

The price of gas is too high, so we don't go for a spin anymore. *Der Spritpreis ist zu hoch, also machen wir keine Spritztouren mehr.*

to spit — *spucken*
   to be the spitting image of — *wie aus dem Gesicht geschnitten; sich aufs Haar gleichen.*
   The child is his spitting image. The DNA analysis will prove paternity.
   Das Kind gleicht ihm aufs Haar. Die DNA-Analyse wird die Vaterschaft beweisen.

to splice — *spleißen*
   to get spliced - *heiraten, sich verehelichen.*
   I hear they got spliced. *Ich höre, sie haben geheiratet.*

   to splice the main brace — *Alkohol trinken, alken, tanken.*
   The sailors came ashore and knew it was time to splice the main brace.
   Die Matrosen kamen ans Land und wussten, dass es Zeit war vollzutanken.

to spoil — *verderben*
   to be a spoilsport — *ein Spaßverderber sein.*
   Aw, don't be a spoilsport. *Ach, sei doch kein Spaßverderber!*

spoke — *die Speiche*
   to put a spoke in s.o.'s wheel — *jmdm. einen Knüppel zwischen die Beine werfen, jmdm. in den Arm fallen.*
   This time I'll succeed, if you don't put a spoke in my wheel again.
   Diesmal wird's mir gelingen, wenn du mir nicht wieder in den Arm fällst.

sponge — *der Schwamm*
   to sponge off/on — *nassauern; jemandem auf der Tasche liegen.*
   Your uncle's sponged off us long enough. *Dein Onkel hat schon bei uns lange genug genaussauert.*

spoon — *der Löffel*
   to be born with a silver spoon in one's mouth — *mit einem goldenen/silbernen Löffel im Munde geboren sein.*

The billionaire was born with a silver spoon in his mouth. *Der Milliardär ist mit einem goldenen Löffel im Mund geboren.*

to spoon-feed — *gängeln.*
I'm grown up and I don't want you to spoon-feed me any more. *Ich bin erwachsen und will mich nicht mehr von dir gängeln lassen.*

---

spot — *der Fleck*
to be in a tight spot — *in der Klemme sein.*
We have neither money nor friends and we're really in a tight spot. *Wir haben weder Geld noch Freunde und sitzen wirklich in der Klemme.*

to hit the spot — *wie gerufen kommen.*
In this heat a glass of beer would hit the spot. *Bei dieser Hitze käme ein Glas Bier wie gerufen.*

---

to spruce up — *verschönern*
all spruced up — *geschniegelt und gebügelt.*
The children were all spruced up for the first day of school. *Für den ersten Schultag waren die Kinder geschniegelt und gebügelt.*

---

spur — *der Sporn; der Ansporn, Antrieb*
on the spur of the moment — *ganz spontan.*
On the spur of the moment I decided to risk it and set the spurs to my horse. *Ganz spontan beschloss ich, es darauf ankommen zu lassen und gab meinem Pferd die Sporen.*

---

square — *viereckig; vierkantig; quadratisch*
to be square — *überholt, altmodisch sein; spießig sein.*
Your parents aren't really all that square. *Deine Eltern sind gar nicht so spießig.*

to be a square peg in a round hole — *am falschen Platz sein; sich fehl am Platz fühlen.*
Our grandkids invited us to the discotheque, but we'd just be square pegs in round holes there. *Die Enkel haben uns in die Diskothek eingeladen aber da fühlten wir uns fehl am Platz.*

to be on the square — *in Ordnung sein; ehrlich, astrein sein.*
That guy isn't quite on the square. *Der Typ ist nicht ganz astrein.*

to give s.o. a square deal — *jmdn. gerecht behandeln.*

His father always gave me a square deal, but his son's a crook. *Der Vater hat mich immer gerecht behandelt, aber der Sohn ist ein Ganove.*

to stab — *stechen*

to stab in the back — *jemnandem in den Rücken fallen.*

His own brother stabbed him in the back. *Sein eigener Bruder fiel ihm in den Rücken.*

stage — *die Bühne*

stage fright — *das Lampenfieber.*

Despite many years on the stage, she still had stage fright. *Trotz vieler Jahre auf der Bühne hatte sie noch Lampenfieber.*

stagestruck — *theaterbesessen.*

Even as a small child she was stagestruck. *Schon als kleines Kind war sie theaterbesessen.*

stake — *der Pfahl*

to be at stake — *auf dem Spiel stehen.*

Our future is at stake. *Unsere Zukunft steht auf dem Spiel.*

to burn at the stake — *auf dem Scheiterhaufen verbrennen.*

Many socalled heretics and alleged witches were burned at the stake. *Viele sogenannte Ketzer und angebliche Hexen wurden auf dem Scheiterhaufen verbrannt.*

to stand — *stehen*

not to be able to stand someone — *jemanden nicht leiden/ausstehen/verknusen können.*

He can't stand most of his relatives. *Die meisten seiner Verwandten kann er nicht ausstehen.*

to stand up and be counted — *Farbe bekennen.*

He was too cowardly to stand up and be counted. *Er war zu feige, Farbe zu bekennen.*

to stand up to someone — *jemandem in die Parade fahren; die Stirn bieten.*

He couln't summon the courage to stand up to the boss. *Er konnte den Mut nicht aufbringen, dem Chef in die Parade zu fahren.*

Don't stand on ceremony, dig in! *Seid nicht so förmlich, greift zu!*

standstill — *der Stillstand*
  to come to a standstill — *zum Stillstand kommen.*
The armistice negotiations came to a standstill. *Die Waffenstillstandsverhandlungen kamen zum Stillstand.*

start — *der Anfang/Beginn/Start*
  to make a fresh start — *von Neuem beginnen.*
She wants to make a fresh start in life. *Sie will alles in ihrem Leben von Neuem beginnen.*

  to start a quarrel/war — *einen Streit/Krieg vom Zaune brechen.*
The dictator started a war without bothering to give any reasons for it. *Der Diktator brach einen Krieg vom Zaun, ohne sich um Gründe dafür zu kümmern.*

state — *der Zustand*
  to be in a state — *aufgeregt, außer sich, genervt sein.*
He's in a state again today. *Er ist heute wieder genervt.*

  state-of-the-art — *auf dem neuesten Stand der Technik.*
These are state-of-the-art electrical appliances. *Diese sind Elektrogeräte auf dem neuesten Stand der Technik.*

to stay — *bleiben*
  to have staying power — *Sitzfleisch haben.*
Joe quit school again; he has no staying power. *Die Schule hat Joe wieder hingeschmissen; Sitzfleisch hat er nicht.*

  to stay in bed — *das Bett hüten.*
He had to stay in bed for a week. *Er musste eine Woche das Bett hüten.*

  to stay at an inn/hotel — *einkehren; übernachten.*
We stayed at a charming inn surrounded by vineyards. *Wir kehrten in einem reizenden von Weinbergen umgebenen Gasthaus ein.*

to step — *treten*

to step on it — *hinter etwas Dampf machen.*

If you don't step on it, we'll be too late. *Wenn du dahinter nicht Dampf machst, kommen wir zu spät.*

to step on someone's toes — *jemandem auf den Schlips treten.*

I don't want to step on anyone's toes, but I must tell the truth. *Ich will niemand auf den Schlips treten, aber ich muss doch die Wahrheit sagen.*

---

to stew — *schmoren*

to stew in one's own juices — *im eigenen Saft schmoren.*

She decided to let him stew in his own sour juices. *Sie beschloss, ihn im eigenen sauren Saft schmoren zu lassen.*

---

stick — *der Stock*

the sticks — *wo sich Fuchs und Hase gute Nacht sagen.*

Once she was a famous globetrotter; but now she lives a secluded life in the sticks. *Einst war sie eine berühmte Weltenbummlerin; jetzt wohnt sie ganz zurückgezogen, wo sich Fuchs und Hase gute Nacht sagen.*

---

to stick — *kleben; stecken*

to stick with — *halten zu.*

"Despite everything, I'm sticking with you," she wrote her husband in jail. *"Trotz allem halt ich zu dir," schrieb sie ihrem Mann im Gefängnis.*

---

to stink — *stinken*

an injustice that stinks to high heaven — *ein himmelschreiendes Unrecht.*

The lawyer is partially responsible for this injustice that stinks to high heaven. *Der Anwalt ist für dieses himmelschreiende Unrecht mitverantwortlich.*

---

stitch — *der Stich; der Faden; die Masche*

A stitch in time saves nine — *Ein Griff zur rechten Zeit spart Müh und Leid.*

to have in stitches — *umwerfend komisch finden, furchtbar zum Lachen bringen.*

The film had us all in stitches. *Den Film fanden wir umwerfend komisch.*

to not have a stitch (of clothing) on — *splitterfasernackt sein.*
Under her mink coat she didn't have a stitch on. *Unter ihrem Nerzmantel war sie splitterfasernackt.*

---

stomach — *der Magen*
The way to a man's (person's) heart is through his/her stomach. *Die Liebe geht durch den Magen.*
Napoleon said, "An army travels on its stomach." *Napoleon sagte: "Das Heer bewegt sich auf dem Magen."*

---

stone — *der Stein*
a stone's throw — *ein Katzensprung.*
It's just a stone's throw from here to downtown. *Von hier zur Innenstadt ist es nur ein Katzensprung.*

---

to stop — *halten*
to stop at nothing — *über Leichen gehen.*
If he's set his mind on something, he'll stop at nothing to get it. *Wenn er sich was in den Kopf gesetzt hat, geht er über Leichen, um sein Ziel zu erreichen.*

---

store — *der Laden*
Mom and Pop store — *Tante-Emma-Laden.*
Because of the supermarkets, things are hard for Mom and Pop stores. *Wegen der Supermärkte haben es die Tante-Emma-Läden schwer.*

---

straw — *der Strohhalm*
That's the last straw! *Das schlägt dem Fass den Boden aus! (Das bringt das Fass zum Überlaufen.)*

---

to strike — *schlagen; streiken; streichen*
to strike a blow for — *eine Lanze brechen.*
In her new book she strikes a blow for society's outsiders. *In ihrem neuen Buch bricht sie eine Lanze für die Außenseiter der Gesellschaft.*

to strike up an acquaintance — *anbandeln.*
He did everything to strike up an acquaintance with her. *Er versuchte alles, um es mit ihr anzubandeln.*

to strike while the iron is hot — *das Eisen schmieden, solange es heiß ist.*

She acted quickly, for she knew that one must strike while the iron is hot. *Sie handelte rasch, denn sie wusste, man muss das Eisen schmieden, solange es heiß ist.*

string — *die Schnur; Kordel; der Bindfaden; das Band*
with no strings attached — *ohne Bedingungen; ohne Haken (und Ösen).*

At first I thought the offer had a catch, but there were absolutely no strings attached. *Zuerst meinte ich, das Angebot hatte einen Haken, aber es war ganz ohne Haken und Ösen.*

stuff — *der Stoff; das Zeug*
Stuff and nonsense! — *Dummes Zeug!*

She knows her stuff! — *Sie versteht ihre Sache.*

to stumble — *stolpern*
to stumble over one's words — *sich verhaspeln.*

Kurt got nervous and stumbled over his words. *Kurt wurde nervös und verhaspelte sich.*

to subscribe to — *abonnieren*

We still subscribe to a few periodicals. *Wir sind noch auf einige Zeitschriften abonniert.*

to subscribe to — *sich Ideen/Meinungen anschließen.*

Since he's become a megalomaniac, we can't subscribe to his ideas anymore. *Seitdem er größenwahnsinnig geworden ist, können wir uns seinen Ideen nicht mehr anschließen.*

to succeed — *gelingen*
If at first you don't succeed, try again. — *Wenn es einem zuerst nicht gelingt, soll man es immer wieder neu versuchen.*

to suffer — *leiden*
  to suffer little aches and pains — *zwicken und zwacken; Wehwehchen haben.*
  My grandfather suffers little aches and pains but his health is surprisingly good. *Meinen Großvater zwickt es und zwackt es, aber seine Gesundheit ist überraschend gut.*

suicide — *der Selbstmord, Freitod*
  suicide mission — *das Himmelfahrtskommando.*
  The terrorist was glad to accept the suicide mission. *Die Terroristin nahm gerne das Himmelfahrtskommando an.*

to suit — *passen*
  to suit to a T — *ausgezeichnet passen.*
  You don't like it, but it suits me to a T. *Euch gefällt's nicht, aber mir passt's ausgezeichnet.*

supply — *der Vorrat*
  to be in short supply — *knapp sein; Engpässe geben.*
  Some foodstuffs are already in short supply. *Bei einigen Lebensmitteln gibt es schon Engpässe.*

sure — *sicher*
  sure as shootin' — *bombensicher; sicher wie das Amen in der Kirche.*
  They'll be looking for it, sure as shootin'. *Sie werden danach suchen, das ist so sicher wie das Amen in der Kirche.*

surprise — *die Überraschung*
  to take by surprise — *über einen kommen.*
  The decision took us somewhat by surprise. *Die Entscheidung ist etwas über uns gekommen.*

swamp — *der Sumpf*
  to be swamped with work — *mit Arbeit eingedeckt sein.*
  Although he's swamped with work, he lived it up till all hours last night. *Obwohl er mit Arbeit eingedeckt ist, sumpfte er gestern die ganze Nacht.*

to swear — *schwören*
  to swear an oath — *einen Eid leisten/schwören.*
  Doctors and dentists must swear the Hippocratic Oath. *Ärzte und Zahnärzte müssen den Eid des Hippokrates leisten.*

  to swear by all that's holy — *Stein und Bein schwören.*
  He swore by all that's holy that he hadn't committed any crime. *Er schwur Stein und Bein, er hätte nichts verbrochen.*

---

to sweat — *schwitzen*
  Don't sweat the small stuff. — *Lass dich nicht im Kleinen ersticken!*

---

to sweep — *kehren*
  to sweep off one's feet — *das Herz im Sturm erobern.*
  Cinderella swept the prince off his feet. *Aschenbrödel eroberte das Herz des Prinzen im Sturm.*

---

sweet — *süß*
  to have a sweet tooth — *eine Naschkatze/ein Leckermäulchen sein.*
  He's lost almost all his teeth, but he's still got a sweet tooth. *Er hat seine Zähne fast alle verloren, aber eine alte Naschkatze ist er geblieben.*

---

swing — *der Schwung*
  to be in full swing — *auf vollen Touren/auf Hochtouren laufen.*
  The electoral campaign is now in full swing. *Der Wahlkampf läuft jetzt auf vollen Touren.*

---

sword — *das Schwert*
  to cross swords — *die Klinken kreuzen.*
  You'd better think it over before crossing swords with the millionaire. *Überleg's dir gut, bevor du mit dem Millionär die Klinken kreuzt.*

  to be at crossed swords — *sich in den Haaren liegen, auf Kriegsfuß sein.*
  The theologians are at crossed swords concerning the interpretation of many Biblical passages. *Die Theologen liegen sich in den Haaren was die Auslegung vieler Bibelstellen betrifft.*

---

sympathy — *das Beileid; das Mitgefühl*
to have no sympathy for — *bei einem nicht ankommen.*
I have no sympathy for that sort of thing. *So etwas kommt bei mir nicht an.*

table — *der Tisch*
to turn the tables — *den Spieß umdrehen/umkehren.*
He had the upper hand for some time, but now I'm going to turn the
tables on him. *Lange hatte er die Oberhand aber jetzt dreh ich ihm den
Spieß um.*

tail — *der Schwanz*
to turn tail and run — *das Hasenpanier ergreifen.*
The whole army turned tail and ran. *Die ganze Armee ergriff das
Hasenpanier.*

to take — *nehmen*
to take after — *durchschlagen.*
Electra took after her father. *Bei Elektra schlug der Vater durch.*

to take amiss — *übelnehmen.*
Don't take it amiss of him if he seems a bit tactless at first. *Nehmen Sie es
ihm nicht übel, wenn er zuerst etwas taktlos erscheint.*

to take hard — *etwas zu Herzen nehmen, zu ernst nehmen.*
Don't take it so hard, things will work out. *Nimm's nicht so zu Herzen, es
wird sich schon richten.*

to take things easier — *kürzertreten.*
The doctor advised him to take things easier. *Der Arzt riet ihm,
kürzerzutreten.*

Take it easy! — *Lassen Sie sich's gut gehen!*

to take lying down — *sitzen lassen.*
He won't take that accusation lying down. *Er wird diesen Vorwurf nicht
auf sich sitzen lassen.*

to take off — *abnehmen.*
She refused to take off her hat, even though it disturbed others. *Sie weigerte sich, ihren Hut abzunehmen, obwohl er die anderen störte.*

to take off — *ausziehen.*
She took off her gloves instead. *Statt dessen zog sie ihre Handschuhe aus.*

to take off — *abhauen.*
I've got to take off now. *Ich muss jetzt abhauen.*

to take priority over — *gehen vor.*
She denied that jobs took priority over environmental protection. *Sie bestritt, dass Arbeitsplätze vor Umweltschutz gingen.*

to take up the cause of — *sich für etwas einsetzen.*
She took up the cause of the war victims. *Sie setzte sich für die Kriegsopfer ein.*

to be taken in by — *sich anführen lassen.*
Don't be taken in by that con man. *Lassen Sie sich nicht von dem Trickbetrüger anführen.*

---

to talk — *sprechen; reden*

to talk big — *Schaum schlagen.*
As usual, he was just talking big. *Wie gewöhnlich hat er nur Schaum geschlagen.*

to talk till one is blue in the face — *sich den Mund fusselig reden.*
I can talk till I'm blue in the face, but my husband does what he wants anyway. *Ich kann mir den Mund fusselig reden, aber mein Mann tut dennoch, was er will.*

to talk nonsense — *dummes Zeug quatschen.*
He got drunk and talked a lot of nonsense. *Er betrank sich und quatschte viel dummes Zeug.*

to talk one's head off — *ein Loch in den Bauch reden.*
He talked his head off at us, but we didn't buy anything. *Er redete uns ein Loch in den Bauch, aber wir kauften doch nichts.*

to talk shop — *fachsimpeln.*
Why do you always have to talk shop? *Warum müsst ihr immer fachsimpeln?*

to talk about this, that and everything — *sich über Gott und die Welt unterhalten.*

They talked about this, that and everything. *Sie unterhielten sich über Gott und die Welt.*

to talk straight — *Tacheles reden.*

Try talking straight to us, for once. *Versuch's doch einmal, mit uns Tacheles zu reden.*

tall — *groß*

tall story — *die Räuberpistole, Räubergeschichte; das Jägerlatein, Seemannsgarn.*

I don't want to hear his tall stories about contacts with extraterrestrials. *Die Räuberpistolen über seine Beziehungen zu Außerirdischen will ich mir nicht anhören.*

task — *die Aufgabe*

to take to task — *ins Gericht gehen mit.*

The lawyer took the judge sharply to task. *Die Anwältin ging mit der Richterin scharf ins Gericht.*

tea — *der Tee*

to take tea and see (what happens) — *Tee trinken und abwarten.*

Now all we can do is take tea and see (what happens). *Jetzt können wir nur noch Tee trinken und abwarten.*

tea and sympathy — *Rat und Trost.*

At first he came to her only for tea and sympathy. *Zuerst suchte er nur Rat und Trost bei ihr.*

to teach — *lehren*

You can't teach an old dog new tricks. — *Was Hänschen nicht lernt, lernt Hans nimmermehr.*

to teach a lesson to — *einen Denkzettel verpassen.*

I hope that'll teach you a lesson! *Ich hoffe, das wird dir einen Denkzettel verpassen!*

tear — *die Träne*

   tearjerker — *die Schnulze; der Schmachtfetzen.*

   He didn't want to admit that he was moved and dismissed the movie as a tearjerker. *Er wollte nicht zugeben, dass er angerührt war, und tat den Film als Schnulze ab.*

---

to tell — *erzählen*

   to be able to tell a thing or two about — *ein Lied singen können.*

   I could tell you a thing or two about busted love. *Ich könnte dir ein Lied von betrogener Liebe singen.*

   to tell fibs — *vorflunkern.*

   You've been telling us fibs again. *Du hast uns wieder etwas vorgeflunkert.*

   to tell an inside story — *aus dem Nähkästchen plaudern.*

   The mayor forgot himself and told an inside story. *Der Bürgermeister vergass sich und plauderte aus dem Nähkästchen.*

   to tell loud and clear — *ins Stammbuch schreiben.*

   I'll never take you along again; I'm telling you that loud and clear. *Dich nehm ich nie wieder mit; das kannst du dir ins Stammbuch schreiben.*

   to tell the same old story — *das gleiche Lied singen.*

   The ancient mariner always tells the same old story. *Der greise Seemann singt immer das gleiche Lied.*

   to tell someone where to get off — *jemandem Bescheid stoßen.*

   He tried to fool me, but I told him where to get off right away. *Er versuchte, mir was vorzumachen, aber ich habe ihm sofort Bescheid gestoßen.*

   to tell someone off — *die Hammelbeine langziehen.*

   He got on my nerves, so I finally told him off. *Er ging mir auf den Geist, da hab ich ihm schließlich die Hammelbeine langgezogen.*

---

tempest — *der Sturm*

   a tempest in a teapot — *ein Sturm im Wasserglas.*

   Everything's calmed down now. The whole thing was just a tempest in a teapot. *Es ist alles wieder ruhig. Das Ganze war nur ein Sturm im Wasserglas.*

---

thin — *dünn*

    thin as a rail — *dünn wie ein Strich (in der Landschaft).*

Thanks to her diet she's as thin as a rail. *Dank ihrem Diät ist sie jetzt dünn wie ein Strich.*

thing — *das Ding; die Sache*

    one thing after another — *Probleme über Probleme!*

First the computer went on the blink, now the fridge. Just one thing after another! *Zuerst ging der Computer kaputt, jetzt der Kühlschrank. Probleme über Probleme!*

to think — *denken; ausgehen*

    to my way of thinking — *für meine Begriffe.*

To my way of thinking, the project would be too costly. *Für meine Begriffe wäre das Unternehmen zu kostspielig.*

thoroughly — *ganz und gar; völlig*

    to be thoroughly exhausted — *völlig fix und fertig sein.*

After looking for a job in vain she was thoroughly exhausted. *Nach vergeblicher Arbeitssuche war sie völlig fix und fertig.*

thorn — *der Dorn*

    to be a thorn in the side — *ein Dorn im Auge sein.*

The one independent newspaper was a thorn in the side of the tyrant. *Die einzige noch unabhängige Zeitung war dem Gewaltherrscher ein Dorn im Auge.*

thread — *der Faden*

    to lose the thread — *aus dem Konzept kommen.*

He came under pressure and lost the thread (of what he was saying). *Er geriet unter Druck und kam aus dem Konzept.*

to throw — *werfen; schmeißen*

    to throw in the towel — *das Handtuch werfen.*

After bitter struggles, they finally threw in the towel. *Nach erbitterten Kämpfen warfen sie endlich das Handtuch.*

to throw off balance — *aus dem Gleichgewicht bringen.*

The news threw him off balance. *Die Nachricht hat ihn aus dem Gleichgewicht gebracht.*

to throw off the scent — *hinters Licht führen.*

The con man succeeded in throwing the detective off the scent. *Dem Trickbetrüger gelang es, den Detektiv hinters Licht zu führen.*

to throw out — *hinauswerfen; rausschmeißen; vor die Tür setzen.*

Her father was cruel and threw out his only child. *Ihr Vater war grausam und setzte sein einziges Kind vor die Tür.*

to throw out the baby with the bath water — *das Kind mit dem Badewasser ausschütten.*

Be careful not to throw out the baby with the bath water. *Gib acht, das Kind nicht mit dem Badewasser auszuschütten.*

to throw up — *sich erbrechen.*

"He makes me want to throw up," said Emma of her former fiancé. *"Er ist ein Brechmittel," sagte Emma von ihrem ehemaligen Verlobten.*

to throw one's weight behind — *sich für etwas stark machen.*

Industry is increasingly throwing its weight behind environmental protection. *In zunehmendem Masse macht sich die Industrie für den Umweltschutz stark.*

---

thumb — *der Daumen*

to be all thumbs — *zwei linke Hände haben.*

Sometimes she thought her handyman was all thumbs. *Manchmal glaubte sie, ihr Heimwerker hätte zwei linke Hände.*

to twiddle one's thumbs — *die Daumen drehen, Däumchen drehen.*

Do something, instead of twiddling your thumbs! *Tu doch was statt die Daumen zu drehen!*

as a rule of thumb — *als Faustregel.*

As a rule of thumb, one should always keep the receipt for the packages. *Als Faustregel sollte man die Quittung für die Pakete immer behalten.*

to have under one's thumb — *unter der Fuchtel haben.*

People say his wife's got him under her thumb. *Die Leute sagen, seine Frau habe ihn unter der Fuchtel.*

to thumb one's nose at — *eine lange Nase machen.*
The warring factions thumbed their noses at the United Nations. *Die kämpfenden Banden machten den Vereinten Nationen eine lange Nase.*

thunder — *der Donner*
thunderstruck — *wie vom Blitz getroffen.*
Thunderstruck, she learned the truth about him. *Wie vom Blitz getroffen, erfuhr sie die Wahrheit über ihn.*

to tick — *ticken*
to be ticked off — *sauer sein.*
He was ticked off at not getting a raise in salary. *Er war sauer, dass er keine Lohnerhöhung bekommen hatte.*
to see what makes s.o. tick — *jmandem hinter die Stirn sehen.*
We'd all like to know what makes him tick. *Wir würden ihm alle gern hinter die Stirn sehen.*

ticket — *der Fahrschein; der Theaterplatz*
just the ticket — *gerade das Richtige.*
We're looking for a new couch. I think this one is just the ticket. *Wir suchen ein neues Sofa. Ich glaube, dieses ist gerade das Richtige.*

tide — *die Gezeiten; Ebbe und Flut*
to swim/go against the tide — *gegen den Strom schwimmen.*
All his life he swam against the tide, against the prevailing artistic currents, and was appreciated only after his death. *Lebenslänglich schwamm er gegen den Strom, gegen die herrschenden künstlerischen Strömungen und wurde erst nach seinem Tod geschätzt.*

The tide has turned. — *Das Blatt hat sich gewendet.*
He kept losing at poker but continued playing in the hope that the tide would turn. *Beim Poker verlor er nur, spielte aber weiter in der Hoffnung, dass sich das Blatt wenden würde.*

tight — *eng*
to be in a tight squeeze — *in der Klemme sitzen.*
The boss is in a tight squeeze. *Der Chef sitzt in der Klemme.*

time — *die Zeit*

Time waits for no man. — *Die Uhr bleibt stehen, die Zeit nicht.*

from time immemorial — *seit eh und je; seit undenklichen Zeiten/Urzeiten.*

Unfortunately there've been wars from time immemorial. *Leider hat es seit Urzeiten Kriege gegeben.*

to do time — *eine Gefägnisstrafe verbüßen, Knast schieben, abbrummen.*

He had to do three years in the slammer for that. *Er musste dafür drei Jahre abbrummen.*

to have a good time — *sich gut amüsieren.*

We had a good time at the folk festival. *Auf dem Volksfest amüsierten wir uns gut.*

in no time — *ruck, zuck.*

The job was done in no time, Ruck, zuck war die Arbeit fertig.

not to give the time of day to — *das Salz in der Suppe nicht gönnen.*

He wouldn't give me the time of day. *Er würde mir nicht das Salz in der Suppe gönnen.*

on time — *auf Pump/Raten/Stottern.*

They bought everything on time (credit). *Sie haben alles auf Pump gekauft.*

on time — *rechtzeitig; zu rechter Zeit.*

Those who don't come on time have to eat what's left. *Wer nicht kommt zu rechter Zeit, der muss essen was übrig bleibt.*

tipsy — *angeheitert; beschwipst*

to feel a bit tipsy — *einen kleinen Schwips haben.*

I felt a bit tipsy after just two little glasses of wine. *Schon nach zwei Gläschen Wein hatte ich einen kleinen Schwips.*

together — *zusammen*

to have it together/have one's act together — *Es im Griff haben.*

He's always got it together. *Der hat immer alles im Griff.*

tongue — *die Zunge*

slip of the tongue — *der Versprecher, Lapsus.*

There's often humor and hidden truth in slips of the tongue. *In Versprechern sind oft Humor und verdeckte Wahrheit zu finden.*

tooth — *der Zahn*

to be (getting) a bit long in the tooth — *nicht mehr der/die Jüngste sein.*
The dentist and her husband are getting a bit long in the tooth. *Die Zahnärztin und ihr Mann sind nicht mehr die Jüngsten.*

to fight tooth and nail — *sich mit Händen und Füßen wehren.*
Work more for less money? No way! We'll fight that tooth and nail. *Mehr arbeiten für weniger Geld? Niemals! Dagegen wehren wir uns mit Händen und Füßen.*

to lie through one's teeth — *nach Strich und Faden belügen.*
The large landowner lied through his teeth to us. *Der Großgrundbesitzer belog uns nach Strich und Faden.*

top — *die Spitze*
The rot starts at the top. — *Der Fisch stinkt vom Kopf her.*

to be on top of the world — *überglücklich sein.*
We loved each other and were on top of the world. *Wir liebten uns und waren überglücklich.*

touch — *die Berührung*
the finishing touch — *der letzte Schliff.*
We should have ordered something for desert; the finishing touch was missing. *Wir hätten etwas zum Nachtisch bestellen sollen — es fehlte der letzte Schliff.*

to get in touch — *sich in Verbindung setzen; sich melden.*
You should have gotten in touch with us right away. *Sie hätten sich sofort mit uns in Verbindung setzen sollen.*
He hasn't been in touch with us for some time. *Seit langem hat er sich bei uns nicht gemeldet.*

to be touch and go — *auf des Messers Schneide stehen.*
It's touch and go whether the law will be passed. *Ob das Gesetz verabschiedet wird, steht auf des Messers Schneide.*

to tow — *ziehen*

    to take in tow — *unter seine Fittiche nehmen; in Schutz nehmen.*

    His father died and I've taken him in tow. *Sein Vater ist gestorben und ich hab ihn unter meine Fittiche genommen.*

    to tow the line — *spuren.*

    If you don't tow the line, you'll get thrown out. *Wenn du nicht spurst, fliegst du.*

town — *die Stadt; das Dorf*

    one-horse town/hick town — *Kuhdorf; Kaff.*

    We were happy living in that hick town. *In dem Kuhdorf lebten wir glücklich.*

toy — *das Spielzeug*

    to toy with — *liebäugeln mit.*

    Some city councilors are toying with the idea of having a new airport built. *Einige Stadträte liebäugeln mit dem Gedanken, einen neuen Flughafen bauen zu lassen.*

track — *die Spur*

    laugh track — *der Lachsack.*

    As a matter of principle, we avoid programs with a laugh track. *Sendungen mit Lachsack vermeiden wir grundsätzlich.*

    to have a one-track mind — *eingleisig denken.*

    He's even proud of having a one-track mind. *Er ist sogar stolz darauf, dass er eingleisig denkt.*

    to have the inside track/dope on — *die Wahrheit für sich gepachtet haben; die Wahrheit mit Löffeln gefressen haben.*

    Those fanatics think they've got the inside track on the truth. *Die Fanatiker glauben, die Wahrheit für sich gepachtet zu haben.*

    to make tracks — *sich aus dem Staub machen.*

    When he was supposed to help me, he made tracks. *Als er mir helfen sollte, machte er sich aus dem Staub.*

trap — *die Falle*
Shut your trap! *Halt die Klappe/Fresse!*

travel — *das Reisen*
Travel broadens the mind. *Reisen bildet.*

trick — *der Kniff*
How's tricks? *Was macht die Kunst?*

to know every trick in the book — *wissen, wo Barthel den Most holt.*
He needs a lawyer who knows every trick in the book. *Der braucht einen Anwalt, der weiß, wo Barthel den Most hält.*

to trim — *schneiden; stutzen*
to trim one's sails before the wind — *nach der Decke strecken.*
The deposed party bosses now have to trim their sails before the wind. *Die abgesetzten Parteibonzen müssen sich jetzt nach der Decke strecken.*

with all the trimmings — *mit allem Drum und Dran.*
For Thanksgiving we had turkey with all the trimmings. *Zum Erntedankfest hatten wir Truthahn mit allem Drum und Dran.*

trouble — *der Ärger*
Everyone has his troubles. — *Jeder hat sein Päckchen.*

to get into real trouble — *in die Bredouille (Teufels Küche) kommen.*
Through his wheeling and dealing he got into real trouble. *Durch seine Mauscheleien kam er in die Bredouille.*

trowel — *die Kelle*
to lay it on with a trowel — *es dick auftragen.*
He really laid the whole story on with a trowel. *Er hat die ganze Geschichte ziemlich dick aufgetragen.*

trumpet — *die Trompete*
to blow one's own trumpet/horn — *sich selbst beweihräuchern; auf die Pauke hauen.*

He's constantly blowing his own trumpet and also wants everybody else to sing his praises. *Ständig beweihräuchert er sich und will auch, dass alle anderen ein Loblied auf ihn singen sollen.*

to try — *versuchen; probieren*
tried and true — *altbewährt.*
Our elixir is brewed accord to a secret, tried and true recipe. *Unser Elixir wird nach einem geheimen, altbewährten Rezept zusammengebraut.*

to try one's hand at — *es versuchen mit.*
I didn't make a go of it with my painting, so now I'm trying my hand at saloon keeping. *Mit der Malerei ging's nicht, daher veruche ich mich jetzt als Kneippenwirt.*

to tug — *ziehen, zerren*
to tug at the heartstrings — *ans Herz gehen.*
The movie tugged at our heartstrings. *Der Film ging uns ans Herz.*

tune — *die Melodie, Weise*
catchy tune — *der Ohrwurm.*
There isn't a really catchy tune among his many songs. *Unter seinen vielen Liedern ist kein richtiger Ohrwurm.*

to turn — *drehen; wenden*
not to know which way to turn — *weder ein noch aus wissen.*
As a single mother with three children, I didn't know which way to turn. *Als alleinstehende Mutter mit drei Kindern wusste ich weder aus noch ein.*

to be someone's turn — *dran sein; an der Reihe sein.*
It's your turn now. *Sie sind jetzt dran.*

to turn a deaf ear — *abschmettern.*
Long did we implore, but he just turned a deaf ear to us. *Lange haben wir gefleht, aber er hat uns einfach abgeschmettert.*

to turn down — *abweisen.*
The boss turned down his request. *Die Chefin hat seine Bitte abgewiesen.*

to turn down/up (radio/TV) — *leiser/lauter stellen.*
It was late and we had to turn down the radio. *Es war spät und wir mussten das Radio leiser stellen.*

to turn in — *schlafen gehen.*
We turned in early. *Wir sind früh schlafen gegangen.*

to turn on — *anmachen.*
Whatever turns you on. *Des Menschen Wille ist sein Himmelreich. (Jeder soll nach seiner Fasson selig werden.)*

to turn out — *ausfallen; ausgehen.*
The matter turned out badly for them. *Die Sache ist für sie schlecht ausgegangen.*

to turn state's evidence — *als Kronzeuge auftreten.*
The petty crook turned state's evidence and got off easy. *Der kleine Gauner trat als Kronzeuge auf und kam glimpflich davon.*

to turn upside down/topsy-turvy — *auf den Kopf stellen, durcheinanderwühlen.*
She turned the whole house upside down before she finally found the ring. *Sie hat das ganze Haus durcheinandergewühlt, bevor sie den Ring endlich gefunden hat.*

without turning a hair — *ohne mit der Wimper zu zucken.*
He's capable of doing anything without turning a hair. *Er ist zu allem fähig, ohne mit der Wimper zu zucken.*

tube — *das Rohr; die Röhre*
go down the tube — *den Bach hinunter gehen.*
All our efforts went down the tube. *Unsere ganze Mühe ging den Bach hinunter.*

boob tube — *die Röhre; die Glotze.*
He spends his whole life in front of the boob tube. *Er verbringt sein ganzes Leben vor der Glotze.*

turtle — *die Schildkröte*
turtleneck — *der Stehbundkragen.*
I'm looking for turtleneck and polo-sweaters. *Ich suche Pullis mit Stehbund- und Rollkragen.*

twinkling — *das Funkeln*
    in the twinkling of an eye — *im Handumdrehen.*
    I'll be back in the twinkling of an eye. *Im Handumdrehen bin ich wieder da.*

two — *zwei*
    There are no two ways about it. — *Da gibt's nichts. (Daran ist nichts zu drehen und zu deuteln.)*
    to put in one's two-cents worth — *seinen Senf dazu geben.*
    Although he doesn't know anything about it, he put in his two-cents worth. *Obwohl er nichts davon versteht, gab er seinen Senf dazu.*

umbrella — *der Regenschirm*
    umbrella organization — *der Dachverband.*
    Is there an umbrella organization for expellees from the east? *Gibt es einen Dachverband für Vertriebene aus dem Osten?*

unfortunately — *leider*
    most unfortunately — *leider leider (leider Gottes.)*
    Most unfortunately, we can't help you. *Leider Gottes können wir Ihnen nicht helfen.*

unknown — *unbekannt*
    an unknown quantity — *eine unbekannte Größe; ein unbeschriebenes Blatt.*
    For the public our candidate is still an unknown quantity. *Für die Öffentlichkeit ist unsere Kandidatin noch ein unbeschriebenes Blatt.*

up — *nach oben; aufwärts*
    What's up? — *Was ist los? (Was gibt's?)*
    up and away — *auf und davon.*
    He was up and away. *Er machte sich auf und davon.*

up and coming — *aufstrebend.*

She's an up and coming member of the firm. *Sie ist ein aufstrebendes Firmenmitglied.*

up to now — *bislang.*

Up to now, Nixon is the only president to resign. *Bislang ist Nixon der einzige Präsident, der zurückgetreten ist.*

to be up against it — *in großen Schwierigkeiten stecken.*

He and his business are really up against it. *Er und sein Geschäft stecken in großen Schwierigkeiten.*

to be up to something/no good — *etwas im Schilde führen.*

I don't know what it is yet, but I sure he's up to something. *Ich weiß noch nicht, was es ist, aber er führt sicher etwas im Schilde.*

to be on the up and up — *astrein sein.*

There's no catch; everything's strictly on the up and up. *Da gibt's keinen Haken; alles ist total astrein.*

up-to-date — *aktuell.*

The astronomer is no longer interested in uptodate fashions. *Die Astronomin interessiert sich nicht mehr für die aktuelle Mode.*

to keep up to date — *auf dem neusten Stand bleiben.*

She makes a considerable effort to keep up to date with the latest research. *Sie gibt sich große Mühe, auf dem neusten Stand der Forschung zu bleiben.*

---

upper — *obere*

the upper crust — *die oberen zehntausend; die Oberschicht.*

Her boutique caters to the upper crust. *Ihre Boutique spricht die oberen zehntausend zu.*

the upper middle class — *der gehobene Mittelstand.*

Heine and Brecht sometimes gave themselves proletarian airs although they really belonged to the upper middle class. *Manchmal gaben sie Heine und Brecht proletarische Allüren, obwohl sie eigentlich zum gehobenen Mittelstand zählten.*

uppers — *die Aufputschmittel.*

He really needs downers, not uppers. *Statt Aufputschmittel braucht er eher Beruhigungsmittel.*

---

use — *der Gebrauch*

   Of what use is that? — *Was nutzt das? (Was soll ich damit anfangen?)*

   to have no use for — *nichts übrig haben für.*

   She has no use for his stingy relatives. *Für seine geizigen Verwandten hat sie nichts übrig.*

   of no earthly use — *völlig unnütz.*

   "All that bric-a-brac you buy is of no earthly use."—"But they're good for my soul." *"Die ganzen Nippsachen, die du kaufst sind völlig unnütz."—"Sie dienen aber dem Wohl meiner Seele."*

to use — *benutzen; gebrauchen*

   If you don't use it, you lose it. *Wer rastet, rostet.*

variety — *die Vielfältigkeit*

Variety is the spice of life. *Abwechslung macht Freude.*

vengeance — *die Rache*

   to take vengeance — *sich rächen.*

   He wanted to take vengeance on his enemies. *Er wollte sich an seinen Feinden rächen.*

   with a vengeance — *gewaltig/tüchtig.*

   He went to work with a vengeance. *Er legte sich tüchtig ins Zeug.*

vent — *die Öffnung*

   to vent one's anger — *seinen Zorn auslassen.*

   I know you're having problems, but don't vent your anger on me. *Ich weiß, du hast Probleme, aber lass deinen Zorn nicht an mir aus.*

very — *sehr*

   the very best — *das Allerbeste.*

   I want to give her only the very best. *Ich will ihr nur das Allerbeste schenken.*

the very one(s) — *gerade der/die/das.*
These are the very ones I've been looking for. *Das sind gerade die, die ich suche.*

VIPs — *alles, was Rang und Namen hat*
All the VIPs appeared for the gala. *Alles, was Rang und Namen hatte, erschien für die Gala.*

vicious — *böswillig*
vicious circle — *der Teufelskreis.*
They're trying to break out of the vicious circle of drug addiction and crime. *Sie versuchen, den Teufels Kreis von Rauschgiftsucht und Kriminalität zu durchbrechen.*

victorious — *siegreich*
to be victorious — *den Sieg davontragen.*
Her party was victorious in the last elections. *In den letzten Wahlen trug ihre Partei den Sieg davon.*

voice — *die Stimme*
to have a voice in — *ein Wort mitreden.*
He wanted to have a voice in the election of the beauty queen. *Bei der Wahl der Schönheitskönigin wollte er ein Wort mitreden.*

to wait — *warten*
to wait and see — *abwarten.*
We'll have to wait and see how it turns out. *Wir müssen abwarten, wie's ausgeht.*

to wait for — *warten auf.*
I've waited long enough for you. *Ich habe schon lange genug auf dich gewartet.*

to wait on — *bedienen.*

Do you know who waited on you? *Wissen Sie, wer Sie bedient hat?*

to wait on hand and foot — *hinten und vorne bedienen.*

He wanted someone to wait on him hand and foot. *Er wollte jemand, der ihn hinten und vorne bedienen würde.*

walk — *der Spaziergang*

to take a walk — *einen Spaziergang machen.*

Every evening we take a walk. *Jeden Abend machen wir einen Spaziergang.*

to tell someone to take a walk — *ablaufen lassen.*

She told him to take a walk. *Sie hat ihn ablaufen lassen.*

to walk — *laufen; zu Fuß gehen; spazierengehen*

to walk the plank — *über die Klinge springen.*

Ruthlessly he made his enemies walk the plank. *Rücksichtslos ließ er seine Feinde über die Klinge springen.*

wall — *die Wand*

It's enough to drive you up the wall! *Es ist zum Aus-der-Haut-Fahren!*

to wash — *waschen*

to be a washout — *ein Schlag ins Wasser sein.*

His attempt to save the company was a washout. *Sein Versuch, den Betrieb zu retten, war ein Schlag ins Wasser.*

to feel all washed out — *durchhängen, sich wie ausgelaugt fühlen.*

When a coworker feels all washed out, the others help him. *Wenn ein Kollege durchhängt, helfen ihm die anderen.*

water — *das Wasser*

to get into hot water — *sich in die Nesseln setzen.*

He acted recklessly and got into hot water. *Er hat waghalsig gehandelt und sich in die Nesseln gesetzt.*

of the first water — *reinsten Wassers or von reinstem Wasser.*

He is an idealist of the first water. *Er ist ein Idealist reinsten Wassers.*

That's water under the bridge/dam; over and done with. — *Das ist alles Schnee von gestern, aus und vorbei.*

---

wave — *die Welle*

to make waves — *hohe Wellen schlagen; Porzellan zerschlagen.*
The actress's memoirs are making waves. *Die Memoiren der Schauspielerin schlagen hohe Wellen.*

---

way — *der Weg*

on the way — *unterwegs.*
They're still underway to grandma's. *Sie sind noch nach Oma unterwegs.*

on the way down/up — *im Aufwind/Abwind.*
Most stocks are still on the way up; only steel stocks are on the way down. *Die meisten Aktien sind noch im Aufwind; nur die Stahlaktien sind im Abwind.*

one way or another — *so oder so.*
One way or another, the besieged city is done for. *So oder so ist es um die belagerte Stadt geschehen.*

to be making one's way (to popularity) — *im Kommen sein.*
These new synthetic fibers are making their way. *Diese neuen Kunstfasern sind im Kommen.*

to yield the right of way — *die Vorfahrt lassen.*
You have to yield the right of way to traffic coming from the right. *Dem von rechts kommenden Verkehr muss man die Vorfahrt lassen.*

to clear out of the way — *aus dem Weg räumen.*
All obstacles are out of the way now. *Alle Hindernisse sind jetzt aus dem Weg geräumt.*

to be well under way — *auf dem besten Weg sein.*
We're well under way to establishing new markets. *Wir sind auf dem besten Weg, neue Märkte zu eröffnen.*

to go out of one's way — *sich besondere Mühe geben.*
She went out of her way to help us. *Sie gab sich besondere Mühe, uns zu helfen.*

to know one's way around — *sich auskennen.*

Sieczysnski knew his way around Vienna—by day and even more by night. *Sieczynski kannte sich in Wien aus—bei Tag und noch mehr bei der Nacht.*

right of way — *die Vorfahrt.*
The right of way is to the right. *Vorfahrt von rechts.*

way back when — *anno dazumal.*
Way back when, men wore bathing shirts. *Anno dazumal trugen Männer Badehemden.*

to wear — *tragen*
to wear down — *abwetzen.*
This sweater is worn down at the elbows. *Dieser Pulli ist an den Ellbogen abgewetzt.*

weather — *das Wetter*
under the weather — *nicht auf der Höhe.*
He's still a bit under the weather. *Er ist noch nicht ganz auf der Höhe.*

weight — *das Gewicht*
to lose weight — *abnehmen.*
He's trying to lose weight. *Er versucht, abzunehmen.*

to gain weight — *zunehmen.*
But unfortunately he's gained weight. *Aber leider hat er zugenommen.*

to throw one's weight around — *sich wichtig machen.*
He's retired but he still tries to throw his weight around. *Er hat sich zurückgezogen, aber er versucht noch, sich wichtig zu machen.*

to weigh — *wiegen*
to weigh anchor — *den Anker lichten.*
Right after sunrise we weighed anchor. *Gleich nach Sonnenaufgang lichteten wir den Anker.*

welcome — *wilkommen*
"You're welcome. It was no trouble." *"Gern geschehen. Es war keine Mühe."*

to welcome — *willkommen heißen; begrüßen*
She welcomed us most cordially. *Sie hieß uns herzlichst willkommen.*

well — *wohl; gut*
    well-balanced — *ausgeglichen,*
    She is a well-balanced person. *Sie ist ein ausgeglichener Mensch.*

    well-groomed — *gepflegt,*
    She always looks well-groomed. *Sie sieht immer gepflegt aus.*

    well-heeled — *gutbetucht.*
    We were looking more for a spa for the well-healed, than for a resort for
       the well-heeled. *Wir suchten eher einen Kurort für Gutgeheilte statt
       eines Ferienortes für Gutbetuchte.*

    well-read — *belesen.*
    She's a very well-read lady. *Sie ist eine sehr belesene Dame.*

    well-versed — *bewandert.*
    She is well-versed in many subjects. *Sie ist auf vielen Gebieten
       bewandert.*

wet — *naß*
Unfortunately, I didn't see the "WET PAINT" sign. *Das Schild: "FRISCH
    GESTRICHEN" habe ich leider nicht gesehen.*

    to be wet behind the ears — *feucht hinter den Ohren (ein junger Dachs)
       sein.*
    He's still wet behind the ears. *Er ist noch ein ganz junger Dachs.*

to wet — *nass machen; benetzen*
    to wet one's whistle — *einen auf die Lampe gießen.*
    During the sermon he felt a strong urge to wet his whistle. *Während der
       Predigt spürte er große Lust, sich einen auf die Lampe zu gießen.*

wheel — *das Rad*
    to wheel and deal — *mauscheln.*
    They accused the mayor of wheeling and dealing with the Mafia. *Dem
       Bürgermeister wurde vorgeworfen, er hätte mit der Mafia gemauschelt.*

to whisper — *flüster*
   to whisper sweet nothings — *Süßholz raspeln.*
He whispered sweet nothings to her, but she didn't believe him. *Er raspelte ihr Süßholz, aber sie glaubte ihm nicht.*

whistle — *pfeifen*
   to blow the whistle on someone — *jemanden verpfeifen.*
Someone should blow the whistle on that crook. *Diesen Gauner sollte man verpfeifen.*

   to whistle Dixie — *sich Illusionen machen.*
If you think the South will rise again and win a new Civil War, you're whistling Dixie. *Wenn du glaubst, die Südstaaten werden wieder hochkommen und einen neuen Bürgerkrieg gewinnen , machst du dir Illusionen.*

white — *weiß*
   a white lie — *eine fromme Lüge; die Notlüge; die halbe Wahrheit.*
It was just a white lie. *Es war nur eine fromme Lüge.*

   to bleed white — *das Mark aus den Knochen saugen.*
The revolutionaries alleged that the rulers were bleeding the people white. *Die Revolutionäre behaupteten, die Herrschenden sögen dem Volk das Mark aus den Knochen.*

   white-collar worker — *der Schreibtischarbeiter, Angestellte.*
The white-collar workers also want to go on strike now. *Auch die Angestellten wollen jetzt streiken.*

   white elephant — *wertloser Gegenstand; nutzloser Besitz; Fehlinvestition.*
The supposed bargain turned out to be a white elephant. *Das vermeintliche Schnäppchen stellte sich als Fehlinvestition heraus.*

whodunit — *der Krimi*
Her last whodunit is suspenseful. *Ihr letzter Krimi ist spannend.*

whole — *ganz*
   the whole kit and caboodle/the whole shebang/the whole nine yards/ the whole enchilada/the whole ball of wax/the whole shooting match/the whole works — *das ganze Zeug/der ganze Kram/das ganze Drum und Dran/ganz und gar alles.*

We bought the store along with its inventory. The whole kit and caboodle is ours. *Wir haben den Laden mitsamt Inventar aufgekauft. Uns gehört der ganze Kram.*

wild — *wild*

to go wild — *außer Rand und Band geraten.*
The crowd went wild at the soccer game. *Beim Fußballspiel geriet die Menge außer Rand und Band.*

in the wild — *in freier Wildbahn.*
Keeping nails trimmed is no problem for these animals when they run in the wild. *In freier Wildbahn ist das Nägelfeilen kein Problem für diese Tiere.*

wild horses —*Wildpferde.*
Wild horses couldn't drag me back to that disco. *Keine zehn Pferde bringen mich wieder in diese Diskothek.*

wily — *listig; gewieft*
a wily devil — *ein Schlitzohr.*
He's a wily devil. *Er ist ein richtiges Schlitzohr.*

to win — *gewinnen*
to win big (in the lottery) — *das Große Los ziehen.*
Millions dream of winning big in the lottery. *Millionen träumen davon, das Große Los zu ziehen.*

wind — *der Wind*
to get one's second wind — *den toten Punkt überwinden.*
The boxer got his second wind. *Der Boxer überwand seinen toten Punkt.*

to throw caution to the winds — *es darauf ankommen lassen.*
He threw caution to the winds and declared his love for her. *Er ließ es darauf ankommen und erklärte ihr seine Liebe.*

wise — *weise*
to be/get wise to someone's tricks — *jmdm. auf die Schliche kommen.*
I've gotten wise to him long ago. *Ich bin ihm längst schon auf die Schliche gekommen.*

to be wise to s.o. — *jemanden durchschaut haben.*

You want to make a sucker out of me, but I've been wise to you for some time. *Du willst mich veräppeln, aber dich hab ich längst schon durchschaut.*

wise guy — *der Besserwisser.*

That wise guy thinks he can do everything better than we can. *Dieser Besserwisser glaubt, er kann alles besser als wir.*

---

wishy-washy — *saft- und kraftlos; fade*

The food always tastes insipid at his place. perhaps because he's so wishy-washy himself. *Bei ihm schmeckt das Essen immer labberig, vielleicht weil er selbst so fade ist.*

---

with — *mit*

to be with it — *ganz bei der Sache sein.*

When Gauguin was a banker he was never really with it. *Als Gauguin Bankier war, war er nie ganz bei der Sache.*

---

woods — *der Wald*

to be out of the woods — *über den Berg sein.*

Many of our problems are solved, and we hope to be out of the woods soon. *Viele unserer Probleme sind gelöst, und wir hoffen bald über den Berg zu sein.*

---

wool — *die Wolle*

to pull the wool over someone's eyes — *hinters Licht. führen; Sand in die Augen streuen.*

The con man pulled the wool over their eyes. *Der Hochstapler hat ihnen Sand in die Augen gestreut.*

---

word — *das Wort*

to get a word in edgewise — *zu Wort kommen.*

The newly elected congresswoman rarely got a word in edgewise. *Die frischgewählte Abgeordnete kam selten zu Wort.*

to get word around — *sich herumsprechen.*

Word has gotten around that this judge is very severe. *Es hat sich herumgesprochen, dass diese Richterin sehr streng ist.*

to have words — *sich streiten.*

They've had words again. *Sie haben sich wieder gestritten.*

not to say/breathe a word about s.t. — *Kein Sterbenswörtchen/keinen Ton davon sagen.*

Tell me if you're planning to leave him. I won't breathe a word about it. *Sag mir, ob du ihn verlassen wirst. Davon sage ich kein Sterbenswörtchen.*

to speak words after one's own heart — *jmdm. aus der Seele sprechen.*

The president spoke words after our own heart. *Der Präsident hat uns allen aus der Seele gesprochen.*

---

work — *die Arbeit; das Werk*

to (still) be in the works — *noch im Werden sein,*

There's nothing definite to report, because everything is still in the works. *Es gibt nichts Bestimmtes zu berichten, da alles noch im Werden ist.*

---

to work — *arbeiten*

to work itself out — *sich richten/schlichten/ausgleichen.*

Don't worry, it'll work itself out. *Keine Bange, es wird sich schon richten.*

to work out — *klappen mit; trainieren, Gymnastik machen.*

We worked out hard in the gym before breakfast. *Vor dem Frühstück haben wir im Fitnesscenter hart trainiert.*

His carefully caculated plan didn't work out. *Mit seinem ausgeklügelten Plan hat es nicht geklappt.*

to make short work of — *kurzen Prozess machen.*

The world champion skier made short work of the competition. *Die Weltmeisterin im Schilaufen machte mit der Konkurrenz kurzen Prozess.*

---

world — *die Welt*

It's not the end of the world. *Es ist noch nicht aller Tage Abend or: Davon geht die Welt nicht unter.*

for all the world — *um alles in der Welt.*

At first he said he wouldn't sell his soul for all the world. *Zuerst sagte er, er würde seine Seele nicht um alles in der Welt verkaufen.*

to think the world of someone — *große Stücke auf jemanden halten.*
They said they thought the world of me, but didn't help me. *Sie sagten, sie hielten große Stücke auf mich; geholfen haben sie mir aber nicht.*

---

worm — *der Wurm*
The early bird gets the worm. — *Morgenstund' hat Gold im Mund.*

---

worth — *wert*
the only thing worth anything — *das einzige Senkrechte.*
This restaurant is the only one worth anything in the whole town. *Dieses Restaurant ist das einzige Senkrechte in der ganzen Stadt.*

not to be worth talking about — *nicht der Rede wert sein.*
Just before he died the hero said his gunshot wounds weren't worth talking about. *Kurz vor seinem Tod behauptete der Held, seine Schusswunden wären nicht der Rede wert.*

---

to be worth(while) — *sich lohnen*
The matter isn't worth investigating any further. *Es lohnt sich nicht, die Sache weiter zu untersuchen.*
The movie is well worth seeing. *Der Film lohnt sich sehr.*

---

to wind up — *aufwickeln*
to be all wound up — *überdreht sein.*
He's all wound up and needs psychiatric care. *Er ist ganz überdreht und braucht eine psychiatrische Behandlung.*

---

wrap — *der überwurf*
to keep under wraps — *geheimhalten.*
They succeed in keep the truth under wraps for a while. *Eine Zeitlang gelang es ihnen, die Wahrheit geheimzuhalten.*

---

to wrap — *einwickeln*
to be wrapped up in — *ganz aufgehen in.*
She is completely wrapped up in her work. *Sie geht ganz in ihrer Arbeit auf.*

to wrap arms around — *die Arme schlingen um.*
When he came back after a long separation, he wrapped her in his arms.
Als er nach langer Trennung zurückkam, schlang er die Arme um sie.

to wrap around one's little finger. *auf der Nase herumtanzen.*
The dancer knew she could wrap the banker around her little finger. *Die Tänzerin wusste, dass sie dem Bankier auf der Nase herumtanzen konnte.*

wrist — *das Handgelenk*
   to get off with a slap on the wrist — *mit einem blauen Auge davonkommen; glimpflich davonkommen.*
   He got off with a slap on the wrist and just paid a fine. *Er kam glimpflich davon und bezahlte nur eine Geldstrafe.*

to write — *schreiben*
   nothing to write home about — *nichts Besonderes.*
   The long awaited new production of Hamlet was nothing to write home about. *Die lang erwartete Neuinszenierung von Hamlet war nichts Besonderes.*

X-rated — *nicht jugendfrei*
   He knew the movie was X-rated. *Er wusste, dass der Film nicht jugendfrei war.*

X rays — *die Röntgenstrahlen*
   to take X rays — *Röntgenaufnahmen machen; roentgen.*
   They took X-rays and didn't find anything. *Man hat geröngt und nichts gefunden.*

year — *das Jahr*

a (per) year — *im Jahr.*

He earns $30,000 a year. *Er verdient $30,000 im Jahr.*

to be getting on in years — *in die Jahre kommen.*

She's getting on in years but still wants to play romantic young heroines (Gretchen, Juliet, etc.) *Sie ist in die Jahre gekommen, will aber noch die Gretchen-Klärchen Rollen spielen.*

to be young/old for one's years — *jünger/älter wirken als man ist.*

She's young for her years and likes to play Juliet. *Sie wirkt jünger als sie ist, und spielt gern Julia.*

---

yesterday — *gestern*

to be born yesterday — *aus Dummsdorf sein; von gestern sein.*

He seemed to think we were born yesterday. *Er schien zu glauben, wir wären aus Dummsdorf.*

---

young — *jung*

You're as old as you feel. — *Jung ist, wer sich jung fühlt.*

young fogey — *der Junggreis.*

That young fogey's always politically correct, never sloppily dressed. *Dieser Junggreis ist stets politisch korrekt, niemals salopp bekleidet.*

---

zilch — *Null Komma nichts*

He'll get zilch from us. *Von uns bekommt er Null Komma nichts.*

ENGLISH INDEX

D

E
N
G
L
I
S
H

I
N
D
E
X

G

English Index

O

3 Foreign Language Series From Barron's!

The **VERB SERIES** offers more than 300 of the most frequently used verbs.
The **GRAMMAR SERIES** provides complete coverage of the elements of grammar.
The **VOCABULARY SERIES** offers more than 3500 words and phrases with their foreign language translations. Each book: paperback.

FRENCH GRAMMAR
ISBN: 978-0-7641-1351-2

GERMAN GRAMMAR
ISBN: 978-0-8120-4296-2

ITALIAN GRAMMAR
ISBN: 978-0-7641-2060-2

JAPANESE GRAMMAR
ISBN: 978-0-7641-2061-9

RUSSIAN GRAMMAR
ISBN: 978-0-8120-4902-2

SPANISH GRAMMAR
ISBN: 978-0-7641-1615-5

FRENCH VERBS
ISBN: 978-0-7641-1356-7

GERMAN VERBS
ISBN: 978-0-8120-4310-5

ITALIAN VERBS
ISBN: 978-0-7641-2063-3

SPANISH VERBS
ISBN: 978-0-7641-1357-4

FRENCH VOCABULARY
ISBN: 978-0-7641-1999-6

GERMAN VOCABULARY
ISBN: 978-0-8120-4497-3

ITALIAN VOCABULARY
ISBN: 978-0-7641-2190-6

JAPANESE VOCABULARY
ISBN: 978-0-7641-3973-4

RUSSIAN VOCABULARY
ISBN: 978-0-7641-3970-3

SPANISH VOCABULARY
ISBN: 978-0-7641-1985-9

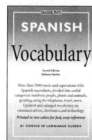

Barron's Educational Series, Inc.
250 Wireless Blvd., Hauppauge, NY 11788
Call toll-free: 1-800-645-3476

In Canada: Georgetown Book Warehouse
34 Armstrong Ave., Georgetown, Ontario L7G 4R9
Call toll-free: 1-800-247-7160

Please visit **www.barronseduc.com**
to view current prices and to order books

(#26) R 12/08

AT A GLANCE Series

Barron's gives travelers instant access to the most common idiomatic expressions used during a trip—the kind one needs to know instantly, like "Where can I find a taxi?" and "How much does this cost?"

Organized by situation (arrival, customs, hotel, health, etc.) and containing additional information about pronunciation, grammar, shopping plus special facts about the country, these convenient, pocket-size reference books will be the tourist's most helpful guides.

Special features include a bilingual dictionary section with over 2000 key words, maps of each country and major cities, and helpful phonetic spellings throughout.

Each book paperback, 256 pp., 3 3/4" x 6"

ARABIC AT A GLANCE, 3rd, Wise (978-0-7641-3766-2)
MANDARIN CHINESE AT A GLANCE, 3rd, Seligman & Chen
(978-0-7641-3556-9)
FRENCH AT A GLANCE, 4th, Stein & Wald (978-0-7641-2512-6)
GERMAN AT A GLANCE, 4th, Strutz (978-0-7641-2516-4)
ITALIAN AT A GLANCE, 4th, Costantino (978-0-7641-2513-3)
JAPANESE AT A GLANCE, 4th, Akiyama (978-0-7641-3555-2)
KOREAN AT A GLANCE, Holt (978-0-8120-3998-6)
RUSSIAN AT A GLANCE, Beyer (978-0-7641-3767-9)
SPANISH AT A GLANCE, 4th, Wald (978-0-7641-2514-0)

Barron's Educational Series, Inc.
250 Wireless Blvd., Hauppauge, NY 11788
Call toll-free: 1-800-645-3476
In Canada: Georgetown Book Warehouse, 34 Armstrong Ave.
Georgetown, Ont. L7G 4R9, Call toll-free: 1-800-247-7160

Please visit **www.barronseduc.com** to view current prices and to order books

(#25) R 8/09